WELCOME to guide to the which will hopefully set you up for a profitable campaign.

Inside these pages we have an in-depth look at the firepower from eight trainers, including Paul Nicholls and Willie Mullins, champions on either side of the Irish Sea.

We also have analysis from the Racing Post's betting experts: James Pyman leaves no stone unturned as he breaks the season down into four parts and finds new angles to give you a winning edge; Paul Kealy unearths a dozen names who have what it takes to score at the big meetings, while Nicholas Watts has invaluable ante-post advice and Dave Orton seeks out a raft of dark horses.

In addition we have handy pen portraits of this season's key contenders, highlighting what they have done so far and the races in which they could do well during the months ahead.

I hope you find the information in these pages useful and that it will help you find some winners throughout the season.

David Dew
Editor

LOWDOWN FROM THE TRAINERS

Published in 2014 by Racing Post Books, Raceform, 27 Kingfisher Court, Hambridge Road, Newbury, RG14 5SJ

ISBN: 978-1-90947147-4 Edited and designed by **David Dew** Printed by **Buxton Press**

RACING POST EXPERTS

THIS SEASON'S KEY HORSES

STATISTICS

Contributors

Tom Bull
Dave Edwards
Dylan Hill
James Hill
Chris Humpleby
Paul Kealy
Jessica Lamb
Steve Mason
Rodney Masters
Kevin Morley
Lee Mottershead
Ben Newton
Dave Orton
James Pyman
Johnny Ward
Nicholas Watts

Return of the big guns will give Henderson major shout of regaining title

SO FAR so good. Nicky Henderson's band of elite troops missing from active service last winter are back from sick leave and being prepared for a march to the frontline. But can Sprinter Sacre, Simonsig, Captain Conan and Finian's Rainbow retrieve the same top level of performance?

The quartet looked in excellent order when paraded before 250 guests at the trainer's open day for owners in September. From then on their work rate was notched up step by step with a harder push on the accelerator pedal, but the litmus test will come when they return to a racecourse.

While, understandably, the focus of ***Sprinter Sacre's*** loss of form centred on a briefly fibrillating heart at Kempton, that problem has not reoccurred, which has given everyone at Seven Barrows renewed belief it will never again impede the fabulous career of the horse who won seven consecutive Grade 1s.

Accordingly, his programme is geared to a launch in Sandown's Tingle Creek Chase on December 6, which, as Henderson points out, could in theory be the first of five showdowns this season with reigning champion Sire De Grugy, although it would be a shame if a pecking order is established before the Queen Mother Champion Chase.

Sprinter Sacre underwent surgery to improve his wind at the beginning of last season and, for some reason, his preparation from then had not been entirely fluent.

Henderson says: "I honestly do not know what caused his heart fibrillation at Kempton that day or, for whatever reason. We were not as happy as we should have been after that, although the one thing we did know was it was nothing to do with his heart or whatever happened that day at Kempton."

He adds: "We now just have to hope, with an element of optimism, that we can get him back to where he was, which was undoubtedly nearly one of the best two-mile chasers of all time. Maybe we need to pretend last season never happened because there are no repercussions and, accordingly, we've started with a clean sheet. His first piece of work will tell us where we stand. If all is fine we can press on from there, most likely with a racecourse gallop. But we'll make sure everything is tickerty-boo before he goes into bat."

Simonsig has been off games even longer, having not run since winning the 2013 Racing Post Arkle Chase, but he takes the eye. He looks sharp and there will be no worry over fitness issues when he returns in the Peterborough Chase on December 7, which is planned as a stepping stone to the King George VI Chase.

Detailing the injury, Henderson says: "A splint [near-fore] problem arose which had been sore for sometime before he actually became lame on it. Although we had a short attempt at a second half of the season, it was advised this was best left alone. Luckily it

Simonsig: has not seen a racecourse since winning the 2013 Arkle, but is back in training and set to return this season

DID YOU KNOW

Nicky Henderson has been champion trainer three times, but that record would have been greatly enhanced in recent times if Paul Nicholls hadn't been around. Henderson has now finished second to Nicholls in five of the last six seasons. He's still got some way to go to match Richard Johnson in the bridesmaid stakes. Johnson has finished second to Tony McCoy in the jockeys' championship an incredible 16 times.

didn't require surgery – we have to draw a curtain under last season."

The trainer adds: "Simonsig has strengthened up, even greyed up a lot in that he's getting lighter and lighter in colour. I still feel he has an enormous future. It's great to have him back and I feel the Peterborough could be a good place for him to start."

Captain Conan, who beat Sire De Grugy at Cheltenham in November 2012 when making his chasing debut, was only third to the future champion when they were sent off joint-favourites for last season's Tingle Creek, and he had a troubled winter.

Henderson says: "It didn't go well with little problems but then things perked up and when Sprinter came out of the Champion Chase we seriously thought we had an able deputy, but it never happened."

And for good reason, too. During the Cheltenham race Captain Conan, who the previous season had netted three Grade 1 chases, fractured his pelvis in two places. As a result, it was some time before he was able to return home to Seven Barrows.

Henderson adds: "It was a long summer of remedial work and there's still some way to go. He looks great and although he hasn't started cantering, he's young enough at seven to hit the headlines."

Little has gone right for ***Finian's Rainbow*** since the spring of 2012 when he completed the Champion Chase-Melling Chase double. Henderson says: "It's been a nightmare that we haven't been able to get him back to that form. He has had a multitude of frustrating injuries that have led to a very stop, start, and mainly stop, campaign. He looks fantastic after a good summer and we can only hope we have mended everything necessary."

Although ***Bobs Worth*** was beaten only four lengths in the Cheltenham Gold Cup, there remains a school of thought at Seven Barrows that he was not at his best that day. Not only did he forfeit his title, but also his unbeaten record at Cheltenham that had embraced the three previous festivals. It was

certainly short of the form he had produced at Christmas when his victims in the Lexus Chase included Gold Cup winner Lord Windermere, beaten 11 lengths at Leopardstown.

Henderson says: "He's returned from his break looking as well as I've seen him and we're very hopeful normal service will be resumed. We're discussing where to start off. It could be under top weight in the Hennessy, or perhaps a return to hurdling over three miles. Having won the Lexus so well that may again be part of the programme as the King George wouldn't be for him. A left-hand course with good ground is ideal.

Of the other leading chasers, dual King George winner **Long Run** will not be back at Kempton this season. He is sidelined until the second half of the campaign having injured the back of a knee when travelling home from the Grand Steeple-Chase de Paris in May.

Both ***Triolo D'Alene***, the Hennessy Gold Cup winner, and **Oscar Whisky** have undergone surgery to improve their breathing, while bet365 winner ***Hadrian's Approach*** might try his luck in the Hennessy.

The mare ***Ma Filleule*** produced one of the jumping exhibitions of the season in the Topham. Still only six, the grey could be a serious player at the highest level this season, although off a mark of 163 handicaps look out of reach. "Accordingly, we'll need to be looking at something like the Charlie Hall or perhaps Down Royal at the beginning of November," says the trainer. "She's still very young but doesn't show it. Over the summer she grew and strengthened again and we'll have to see where all this leads us."

After much debate between the trainer and JP McManus it has been agreed to give ***My Tent Or Yours*** another shot at the Champion Hurdle. He was beaten only a neck for the title last season, which was remarkable considering how hard he pulled in the middle section of the race. Attempting to solve that

Captain Conan: on the way back to full fitness after breaking his pelvis

problem is proving difficult, as Henderson explains: "He doesn't take a hold at home – he could be ridden out in a head-collar without a bit. Our priority must be to get him to settle because he has been going the wrong way in that respect. It's a difficult one."

As last season, he could start again in Newcastle's Fighting Fifth, although there is another option available with the introduction of a similar £100,000 race on Haydock's Betfair Chase day the previous weekend. If Haydock is the choice, it will then free up Tony McCoy for Newbury's Hennessy Gold Cup meeting, which invariably clashes with Newcastle. My Tent will again contest the Christmas Hurdle, in which he beat The New One last season.

Vaniteux, third to Vautour in the Supreme Novices' Hurdle following a classy win at Doncaster, is high up the order of merit at the yard and is likely to reappear in one of those Newcastle/Haydock trials. "He's only five and was still weak last season, but I'd be very hopeful he's close to top class," says the trainer.

Josses Hill, who finished one place ahead of Vaniteux in the Supreme before winning a Grade 2 at Aintree, is heading for novice chases and is confidently expected to be one of the season's leading lights in that division, but he was troubled by a splint in mid-September which means his preparation is

on hold for a month. "He's a gorgeous big horse with bags of scope for two-mile chases," says Henderson: "The splint problem looks only a minor one, certainly not like Simonsig's last year."

Over longer trips, the hardy ***Whisper***, who completed a big-race double at Cheltenham and Aintree last season, is expected to prove a major force.

The Queen's ***Close Touch*** missed last season due to injury, but is regarded as a leading hope in the novice chase ranks. "He loves soft ground," says Henderson. "He's been beaten just once and I believe he has an enormous future."

Grandouet has undergone a breathing operation and the plan now is to win a couple of minor chases before moving back to the top league.

West Wizard has a massive reputation at the yard and tops the novice hurdle division, having recovered from a knee problem which sidelined him for the most part of last season. Also expected to make an impact is JP McManus's ***Cup Final***, who looks nicely handicapped on a mark of 125, and three of the Queen's homebred bumper winners, ***Jack Frost***, ***Special Agent*** and ***Summer Storm***, along with ***Bringithomeminty***, ***Clondaw Banker***, ***Native Display***, ***Lolli*** and ***Forever Field***.

Reporting by Rodney Masters

Josses Hill: Aintree winner picked up a splint problem in September but should make his debut over fences this season

HENDERSON: ASSESSING THE STATS

An influx of serious talent at Seven Barrows in recent years enabled Nicky Henderson to win the trainers' championship in 2012-13, his first for 26 years, *writes Kevin Morley*. However, last term he managed to rake in a little over £2 million in prize-money, below the total amassed in the previous five seasons and significantly lower than the last two, and found the title wrested away from him by Paul Nicholls.

Henderson's biggest earner last term was My Tent Or Yours, winner of the Fighting Fifth and the Christmas Hurdle. He was also a close second in the Champion Hurdle. However, he didn't have as many horses on that level at his disposal in 2013-14 as injury scuppered plans for Sprinter Sacre and Simonsig. Both dominated their respective divisions the previous season and were expected to prove big players in Grade 1 chases last term but their absence dealt Henderson a sledgehammer blow in terms of retaining the trainers' championship.

The Seven Barrows handler still managed to notch up 124 victories last term. That might have been only one below his tally the previous season, but lack of success at the top level cost him dear. While Henderson's strike-rate is generally higher than Nicholls, he doesn't run his string as often.

Similarly to his main training rival, Henderson has plenty of regular success in hurdles, chases and bumpers alike, although a more refined approach is required for betting purposes as backing all of his runners in any given code will result in a loss.

Stable jockey Barry Geraghty is riding as well as ever and can be expected to maintain his healthy association with the yard, much to the benefit of punters, although an even better source of profit is when Tony McCoy is called upon.

There is normally a good claimer who is worth following at the yard and last season it was the turn of Nico de Boinville. The amateur-turned-conditional excelled and his allowance proved a valuable asset in handicaps, most notably on Whisper in the Coral Cup.

Henderson can be followed at most tracks with confidence but his favourite course is Kempton. He regularly sends out plenty of winners to a high strike-rate and a handsome level-stake profit. His runners at the Surrey venue over Christmas are particularly worth a look. It is also worth noting his figures at Newbury last term, which were outstanding considering the competitive nature of racing at the Berkshire track.

With Henderson's stable stars all seemingly fit and well, he seems on course for a successful campaign and would be a strong favourite to regain the trainers' championship.

Novice chase prospects set the pulse racing for an exciting campaign

PHILIP HOBBS admits he is slightly weaker in the novice hurdle department this year, but few stables can boast the raft of top-notch novice chase prospects like those at Sandhill.

With seven 140 plus-rated hurdlers likely to embark on a career over fences, alongside a host of returning stars, Hobbs has plenty of tools to build on last winter's exploits, which yielded two Cheltenham Festival victories and over £1.5 million in prize-money.

Triple Grade 1-winning chaser ***Captain Chris*** spearheads the familiar faces, with the ten-year-old returning from a suspensory injury that ruled him out of a second tilt at the Cheltenham Gold Cup last season.

While his habit of jumping right-handed has proved troublesome since success in the 2011 Arkle, Captain Chris has since established himself as a chaser of the highest magnitude racing in that direction, narrowly succumbing to Long Run in the 2012 King George and spectacularly pummelling seven rivals in the Ascot Chase last season.

Having been given the all-clear following a mid-September scan, Captain Chris is set to return to the track in January.

"He'll be back in training with us in November and we'll go for the Grade 1 again at Ascot," Hobbs says. "Regarding spring plans, I think we'll see nearer the time. I imagine he would retain the habit of jumping right-handed, but we'll go to Ascot first and take it from there."

If Cheltenham has proved troublesome for Captain Chris, then the opposite is true of ***Balthazar King***. A seven-time winner around Prestbury Park, including the most tenacious of victories in this year's festival Cross Country – a race he also won in 2012 – the ten-year-old followed that run with a fine second behind Pineau De Re in the Grand National.

He has already been busy in France, defending his crown in the Crystal Cup at Craon, having ended last season with a fall at Lion-D'Angers in May.

"The plan would be to go to Cheltenham in November for the level-weights cross-country chase," Hobbs says. "I don't think he'll go to the festival this year because he's probably better fresh, so he's likely to go straight for the Grand National, or if the ground was soft there, the Scottish National."

Chance Du Roy also enjoys Aintree having landed the Becher Chase before finishing sixth in the Grand National last season. He will go for both races again.

Menorah has proved a frustrating customer on occasions, displaying a raft of class to land the 2010 Supreme Novices' without showing the same spark in top-flight chases in subsequent seasons.

However, he returned to his best when a three-quarter-length second behind First Lieutenant in the 2013 Aintree Bowl, while his sole success last season came courtesy of a 17-length romp in Listed company at Sandown.

Chance Du Roy: has the Becher Chase and Grand National on his agenda

DID YOU KNOW

Philip Hobbs has passed the win prize-money barrier of £1 million on three occasions and came close to repeating the feat last year. What is noticeable is the tremendous record he has with stable jockey Richard Johnson. A look at Hobbs's big-race wins on the Racing Post website shows Johnson having ridden 24 of the last 26. Fairly extraordinary given the yard has Tom O'Brien as its No.2. Johnson was also aboard Hobbs's two festival winners last term.

The nine-year-old returned to that venue in May, making his Flat debut in Group 3 company, but future plans in that sphere were aborted on account of the ground.

Hobbs says: "The plan was to run him in the Queen Alexandra Stakes at Royal Ascot, and that could have worked very well, but we didn't want to run him on very firm ground. I suppose his Flat racing career is finished already, although it was a promising first run.

"We're thinking of starting him off in the Charlie Hall. His right trip is probably the two miles six furlongs he won over at Sandown, but he would have won over any distance that day because he travelled so well, which sometimes he doesn't. He ought to stay three miles, but that would be my concern about the Charlie Hall – that extra furlong might be a bit far to be going. The problem with a horse of his rating is there aren't many options."

Fellow Diana Whateley-owned stalwart ***Wishfull Thinking*** is another for whom the optimum trip is not glaringly obvious, with the 11-year-old having landed a 2m5f handicap on Festival Trials Day before running creditably in the Queen Mother Champion Chase.

"I imagine he'd run at Aintree in the Old Roan Chase," Hobbs says. "He started in that race last year. He didn't run that well, but nevertheless it's the right race for him – a limited handicap – and then we'll go from there.

"Most years when we come round to Cheltenham, his handicap mark has gone up and down a bit over the season. We were in the Ryanair and the Champion Chase last year, and we left the decision to the last minute, but we ran him in the Champion Chase – he picked up really good prize-money for finishing fifth. Now he's a bit older, he's more likely to end up in the Ryanair."

Roalco De Farges has not been the easiest to train, picking up an injury following the 2012 bet365 Gold Cup at Sandown – in which he finished second behind a rejuvenated Tidal Bay – but the nine-year-old made a mockery of a mark of 127 at Newbury in March.

While two subsequent efforts over stamina-sapping trips were fruitless, he has fallen in the weights

Wishfull Thinking (right): could have Ryanair Chase as his main target

to a mark of 134 and Hobbs is keen to test the water back in trip this time.

"I think we completely messed up with him," Hobbs says. "Having been second in the bet365 Gold Cup, I presumed he'd be better over a longer trip, but both in the Scottish National and the bet365 again, he didn't get home.

"I think we'll change tack and go back to three miles. The Hennessy could be a possibility. I suppose the race is often won by a second-season novice, but there has always been exceptions, and I think it would be an option."

Duke Of Lucca was down the field in the 2012 renewal of the Newbury showpiece, but he won't be bidding to avenge that defeat, with Hobbs reporting his charge to have emerged unscathed from a fall at Craon having tipped up when looking set to challenge Balthazar King.

The nine-year-old had recorded his first victory in over two seasons when gallantly repelling Vino Griego in an Aintree handicap, while he travelled smoothly in cross-country company at Punchestown before appearing not to get home.

Hobbs says: "He jumped very well at Punchestown and jumped well in France until his fall. It was an unusual fence where he fell – they jump off a level platform before jumping down about eight foot and it caught him unawares.

"He doesn't want the ground too soft, so I imagine he'd run in October, either at Cheltenham or Chepstow where there are two long-distance handicap chases, or possibly the 3m handicap chase at Ascot [second last year]."

Fingal Bay, the only horse to have beaten Simonsig under rules, was off the track for 14 months before victory in an Exeter handicap hurdle in February, but that success paved the way for a huge performance in the Pertemps Final at Cheltenham, in which he defied top weight to prevail by a nose before finishing fifth in the World Series Hurdle at Punchestown.

Despite three inauspicious performances over fences the season before last, which included running out when long odds-on at Exeter, a return to chasing is likely for the eight-year-old.

"Realistically, he showed at Punchestown he's not a Grade 1 horse over hurdles, so I think he'll probably go chasing again," Hobbs says. "Graduation chases would be the obvious route for him as he's only won one race over fences."

If In Doubt, who finished second behind Fingal Bay at Exeter before a respectable ninth in the Pertemps Final, is one of a plethora of high-quality prospects for novice chases.

Hobbs says: "He wasn't beaten far in the Pertemps – he's not that slow and yet he didn't really travel. He's been very backward and has taken plenty of time and I hope there is room for improvement. Whether he goes straight over fences or takes in a hurdles race first I'm not sure at this stage."

2011 Champion Bumper winner ***Cheltenian*** could also join rank over fences after beginning his campaign with a spin over hurdles.

"I imagine Cheltenian will be going chasing this year, but whether he runs in a hurdle race first I'm not sure," Hobbs says. "He has enough pace for 2m, but 2m4f is probably his trip."

Hobbs also plans to send Albert Bartlett fourth ***Champagne West*** chasing after a productive season over hurdles, while a revitalised ***Dunraven Storm*** could dip his toe in that sphere alongside ***Horizontal Speed***, who won four times over hurdles last winter and finished out of the frame only once in seven runs.

Hobbs says: "Horizontal Speed is a big, strong horse and chasing is likely to be his job. He's the sort of horse who should better his form over fences.

Whateley has an enviable quartet of high-quality hopes for the novice ranks, including quadruple hurdles winner ***Garde La Victoire*** and the lightly raced ***Mountain King***.

"I think good ground is important to Garde La Victoire," Hobbs says. "He's only a five-year-old and he'll probably run in the Silver Trophy at Chepstow – we'll decide after that if we go novice chasing with him.

"Mountain King is also five and looks fantastic. I imagine he'd run in a handicap hurdle first because I think there might be more room for improvement, and then he'll go novice chasing.

Royal Player and ***Sausalito Sunrise***, both of whom Hobbs describes as "big, strong horses who will go straight over fences" will also carry the Whateley silks, with the trainer hopeful Sausalito Sunrise can "perform at a high level in novice chases".

A gallant winner at Cheltenham's New Year's Day fixture, ***Return Spring*** will also tackle fences despite being "not a big horse", as will ***The Skyfarmer***, who was rapidly progressive in the first half of the campaign before registering a couple of blips in the new year.

Hobbs says: "Maybe we would blame The Skyfarmer's Ascot run on heavy ground, but there were no issues after that. I think we'll forget his Cheltenham run and start again. For a novice chase at the festival you need to be rated 140-odd. If he progresses from where we are, a mark of 137 over hurdles – we're not that far off."

The novice hurdling division includes ***Brother Tedd***, who landed an ordinary bumper at Huntingdon before running creditably under a penalty at Wincanton, alongside point-to-point recruit ***Ink Master*** and 77-rated Flat performer ***Sternrubin***, who Hobbs believes "will be a nice sort for juvenile hurdles" having been purchased from Peter Chapple-Hyam.

Neck Or Nothing, who showed plenty of ability in two starts for Hobbs in the spring, and Sandown bumper winner ***Hello George*** will also go hurdling in the new campaign.

Hobbs says: "I hope Neck Or Nothing has improvement to come. He's schooled well over hurdles already and two-mile novice hurdles would be the plan with him.

Chepstow second ***Rock The Kasbah*** is another potentially bright young prospect who could fly the flag in bumper company.

"He is only four and is a really nice horse who should improve," Hobbs says. "We'll try him in a bumper first."

Reporting by Chris Humpleby

Fingal Bay (right): likely to run in graduation chases

HOBBS: ASSESSING THE STATS

Before last season, numbers had been on the decline at Withycombe with the 68 winners sent out in 2012-13 the lowest for 15 years, *writes Kevin Morley*. However, there was a big turnaround in fortunes for Philip Hobbs in the 2013-14 campaign which saw him send out 106 winners, earning over £1.5 million. That prize-money total was his second highest and saw him finish third in the trainers' championship.

Hobbs's highest-class performer was Captain Chris, who landed Ascot's Grade 1 Betfair Chase, but his top moneyspinner was Balthazar King, who picked up three valuable contests, including the festival's cross-country chase for the second time, while he also finished runner-up in the Grand National.

Along with those two stalwarts, it was the established stars who did Hobbs proud last term, with Menorah and Wishfull Thinking picking up the odd valuable chase while the return of Fingal Bay from injury was also welcome as he won Cheltenham's Pertemps Final.

Hobbs generally enjoys more success over hurdles, but the gap was narrowed last term as his chasers excelled. His bumper runners also continue to oblige at a healthy rate. Having seemingly been on the slide, the dramatic reverse in amount of winners also caught the layers unaware as backing all of his runners last season would have returned a level-stake profit.

Stable jockey Richard Johnson also felt the benefits of Hobbs's success as his tally of winners for the season was also an improvement on the previous three totals. And his rides for Hobbs last term returned a massive profit. Tom O'Brien and conditional James Best fill in admirably when required although the benefits of backing them blind is negligible.

Over the last five seasons, Hobbs has sent out most winners at Exeter, although the strike-rate there is lower compared to other tracks. He has reasonable records at most of the leading courses such as Cheltenham, Newbury and Sandown but seems best followed at Chepstow.

Lower down the racing scale, Hobbs's frequent raids at Bangor are often successful, while rare visits to Lingfield and Towcester are also worth noting.

If Hobbs is to replicate the success of last term, he will need his proven performers to step up to the plate again as the novices coming through the ranks need to improve on what they have shown so far.

Philip Hobbs keeps an eye on the string at his Somerset stables

MY WAY DE SOLZEN, Voy Por Ustedes and Medermit are familiar names to racing fans. They have also provided Alan King with chasing victories at the highest level in recent years, flying the flag for Barbury Castle and proving year on year that King can keep producing top-class horses. And the trainer is confident of a good showing this season.

Last year the trainer introduced ***Balder Succes*** *(below)* to fences and the six-year-old made an immediate impact, beating some very smart yardsticks in high-class races. King hopes he can continue improving and stamp his class on the 2m chasing scene.

"Balder Succes had a marvellous season last year which culminated in his win in the Maghull Novices' Chase at Aintree," King says. "We have high hopes he can build on that this season and I'm going to start him off down the two-mile route and he'll probably head for the Haldon Gold Cup at Exeter or the Schloer Chase at Cheltenham. He's done really well over the summer and has come back more powerful."

Another first-season novice chaser who won a Grade 1 at Aintree was the JP McManus-owned ***Uxizandre***.

The six-year-old started off over fences with two small-field victories at Plumpton before proving a revelation at the Cheltenham Festival, finishing second in the JLT Novices' Chase at 33-1. He proved that was no fluke with a win at the highest level in his final run of the season, and King is looking to start him off gradually this year.

"Uxizandre is very well

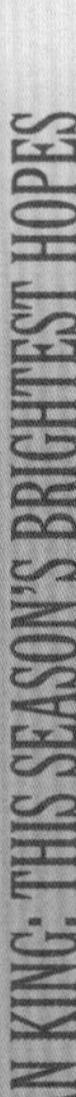
ALAN KING: THIS SEASON'S BRIGHTEST HOPES

Balder Succes flying flag for yard with fine record on the big stage

and has had a good summer," he says. "We discovered last year he wants to be ridden aggressively, and he's an interesting horse because he gets three miles but we can also bring him back to two. Our hands are slightly tied as he only wants to race left-handed. There's an intermediate chase at Newton Abbot which we might look at for his first outing."

Smad Place has consistently been competing against the most talented staying hurdlers for the last few years and, after a most successful first season over fences, an ambitious second-season chasing campaign is planned.

Godsmejudge: will be campaigned with the Grand National as his main target

Following an excellent second in the RSA Chase at the Cheltenham Festival last year, there is little doubt his future lies in the top races over three miles-plus.

"Smad Place enjoyed a very good first season over fences," King says. "He doesn't want a huge amount of racing and the plan is start him off in the Hennessy Gold Cup at Newbury."

One who went somewhat under the radar at the Cheltenham Festival was **Valdez**. The seven-year-old held his own over hurdles but it was clear when he jumped a fence that chasing would be his game.

After three straight victories he lined up in the Arkle Chase with connections hopeful of a good run, but things didn't quite work out and he finished fifth of nine to Western Warhorse. King, though, is hopeful he can prove competitive in more top races this season.

"Valdez seems to be back in very good form now. Any distance from two to two and a half miles will suit him and it's likely he'll head down the handicap route this season," Kings says. "The Paddy Power Gold Cup at Cheltenham is a possible early target for him."

King has a live chance for the Aintree showpiece in April at the end of the season in **Godsmejudge**. The hardy stayer has shown he is made of stern stuff, and his trainer hopes he can add the Grand National to his CV, having already scored a victory in the Scottish Grand National as well as finishing a good third in Sandown's bet365 Gold Cup.

"I was thrilled with the way Godsmejudge came back to finish second in the Scottish National." King says. "I'd hoped to run him in the Grand National last year but he didn't get there but this year all roads lead to Liverpool. He's very well and he could go for the Scottish National again but that would be an afterthought as his main target is Aintree."

Another staying chaser who provided his trainer with success last season is ***Midnight Prayer***, winner of the National Hunt Chase over four miles at the Cheltenham Festival.

"Midnight Prayer had a marvellous year last season and he's come back in good form," his trainer says. "He could have one run in early December and it's possible he could be our main hope in the Welsh National at Chepstow."

A chaser who has yet to see a fence in public is ***Carraig Mor***. The lightly raced six-year-old burst on to the hurdling scene last year with a fine performance in a Uttoxeter novice hurdle, bolting up by 25 lengths. Things didn't quite work out after that, but King believes he will bounce back to his best this year.

"Carraig Mor was very impressive at Uttoxeter but wasn't quite right after that. He's had the sun on his back which has helped him. He doesn't have any targets yet as he needs two and half miles or possibly three, and also a bit of rain. The plan is to go chasing."

Turn Over Sivola is perhaps one of King's most frustrating horses. There is no doubting his ability, with close seconds in a number of races last season, including a fiercely competitive handicap chase at Aintree.

His trainer says: "Turn over Sivola needs a flat track as we saw when he finished second in the Red Rum Chase. He's more of a speed horse and will be aimed at either a decent novice or a good handicap."

As well as a formidable group of chasers to go to war with this season, King also has a plethora of hurdlers, some of whom could be very smart. Perhaps his most exciting prospect is **Ordo Ab Chao**. After an impressive bumper victory, he was aimed high, and King is confident he can improve again.

"Ordo Ab Chao will go straight to hurdling now he's had his experience in bumpers. I was very pleased with his two runs last season, and when he came fourth at Aintree

DID YOU KNOW

Alan King is increasingly becoming a Cheltenham Festival specialist. Last term saw four of his runners finish in the first five on day one and he had two seconds and a third later on in the meeting. Before Cheltenham last season the Racing Post's James Pyman worked out that King was the top British trainer on Racing Post Ratings in terms of his horses improving at the meeting, showing his skill at getting one to peak for the big day.

he had to come from a long way back. He probably needs a stiff two miles. He's a very smart horse."

A more experienced hurdler, and one already successful at the highest level, is the mare **L'Unique**. After winning a novice Grade 1 at Aintree two years ago, she never quite reached that level again until the Cheltenham Festival last season, where she ran a mighty race to finish third to Quevega. With no Quevega this year, King hopes she can improve two places and take the victory in the Mares' Hurdle.

"L'Unique will be staying hurdling this year as she finished off her season last year very well," he says. "The David Nicholson Mares' Hurdle at the Cheltenham Festival is her target again this year as I think the race will be tailor-made for her. She'll make a lovely chaser in time."

Another exciting prospect is the scopey **Ulzana's Raid**. One of the larger horses at Barbary Castle, the five-year-old impressed in a maiden hurdle and a handicap last year, winning twice despite looking in need of the experience. The fact King is keen to keep him over hurdles for the time being is surely a reflection of how talented his trainer thinks the horse is, when clearly the gelding could also be making his mark as a chaser.

"Ulzana's Raid will stay hurdling this season but I'm certain he'll make a gorgeous chaser," the trainer says. "He won his last two races and has improved physically over the summer. He'll keep progressing and never win by very far."

Wilde Blue Yonder also looked a horse of considerable talent last season, running very well to finish fifth in the Supreme Novices' Hurdle at Cheltenham in only his second completed start over hurdles before finishing off with a fourth in a Grade 1 at Aintree. He had two falls as well but apparently felt no ill-effects.

"Wilde Blue Yonder will also stay hurdling this season," says King. "He finished last season well but had two unfortunate mishaps, falling at Ascot and Newbury. He was fifth in the Supreme Novices', and whether he didn't get home over two and a half miles at Aintree I don't know, but I'll keep him at that trip this season as he'll probably get it."

One horse who has proved most consistent in recent seasons is also one of the smallest in the yard. **Medinas** has demonstrated that size isn't everything with victories in top handicaps, including the Coral Cup at the Cheltenham Festival and the Welsh Champion Hurdle at Ffos Las.

"Medinas seems very well but I'm not sure what to do with him. I'm not convinced he's big enough for fences so I might aim him at a three-mile handicap hurdle at Wetherby at the start of November as we can use a claim which he needs as he is so small. He was second in the race last year, so we know he goes well there."

The Pirate's Queen is another novice who contested some top-class races over hurdles last season but didn't manage to score, despite coming very close behind the smart Run Ructions Run in a Listed handicap at Newbury. It is likely the five-year-old will be able to pick up some prize-money if she carries on this season is the same vein.

"The Pirate's Queen is still a novice but has very good form in the book. We'll continue down the mare's route with her and there is a good programme this year that she can be aimed at. She's quite decent."

Reporting by Tom Bull

L'Unique: Grade 1 winner will have another crack at the festival Mares' Hurdle this season

KING: ASSESSING THE STATS

In recent years Alan King has failed to match his exploits in 2007-08 and 2008-09, seasons in which he broke the century barrier with big-race wins galore, *writes Kevin Morley*. However, he doesn't quite possess the same ammunition these days although a tally of 75 last term was a reasonable effort in the circumstances while King's prize-money total of over £1.1 million was a superb return.

That success owed much to novice chasers. The likes of Balder Succes, Uxizandre, Manyriverstocross, Pantxoa and Valdez were all among King's top moneyspinners, while Midnight Prayer recorded the trainer's sole victory at the festival in the four-mile National Hunt Chase.

King is a rounded trainer and generally enjoys a greater frequency of success over hurdles. That was the case last term although the victories came in a lower grade more often than not. The Barbury Castle handler usually has a fair strike-rate in bumpers and his runners returned a level-stake profit in this area last term.

King employs two main riders in Robert Thornton and Wayne Hutchinson. Thornton has struggled with injuries in recent times, which has seen Hutchinson step in to ride more winners in each of the last two seasons. He has also returned a huge level-stake profit on all his rides for King during this period and continues to remain underrated by the layers.

Like many of the other leading yards, King utilises Tony McCoy to excellent effect and this was evident last term when the champion jockey scored on four of his eight mounts.

King has some success at the top tracks – Ascot fares best in this respect – but not on a consistent basis. He is best followed at some of the smaller circuits, with his strike-rates at Hereford, Towcester, Stratford and, in particular, Plumpton taking the eye.

One of the problems King will face this term is placing his leading novice chasers from last season. Having enjoyed a fair amount of success they have lofty official ratings and some will have to find some improvement to cut it in the top races. That's not out of the question though as age is on their side – and King usually has a few smart novices coming through the ranks each season.

ultima
BUSINESS SOLUTIONS

Exciting Corrin Wood heads quality team that looks sure to do well

SINCE he first took over the reins from his father, Donald McCain has regularly increased the size of his Cheshire stable, and the Cholmondeley-based trainer now has 200 horses in his care.

Operating last season at a strike-rate of 18 per cent, McCain has started the 2014-15 season in a similarly successful vein, and it is a testament to his conscientious and methodical approach that he is able to run so many horses so many times and still achieve good results – last year his horses raced, collectively, 775 times, and he picked up win or place prize money in nearly half of those contests.

Perhaps the horse most likely to help McCain accomplish high-profile success this time is his second-season chaser ***Corrin Wood***, who last year burst onto the novice scene with back-to-back victories in decent contests before proving slightly disappointing at the Cheltenham Festival.

"Corrin Wood has summered well and I'm really chuffed with him. Cheltenham was a bit of a disaster and it didn't really happen for him, but he's come back to form now and looks great."

As far as a target is concerned for the seven-year-old, McCain is eager to test the waters in graded company to find out where he stands.

"The first thing I need to find out is if he's a conditions chaser or a handicapper, and the plan is to start him off in the Charlie Hall Chase at Wetherby."

Another promising inmate is ***Diamond King***, who last year won hotly contested novice hurdles at Wetherby and Doncaster. Aside from a blip at Bangor, which his trainer believes was due to the ground, hopes are high at Cholmondeley he can progress to a new level this year.

"I think Diamond King could be my brightest prospect for the season. I imagine we'll be starting him off novice chasing. He's pretty smart and would have remained unbeaten but for a mistake at the last at Bangor in December. He's missed two festivals at Cheltenham due to injury and I hope this year I'll be able to get him there."

Six-year-old ***Stonebrook*** showed significant ability last season. By Flemensfirth, the JP McManus-owned gelding demonstrated he had inherited some of his sire's Group 1-winning speed with bloodless wins at Ayr and Newcastle before starting favourite for a competitive handicap hurdle at Aintree.

"He's been cantering away over the summer. He's not very big, but he's a nice, genuine little horse. He won his novice hurdles and was on the bridle when he had the rest of them all off it. At Aintree he raced in a competitive handicap hurdle, but nearly got brought down two out and there wasn't a lot he could do about it. I think he'll stay further in time."

One who made headlines at the Grand National meeting for the wrong reasons last year was ***Across the Bay***. Leading the field

Corrin Wood: set to start off in the Charlie Hall Chase at Wetherby

and going comfortably past the stands, McCain's ten-year-old looked as though he was going to figure prominently at the finish only to be carried very wide by a loose horse, losing any chance.

"The plan again this year for Across The Bay is definitely another go at the Grand National. I was devastated with his run in the race last year when he got carried wide."

In terms of a target for his first run of the season, McCain believes another crack at the National fences is the most sensible plan.

"From what I saw in the race last year I think he'll stay the Grand National distance, and the plan is to start him off in the Becher Chase. He surprised us when he won at Haydock at Christmas as we rode him differently and held him up, but he still stuck his neck out in the deep ground. He's a smashing horse who performs all the time and always does his best."

Another promising sort for this season who

ran at Aintree was ***Clondaw Kaempfer***. The six-year-old provided a refreshing antidote to McCain's Grand National woes, showing great tenacity to win the same handicap hurdle for which Stonebrook started favourite. Fences are possibly on the agenda or him, but McCain doesn't rule out trying to find other suitable handicaps over the smaller obstacles.

"He's been working well at home. We've never schooled him over fences, but I will at some point soon as I think chasing could be good for him. His targets are flexible and I'll also take a look at some handicap hurdles. Although he won at Aintree and his mark went up he'll still be competitive in good handicaps."

Desert Cry finished off his season well, coming second to an improver in a Listed chase at Ayr. He had won his first two races, so wherever his trainer opts to send him first, he will be worth keeping an eye on.

Across The Bay: all roads lead back to Aintree

He ended last season with a career-high Racing Post Rating of 160, and his trainer hopes he'll be able to pick up some good prize-money.

"Desert Cry goes on better ground but is also very effective in bad conditions, so I'll follow the ground over the course of the season. We'll aim at more listed chases, depending on the ground, and maybe put him over hurdles as there are so many good races over two miles. He can jump a fence well but he doesn't need a fence so his options are open."

Staying chasers have become a standing dish at McCain's stable. Often tough and tenacious, past winners over a longer distance have included Will Be Done, Cloudy Lane, and Ballabriggs. The latest in a long line of hardy chasers from the yard emerged in impressive style last season, in the form of ***Sydney Paget***.

At Haydock last November he trounced a strong field on soft ground over 3m1f, earning the enviable formbook description 'eased down run-in' and, although slightly disappointing afterwards, McCain believes he can bounce back this year given the right conditions.

"The plan is to leave him until the second half of the season as he's had a setback. I think the longer staying chases will be the target for him. As he showed at Haydock, he runs well fresh and performs best on very soft ground. At this stage I think the Welsh Grand National could be a race for him."

Swatow Typhoon takes after Sydney Paget in that he is a promising staying chaser, but that is where the similarities end. McCain's enigmatic seven-year-old tends to either run very well or very lazily, but there is no denying his ability, with two wins from five races last year.

"Swatow is an enigma who is never on the bridle but he travelled well in the Eider Chase when he was equipped with first-time blinkers – in fact, he travelled too well and eventually pulled up."

The target following that enthusiastic run at Newcastle is likely to be another marathon chase, although a specific race is yet to be decided.

"He'll get long distances this season but has his own ideas and we have to put up with him as he can be very hard to ride. But we'll aim him at big staying chases, probably in the north – he'll tell us as he's different."

Another horse McCain hopes can bounce back is ***Red Merlin***. Winner of what is formerly known as the Swinton Handicap Hurdle in 2012, the smooth-travelling nine-year-old picked up an injury after the race and we did not see him again until June.

He clearly retains a lot of his ability, finishing second in two outings this season, but he probably needs to find another five or six pounds before he gets back to his best.

"Red Merlin looked pretty smart at one point, and he's still very talented. I would think the first port of call for him would be Market Rasen and then big galloping tracks which I think are more suitable for him. He's more effective arriving late off a strong pace in a large field and I imagine he'll be aimed at handicaps, but we'll play it by ear as he's fragile and we have to ensure he's healthy."

More success last season came from ***Dispour***, who won a decent Sandown handicap hurdle in April. Following a good

The McCains are steeped in Grand National history, but Ginger's son Donald has become renowned for training hurdlers. A good look at McCain's gallery of big-race wins on the Racing Post website shows 17 of the 23 listed have been in hurdle races. At the Cheltenham Festival McCain has a fine record in the Kim Muir, but outside that handicap chase his wins at the meeting have all come over the smaller obstacles. Three of his winners – Peddlers Cross, Whiteoak and Cinders And Ashes – all went on to run in the Champion Hurdle with Peddlers Cross finishing second in 2011.

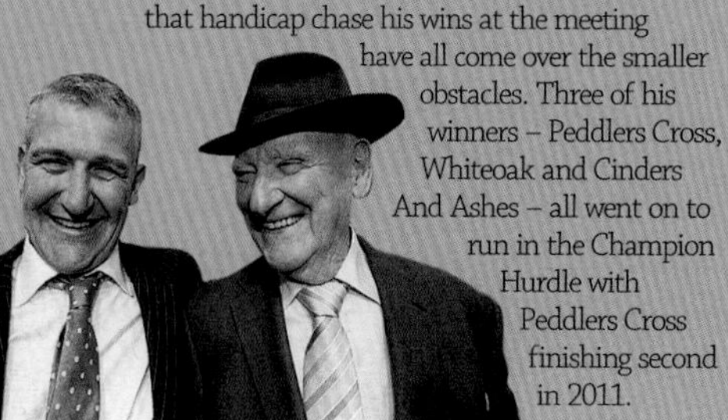

run in the Grade 1 juvenile hurdle at Aintree the four-year-old won off a mark of 131, and has since been raised six pounds to a career-high figure, but it is unlikely we have seen the end of his improvement.

"He's doing great at home and we probably shouldn't have run on the Flat at Chester in May. The plan is to start him off in a four-year-old handicap hurdle at Chepstow."

Gabrial The Great has shown significant ability. He was fairly useful on the Flat and could be even better over hurdles. On his debut over obstacles he looked fairly ordinary but the form was franked as the winner went on to win the Betfair Hurdle, and his subsequent three novice hurdle wins produced a combined winning margin of over 80 lengths. McCain's promising five-year-old didn't find conditions to his liking when struggling in the Summer Hurdle at Perth, but the potential is still very much there.

"Gabrial The Great was very promising before we ran him in ground that was too soft, but he seems fine now. He gets very keen in his races and I want to get him to relax although there seems to be nothing capable of leading him. I'll take him back to basics and try and get him to switch off. He's a smashing horse and is very economical over hurdles, so I think he'll be even better over fences."

Another slightly unknown quantity for this season is the Diana Whateley-owned ***King's Bandit***, for whom the future looks bright after a trio of workmanlike victories in novice hurdle company. In the most recent of those, King's Bandit took the scalp of the smart chaser King Edmund without much fuss, demonstrating he is a smart recruit for the yard.

"King's Bandit is relaxed at home," says McCain. "But he tends to hang his head to one side when he gets on the racecourse and consequently he'll probably only go on left-handed tracks. You have to know where the right races are, and there are one or two suitable novice events further down the line for him. I think he's improved."

Reporting by Tom Bull

Dispour: Sandown winner is capable of improvement

McCAIN: ASSESSING THE STATS

With 142 victories on the board, no trainer sent out more winners than Donald McCain in the 2013-14 campaign, a feat he also achieved the previous term, *writes Kevin Morley*. However, he failed to break the £1 million prize-money mark for the second season running.

While quantity is hardly an issue for the Cholmendeley handler, the quality has generally been lacking over the past couple of years and McCain's string has been worryingly absent from the top-grade races during this period.

The exploits of Corrin Wood, one of the stable's best chasers, was indicative of McCain's performance last term. The seven-year-old grey had no trouble dispatching his rivals in weakly contested novice chases in the north but came up well short when upped in class at the festival. In fact, McCain's biggest success came at the Grand National meeting when Clondaw Kaempfer landed a Grade 3 handicap hurdle, which is disappointing considering the amount of ammunition he has at his disposal.

If he is to have more success at the top level, an advantage McCain does have is that he is equally skilled in all disciplines of the jumping game as victories in hurdles, chases and bumpers all come with a similarly high frequency.

Jason Maguire has had more than his fair share of injuries in recent times, but the durable jockey can be expected to pick up the lion's share of rides now he is back in action. A level-stake loss is likely to occur if backing his mounts blindly although that could improve if McCain's fortunes in the top-class races take a sudden turn for the better. As with plenty of the top trainers, they turn to Tony McCoy when in need, and the champion jockey usually comes up trumps while, to a lesser extent, Noel Fehily is also utilised to good effect.

Henry Brooke was the yard's top conditional last term although it remains to be seen how he fares now he no longer claims. James Cowley is a rider on the up and he could prove a useful weapon for the yard with his 7lb claim still intact.

McCain sends many runners to nearby Bangor and he has a decent strike-rate and level-stake profit at the Welsh venue. He also boasts impressive figures north of the border, with his raiders at Kelso and Musselburgh standing out in particular.

Expect McCain to send out plenty of winners again, particularly on the northern circuit, but more success at the top level. Diamond King, a promising novice hurdler last term and embryonic chaser, looks his best hope in that respect.

On the gallops at McCain's Cheshire stables

Huge array of talent sure to provide another exciting season for Irish champion

WILLIE MULLINS' closing statement of the season was: Hurricane Fly is not finished. As he retired five-time Cheltenham Festival-winning mare Quevega, Mullins was adamant his flagbearer would continue to hold that title in the new campaign. But that was the only thing the champion trainer was certain of, leaving three major questions to ponder.

Is Hurricane Fly, the dual Champion Hurdle winner, to emulate Solwhit and migrate into the staying ranks? Will Supreme Novices' Hurdle winner Vautour be Mullins' challenger to Jezki, who lowered the Fly's crown at Cheltenham and Punchestown? Or will he target the Arkle and leave Neptune Novices' Hurdle star Faugheen to have a crack at big 2m hurdles?

Mullins always keeps his cards close to his chest. His mind churns constantly with ideas and plans, but he voices few of them because so many are fleeting thanks to the ever-changing landscape of each jumping division – and his own team.

So, at this early stage, even he does not fully know the answers to the questions above. What he does know is this.

"Hurricane Fly is only ten and he's still a relatively young horse in jumping terms, and he is injury free," he says. "I think he's still got one or two Grade 1s left in him and we might just go up in trip.

"The older he's got, the better he's settling in his races and his body language tells me he's settled down. Going up in trip might be the way to go. I certainly wouldn't be writing him off just yet."

His swagger in a parade at the Curragh on Irish Champions Weekend in September showed what Mullins believes – there is life in the old dog yet. Hurricane Fly was bright-eyed and gleaming after a summer break. This thought of a step up to 3m raises a further exciting issue, the possibility he will race against this year's World Hurdle runner-up, stablemate ***Annie Power***.

That Cheltenham run is the only defeat Annie Power has suffered in 12 outings, and she has been carefully placed by Mullins to win Grade 1 and 2 hurdles from 2m to 2m4f. Owners Rich and Susannah Ricci are not keen on a switch to fences, so she could be returning to meet More Of That – and maybe Hurricane Fly – in next year's World Hurdle.

The main fences-or-not conundrum Mullins has is his star novice hurdlers ***Vautour*** and ***Faugheen***. The pair are unbeaten in Britain and Ireland and have five Grade 1 wins between them, and showed in those top-level wins at Cheltenham and Punchestown they are as good over longer trips as they are over 2m.

Mullins says: "I thought Vautour's win at Cheltenham was hugely impressive. He blew me away in the Supreme Novices'. He wasn't 100 per cent right at the start of the week of

Vautour: could be a big player in the Champion Hurdle following his smooth win in the Supreme Novices' last season

Punchestown and had a few easy days, forcing us to switch him to the longer race. His run there wasn't in keeping with his Cheltenham form – maybe everything took its toll. With his owner also having Faugheen and so many other nice novices we have a lot of thinking still to do."

Faugheen was bought as a chaser, but Mullins was eyeing the Champion Hurdle after his win over 2m at Punchestown, although his sloppy hurdling is a worry.

Son Patrick Mullins feels lessons could be learnt from the moves they made with 2013 Supreme Novices' Hurdle winner Champagne Fever. He switched to fences and was well beaten in two of his three Grade 1 starts, finishing a head second in the Arkle on the same day that the Supreme second and third finished second and first in the Champion Hurdle.

Patrick says: "Vautour went from strength to strength last year. He won the Supreme Novices' and looked like a chaser. He could still go chasing, but after Champagne Fever maybe you could do the obvious thing – win the two-mile novice race then go for the two-mile open race. I think he could be a live Champion Hurdle contender, but Dad will make that decision later."

Of Faugheen, he adds: "He's incredibly versatile. He's won a point-to-point and doesn't particularly seem to respect his hurdles, so I'd like to see him over fences, but he's a bit like The New One – he could go for the Champion Hurdle instead, but he's won a point-to-point so we know he jumps fences."

Mullins has trained eight Champion Bumper winners, dominating the festival race like he has no other, and last season he had 43 bumper winners in Ireland and 38 per cent strike-rate. He does not perform better in any other area

Sir Des Champs: will be on the Gold Cup trail if recovering from injury

and Patrick already has his eye on a newcomer.

He says: "We have a lot of pointers in. We haven't done any fast work with them yet but I've ridden a horse called ***Fulham Road***, who is by Shantou and fell at the second-last in a point-to-point when going well. I like him. I think he's very athletic – hopefully when we start doing fast work with him he'll show he has an engine too."

A major chase that has eluded Mullins is the Cheltenham Gold Cup and this season he looks to have two live contenders to right that, should last year's second ***Sir Des Champs*** return from injury and ***Boston Bob*** continue the transformation he underwent last term.

After a frustrating novice chase campaign that saw him fall more times than he completed, Boston Bob won Aintree's Melling Chase and the Punchestown Gold Cup. Ruby Walsh had been ready to ride owner Andrea and Graham Wylie's On His Own in the latter event, but Mullins knew better and pushed the jockey to reconsider. He did and now Boston Bob is shaping up as a leading Gold Cup contender.

Mullins says: "He's improving and he's turning into the horse I hoped he would. I'll be going down the Gold Cup route with him."

Djakadam is the dark horse in the staying chaser ranks. He was coached gently through his novice campaign, keeping to smaller events, just like how Sir Des Champs was brought forward. He fell in

the JLT Novices' Chase at Cheltenham, but it was a minor blip in an otherwise exciting start to chasing.

His trainer says: "He's just such a natural jumper and galloper. He has so much scope and I was really happy with his first two runs over fences. His pedigree suggests he'll have no problem staying three miles, and he'll get some big entries."

Mullins was so taken by him that he has his four-year-old brother ***Sambremont***, who began his career over hurdles with Anthony Chaille-Chaille in France last year.

Patrick is already excited about the novice, and says: "Sambremont could turn out to be a three-mile Grade 1 chaser. He does everything right at home, moves lovely and is a fantastic looker. He's one we're looking forward to getting out on the track."

Sambremont could form part of Mullins' novice hurdle team, with his brightest bumper stars ***Shaneshill***, ***Killultagh Vic*** and ***Black Hercules*** already poised to make the change to obstacles. His novice chasers could include Faugheen or Vautour together with Champion Bumper winner ***Briar Hill*** and unbeaten front-runner ***Un De Sceaux***, who won seven hurdles last term by a combined total of more than 130 lengths. Four-year-old ***Abbyssial*** is likely to head over fences too after confirming his superiority in the juvenile hurdling ranks with victory in Punchestown's Grade 1 contest. It came as compensation for a heavy fall in the Triumph Hurdle at Cheltenham a month earlier.

Mullins says: "That was a fantastic performance. You wonder what he would have done had he stood up at Cheltenham, although in the build-up to Punchestown he did the best piece of work I've seen from him. He has stamina and is a chaser for the future."

There is also ***Don Poli***. Gigginstown House Stud's winner of the Martin Pipe Conditional Jockeys' Handicap Hurdle was beaten less than a length when trying Grade 1 class in a 3m event at Punchestown in April and Patrick saw in him that day the potential to go further.

He says: "Don Poli is one I'm really looking forward to. Mikey Fogarty gave him a fantastic ride to win at Cheltenham last season. He's going to keep improving.

DID YOU KNOW

Willie Mullins has been champion trainer in Ireland since 2007-08. Since 2008-09, his winning margins have averaged 94, increasing to well over 100 for the last two years when he has surpassed the €3 million mark in the Irish championship. He also managed to finish 11th in the British trainers' championship last year and also had success with his horses in France, making him perhaps the most dominant jumps trainer in Europe currently.

"He got beaten first time out in a maiden hurdle and didn't show a whole lot at the start of the season, but progressed as it went on. He's 16.3hh and built like a tank – he should love jumping fences. If I get my way he might be my horse for the four-mile chase at Cheltenham, but he might have too much class for that and end up in the RSA Chase."

Don Poli features in a huge group of potential improvers who could progress from the lower ranks at Closutton to stardom this season. That is hard to do in the most powerful jumps yard in Ireland but, as highlighted before, often Mullins does this with his most promising charges. It could be worth keeping your eye on the likes of Guinness Galway Hurdle third ***Make Your Mark*** and ***Arctic Fire***, who was racing for just the fifth time over hurdles when runner-up in the County Hurdle at the festival.

As well as exciting improvers and new recruits, Mullins also has a new owner in Sheikh Fahad, who has sent him an unraced son of Milan. Adding one of the most powerful men in Flat racing to your ownership roster just proves further the dominance Mullins has. Last term he finished with a record 185 winners in Ireland. Bank on him bettering that this season.

Reporting by Jessica Lamb

Djakadam (right): has been exciting his trainer

MULLINS: ASSESSING THE STATS

Willie Mullins continues to dominate the Irish scene and sent out an incredible 185 winners in his homeland last term, earning a shade under €4 million in prize-money. He boasts an impressive array of talent in his yard which no trainer can match in Ireland, *writes Kevin Morley*.

Mullins is a rare visitor to Britain but always sends over a huge team for Cheltenham. He sent out four winners at last season's Festival and, while this would be seen as an impressive haul by most trainers, it was standard for the County Carlow handler. Quevega landed a sixth Mares' Hurdle and, while some question those merits, it is an incredible achievement to produce a mare who has had injury problems to peak consistently for the big occasion.

What caught the eye more at Prestbury Park though were the performances of Vautour and Faugheen, who were both impressive in winning the big novice hurdles. The sky is the limit with this pair and they are likely to figure prominently on the big stage.

Despite having just 11 winners in Britain last season, prize-money of over £800,000 was enough to see Mullins finish just outside the top ten in the trainer's championship, figures that were a personal best last term.

With his British raiders it tends to be the hurdlers who are best followed, and that was evident last term with ten of his 11 winners coming over the smaller obstacles.

Mullins is fortunate enough to be able to call upon the superb Ruby Walsh. Having had to share his services with Paul Nicholls previously, Mullins had him as full-time stable jockey last term. Although the strike-rate is predictably high, the layers keep this combination well onside and backing them blind is not suggested.

Mullins gets sent plenty of the Gigginstown Stud horses and those ridden by their retained rider Bryan Cooper are well worth a look.

In Ireland, Mullins has proved best to follow at Gowran Park over the last five seasons, while his figures at Limerick, Naas and Tipperary are impressive. In Britain, it is mainly about Cheltenham, although the vast amount of runners he has makes it difficult to secure a level-stake profit. It is worth pointing out he had four runners at Warwick last term, two of whom obliged.

Mullins has a huge conveyer belt of talented horses at his disposal and domination in his homeland and a few winners at Cheltenham are almost a given once again.

World Hurdle runner-up Annie Power leads the string at Willie Mullins' Closutton stables

Could this be the year O'Neill challenges for championship honours?

IT should come as no surprise Paul Nicholls fears a title challenge from Jonjo O'Neill. Consider what O'Neill did last season, then consider what O'Neill has the potential to do this season, and you will probably end up thinking the same.

No trainer seems to succeed at the Cheltenham Festival as potently and consistently as the master of Jackdaws Castle, who in March struck on three occasions, landing the Ladbrokes World Hurdle with More Of That, the Jewson Novices' Chase with Taquin Du Seuil and the staying handicap chase last season backed by Baylis & Harding with Holywell. All three are back this season and all three have genuine championship credentials with Holywell having gone on to establish himself as a likely player in this season's Gold Cup, a race that could also end up on Taquin Du Seuil's agenda.

O'Neill's principal rider Tony McCoy revealed a confidence about O'Neill's own belief in himself last season, saying: "I think it's realistic for him to become champion trainer in the next few years but this is the first season I genuinely think he has started to believe he can do it. It won't be easy but everyone in life should want to be the best at their sport or business and Jonjo isn't any different."

At the end of the 2013-14 campaign O'Neill was in fourth place in the championship table, around £900,000 behind Nicholls but with 134 winners, a personal record, on the board. His string continues to be vast, and although at this stage he is unable to identify any equine names we might not know about, we should expect plenty of come along. Fortunately, there are plenty we do know about, few having achieved so much and so quickly as ***More Of That***.

Having won a Folkestone maiden hurdle on his sole outing in the 2012-13 campaign, JP McManus's son of Beneficial remained unbeaten in four outings last term. He kicked off by winning a Wetherby handicap off a mark of 130 on his reappearance in November and ended his season's labours by inflicting a length-and-a-half defeat on Annie Power in the World Hurdle. That, intriguingly, was his first appearance since mid-December, highlighting how well he runs fresh.

One of the sport's tallest reputations must now be defended, but whether that defence is over hurdles – More Of That is ante-post favourite for a second World Hurdle victory – or over fences is unclear. Bookmakers also make the six-year-old market leader for the RSA Chase.

"I don't know if it will be hurdles or fences and it hasn't been discussed yet," says O'Neill. "He could go either way. We have a lovely horse to go to war with whichever way we do go. He's still a bit of a baby in terms of how much racing he has had.

"I'd say he'll probably stay hurdling, but he's a massive horse and very strong so just

***More Of That:** World Hurdle winner is ante-post favourite for a repeat but also has the option of going novice chasing*

the right type for fences, although that means nothing until you start schooling them. He's done fantastically well over the summer and is healthy and happy so we'll try to look after him. We love him and are lucky to have him."

O'Neill is also lucky enough to have two of those most fancied by bookmakers and punters for the Gold Cup.

He says: "You can't argue with ***Holywell's*** rating because he put up a performance at Aintree to earn it, but we all know that at Aintree some horses aren't at their best. I just hope he lives up to his rating and how good he looked that day.

"I imagine he'll start off in the Charlie Hall or maybe the Betfair Chase and then move on towards the Gold Cup. That's the plan and if it looks like failing we'll have to think again. On ratings he has to be a Gold Cup horse but you have to remember Aintree sometimes gives a false impression of a horse. I just hope he's as good as he looked that day.

"***Taquin Du Seuil*** will hopefully be a Gold Cup or Ryanair Chase horse. I don't see him having a problem staying three miles-plus, but until you actually try you don't know. He might start off in a graduation chase and then he could easily be a King George horse – of the two you'd think Kempton would be more his thing than Holywell's, although Holywell showed at Aintree he isn't short of pace, either."

Not that those two are O'Neill's only prospects of training his second Gold Cup winner three years on from Synchronised's gritty triumph. The latter was essentially a marathon runner and so, too, is ***Shutthefrontdoor***, who heads Crabbie's Grand National markets after taking out the Irish equivalent under Barry Geraghty in April. However, although Aintree is the obvious aim, we should not rule out the 150-rated chaser lining up in the Gold Cup first.

"He's in brilliant form and we're looking forward to him this season," says O'Neill. "He's a galloper and a stayer. Hopefully he'll be heading towards the Grand National and maybe the Gold Cup, but he's another who could start off in a graduation race."

Having ended his own Grand National hoodoo by at the same time ending McCoy's, Don't Push It's winning trainer is forever to be feared in the world's most famous jumps race and his potential 2015 squad also includes ***Burton Port***. The ten-year-old was an early casualty at Aintree last season and then frustratingly waved the white flag after the final fence of the bet365 Gold Cup.

"Burton Port has come back looking better than ever," says O'Neill. "He will have another go at the National and might start off at Aintree as well in a 0-150 veterans race. He didn't quite get home at Sandown but he ran a blinder. We'd been hoping he would

Taquin Du Seuil (main picture and top centre) could develop into a Gold Cup candidate, while Holywell (left) also has that race on his agenda. Shutthefrontdoor (right) will have a crack at the Grand National

run well in the National as well but unfortunately he didn't last very long.

O'Neill also has 2012 nose Grand National runner-up ***Sunnyhillboy*** (ruled out of Aintree last term). "I hope Sunnyhillboy will also get to Aintree and I certainly wouldn't be ruling him out as he loves the place. He just lost his way a bit in the spring and wasn't right. He had a few little niggles, silly little problems of no great consequence, but they held him up and you can't have that when you're going for big races.

Scottish National fourth ***Merry King*** is another who could head to Aintree, as O'Neill explains: "He didn't seem to quite get home at Ayr. That was at the end of a long season, though, and you would want to give him another chance. He could go to Ascot for a £100,000 chase early on and he might have another go in the Hennessy."

Before that big Newbury race is the Paddy Power Gold Cup, a prize O'Neill landed last season with ***Johns Spirit***, who will very probably return to Cheltenham with a rating now 8lb higher than that which he won off last November.

Among others under consideration for the winter's first true classic is ***Festive Affair***, ninth when last seen in the Rewards4Racing Novices' Handicap Chase at the festival.

O'Neill said: "Festive Affair could easily be a Paddy Power horse and Johns Spirit will be going for that again as well, although he could also go to the first Cheltenham meeting. He's rated 147 now, which doesn't make it easy."

One of the other established names coming back for more is ***Get Me Out Of Here***, who finished second at the festival for the fourth time when narrowly denied in the most recent running of the Coral Cup.

"He's bucking, kicking and farting around the place as well as ever," says O'Neill of the ten-year-old. "We tried him over a fence, but he didn't like it so he'll stay hurdling but he isn't easy to place as he's high in the handicap and not really good enough for the conditions races."

Also very much worth noting for a handicap is ***Goodwood Mirage***, who cost his current connections 380,000gns but has so far looked to be a disastrous purchase having repeatedly flopped after winning an ordinary Kempton novice hurdle on his jumping debut. However, he was quietly fancied by McCoy for the Fred Winter Juvenile Hurdle – for which he was sent off at just 15-2 – only to be brought down at the second flight. Should he ever get his act together he should surely be able to exploit a rating of 132.

O'Neill describes him as "awkward to work out" but there is a very good chance he will find a way of working him out.

Goodwood Mirage almost certainly has a decent future, as might any number of the trainer's most unexposed inmates, including ***Mountain Tunes***, who gave McCoy his 4,000th career jumps win last November at Towcester before following up at the same venue the following month.

Also worth noting are ***Oscar Fortune*** – who was too good for Deputy Dan at Carlisle last November – and Sefton Novices' Hurdle fourth ***Capote***. All three are expected to make their mark in novice chases, although Mountain Tunes could be tried further over hurdles first.

Of those who have not even jumped in public under rules are ***Fort***

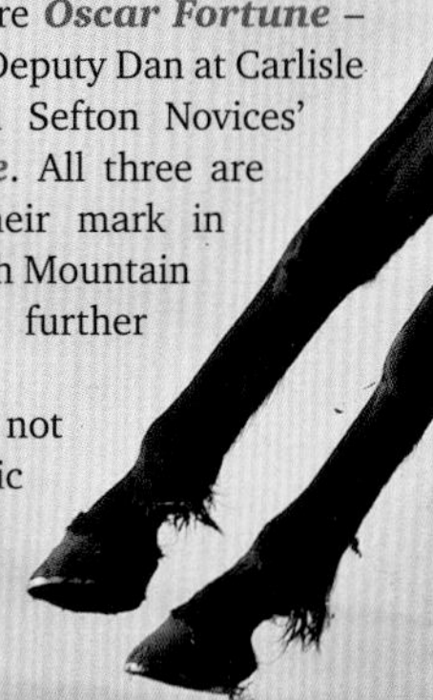

Worth, an easy Huntingdon bumper winner last November.

O'Neill adds: "Fort Worth has come back in good form and could be anything. Overall, we've got quite a few nice young horses we had ready for bumpers but didn't run. Hopefully they will be stronger this season and can do well."

Reporting by Lee Mottershead

DID YOU KNOW

Last season Jonjo O'Neill bagged 100 winners between April and December. For the last four seasons he averaged over 70 successes during that period, which helps explain Tony McCoy's recent fast starts. O'Neill was champion jockey twice and was closest to becoming champion trainer in 2006-07 when finishing second to Paul Nicholls.

Festive Affair (near): could be just the type for the Paddy Power Gold Cup

O'NEILL: ASSESSING THE STATS

Only Donald McCain sent out more winners than Jonjo O'Neill last term when his tally of 134 was a personal best, *writes Kevin Morley*.

Not only was it a success on the numbers front, but O'Neill also amassed over £1.5 million in prize-money which saw him finish fourth in the trainers' championship.

The Jackdaws Castle handler is one of the best at peaking his string for the big occasion and three winners at the festival was evidence of that.

O'Neill has a balanced strike-rate in all disciplines but it is clear he excels with stayers and there is often improvement from his inmates when they are upped to extreme distances.

That was the case with Synchronised in the 2012 Gold Cup, who progressed from handicapper to Grade 1 winner, while the step up in trip saw More Of That develop into a World Hurdle winner last season. This term, Holywell and Taquin Du Seuil, both festival winners in March, appeal as potential improvers in the staying chase division and could develop into Gold Cup contenders.

Although he doesn't quite possess the ammunition of Nicholls and Henderson, O'Neill matches them for total winners by

remaining busy during the summer months, a period when the big yards are usually quiet, and he often proves profitable to follow in this period.

With plenty of O'Neill's string owned by JP McManus, it is unsurprising to learn Tony McCoy rides the lion's share of the winners. The strike-rate is decent but the level-stake profit isn't, and any punter backing them blind will lose out, particularly at the smaller meetings.

Conditional Maurice Linehan returned a small profit last term to a fair ratio, and his mounts are worth looking out for as he is well worth his 3lb allowance.

Also keep an eye out for the rare occasions Barry Geraghty is called upon, as seen last term on More Of That in the World Hurdle.

There is no better trainer than O'Neill at priming them for Prestbury Park in March, so it makes sense his runners at Cheltenham return a profit. For the lower-grade racing, his runners are best followed at Newton Abbot and, to a smaller scale, Catterick, Sedgefield and Cartmel.

O'Neill seems to have good mix of proven performers and emerging talent and looks set for another solid campaign.

On the gallops at Jackdaws Castle

Champion has high hopes of making it third time lucky with Silviniaco

SILVINIACO CONTI, the top-rated chaser in Britain and Ireland who has not had things go right in the last two runnings of the Cheltenham Gold Cup, has every chance of making it third time lucky, his trainer Paul Nicholls believes.

The eight-year-old, a faller at his first attempt in 2013, ran a puzzling race at Cheltenham last March, finishing only fourth having led halfway up the run-in.

"For a long time I couldn't get my head round the performance," says Nicholls. "And although he bounced back and won the Bowl next time, he still stopped a bit after the last like he had done at Cheltenham.

"I don't think we had him at his best in the spring and he wasn't seeing out his races as well as he should have done. I hope there's still a lot of improvement to come and I'm really looking forward to having another crack at the Gold Cup. It looks a very open year, with no horse standing out at this early stage."

Before his Gold Cup defeat, Silviniaco Conti had won the King George VI Chase, a performance that earned him the champion chaser accolade with a top seasonal rating of 174. His efforts this winter will help determine whether Nicholls is able to successfully defend the trainers' title he grabbed back from Nicky Henderson last season.

Rarely can there have been a stronger-looking squad of juvenile hurdlers at Manor Farm Stables. Boasting the best Flat form is 102-rated ***All Set To Go***, last seen finishing third to Fascinating Rock in the Group 3 Ballysax Stakes in April.

"He was gelded and spent the summer here at Ditcheat and he could be an exciting prospect," says Nicholls. "Like all our juveniles he'll need to school on grass, so the weather will help determine when they can start."

Chartbreaker showed smart form on the Flat in Germany, finishing fourth to Sea The Moon in a 1m3f Group 2 at Cologne in June. "He's just been gelded and will be out after Christmas," says Nicholls.

Also boasting useful German Flat form is ***Lac Leman***. "He won his first two starts impressively and arrived here in August after finishing third in the Slovakian Derby," the trainer says. "We gelded him straight away and he's got over it pretty quickly. He could be exciting in the new year for Graham Wylie."

Ibis Du Rheu catches the eye on breeding as a half-brother to the smart Saphir Du Rheu.

"He was an impressive winner over hurdles for Guillaume Macaire at Bordeaux in April, but I don't see him as a Triumph horse so we won't be too hard on him this season," says Nicholls. "He's like his half-brother – a future chaser."

San Benedeto joined the yard after finishing second in the Listed Prix Wild Monarch, France's top juvenile hurdle for

Silviniaco Conti: last season's King George winner will be aimed at the Cheltenham Gold Cup again

DID YOU KNOW

Paul Nicholls strength is with staying chasers. This is highlighted by his record in the Gold Cup, and Silviniaco Conti's fourth place last March was the seventh year in the last ten runnings that the Ditcheat master has made the frame with at least one of his horses. In this period Nicholls has won the race three times, had four seconds, two thirds and four fourth places. Some record to have in the blue riband event.

unraced colts and geldings.

"He's one for the better meetings early on," says Nicholls, "although I'm not sure the form of the French race was as strong as it usually is."

Albahar won twice on the Flat in the France, his latest success coming at Deauville in July, and is schooling well, ***All Yours***, a half-brother to the useful Lac Fontana, joined the yard after finishing fourth on his only start on the Flat at Chantilly in June, and ***Annalulu*** will race for Highclere after winning twice on the Flat in France for Jean-Claude Rouget.

Although a maiden in France on the Flat and over hurdles, ***Celestino*** showed promise on both hurdle starts behind the exciting unbeaten juvenile Top Notch.

Full Blast was still technically a two-year-old when making an eyecatching hurdling debut in third at Enghien in March and Nicholls says: "He could be our first juvenile runner – he jumps that well I could run him in a chase now."

The most recent arrival is ***Old Guard***, successful over 1m2f at Lingfield in July for Roger Charlton and rated 81 on the Flat.

"He loves his jumping and has taken to it like a duck to water," reveals Nicholls.

There is no disguising Paul Nicholls' soft spot for ***Alcala***, owned by Graham Wylie.

"We like him a lot – he's a real beauty," he says. "He ran with a lot of promise on his only outing for us in the Adonis and it's good he's a novice for the whole season. He's going to make some chaser in a year's time."

Wylie can also look forward to ***Simon Squirrel***, the first foal out of a sister to Rock On Ruby who was bought after winning a Chepstow bumper for Charlie Brooks, and ***Urubu D'Irlande***, a bumper and point-to-point winner.

Ptit Zig's half-brother ***Earthmoves*** was green when making a winning debut in a Wincanton bumper in March.

"He's strengthened up over the summer and should do well," says Nicholls.

Emerging Talent is an interesting recruit from Ireland for Paul and Marianne Barber. He shaped with a lot of promise when winning his only start in a bumper at Naas in March and will be suited by two and a half miles.

Great Try, whose dam is a half-sister to smart chaser The Nightingale, was put away after making a successful debut in a Southwell bumper in February. He is an interesting prospect by a sire, Scorpion, Nicholls likes.

Port Melon looks a potentially very useful second-season novice, having run with eyecatching promise in a Grade 2 at Cheltenham last November. "He lacked experience when stepped up to Grade 1 company next time, but we do like him," says Nicholls.

Silsol retains his novice hurdle status until November 1 so should be noted if running before then, although he came back a bit later than the others.

Already on a stiff-looking rating of 144, Nicholls says: "He's nicely handicapped on the Flat and there's a suitable race at Newbury at the end of October – at least that's what my daughter Megan keeps telling me!"

Another who is still a novice until November 1 is ***Vivaldi Collonges***, and he is being aimed at the Grade 2 Persian War Novices' Hurdle at Chepstow before a likely switch to fences.

Southfield Vic, a half-brother to the smart Southfield Theatre, made a promising start to his hurdling career at Wincanton in March. He was then put away to keep his novice status intact for this winter.

"We've minded him as the family get better as they mature," says Nicholls. "We haven't seen the best of him yet."

The Brock Again, placed on all three hurdle starts at Cagnes last winter, was bought at the Arqana Sale in February and could prove another shrewd purchase for Axom, who have enjoyed so much success with stablemates Irving and Far West.

There were high hopes for ***On Blueberry Hill*** this time last year, but the winner of the big Fairyhouse point-to-point bumper sustained a leg injury that kept him off all season.

"He was very weak, but he's matured physically for the break and will go novice hurdling over a trip," says Nicholls.

Arenice Et Pictons was third on his hurdling debut at Auteuil in April behind the very smart Geluroni.

"He's tall and scopey and is one to look out for first time out," his trainer says.

Arpege D'Alene is a half-brother to Hennessy winner Triolo D'Alene and finished third on his only run last December in a bumper at Deauville.

"He's a big strong sort and I can't believe he got to the track last season," Nicholls says. "He'll want a trip."

The Ex-German ***Amanto*** was touched off on the Flat at Newbury in the Ladies' Derby in August under the trainer's daughter Megan.

"He jumps well and should be ready to make his jumping debut in October," the trainer says.

Don't be surprised if at least one of the big staying handicap chases prizes makes its way back to Ditcheat, as Paul Nicholls looks especially strong in that division.

Grand National fifth ***Rocky Creek*** will have a second tilt at the world's most famous race at the top of his agenda.

His trainer says: "This is a true staying chaser we hold in the highest regard. He could start off again in the Hennessy, in which he ran a massive race last season, and I wouldn't be afraid to enter him for the Gold Cup, but the National is our number-one goal.

"He ran a bit free there last April, and he wasn't quite seeing his races out during the season, but I hope he's that bit stronger now."

A number of others are also expected to get a Crabbie's Grand National entry. ***Just A Par*** did not quite live up to expectations as a novice chaser, but Nicholls predicts: "He'll be seen to best effect in long-distance chases. He could start in a £100,000 three-mile handicap at Ascot at the end of October

Port Melon: well regarded by his trainer and expected to do well in novice hurdles

Unioniste: will be campaigned with a crack at the Grand National in mind

or the Badger Ales at Wincanton, and he'll get an entry for the Welsh National."

Unioniste, successful just once last winter, looks well suited by a stiff test of stamina now, so the yellow and red silks of Neptune Collonges could be seen at Aintree once again next spring.

"Sam [Twiston-Davies] and Ruby [Walsh] have both come back and told me he'd be ideal for the National," Nicholls says. "We'll be in no rush with him and he'll be ready early December."

Nicholls has long held a liking for the Hennessy Gold Cup as a launching pad for his up-and-coming stayers, and the Newbury chase could feature on the agenda for ***Easter Day*** and ***Sam Winner***.

Easter Day is fully recovered from a setback that put him on the sidelines after Ascot in December, when he beat subsequent RSA winner O'Faolains Boy. Nicholls says: "He could have the ideal profile for the Hennessy."

Sire Collonges has found his niche in cross-country races and will be back at Cheltenham for one of those races in November before going on trial for the Grand National in the Becher Chase.

Al Ferof will kick off either in the Grade 2 Amlin Chase, a race he won 12 months ago, or the Peterborough Chase, before having another crack at the King George, in which he finished third last season.

Caid Du Berlais will come back in trip to two and a half miles after failing to stay in the Galway Plate, and ***Benvolio***, who goes very well fresh, has the Badger Ales Chase at Wincanton as his first target.

Things did not go according to plan for ***Hinterland*** in the second half of last season. He was still going well when badly hampered in the Champion Chase and was then probably over the top at Aintree.

Nicholls says: "He has to be fresh and we need to space his races out, so he'll either go for the Haldon Gold Cup and then the Tingle Creek or go straight to Sandown, with another crack at the Champion Chase a distinct possibility."

Of Racing Post Arkle fourth ***Dodging Bullets***, Nicholls says: "He can be a bit stressy so we have to pick his targets carefully. The idea is to start off in the Haldon Gold Cup or the Shloer Chase at Cheltenham."

Surprisingly, since Kauto Star landed the second of his two Gold Cups in 2009, Paul Nicholls has not won a chase of any description at the Cheltenham Festival. You can be sure he will be pulling out all the stops to rectify that in March and in smart hurdlers ***Saphir Du Rheu***, ***Ptit Zig***, ***Southfield Theatre*** and ***Irish Saint*** he has a quartet who have the potential go to the top over fences.

There is no set plan yet for Saphir Du Rheu, whose rapid rise through the hurdling ranks led to his rating leaping 35lb to 165, but he could have one outing over hurdles in top company – "I just want to see where we stand with him", says Nicholls – before a final decision is taken whether to go chasing this season. He looks the part.

Nicholls has high hopes of Ptit Zig, "provided he jumps fences okay". The trainer adds: "He wasn't the most fluent jumper of hurdles to start with, although he's got better in that department, so I hope he takes to fences. We'll find a beginners' chase somewhere and work up from there."

Southfield Theatre is rated a "really exciting prospect" for staying novice chases.

Nicholls says: "He started last season winning a small novice hurdle and ended it when going down by a very small nose in the Pertemps Final and winning a Listed race.

"He could start over fences next month in the Chepstow race in which Silviniaco Conti made his chasing debut, and then I'd have a look at the Rising Stars Novices' Chase."

Irish Saint is another who should step up markedly on his hurdling form, which was pretty decent, now he goes over fences.

"He ran two really good races over hurdles last season but to my eyes he's always been a chaser in the making," Nicholls says.

Salubrious was due to go chasing 12 months ago but he had a fall schooling so stayed over hurdles. He jumped fences better when schooled at the end of the season and that is where he goes now.

"The aim will be to build his confidence up in a beginners' chase and not go too big too soon with him," his trainer says.

Far West, a very smart juvenile two seasons ago, failed to win last winter but should not be written off.

Nicholls says: "He scoped with gastric ulcers following a disappointing run at Haydock before Christmas and was travelling well when falling at Newbury in February. I still think there's a good race to be won with him over hurdles, but ultimately he's a chaser."

The lightly raced ex-French ***Brother Du Berlais*** was ruled out of the EBF Final by a small injury but gave a hint of what is to come

when winning an Ayr handicap on only his second outing for the yard. His trainer predicts "a bright future" over fences.

The application of a tongue-tie helped transform ***Caesar Milan's*** form over hurdles and after his breathing was tweaked over the summer he is expected to make a successful transition to fences.

Aldopicgros took time to find his form as a novice hurdler but ended the season on a high.

"His jumping has improved enormously and, although he could start in a handicap hurdle, he looks a readymade novice chaser," says Nicholls.

Another slow starter who later caught the eye was ***Virak***, one to look out for mid-season having done all his winning on soft or heavy ground.

Vibrato Valtat was not really getting home in his races over hurdles but, reported stronger now, is expected to do better over fences.

See More Business, Paul Nicholls' first Gold Cup winner who died in the summer, first showed his ability in point-to-points and the trainer highlights a handful of graduates from that sphere who can display their talent in staying novice hurdles this winter before graduating to fences in a year's time.

Mr Dinosaur was bought in May for Graham Wylie after winning his only start at the Berkeley.

Nicholls says: "He's a big, strong

Dodging Bullets: his targets will be picked carefully this season

Pearl Swan: set to return this season with the Greatwood Hurdle a possible early target

individual from the family of Battlecry and Hey Big Spender, and it was his jumping that impressed me in his point."

It's A Close Call, also a Berkeley winner on his debut, was bought at the 2012 Derby Sale in Ireland and spent last season with the Richard Barber team.

There is a strong word for ***Rock On Oscar***, a graduate from last year's Derby Sale who won his only point for Jack Barber with ease in the spring, and Nicholls says:. "He looks promising."

Pepe Simo's half-brother ***The Eaglehaslanded*** won his only point-to-point impressively last season and will have one bumper run before going hurdling.

The rangy ***Present Man*** was recruited to the Ditcheat squad after finishing second on his debut at Lemonfield in March, and ***Ballycoe***, winner of his second start in an Irish point, is "big, still unfurnished and a staying chaser of the future".

Reporting by Ben Newton

FIVE DARK ONES

Black River Came over from France with a big reputation – he had beaten Vautour second time out – but he was disappointing. He's taken time to acclimatise and I hope he'll reveal his potential over fences.

Keppols Hill Missed last season. He was a bit weak in his first season under rules and didn't jump that well, but has come back a stronger horse. If I can get a run into him beforehand, possibly in a three-mile novice hurdle, I'd like to go for the Badger Ales Chase in November.

Marracudja A three-year-old who was disappointing in France after a promising debut in a hot race. He arrived very light in condition and had a little problem which we've now sorted. He jumps really well and I couldn't be more pleased with him.

Pearl Swan Missed 18 months with a leg but was a smart juvenile. Could go straight for the Greatwood Hurdle.

Vago Collonges Had a little niggle so we gave him last season off. He'd run very well for us in a Graded and Listed bumper and could be a serious prospect for novice hurdles. We like him a lot.

NICHOLLS: ASSESSING THE STATS

After a dominant spell at the top of the trainer's championship, Paul Nicholls faced some serious competition for the title in the 2012-13 campaign and duly lost out to Nicky Henderson, *writes Kevin Morley.* However, he is not one to take defeat lying down and regained his crown last term. That was some achievement considering he was lacking in numbers for the top graded races.

With Big Buck's returning from injury a shadow of his former self and the likes of Kauto Star and Denman long gone, it was left to Silviniaco Conti to carry the mantle of stable flagbearer. While few would argue he possesses as much talent as the aforementioned trio, he is clearly a high-class performer in his own right and proved as much last term, landing the King George and Betfair Bowl while also finishing a close fourth in a thrilling Gold Cup.

Nicholls accrued just under £2.5 million in prize-money in 2013-14 with Silviniaco Conti accounting for over ten per cent of that. A tally of 118 winners last season wasn't even an outstanding one, especially he had sent out 131 when losing to Henderson in the previous campaign.

But Nicholls has no superior when it comes to running his string regularly and to a consistently high level, and it was this trait that enabled prize-money to keep ticking over. For example, Zarkandar failed to win a race last term but was always finishing in the money and racked up over £80k.

A problem Nicholls had to overcome was the loss of Ruby Walsh as stable jockey. The position was filled by Daryl Jacob last term although he often found himself jocked off for the big occasions. Jacob rode most of the winners but to a level-stake loss, and there was a better return on the mounts of Noel Fehily and Tony McCoy.

However, Sam Twiston-Davies has now replaced Jacob as the number-one rider at Ditcheat. He had good association with the yard last term and the trainer's acquisition of a young, hungry, talented jockey looks shrewd.

Formerly known as a trainer of chasers, Nicholls is much more rounded these days and now to the point where the hurdling victories outnumber those over fences. A selective approach is required, though, as backing his string blind will likely result in a heavy deficit.

Nicholls will always have his share of winners at the top tracks but most of his winners and best strike-rates are at venues close to his West-Country base. Wincanton, Newton Abbot, Taunton and Worcester are successful ports of call on a regular basis and maintaining his record at these courses will be crucial in retaining the trainers' title.

Saphir Du Rheu (left) at Paul Nicholls' owners' open day in September, and the trainer heading to the gallops at Ditcheat

Dynaste set for another big one with King George and Ryanair the targets

BAROMETERS of success come in many forms, but David Pipe readily admits "Cheltenham is the place you want to win at". By that gauge, last season must be catagorised as triumphant, with three festival victories signalling Pipe's best return since taking over the licence at Pond House in 2006.

While he will be without the services of one of those horses this campaign, as surprise Arkle winner Western Warhorse has been sidelined through a leg injury, Pipe has assembled a strong squad of proven graded performers, intriguing handicap prospects and potentially top-class novices to be unleashed over the coming months.

Dynaste, who suffered his only defeat in a five-race novice chase campaign when second at the 2013 festival, handsomely rectified that reverse with a two-and-a-quarter-length victory in the Ryanair in March, staying on powerfully to repel Irish challenger Hidden Cyclone having been nursed into contention by Tom Scudamore.

Runner-up behind Cue Card in the Betfair Chase on his seasonal reappearance, Dynaste occupied the same position behind Silviniaco Conti as he closed his campaign in the Betfair Bowl.

A well-held fifth in the King George proved the sole disappointing run of the year, but the eight-year-old was subsequently found to have pulled muscles in his back, and Pipe is eager to have another crack at the Christmas showpiece before defending his Cheltenham crown.

"The Ryanair will be his target again this year – the races are easy to map out for him," Pipe says. "The 3m1f of the Betfair Chase and Bowl might just stretch his stamina a little, but he wasn't right after last year's King George – he wouldn't have won over any trip that day. We'll try the King George again and see what happens."

Ballynagour will also be seeking Grade 1 plaudits having finished runner-up behind a revitalised Sizing Europe in the Champion Chase at Punchestown.

The eight-year-old had previously advertised his credentials as a top-flight performer with a third-place finish in Aintree's Melling Chase, before which he had blown apart the Byrne Group Plate field at Cheltenham off a mark of 140, a race for which he had been heavily supported 12 months earlier only to bleed when travelling ominously into contention.

Pipe says: "He had a fantastic season, but it'll be tough for him this year. Even if he doesn't win, he'll hopefully be picking up lots of prize-money. I would have thought we'll be targeting Grade 1 races – he could run over anything from two miles to three miles. He's come back fairly fat, so we'll see how we get on before making any plans."

Red Sherlock was one of a few not to run up to scratch at the festival, finishing ninth behind Faugheen in the Neptune Novices' Hurdle having arrived at Cheltenham

Dynaste: will take in the King George before defending last season's win in the Ryanair Chase at Cheltenham

unbeaten in six bumper and hurdle starts, but Pipe believes his charge was better than that performance implies.

"I don't think he ran up to his best at Cheltenham, but he had a terrific season and hopefully we can build on it this year," Pipe says. "He could go chasing, but he's most likely to start over hurdles first. He handles cut in the ground well, but the ground is just the way it's been with him."

Kings Palace made a deep impression in the first half of last season, bolting up in a novice hurdle at Cheltenham's October meeting before routing some useful yardsticks in Grade 2 company on the New Course in December.

Kept fresh for a tilt at the Albert Bartlett, the son of King's Theatre looked certain to play a part at the business end jumping the second-last, but he weakened turning for home and fell at the final flight.

"He came out of his Cheltenham fall fine – we called it quits after that," Pipe says. "He's come back in looking well and he'll probably start off over hurdles and we'll see where we go after that. A drop in trip hasn't been talked about yet."

Running first over hurdles before mapping out the rest of the campaign is a ploy Pipe plans to use with a number of his recruits, with the "handicapper deciding which route they will go."

They include French import ***Balgarry***, who landed a Newbury handicap off a mark of 129 on his British debut in March 2012 before finishing a creditable seventh when sent off joint-favourite for the Coral Cup less than two weeks later.

Not seen on the track since, connections

DID YOU KNOW

David Pipe has yet to become champion trainer like his father did on so many occasions, but similarities remain to the days when Pond House ruled the jumping world. The Open meeting in November remains a happy hunting ground for the Pipes. In the Paddy Power Gold Cup the old master won the race a record eight times along with countless other races over the three days. And his son has continued the tradition in recent times with 12 winners at the meeting in the last three years.

Kings Palace: fine after Cheltenham fall and ready to regain the winning thread

have persevered with the seven-year-old, who is back in training.

Pipe says: "Maybe his effort in the Coral Cup was a combination of him not getting home and the run coming too soon. We've had the horse for a long time but we're still learning about him.

"He's just very hard to keep in one piece – he's in good form at present and I think we'll probably start him off over hurdles and see how we go, with novice chasing a potential option."

A similar tack could be adopted with ***The Liquidator***, one-time favourite for the Supreme Novices', in which he finished 11th, and Greatwood Hurdle winner ***Dell' Arca***, whom Pipe describes as "very tough – a good horse."

Imperial Cup winner ***Baltimore Rock***, who finished fourth in Grade 2 company at Aintree, is also likely to begin his season over the smaller obstacles. So too are the unexposed duo of ***Knight Of Noir*** and ***Vieux Lion Rouge***, a "big horse" who couldn't land a blow when seeking to record a historic first victory for Pipe in the race run in honour of his father – the Martin Pipe Conditional Jockeys' Hurdle – at the festival, but is set to go chasing after his first run.

Record-breaking purchase ***Un Temps Pour Tout***, who was bought from France for £450,000, built on a promising first run on British soil over 2m at Haydock when comprehensively landing a 2m4f novice heat at Ascot.

He finished his season with a remarkable run off top weight in a Punchestown handicap, beaten just over seven lengths into third when conceding 15lb to the progressive Deep Trouble.

Pipe says: "He's another who could go novice chasing, but I'd like to step him up to 3m over hurdles first and see how he gets on."

Doctor Harper, a winner in Grade 3 handicap company at Aintree, is another who could join rank over fences.

"He hasn't done much wrong and I imagine he'll go novice chasing," Pipe says. "He got the three-mile trip well at Aintree."

Ninth in the RSA Chase having been pulled up on his chasing debut at Ascot, the 143-rated ***Gevrey Chambertin*** has shaped much better than the bare result implies over fences, and he retains his novice status for the current campaign.

A brother to stable companion ***Grand Crus***, whose future is yet undecided, the six-year-old boasts plenty of ability on a going day, as demonstrated when landing a red-hot handicap hurdle at Haydock on his seasonal bow.

Pipe says: "He's maybe best fresh – he struggles to hold his form. He's a novice chaser still for this year and we'll start him off somewhere low key."

Top Wood, the prolific ***Ainsi Fideles*** and ***Broadway Buffalo***, who was beaten at short odds on his chasing debut at Wetherby, are three to have already tried their hand over fences.

Pipe says: "Top Wood loves the mud. Ainsi Fideles appreciates the better ground or appears to – he did really well over summer, bringing up a five-timer at Perth at the end of September. It's going to be tougher for him through the winter.

"It was a three-runner race when Broadway Buffalo was beaten, and three-runner races can be strange things. It was the end of a long season as well. He's had a break now and is on the way back. I'd have thought he'd continue novice chasing this season."

Swing Bowler, unbeaten in her first five starts and a stalwart in top-flight handicap hurdles since, and ***Shotavodka***, a second-season novice who performed admirably in the spring, are two of his string Pipe believes to be facing an uphill struggle with the assessor.

"Swing Bowler ran a cracking race in the Betfair Hurdle and went up 6lb for that," Pipe says. "Once again, she's in the grips of the handicapper and it's difficult for her but she's a good mare.

"Shotavodka is going to find it hard this winter, but he tries very hard. He's probably his own worst enemy, but he's been fantastic for the owners and I'm sure he'll win again."

Formerly trained by Emma Lavelle, ***Easter Meteor***, who was set to go very close in last season's Paddy Power when falling two out, has joined the list of established chasers at Pond House, which include the enigmatic ***Our Father***, whose record fresh was latched on to by punters when sent off favourite for the Hennessy, but he continues to prove a conundrum.

"We haven't had Easter Meteor long," Pipe says. "He's a good chaser at up to two and a half miles and he'll be going for some nice handicaps. He'll probably have an entry in the Paddy Power."

Pipe knows what it takes to land the Grand National having won the 2008 renewal with Comply Or Die, and he has a number of horses who could be targeted at the Aintree showpiece, spearheaded by comprehensive Midlands National winner ***Goulanes***.

Pipe says: "Goulanes will be a Grand National type. He probably won't come back until the second half of the season, but he stayed well in the Midlands National and you have to think of him along the lines of Aintree. He goes on most types of ground."

Other contenders for the Grand National could include veteran ***The Package***, who finished mid-division last year having unseated his rider in 2010, and ***Big Occasion***, who missed last season having picked up a knock when runner-up behind Godsmejudge in the 2013 Scottish equivalent.

"The Package may well go for another tilt at the Grand National. He's tricky to keep sound, but he'll be aimed at long-distance chases.

"We're in no rush with Big Occasion, so he'll hopefully have a busy second half of the season," Pipe says. "The distance for the National would be fine, but he would have to go up in the ratings to get in the race."

The novice hurdle ranks are set to be populated by a number of exciting types, including first-time-out bumper winners ***Lady Of Longstone***, ***Molo***, ***Mount Haven*** and ***Cloughernagh Boy***, with that quartet likely to have one more start in bumpers before embarking on a career over the smaller obstacles.

Taj Badalandabad, unbeaten in two bumpers, will also go novice hurdling. "They were only two small bumpers he won, but he couldn't have won them any easier," Pipe said. "He'll go over hurdles now."

Reporting by Chris Humpleby

The Package: long-distance races are his bag, and he will be aimed at the Grand National

PIPE: ASSESSING THE STATS

David Pipe's tally of 90 winners last season may have been 14 less than the previous term but the 2013-14 campaign saw him earn a greater amount of prize-money, clocking just shy of £1.5 million, *writes Kevin Morley.* While he had less runners overall, Pipe managed to deliver on the big stage on more than one occasion making it a more successful season.

The Nicholashayne handler managed to strike in two Grade 1 contests at the festival, courtesy of Dynaste in the Ryanair and Western Warhorse in the Arkle. Success in big handicaps was also a common occurrence throughout the campaign with Ballynagour bolting up in the Byrne Group Plate at the festival while Dell' Arca won the Greatwood. Pipe also landed Uttoxeter's Midlands National with Goulanes, a race the trainer has now taken for the last four years.

Pipe sends out his fair share of winners in all disciplines. Hurdlers provide the most winners but the lowest strike-rate, while the polar opposite is true of his runners in bumpers.

Tom Scudamore rides the vast majority of the yard's winners, but don't expect to make money backing all his mounts. Instead, look out for those ridden by Tony McCoy, who had such a successful spell at the yard when stable jockey to his father. And the booking of Timmy Murphy also proves significant.

Pipe is also known to give plenty of opportunities to conditional riders and has even utilised them to good effect in handicaps at the festival. Expect the likes of Michael Heard, Kieron Edgar and Mikey Ennis to put their claims to good use in the coming months.

Cheltenham aside, Pipe has sent out most winners at Exeter over the last five seasons. However, expect plenty of his runners to start at short odds at the Devon course. His figures are more impressive still at Chepstow and Uttoxeter, with his record at the latter last term standing out in particular. Look out for his rare visits to Fakenham and Musselburgh with respective strike-rates suggesting his raiders are more likely than not to oblige.

Pipe's established stars remain at a relatively young age, and he appears to have enough talent coming through the ranks to enjoy another solid campaign.

Out on the gallops at Pond House

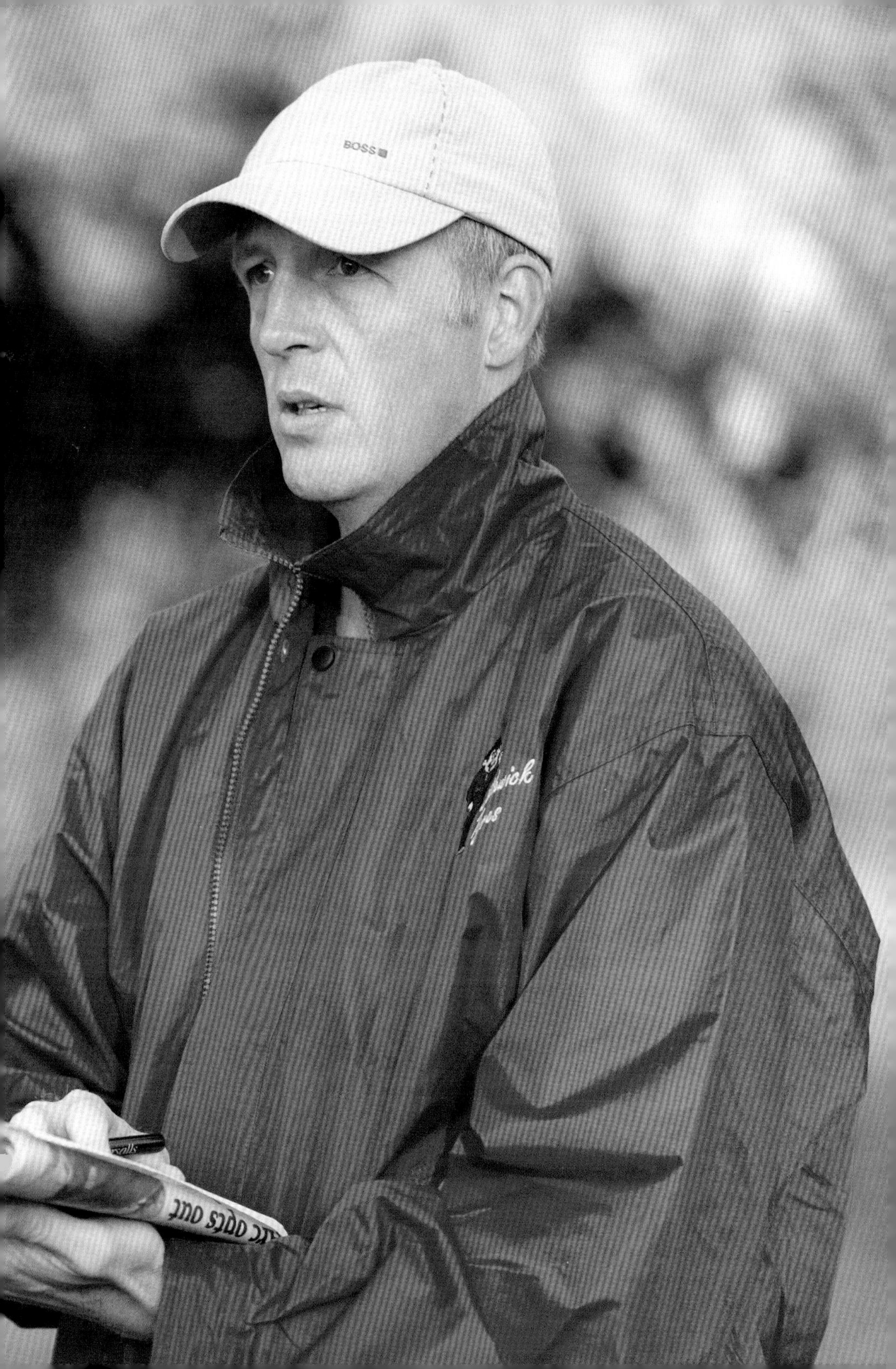
BOSS

With awesome firepower Mullins holds the key to so many of the big races

PERHAPS more than ever, Willie Mullins holds the key when it comes to Ireland's jumps prospects for 2014-15 – and there could hardly be a more reliable lockmaster.

Although the recession has challenged the horseracing scene in Ireland over the past half-decade or so, the principle owners have stuck it out impressively and Mullins has been able to pick up the pieces due to the struggles of others. Graham Wylie brought many of his horses to Ireland and, specifically to Closutton after Howard Johnston's demise. Mullins also ran horses for Gigginstown, Rich Ricci, JP McManus and Alan Potts last season – among others.

Even an ephemeral study of ante-post lists for 2015 at the Cotswolds will underline Mullins' stranglehold. Not long ago, bookies would have offered something like 50-50 Mullins or Noel Meade to be champion trainer in the following season. There is no competition between the pair now, although Meade managed a long-priced winner at the 2014 festival with Very Wood.

Gordon Elliott and Tony Martin are in fine fettle; Dessie Hughes, Jessica Harrington and Dermot Weld continue to thrive. However, Mullins is the high king of Ireland.

Overall, these are days of immense prosperity for Irish racing. The Flat's health was showcased on a stunning Irish Champions weekend, while the figures, albeit a bit crude, are startling regarding our jumpers: of the 54 Cheltenham races run throughout the past two festivals, 26 of the winners were trained in Ireland – an incredible statistic given how numerically up against it the Irish are year-on-year.

Moreover, as we attack a fascinating new season, there is depth of talent from top to bottom.

SENIOR CHASERS

The 2014 Gold Cup was nothing shy of unbelievable, two longshots fighting out a controversial finish. ***Lord Windermere*** had achieved nothing to give him any chance all season, while ***On His Own*** then ran a shocker in the Punchestown Gold Cup. To Lord Windermere's credit, his RSA win the previous season proved how much he likes Cheltenham, and no doubt Jim Culloty will aim him specifically at the big one again this year.

Sir Des Champs suffered a slight tendon injury and it remains to be seen how he will recover from that, but there are some big prizes to be won and he still has time on his side as an eight-year-old.

Tony Martin, meanwhile, reported ***Flemenstar*** to be coming along well in the care of his owner during the summer, and it will be fascinating to see how he fares. His trainer will give him all the time he needs. The chances are at least one of this pair will not be at his best, but they are names to look forward to.

The novice chasers from last year were far from a vintage lot, with ***Carlingford Lough*** proving a remarkably durable type, and perhaps he can go on to stake a Gold Cup claim. However, the one to keep an eye on could be the five-year-old ***Djakadam***. He won his first two starts over fences and was travelling powerfully it seemed when falling in the JLT Novices' Chase. He is a strapping youngster who jumps well and could yet be a Gold Cup contender.

The most hyped of last year's novices, ***Champagne Fever*** proved far from durable and ended the campaign with the bubble truly blown. Willie Mullins will surely think about stepping him up in trip, yet it is hard to know what to make of the two-mile championship division. Certainly there are few horses in Ireland one would be rushing to back for the Champion Chase.

If there is to be a worthy Grade 1 winner it is ***Hidden Cyclone***. Speaking to Shark Hanlon before the Listowel festival, he pointed out that as his horses were generally out of form last season, it is possible that Hidden Cyclone could be a bit healthier this year. While he certainly did not look a sick horse, he has not had a huge deal of experience at the top level and Hanlon's hit-rate was notably poor last term. He has obvious Ryanair claims, with ***Ballycasey*** and ***Boston Bob*** likely sorts for that race too.

SENIOR HURDLERS

The plans of Willie Mullins will be fascinating here as a palpable changing of the guard takes place. ***Hurricane Fly*** has had his day at the top level over the minimum distance; he will likely try further, leaving room for the likes of ***Un De Sceaux***, ***Annie Power*** and ***Faugheen*** to take his place – all from the

Lord Windermere: Cheltenham specialist and surprise winner of the Gold Cup will be back for more this season

WATCH OUT FOR . . .

Annie Power, Djakadam, Faugheen, Hidden Cyclone, Pont Alexandre, Shaneshill, Sir Des Champs, The Tullow Tank, Un De Sceaux, Vautour

same stable, although all three could also go chasing.

Faugheen was rarely thought of as a potential Champion Hurdle horse last season but his Grade 1 rout at Punchestown, when he dropped back in distance after winning the Neptune, suggested he might have the pace to win a Champion. The way he quickened for a squeeze in the Neptune was one of the visual delights of the 2014 festival and, with such talent elsewhere, Mullins might tackle top hurdle races with the six-year-old, who can go novice chasing if needs be.

Jezki ended the campaign with three Grade 1 victories to his name, including the Champion Hurdles at Cheltenham and Punchestown. He shows a fine attitude and is likely to come into his own in the second half of the year, especially when he gets more lively terrain.

Annie Power's World Hurdle defeat reignited the trip debate that seemed to dominate the narrative for the months leading up to Cheltenham. Clearly she was beaten by a star and, if More Than That stays hurdling, it is difficult to see what will beat him in the stayers' showpiece, but it remains to be seen what happens with Annie Power. Be it chasing or hurdling, two miles or three, she will be one of the superstars of the season.

Solwhit, rising 11, is due to return to action but anything he achieves now is bonus territory.

NOVICES

The novice chase division looks formidable. Perhaps the most exciting this year is ***Vautour***, since the manner of how he negotiated hurdles last season screamed out the potential to improve for fences. Given his dominance in the Supreme, that entitles him to belong to the "could be anything" bracket. Again, however, Willie Mullins has taken his time to decide where his aces will go, and the Champion Hurdle is another option.

Or will something from his stable usurp him? Un De Sceaux might easily go chasing, as could Annie Power, and no doubt Mullins will ruminate hard and deep about how to keep his plethora of super steeds apart.

Briar Hill – a faller in the Albert Bartlett won by Very Wood – is not one to discount, and arguably more promising is ***The Tullow Tank***, an ex-pointer who has joined Dessie Hughes. He looks a prime Arkle candidate.

Abbyssial is one to look forward to as well. He was far from the archetypal juvenile hurdler last season, as he is very much jumps-bred, and Mullins said after he won a Grade 1 at the Punchestown festival that the horse would

go chasing this season. Getting the age allowances, and given his size, he can only improve.

The novice hurdling division can hardly lack depth, since Ireland provided five of the first six home in a Champion Bumper in 2014 that seemed right up to scratch.

Silver Concorde, the winner, is exciting, since he is considered to have the pace to win a smart Flat race, the sort of toe that should make him a top hurdler if he jumps – and he certainly will not lack tutelage, given Dermot Weld's amazing record with jumpers.

Willie Mullins provided the second, third and sixth in the Cheltenham Bumper, with the Weld-trained ***Vigil*** fifth.

Shaneshill, who chased home Silver Concorde, then reversed the form at Punchestown. He looks a proper jumper in the making, one with pace and stamina and who can be ridden positively.

There could be an intriguing Triumph Hurdle candidate in ***Timiyan***, who cost €470,000 at Goffs after winning two handicaps for Dermot Weld. It is understood the Ghostzapper gelding will stay in training for new owner JP McManus with the master of Rosewell and, having attained a mark of 104 on the Flat, it will be interesting to see how he takes to hurdling. He will be one of many to move markets ahead of Cheltenham.

Jezki: will surely be winning top contests in Britain and Ireland again

Why you must side with unlucky New One and go against Sire De Grugy

OPINION seemed divided after the Champion Hurdle as to whether The New One was unlucky. He was severely hampered at the third following the fatal fall of Our Conor and was beaten only two and three-quarter lengths after storming up the hill.

Straight after the race the consensus seemed to be he was hampered more than the distance he was beaten by, but in time some offered the view he had plenty of time to work back into the race and couldn't do so, merely staying on when the race was over.

CHAMPION HURDLE

So which is it? My inclination at the time, and it still holds true, is that he was unlucky. In a championship race everything needs to go right and on this occasion it didn't work out for ***The New One***. Yes, the incident happened early in the race when no cards had been played, but it disrupted his rhythm,

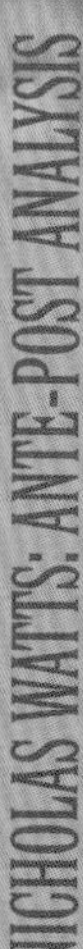

he was careful at many of the following hurdles, and Sam Twiston-Davies had to make sure the horse was all right before he could safely launch a challenge.

If you deem him unlucky, as I do, then you have to go in again this season. He is an awesome hurdler when in full flow, skimming over hurdles with ease, and no horse in training gets up the Cheltenham hill as well as he does. This season is likely to be very similar to last – starting off at Kempton in October, before taking in the International Hurdle (which he won last season), Christmas Hurdle, Cheltenham, then Aintree.

His Prestbury record, on both courses, is 1612113, and it is entirely possible he can improve again this season on the very good form he showed in the last campaign. He is a confident selection to see off whatever Willie Mullins throws at the race.

Mullins has considerable ammunition. Faugheen and Vautour both won easily at last season's festival, while Un De Sceaux is still lurking, still unbeaten, and still being campaigned in such a way that we have little idea how good he might be.

One, or maybe all three of the above could conceivably represent Mullins or, possibly, Vautour and Un De Sceaux will try chasing leaving Faugheen a clear passage through to the Champion Hurdle.

It will be interesting to see how the three are campaigned, but for now it is pure guesswork as to what each will do. That is another reason to play safe with The New One – we already know what he will be doing this season.

CHAMPION CHASE

The Champion Chase was won in thrilling style by Sire De Grugy, and it was a result that warmed the hearts of all jumps fans, showing smaller trainers and jockeys can beat the big guys every now and then.

Sire De Grugy *(below)* is clearly an exceptional talent and will be back for more

this season, where he might have to contend with a rejuvenated Sprinter Sacre, who is due to return following his health woes.

They are both skinny prices for the Champion Chase, however, and it is not much fun lumping on either at around the 3-1 mark before a fence has been jumped.

More imaginatively, it might be worth following the Henry de Bromhead-trained ***Moscow Mannon***, who has only one quote for the race – 33-1 – but who could force his way into the reckoning if he can win a few graded chase in Ireland over the winter.

That is not impossible. He had a positive start to life over fences last season, winning easily at Naas before running Gods Own to half a length in a Grade 1 on his most recent start at the Punchestown festival. Behind him that day were Balder Succes, Felix Yonger, Trifolium and Champagne Fever, so it was a hot race and he excelled.

Now he has more experience under his belt he could develop and become a natural successor to Sizing Europe, De Bromhead's other great two-miler of recent seasons.

The two-mile chase division in Ireland this season might not be the strongest with Champagne Fever a likely candidate to step up in trip, and Moscow Mannon, who was fourth in the 2012 Champion Bumper, could really come of age.

WORLD HURDLE

The World Hurdle order has most definitely changed. More Of That romped away from hot favourite Annie Power last March, while Big Buck's could manage only fifth and was promptly retired.

So what will happen this season? A lot will depend on who stays over hurdles. If More Of That does, he would be a logical choice to follow up, but the one who interests me most is ***Briar Hill*** at 12-1. Of course, he could also go chasing, but Mullins isn't short of options in that department, and bearing in mind the awful fall he suffered in the Albert Bartlett last season, it might make sense to keep him over hurdles for now.

He certainly has unfinished business in that department. His three hurdle wins were achieved at odds of 1-9, 1-4 and 1-3, so we didn't learn much about him – although his win at Naas when beating Apache Jack and Very Wood is better than it appeared.

Briar Hill is a strong stayer, bred for stamina, and will have no trouble with better ground or the Cheltenham hill – as he proved when winning the 2013 Champion Bumper.

WATCH OUT FOR . . .

Briar Hill, Cause Of Causes, Colour Squadron, Cue Card, Dynaste, Moscow Mannon, Sire De Grugy, The New One, Very Wood, Vigil

Briar Hill: the 2013 Champion Bumper winner looks value for the World Hudle at 12-1

Interestingly, Mullins put Boston Bob back over hurdles last season for a time (also owed by the Wylies) and it could be that he keeps Briar Hill back for one more year over hurdles. After all, he is only six.

At 12-1 he will do for me, although a note should be made of Whisper. He is due to go chasing, but these things don't always work out (remember Big Buck's?) and he is another who would be interesting if reverting to hurdles.

CHELTENHAM GOLD CUP

The most open division this season is the Gold Cup. It's currently 10-1 the field after a strange renewal last season where the unheralded Lord Windermere trumped the better-fancied Bobs Worth and Silviniaco Conti. That trio are hard to fancy this season and it could be this is ***Cue Card's*** season. He missed the race this year due to injury but before that had won the Betfair Chase easily and finished second in the King George.

That defeat led to the assumption Cue Card doesn't stay, but the soft ground was against him that day, and if it is good, like it normally is at Cheltenham, then his stamina could well be eked out to a Gold Cup trip.

His defeat of Dynaste, Silviniaco Conti, Tidal Bay and Bobs Worth at Haydock was one of the best performances of the season and he wasn't stopping, so it is not impossible the Gold Cup trip at Cheltenham on good ground is beyond him. He is available at double-figure odds and only sixth in the betting, but he has a much better chance than that implies.

KING GEORGE VI CHASE

He is likely to go for the King George again this season and is likely to run very well. However, for this race I'm going to give ***Dynaste*** another chance to prove his running in the race last season was all wrong.

He was a great second to Cue Card at Haydock, but it is quite possible that effort took the edge off him with Kempton in mind. He was reported to have back problems after the race which wouldn't have helped either, but he showed what he could do when an easy winner of the Ryanair Chase.

The fact he couldn't follow up at Aintree was disappointing, but again highlights the fact he is probably best when fresh.

I would like to see David Pipe's charge go for the King George first time up so it gives Dynaste no option of bouncing or running below par. Instead, get him ready at home, send him to Kempton mad fresh and you might see a performance more akin to the one he put up when winning the Feltham Novices' Chase the previous season.

At 12-1 with Boylesports he is a juicy price for one of his class.

From start to finish: a guide in how to play the jumps season for a profit

PART 1:
OCTOBER TO NOVEMBER

At this early juncture of the season, the first consideration when analysing any jumps race with a view to placing a bet is the likely fitness states of the runners involved.

An overwhelming majority of trainers have access to all-weather gallops so are capable of readying a horse to make a winning resumption from a summer break, but many still prefer the traditional method of bringing their runners to match fitness on the track and their horses can lack a competitive edge first time out.

Consequently, jumpers coming back from layoffs at this time year can be tricky to assess. You can choose to ignore them and focus only on runners with a recent run under the belt, but last October around half of the winners of jumps handicaps in Britain went to horses returning from 50-plus day absences.

Instead, I suggest you stick to either returning runners from stables with high strike-rates with their longer-layoff runners, or horses who have performed well in the past when fresh.

Table 1 reveals a number of British-based trainers whose fresh runners are typically fit enough to do themselves justice. Each are showing a better strike-rate in October-November jumps handicaps run in the previous four seasons with runners returning from 50-plus day breaks than with horses who had been off for fewer than 50 days.

Fitness was rarely an issue with legendary trainer Martin Pipe's runners, and son David has evidently embraced this methodology. Pipe's runners who had been off for at least 50 days are generating a monster £1 level-stake profit of £80.50. By contrast, those returning within 49 days of their last run are showing huge losses of £111.88.

Paddy Power Gold Cup meeting and the Hennessy Gold Cup

Since taking the reins from his father, Pipe is upholding family traditions by landing big handicaps – he's already won the Paddy Power Gold Cup, Hennessy and Grand National – and targeting the Open meeting at Cheltenham in November.

Pipe has enjoyed 16 winners at the meeting with 12 achieved in the last three seasons – and when you analyse his winners' profiles it's possible to detect a clear MO.

Interestingly, all bar The Liquidator, who won a novice hurdle at the fixture last year having scored 18 days earlier at Carlisle, were running for the first time in Britain that season, so he evidently prefers priming horses for the meeting on the Pond House gallops rather than bringing runners to the boil with a pipe-opener.

Evan Williams and Nigel Twiston-Davies are other trainers in the table who have captured big pre-Christmas handicaps with fresh horses. Williams' popular chaser State Of Play defied an absence of 232 days when winning the 2006 Hennessy. Twiston-Davies has won the Paddy Power Gold Cup twice in the last six seasons and his earlier winner Imperial Commander (2008) had been off

Table 1: TOP STRIKE-RATE TRAINERS WITH GB JUMPS HANDICAP RUNNERS RETURNING FROM 50-PLUS DAYS OFF

	OFF 50-PLUS DAYS		OFF FEWER THAN 50 DAYS		
Trainer	*w-r*	*profit-loss*	*w-r*	*profit-loss*	*strike-rate diff*
Keith Reveley	7-34	17.5	3-37	-19	13
Jeremy Scott	8-41	6.13	4-50	-34.88	12
David Pipe	21-116	80.5	14-169	-111.88	10
Alex Hales	6-39	28	2-34	-28.13	9
Nick Williams	7-34	11	4-32	-18.88	8
Nigel Twiston-Davies	21-129	-4.95	20-214	-84.51	7
Peter Bowen	7-42	21.83	15-148	-45.7	7
Evan Williams	13-82	42.58	15-149	-72.68	6
Oliver Sherwood	7-41	-2	2-34	-15.88	5
Nick Alexander	7-31	11	7-38	35.5	5
Alan King	20-115	36.18	11-91	-25.17	5
Charlie Longsdon	15-74	-17.34	20-126	-61.58	4
Kim Bailey	10-59	5.75	9-64	-6.63	3
Richard Lee	10-54	34	9-58	11.5	3

(Date: previous four seasons, October and November races only)

for 337 days. Little Josh provided the second success in 2010 just 13 days after dead-heating on his reappearance in an intermediate chase at Carlisle.

In fact, the majority of recent runnings of these two landmark handicaps have gone to seasonal debutants with such runners accounting for nine of the 14 Paddy Power Gold Cup winners this century, and six of the last ten Hennessy winners.

We shouldn't lose sight of how well handicapped a horse needs to be to win a fiendishly competitive handicap chase.

It takes a Gold Cup horse to win the Hennessy off a big rating. This century, Gold Cup winners Denman and Bobs Worth are the only chasers to claim the Newbury handicap from marks of 160-plus, while it's equally hard for a horse towards the top of the ratings to land the Paddy Power Gold Cup with Al Ferof, who won off 159 in 2012, the sole winner to defy a rating above 154 in this period.

Al Ferof has since won a Grade 2 chase, although injuries have hindered his progress over fences. This talented grey turns ten in January, but his trainer Paul Nicholls is a dab-hand with veteran chasers so perhaps this will be the season when Al Ferof earns a breakthrough success in Grade 1 chase company.

The welcome introduction of the Grade 1 2m4f JLT Novices' Chase at the Festival has impacted on the Paddy Power Gold Cup with regards to the handicaps marks of the second-season chasers who have the option of competing in the Cheltenham handicap.

Second-season novices who run well in the JLT have high ratings leaving them vulnerable in races like the Paddy Power Gold Cup to lower-weighted improvers, so many are bypassing handicaps for graded races. You suspect the first two home in last season's JLT, Taquin Du Seuil and Uxizandre, who start this campaign with respective ratings over fences of 159 and 158, need to be Grade-1 chasers to win this season's Paddy Power Gold Cup.

I'm inclined to believe the 2m4½f novices' handicap chase at the Festival will prove a richer source of future Paddy Power Gold Cup winners as horses who finish in the money in this 0-140 race are often then able to return to Cheltenham the following November on workable marks.

The latest running was won by hugely progressive chaser Present View. He ended the season with a chase rating of 144 and would make considerable appeal in the Paddy Power Gold Cup if going straight for the race off this mark.

Novice chasers and hurdlers

The lions' share of fresh chasing and hurdling talents each season launch their careers in the autumn and winter months.

Despite the BHA's on-going efforts to make novice chases more competitive, a sizeable chunk in these months will look one-sided on paper featuring a strong favourite entitled to enjoy a class edge if running to form and, crucially, negotiating the fences.

Jumping is always a worry with a chase debutant and, based on stats from British chases since 2010, around one in every eight/nine newcomers (11.7 per cent) will fall or unseat. This figure doesn't include runners who are pulled up as a consequence of poor jumping. The percentage of chase newcomers overall who pull up each season is typically 17 per cent.

As you may have anticipated, chasers are less likely to commit major jumping errors as they gather experience over fences. A chase debutant is twice as likely to succumb to the fences than an experienced chaser with at least ten runs over fences on their CV.

Although chase debutants are inherently more likely to fall, this risk factor is often accounted for in their prices and makes chase newcomers from stables whose inexperienced chasers infrequently fall/unseat and are rarely pulled up interesting betting propositions.

For every trainer (minimum of 20 qualifying runners) I have worked out a 'blowout' percentage with chase debutants in

Uxizandre will to be a top-class chaser to strike a blow in the Paddy Power Gold Cup

British races in the past four seasons by calculating the share who received F, U and P form figures.

The ten most reliable in this period are Emma Lavelle (just 9.1 per cent of chase debutants fell/unseated or pulled up), Fergal O'Brien (9.5%), Tim Vaughan (15.8), Colin Tizzard (16.7), Alan King (17.8), Evan Williams (18), Charlie Longsdon (19), Lucinda Russell (19), Nick Williams (19) and Nicky Henderson (19).

Generally speaking, a hurdling debutant is about twice as likely to hit the deck than an experienced one (ten-plus starts), but hurdlers first time out are considerably less likely than chase newcomers to be beaten by the jumps with 4.8 per cent falling/unseating in Britain in the last four seasons.

Consequently, you can back a hurdles newcomer who you suspect might have a big class edge with conviction. In the past four seasons, six British trainers have excelled with these runners in the last four months of the calendar year with each showing at least a 20 per cent strike-rate from a minimum of 25 qualifying runners.

They are Nicky Henderson (44 winners from 123 runners, 36 per cent strike-rate, £1 level-stake profit of £2.89), John Quinn (9-26, 35%, +£4.95), Emma Lavelle (15-55, 28%, +£70.83), John Ferguson (14-52, 27%, +£5.60), Paul Nicholls (30-123, 25%, -£12.24) and Charlie Longsdon (14-64, 22%, +£6.75). The only trainer not showing a profit is Nicholls.

Quinn and Ferguson inherit a lot of classy Flat horses and, provided such runners are able to negotiate the hurdles on their debuts, often they use their natural speed and superior gears to gain an upper hand over the National Hunt breds and chasing types.

PART 2: FESTIVE PERIOD (DECEMBER 26 TO JANUARY 7)

The volume and variety of races makes this busy period a window of opportunity for stables of all sizes.

Your first port of call should be horses connected to trainers and owners who routinely enjoy festive winners. Two leading trainers synonymous with such success are Henderson and Willie Mullins.

Henderson's exploits at Kempton's two-day meeting are legendary. In the last four seasons he has won 35 per cent of the races and his runners are producing a £1 level-stake profit £12.54 on the back of 17 wins from 49 runs.

Since 2010, one in eight Irish jumps races run in this festive period have gone the way of a Mullins-trained runner. Interestingly, his runners in Ireland outside of Leopardstown's Christmas meeting seem to be offering a better chance of making a profit.

At Leopardstown, he has achieved 25 wins from 117 runs for a £1 level-stake loss of £43.18 – his stats with runners outside of the home of the Lexus Chase are 43 wins from 129 runs (33 per cent) for a loss of just £10.90.

Mullins, who has won the Cheltenham Festival Champion Bumper eight times since its inception in 1992, loves to target bumpers at this time of year.

In the last four seasons, he boasts a record of ten wins from 24 runs (+£3.28) in these races and has used festive bumpers to launch the careers under rules of a number of his recent star performers, notably Champagne Fever, Ballycasey and Briar Hill.

A collection of trainers evidently placing their horses well at Christmas time can be found in table 2. To make this list, since 2010 a trainer in our festive window needs to have achieved at least ten wins, and be showing a strike-rate of 20-plus per cent and a £1 level-stake profit.

You would have enjoyed handsome rewards from blindly following runners trained by Pipe, Eoin Doyle and Denis Gerard Hogan.

Malcolm Jefferson is another producing a healthy balance sheet and, interestingly, this profit stems from his record at Wetherby's two-day December meeting where he has registered six wins from 13 runs (+£47.85), while four of his seven beaten horses finished in the money.

Table 2: TRAINERS TO FOLLOW IN FESTIVE PERIOD

Trainer	*w-r*	*%*	*profit-loss*
David Pipe	37-174	21	68.96
Eoin Doyle	11-55	20	66.67
Denis Gerard Hogan	10-37	27	60.33
Nicky Henderson	64-184	35	43.3
Malcolm Jefferson	13-42	31	42.2
Nick Williams	10-43	23	22.54
John Ferguson	10-29	34	13.07
Venetia Williams	33-162	20	8.2

(Data: records in last four season with runners between December 26 and January 7)

PART 3: JANUARY TO FEBRUARY

These core winter months are treated by some trainers as the calm before the storm (March's Cheltenham Festival) and provide a chance for soft-ground specialists to thrive before the going dries out in the spring.

This period is characterised by deep, holding ground. Trainers are understandably reluctant to run horses they are preparing for Cheltenham on this testing going so close to the Festival and keep these runners under wraps.

Past performances can offer clues to whether horses are likely to be suited by attritional conditions, and a desirable profile is a runner with excellent form on softer ground in their back catalogue who has been running well on quicker going.

A prime example is Vieux Lion Rouge. This exciting young horse is unbeaten in six starts on going described as soft or slower and has lost all three times he has encountered ground with good in the description.

PART 4: SPRING
Cheltenham Festival

The festival is the pinnacle jumps meeting and this season gets under way on March 10. Finding winners across four days of the most competitive jumps action on the planet is a serious challenge, even for us experts, so to aid your quest for Festival riches I've come up with some do's and don'ts.

DO . . .

. . . focus on horses from stables with a proven track record at getting their runners to peak at the meeting. Three trainers who spring to mind are Alan King, Dessie Hughes and Charles Byrnes. Three-quarters of Cheltenham Festival winners produce their season-best Racing Post Ratings.

. . . brush up on Irish jumps form before the meeting. Generally speaking, Irish trainers are Cheltenham Festival-centric. In fact, for many of these stables, success at Prestbury Park is an even higher priority than winning big prizes on home soil.

. . . side with last-time-out winners towards the top of the market in handicap chases. This century such runners are showing a £1 level-stake profit of £25.50 courtesy of 20 wins from 112 bets.

. . . be willing to afford a promising young horse who has suffered a blip en route a second chance. About two-thirds of the winners of Grade 1 novice races at the Festival this century had previously tasted defeat that season.

. . . check the winner's time of the Supreme Novices' Hurdle if there is a degree of doubt over the state of the going. If it takes the winner more than four minutes to win this Festival opener, the ground is likely to be soft.

. . . take advantage of bookmakers' offers.

DON'T . . .

. . . opt for the computer-straight forecast (CSF). Instead, choose the Exacta. At last season's festival, the Exacta produced the bigger dividend in all 27 races.

. . . back a horse at short-odds in the Fred Winter. The handicap for juvenile hurdlers can lay claim to being the hardest race of the meeting for punters to get a handle on. The last three runnings prove unfathomable to most with the winners returning starting prices of 33-1, 25-1 and 40-1.

Crabbie's Grand National

Grand National fever takes hold in April with the historic Aintree race staged on the second Saturday.

This famous chase has undergone a radical transformation in recent seasons – weights are now compressed and the course and fence design have received much-needed makeovers, and these changes have evidently altered the typical National winner profile.

When the course was more challenging in the 1990s and 2000s most winners were strong stayers carrying low weights – good jumpers had been prepared with a view to preserving their handicap ratings and were towards the top of the betting.

Weight is no longer an issue – four of the last six winners carried at least 11st – and jumping ability is less important, while the betting, too, has seemingly become an unreliable guide with four of the last seven winners returning SPs of 25-1 or bigger.

Stamina and a runner's preparation remain essential considerations, while recent runnings suggest proven class, a good run in a graded race as a novice, and form at the Grand National meeting, not necessarily over the big fences, are desirable features in the profile of a contender for the Aintree marathon.

Silviniaco leads the way when it comes to sorting out big-race contenders

WHEN you are asked to provide a list of 12 horses likely to be contenders at the big meetings it can be very hard to avoid the obvious.

That was the case 12 months ago when, try as I might, I really couldn't justify leaving out Sprinter Sacre – and look what happened to him.

That serves as a reminder you can never take anything for granted in the jumps game, so while almost every name in this list will be familiar to jumps fans, I've tried not go to be too obvious. That means there us no room for any of Willie Mullins' 2014 Cheltenham Festival winners like Faugheen and Vautour – of course I expect them to be challenging for major honours this season, but so does everyone else.

There will also be no room for Sprinter Sacre, Simonsig or Cue Card, who all have plenty to prove after their difficulties. In the case of Cue Card, I really do I hope I'm wrong, as I'd love to see him run in a Gold Cup, but there is no room for sentiment and it remains to be seen if he can return in the same shape as before his injury.

BEAT THAT Nicky Henderson

If Nicky Henderson has a staying chaser to follow in the footsteps of the likes of Long Run and Bobs Worth it is probably this six-year-old. He carried a fair reputation when running in bumpers early in 2013 but, clearly yet to grow into his frame, was beaten as favourite twice before being put away. That worked wonders as he won three of his four hurdles starts last season, winding up with victories at the Aintree and Punchestown festivals, in the latter beating Cheltenham winner Don Poli. He showed a good attitude that day, proving he has the courage to go with his ability and now all he needs to do is learn to jump a fence. He should take high rank in staying novice chases.

BUYWISE Evan Williams

Had his first full season last year and made rapid strides when sent novice chasing, winning four of his five starts. The only defeat came in a novice chase at the Cheltenham Festival and while most people were concentrating on how unlucky second-place Attaglance was, the chances are Buywise would have won easily had he not nearly fallen at the second-last. He had already made a couple of mistakes before that and was only tenth three out, but he was powering into contention when they straightened up only to nearly come down. That must have cost him ten lengths, but he flew home to finish fifth, and returned to Cheltenham a month later to win easily off the same mark. He still needs to learn a bit about jumping, but we know he stays well and has pace and he looks the ideal type for the Hennessy, with a mark of 146 looking pretty fair.

IRVING Paul Nicholls

I was heavily involved in this one for last

Irving: appeals as a Champion Hurdle contender

season's Supreme Novices' Hurdle and he could not have been more disappointing when finishing only ninth as joint favourite with winner Vautour. His trainer was apparently not overjoyed with the ride given by Nick Scholfield at the time, but I thought the horse was never travelling like he can, and Nicholls may have changed his mind given Irving was subsequently found to be coughing. He has been earmarked for a possible early return in the Elite Hurdle at Wincanton, a race Nicholls has won six times this century, including with the classy Azertyuiop, Celestial Halo (twice) and Zarkandar. The last two have represented him well in Champion Hurdles and Irving could well prove to be his main contender this time, although it does look a particularly hot year, although that's something we often say at this time of year.

JOSSES HILL Nicky Henderson

Five runs in Britain last season yielded three wins plus a close second in the Grade 1 Tolworth Hurdle and the same berth at a respectable distance of six lengths to the brilliant Vautour in the Supreme Novices' Hurdle. He is no exactly a horse who has gone under the radar, then, but if there is a more obvious contender for top 2m chasing honours in Britain I haven't seen it. As early as December last season Nicky Henderson was saying he would be minded for a chasing campaign, so the fact he ended up going to Cheltenham and Aintree, where he powered clear for a six-length win, suggests he progressed more rapidly than expected. He is every inch a chaser, though, and if all goes well he should take high rank among the novices.

MA FILLEULE Nicky Henderson

Mares do not win Gold Cups, the last one being Dawn Run in 1985, which has to be the reason there is such a discrepancy between Ma Filleule and Holywell in the Gold Cup

market. But based on their form last year, there just shouldn't be. First and second in the staying handicap chase on day one of the Festival, there was just 2lb between them in the ratings that day and now there is nothing after both scored at Aintree. Ma Feilleule was particularly impressive when an eight-length scorer off a mark of 150 in the Topham Trophy at Aintree, earning a Racing Post Rating of 164 which, given she would receive a mares' allowance of 5lb in the Gold Cup, put her right on the mark achieved by this year's winner. If she can improve just a little on that, she would be a major contender in what looks a very open year. Whatever the case, her allowance will surely make her of interest in graded races.

MILSEAN Willie Mullins

Willie Mullins has the most powerful yard in Britain or Ireland and has so many potential stars it's hard to know where to start. The likes of Faugheen and Vautour are obvious,

Ma Filleule: would not have to improve much to have a chance in the Gold Cup

but one who could fill their boots in the novice hurdle division could be Milsean, whose only defeat came at the hands of No More Heroes. Following that defeat he was allowed to his own thing front next time and a relentless display of galloping saw him draw clear at Limerick for a 25-length success and earned him a Racing Post Rating of 145. To put that into context, only three horses have bettered that mark in a bumper since 2007 – Dunguib, Pandorama and Don Cossack – al of whom went on to Grade 1 glory over hurdles or fences. He has plenty to live up to then, but don't be surprised if he takes high rank among the staying novices.

MONTBAZON Alan King

Not exactly an obvious one as he's been around the block a few times and not won since February 2012 but, having missed a year after running fourth in the Supreme, he showed what he could be capable of when third in the County Hurdle in March. He could not match that form on the rest of his outings but he has never been asked to go further than 2m1f and he looks to me like he is crying out for 2m4f at least. He has only twice finished out of the first four and the ability is there for him to pick up a decent prize if a rise in trip is what he needs.

NO MORE HEROES Gordon Elliott

There is no horse in training I am more excited about than Gordon Elliott's five-year-old, who I made a horse to follow in the Weekender following a hugely eyecatching maiden hurdle run in November last year. He ran only twice more, but paid for Christmas when winning a bumper by 39 lengths at

giveaway odds of 15-8, and he followed up by giving the very decent Milsean 5lb and a beating at Naas in February. The Racing Post Rating he earned for both those wins was 140, which is identical to that awarded to Champion Bumper winner Silver Concorde, so he is clearly a high-class horse in the making. Long term he has the potential to be contesting Gold Cups, but I will be bitterly disappointed if he doesn't make his mark in good staying novice hurdles this season. Being by Presenting, you'd hope he'd handle good ground, but trainer Gordon Elliott was in no rush to try him on it last season.

SAPHIR DU RHEU Paul Nicholls

Having won a weak maiden hurdle in January 2013, Saphir Du Rheu was not a novice last season, but he is younger than Cheltenham Festival winner Faugheen and the same age as Vautour and finished last season rated considerably higher than both over hurdles. Having run only ten times, he clearly remains of huge potential and it will be interesting to see what the plan is with him. Apparently connections are keen to have one go over hurdles before deciding whether to go chasing, but whatever he does he wants to be kept on side. The way he sluiced through the field to win the Lanzarote Hurdle at Kempton in January marked him down as potentially top class and, while he had to battle to give 11lb (not including jockey's claim) to beat Whisper a head in the Welsh Champion Hurdle (pair 19 lengths), the winner went on to land the Coral Cup and Grade 1 stayers hurdle at Aintree. You can forget his odds-on defeat in the Game Spirit at Fontwell as he was clearly over the top and Nicholls was probably right to give this young horse the rest of the season off. He is exciting.

SILVINIACO CONTI Paul Nicholls

Can lay claim to be being the best staying chaser in training on the form of his King George win and reportedly wasn't at his best afterwards despite leading over the last in the Gold Cup and winning the Bowl at Aintree. There must have been a physical

reason for those two performances, though, as he had never previously hung the way he did at Cheltenham and he was also tying up late at Aintree. He has already had two attempts at the Gold Cup, so is running out of time even at the age of eight, but if there is one trainer you can trust to bring a horse back year after year it is Paul Nicholls and Silviniaco Conti's latest season was hardly a disaster. We can expect a similar campaign this term with the Betfair Chase being a primer for the King George, for which I reckon he is easily the best value at this stage despite being 5-1 market leader. All roads will then lead to the spring festivals.

TAQUIN DU SEUIL Jonjo O'Neill

Paun Nicholls mentioned Jonjo O'Neill as the

Trustan Times (right): could do well in staying chases and can make up for not scoring last season

one to beat for this year's trainers' championship and he might not be far wrong. According to the market, O'Neill's Hollywell – already a dual festival winner – is his most likely Gold Cup contender, but it would not be a great surprise should Taquin Du Seuil prove a better horse when stepped up in trip. He raced at up to 2m in a few Flat starts in France (got within three lengths of Tac De Boistron on one occasion) a few years ago and, having won at Grade 2 level over hurdles and fences at 2m5f on heavy ground, clearly stays that trip very well. He also proved he was not ground dependent when winning the Jewson at Cheltenham in March (surprise runner-up Uixizandre franked the form with victory at Aintree) and he has just as much promise as his much shorter-price stablemate.

TRUSTAN TIMES Tim Easterby

Failed to register a win last season, but that might not have been the case had he not been 6lb out of the handicap when beaten less than two lengths in the Scottish National. That was his first try at a marathon trip and, while he paid for it with an 8lb rise (only 2lb higher than he ran off), he was rated higher over hurdles. He has gone particularly well at Haydock on soft ground and races like the Tommy Whittle or Grand National Trial at the course ought to be on his radar, although there is room for improvement in his jumping. He's no one-trick pony, though, as he ran a close third in the Pertemps Final over hurdles before his Ayr effort, and he could run again over hurdles. Either way, he can find a decent prize this term.

A dozen to follow who have made an impression away from the limelight

ALLEZ COLOMBIERES Willie Mullins

Ireland's champion trainer has an enviable record with acquisitions from the French jumping sphere and this €300,000 purchase rates a very exciting prospect, having won three of his four bumpers. They came from 1m4f to 1m6f on testing ground, so it will be fascinating to see if he is viewed as a stayer or more of a speedier hurdler in the making, as there is stamina in his pedigree. He's one to look forward to in Ireland through the winter and is expected to take a high rank.

ART OF SECURITY Dessie Hughes

This four-year-old shaped like a useful horse in the making on his debut in a bumper at the Punchestown festival last term, when placed behind highly impressive winner Forgotten Rules. It will be a surprise if he doesn't land a bumper and he's certainly got the pedigree. He is in good hands to make the grade once switched to hurdles and trainer Dessie Hughes is hoping his charge will cross the sea for one of the spring festivals.

BLAKEMOUNT Sue Smith

Each season Sue and Harvey Smith unleash an unexposed youngster to graduate from the novice hurdle division to the chasing equivalent, and hopes are very high Blakemount will more than make the grade. The son of Presenting had some very useful form over hurdles, winning twice and pushing Urban Hymn close in the Grade 2 River Don over an extended 3m at Doncaster in January on testing ground. That was to be his final outing as he was a late withdrawal from the Albert Bartlett at the Cheltenham Festival, for which he had been quietly fancied. He'll arrive back this season fresh and ready for a crack at fences. He is built for the job, stays very well and will be treated as a candidate for the RSA Chase.

EDUARD Nicky Richards

A one-time classy novice hurdler, this six-year-old was steadily campaigned after a somewhat unfortunate defeat to Pendra on his chasing debut at Carlisle last season. Nicky Richards sent him out to win his next two starts in ordinary company, and patience was rewarded when he signed off by landing the hat-trick in a Grade 2 over 2m4f at Ayr's Scottish National meeting. Eduard has got relatively few miles on his clock and connections have mapped out an ambitious campaign. Expect him to ruffle a few feathers, provide some value and take a high ranking.

FAYETTE COUNTY Tim Vaughan

Leading owner JP McManus snapped up this unexposed seven-year-old after he ran one of his hurdlers close at Carlisle on his British debut. He gained immediate reward on his investment when Fayette County recorded back-to-back wins in the famous green and gold hoop colours. His form bears close inspection, and Tim Vaughan thinks the world of him and will likely try to bag a decent handicap hurdle before sending him over a fence this season. He's one to follow along the way.

Eduard (red and yellow): progressive novice chaser last season is expected to take high rank over fences this term

GREAT TRY Paul Nicholls

A son of up-and-coming jumps sire Scorpion, Great Try created a fine impression on his debut in a jumpers bumper on Southwell's Fibresand surface last season. He moved strongly before coming away once the penny dropped, and the form was given substance when the runner-up went one better next time. His dam is from the same family as The Nightingale, so Paul Nicholls knows the family well and it will be fascinating to see how high he can climb up the novice hurdle division. Expect him to kick off around 2m4f.

SHANTY TOWN Suzy Smith

Narrowly denied in his sole Irish point before heading to Suzy Smith's yard in East Sussex, Shanty Town needed his rules debut in a Taunton bumper and was well held when switching his attention to hurdling at Kempton over 2m5f. However, on both occasions he left the impression he could do better. The pedigree suggests he is a stayer in the making and there is no doubt he is up to winning races this season.

SWNYMOR John Quinn

Having rather lost his way over hurdles last term, the move to John Quinn's stable brought about total rejuvenation as he bolted up returned to the Flat at Chester on his debut for the North Yorkshire handler. Quinn is renowned for taking care of such characters and the five-year-old's next outing at the Galway Festival, in a prestigious amateur rider's handicap off a stone higher mark, fully confirmed he is back up and running. Connections are excited about a return to hurdling, considering he has dropped a stone in the handicap from a 2012 peak, and there should be a decent prize in him.

TARA POINT Paul Nicholls

Having fallen on her point debut, Tara Point made amends next time when thrashing an improving sort at Mollington. She was then sent to leading trainer Paul Nicholls but went missing after enduring a problem and proved easy to back ahead of her rules debut in a mares' bumper at Wincanton a year later. She bolted up, heavily easing down at the finish, and confirmed herself a classy operator. Nicholls will look to the Listed mares' bumper at Cheltenham's Open meeting in November before a hurdles campaign.

TELL US MORE Willie Mullins

An impressive Irish point winner in December 2013, this five-year-old was knocked down to Giggingstown Stud for £290,000 at the Cheltenham sales later that month and sent to Willie Mullins. He hacked up on his debut for the champion trainer in a soft-ground Gowran bumper in March and stamped himself an exciting jumper in the making. He was lame when an intended runner at the Punchestown festival when again strongly fancied, but reports remain bullish about his home work. He is versatile regards ground, we know he can jump and he stays well. He should take high rank among Ireland's best novices this term.

TIME FOR A PINT Gordon Elliott

This progressive six-year-old won his first two bumpers before getting found out by deep ground in a decent winner's event at Fairyhouse in April. He then confirmed himself a sound-surface performer when winning readily over an inadequate 2m back there on his hurdling bow. He was given time to get over that and is expected to make into a very useful performer. He will jump a fence in time and wants 2m4f at least to shine.

USTICA Jonjo O'Neill

After scoring on his debut in a bumper for Phillip Kirby on soft ground last season, Ustica got snapped up to join Jonjo O'Neill and was sent to the Punchestown festival for the Goffs Land Rover Bumper. He was sent off 12-1 in a warm contest and emerged with credit considering fellow prominent racers dropped away. From a successful staying jumps family, he strongly appeals as the type to make into a useful hurdler during the winter months.

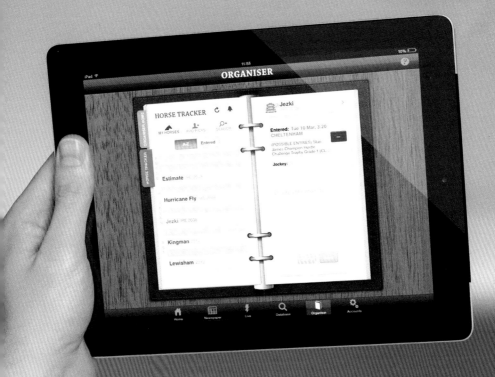

Abbyssial (Ire)

4 ch g Beneficial - Mega D'Estruval (Garde Royale)

Willie Mullins (Ir) — **Mrs Violet O'Leary**

PLACINGS: 3111F-16 — **RPR 148+h**

Starts	1st	2nd	3rd	4th	Win & Pl
7	4	-	1	-	£100,899

	5/14	Punc	2m Gd1 Hdl 4yo gd-yld	£51,667
	2/14	Fair	2m Gd2 Hdl 4yo sft-hvy	£20,313
	1/14	Gowr	2m Hdl 4yo soft	£11,375
	12/13	Fair	2m Mdn Hdl 3yo gd-yld	£4,207

Hugely impressive winner of Grade 1 juvenile hurdle at Punchestown in May before disappointing at Auteuil; had previous won first three races following move from France before suffering early fall in Triumph Hurdle; likely to go novice chasing.

Ackertac (Ire)

9 ch g Anshan - Clonsingle Native (Be My Native)

Tim Vaughan — **The Mount Fawcus Partnership**

PLACINGS: 3325P/231P521/26P79- — **RPR 147c**

Starts	1st	2nd	3rd	4th	Win & Pl
32	5	8	3	-	£71,050

	4/13	Chel	3m1½f Cls2 Nov Ch gd-sft	£12,512
131	11/12	Asct	2m3f Cls3 122-132 Ch Hcap soft	£12,512
	10/10	Uttx	2m6½f Cls4 Nov Hdl good	£2,212
	9/10	Uttx	2m4½f Cls4 Nov Hdl good	£2,212
	11/09	Ludl	2m Cls5 Mdn NHF 4-6yo soft	£2,602

Has run well at Cheltenham Festival for last two seasons, finishing second in novice handicap chase in 2013 before good seventh to Holywell in very strong handicap chase last season; won at the same track in between and could exploit falling handicap mark.

Activial (Fr)

4 rg g Lord Du Sud - Kissmirial (Smadoun)

Harry Fry — **Potensis Limited**

PLACINGS: 1218- — **RPR 128+h**

Starts	1st	2nd	3rd	4th	Win & Pl
4	2	1	-	-	£22,787

	2/14	Kemp	2m Cls1 Gd2 Hdl 4yo soft	£15,661
	9/13	Stra	1m4f NHF 3yo	£4,878

Promising second to Calipto on hurdling debut at Newbury last season before running away with a Grade 2 at Kempton; missed Triumph Hurdle and seemed to find ground too quick when disappointing at Aintree; looks type to improve with age.

Adriana Des Mottes (Fr)

4 br f Network - Daisy Des Mottes (Abdonski)

Willie Mullins (Ir) — **Mrs S Ricci**

PLACINGS: 8/6312B1-9 — **RPR 131+h**

Starts	1st	2nd	3rd	4th	Win & Pl
8	2	1	1	-	£65,760

	4/14	Fair	2m4f Nov Gd1 Hdl soft	£48,750
	12/13	Punc	2m Mdn Hdl 3yo heavy	£5,610

Grade 1 winner over hurdles last season, although that came in a desperately soft mares' contest at Fairyhouse; had run Abbyssial close previously before being brought down by same horse in Triumph Hurdle; big mare who has plenty of scope for chasing.

Ahyaknowyerself (Ire)

8 b g Milan - Summer Break (Foxhound)

Dr Richard Newland — **G Carstairs & R Marker**

PLACINGS: 7161F3121/413F2314P- — **RPR 148h**

Starts	1st	2nd	3rd	4th	Win & Pl
28	7	4	3	3	£61,188

	1/14	Leic	2m Cls3 Nov Ch soft	£6,498
128	9/13	MRas	2m1f Cls1 List 111-136 Hdl Hcap good	£19,933
124	10/12	Carl	2m1f Cls3 107-124 Hdl Hcap soft	£4,549
	10/12	Sedg	2m1f Cls4 Nov Hdl good	£2,534
	7/12	Strf	2m½f Cls4 Nov Hdl good	£3,165
	7/12	Uttx	2m Cls4 Nov Cond Hdl heavy	£2,534
	7/11	Wxfd	2m2f NHF 5-7yo good	£4,164

Quickly took form to another level last season after nearly a year out through injury; good third in Elite Hurdle and progressed well when sent chasing, finishing fourth in novice handicap chase at Cheltenham Festival; should be a smart handicapper.

Al Co (Fr)

9 ch g Dom Alco - Carama (Tip Moss)

Peter Bowen — **F Lloyd**

PLACINGS: 0/0404/1128/3510201- — **RPR 151+c**

Starts	1st	2nd	3rd	4th	Win & Pl
30	7	2	3	5	£191,681

140	4/14	Ayr	4m½f Cls1 Gd3 140-166 Ch Hcap gd-sft	£113,900
136	10/13	Chep	3m Cls2 126-148 Ch Hcap good	£16,245
	5/12	Ffos	3m Cls4 Nov Ch gd-fm	£3,054
	5/12	Fknm	3m½f Cls3 Nov Ch soft	£6,324
130	2/11	Donc	3m½f Cls3 109-130 Hdl Hcap gd-sft	£4,554
126	4/10	Uttx	2m6½f Cls3 106-130 Hdl Hcap gd-fm	£4,816
	1/09	Pau	2m1½f Hdl 4yo soft	£17,709

Sprang 40-1 surprise when winning last season's Scottish National, relishing big step up in trip (first run beyond 3m2f) and long break since previous run (best when fresh according to trainer); thorough stayer and likely to be aimed at Grand National.

Al Ferof (Fr)

9 gr g Dom Alco - Maralta (Altayan)

Paul Nicholls — **J Hales**

PLACINGS: /F3111/11343/1/1325- — **RPR 168+c**

Starts	1st	2nd	3rd	4th	Win & Pl
19	9	2	5	1	£320,095

	11/13	Asct	2m3f Cls1 Gd2 Ch gd-sft	£28,475
159	11/12	Chel	2m4½f Cls1 Gd3 137-163 Ch Hcap soft	£91,120
	12/11	Sand	2m Cls1 Nov Gd1 Ch gd-sft	£20,787
	11/11	Chel	2m Cls1 Nov Gd2 Ch gd-sft	£13,668
	3/11	Chel	2m½f Cls1 Nov Gd1 Hdl good	£57,010
	2/11	Newb	2m½f Cls3 Nov Hdl gd-sft	£5,204
	1/11	Tntn	2m3½f Cls4 Nov Hdl 4-7yo gd-sft	£3,426
	2/10	Newb	2m½f Cls1 Gd2 NHF 4-6yo gd-sft	£10,832
	12/09	Fair	2m NHF 4yo heavy	£6,038

Made winning return last season after more than a year out following victory in 2012 Paddy

Power Gold Cup; slightly disappointing subsequently, failing to convince over 3m and getting struck into when fifth in Ryanair Chase; capable of better.

Alderwood (Ire)

10 b g Alderbrook - Clamit Falls (Homo Sapien)

Thomas Mullins (Ir) — **John P McManus**

PLACINGS: **10120111/S31213P/4-B** — RPR **125c**

Starts	1st	2nd	3rd	4th	Win & Pl
26	8	3	3	3	£220,784

140	3/13	Chel	2m½f Cls1 Gd3 133-155 Ch Hcap soft	£51,255
	1/13	Navn	2m1f Ch heavy	£8,976
	4/12	Punc	2m Nov Gd1 Hdl sft-hvy	£41,333
	4/12	Fair	2m Nov Gd2 Hdl gd-sft	£21,667
139	3/12	Chel	2m1f Cls1 Gd3 132-150 Hdl Hcap good	£39,865
123	8/11	Klny	2m6f 103-125 Hdl Hcap yld-sft	£12,888
116	7/11	Klny	2m1f 98-123 Hdl Hcap good	£8,625
	5/11	Klny	2m6f Mdn Hdl good	£4,759

Dual Cheltenham Festival winner who landed County Hurdle in 2012 and followed up by winning Grand Annual Chase as a novice 12 months later; missed much of last season and brought down on return in Galway Plate; may still be capable of winning good races.

Aldopicgros (Fr)

4 b g Tirwanako - In'Challha (Bad Conduct)

Paul Nicholls — **Million In Mind Partnership**

PLACINGS: **1/324111-** — RPR **135+h**

Starts	1st	2nd	3rd	4th	Win & Pl
7	4	1	1	1	£22,145

	4/14	Winc	2m4f Cls4 Nov Hdl good	£3,899
126	3/14	Newb	2m3f Cls3 104-130 Hdl 4yo Hcap gd-sft	£5,848
120	2/14	Winc	2m Cls3 99-125 Hdl Hcap heavy	£6,330
	4/13	Lrsy	1m4f NHF 3yo	£4,065

Took time to find form last season but progressed rapidly once sent handicapping, winning twice; well below that form on quicker ground next time when struggling to defy odds of 1-5; subsequently bought by JP McManus as a good chasing prospect.

Alelchi Inois (Fr)

6 b g Night Tango - Witness Gama (Take Risks)

Willie Mullins (Ir) — **Mrs M McMahon**

PLACINGS: **P33/1174-111** — RPR **146+c**

Starts	1st	2nd	3rd	4th	Win & Pl
10	5	-	2	1	£49,773

	7/14	Gway	2m1f Nov Ch good	£12,188
	7/14	Klny	2m6f Nov Ch good	£8,913
	5/14	Tram	2m Ch good	£5,175
	11/13	Fair	2m4f Nov Hdl soft	£6,732
	5/13	Kbgn	2m Mdn Hdl 4-5yo soft	£4,207

Twice found out in Graded company over hurdles last season but looked a much better chaser this summer and notched a quickfire hat-trick from 2m to 2m6f; gained all those wins on good ground but had won twice on soft as a novice hurdler.

All Set To Go (Ire)

3 gr g Verglas - Firecrest (Darshaan)

Paul Nicholls — **A Oliver**

PLACINGS:

Starts	1st	2nd	3rd	4th	Win & Pl
0	-	-	-	-	£2,799

Bought to go jumping after finishing third in a strong Group 3 at the Curragh in April; battle-hardened (ran eight times on Flat) and has proved himself on different types of ground; should make a leading juvenile hurdler.

Amore Alato

5 b g Winged Love - Sardagna (Medaaly)

Nick Williams — **Mrs Sarah Faulks**

PLACINGS: **81/411320-** — RPR **139h**

Starts	1st	2nd	3rd	4th	Win & Pl
8	3	1	1	1	£25,989

	12/13	Kemp	2m Cls2 Nov Hdl soft	£9,384
	11/13	Winc	2m Cls3 Nov Hdl 4-6yo gd-sft	£6,498
	4/13	Chep	2m½f Cls6 NHF 4-6yo gd-fm	£1,560

Useful front-running novice hurdler last season who did particularly well at Kempton, winning on Boxing Day and finishing second to Irving in a Grade 2; may have found quicker ground against him when disappointing at Aintree on final start.

Analifet (Fr)

4 b f Califet - Viana (Signe Divin)

Willie Mullins (Ir) — **Gigginstown House Stud**

PLACINGS: **111P-** — RPR **137+h**

Starts	1st	2nd	3rd	4th	Win & Pl
4	3	-	-	-	£30,410

	12/13	Fair	2m Gd3 Hdl 3yo gd-yld	£14,533
	11/13	Punc	2m Hdl 3yo yield	£7,293
	5/13	Comp	2m Hdl 3yo v soft	£8,585

Looked a potential superstar early last season but fractured her pelvis when pulled up at Leopardstown over Christmas; had been sent off 3-10 to win a Grade 2 that day to underline huge impression made in winning first three races; top-class prospect.

Annacotty (Ire)

6 b g Beneficial - Mini Moo Min (Ardross)

Martin Keighley — **Mrs Peter Prowting**

PLACINGS: **33/13114/55162128-** — RPR **155+c**

Starts	1st	2nd	3rd	4th	Win & Pl
12	4	2	1	1	£62,385

	12/13	Kemp	3m Cls1 Nov Gd1 Ch soft	£39,865
123	11/13	Kemp	3m Cls3 Nov 111-124 Ch Hcap gd-sft	£6,657
	3/13	Hayd	2m4f Cls4 Nov Hdl gd-sft	£3,899
	2/13	Chep	2m4f Cls4 Mdn Hdl gd-sft	£3,899

Defied lowly handicap mark of 130 when winning Grade 1 novice chase at Kempton by ten lengths last season and proved that was no fluke when second in strong novice handicap at Cheltenham; jumping fell apart when well beaten in RSA Chase.

Annie Power (Ire)

6 ch m Shirocco - Anno Luce (Old Vic)

Willie Mullins (Ir) **Mrs S Ricci**

PLACINGS: 1111111/1112-1 **RPR 164+h**

Starts	1st	2nd	3rd	4th	Win & Pl
12	11	1	-	-	£298,302

5/14	Punc	2m2f Gd1 Hdl gd-yld	£51,667
1/14	Donc	2m½f Cls1 Gd2 Hdl gd-sft	£21,031
1/14	Chel	2m4½f Cls2 Hdl soft	£15,640
11/13	Asct	2m3½f Cls1 Gd2 Hdl gd-sft	£52,233
3/13	Fair	2m4f Nov Gd1 Hdl soft	£47,561
2/13	Naas	2m Nov Gd2 Hdl sft-hvy	£21,931
2/13	Clon	2m½f Hdl heavy	£5,610
11/12	Thur	2m Mdn Hdl soft	£4,313
9/12	List	2m NHF 4-7yo heavy	£8,050
8/12	Wxfd	2m NHF 4-7yo soft	£5,750
8/12	Gway	2m NHF 4-7yo sft-hvy	£5,750

Brilliant mare who suffered sole defeat in last season's World Hurdle at Cheltenham when second to More Of That; seemed to stay 3m well enough but has also won good races over minimum trip, giving trainer plenty of options; could even be sent chasing.

Apache Jack (Ire)

6 b/br g Oscar - Cailin Supreme (Supreme Leader)

Dessie Hughes (Ir) **Mrs P Sloan**

PLACINGS: 76/7319/3123-4 **RPR 149h**

Starts	1st	2nd	3rd	4th	Win & Pl
11	2	1	3	1	£32,002

12/13	Punc	2m4f Mdn Hdl gd-yld	£5,610
2/13	Fair	2m4f NHF 5-7yo soft	£3,927

Useful novice hurdler last season; benefited from step up to 3m for first time when finishing third in Albert Bartlett Hurdle at Cheltenham, though only fourth behind Beat That in stronger Grade 1 at Punchestown; could develop into a good staying chaser.

Apache Stronghold (Ire)

6 b g Milan - First Battle (Un Desperado)

Noel Meade (Ir) **Mrs Patricia Hunt**

PLACINGS: 133/114-2 **RPR 149+h**

Starts	1st	2nd	3rd	4th	Win & Pl
7	3	1	2	1	£54,716

11/13	Navn	2m4f Nov Gd2 Hdl gd-yld	£19,817
10/13	Punc	2m4f Mdn Hdl good	£5,610
11/12	DRoy	2m NHF 4-7yo yld-sft	£7,475

Missed much of last season through injury but made big impression from limited opportunities, winning early Grade 2 at Navan and finishing good second to Vautour at Punchestown on second run after long absence; likely to go novice chasing.

ONE TO WATCH

Balder Success Side-stepped Cheltenham and vindicated the decision with success at Aintree. He could be a Champion Chase contender.
[Dave Edwards, Topspeed]

Arctic Fire (Ger)

5 b g Soldier Hollow - Adelma (Sternkoenig)

Willie Mullins (Ir) **Wicklow Bloodstock Limited**

PLACINGS: 1S342-1 **RPR 150h**

Starts	1st	2nd	3rd	4th	Win & Pl
6	2	1	1	1	£40,929

5/14	Punc	2m Nov Hdl gd-yld	£12,188
10/13	Tipp	2m Mdn Hdl 4-5yo good	£4,207

Very smart novice hurdler last season; disappointed on only run on soft ground but bounced back after a break to finish close second in County Hurdle at Cheltenham, relishing quicker conditions; easy winner of modest race at Punchestown next time.

Ardkilly Witness (Ire)

8 b g Witness Box - Ardkilly Angel (Yashgan)

Dr Richard Newland **C E Stedman & Dr R D P Newland**

PLACINGS: 1122/173220/2312510- **RPR 141c**

Starts	1st	2nd	3rd	4th	Win & Pl
14	3	5	2	-	£46,527

4/14	MRas	3m1f Cls3 Nov Ch good	£7,798
12/13	Winc	2m5f Cls3 Nov Ch heavy	£6,564
11/12	Towc	2m5f Cls4 Nov Hdl gd-sft	£2,534

Useful staying novice chaser last season, winning twice and running well in two major handicaps, notably when unlucky fifth in BetBright Chase at Kempton; also sent off co-favourite for bet365 Gold Cup but failed to stay having travelled well.

Argocat (Ire)

6 b g Montjeu - Spirit Of South (Giant's Causeway)

Tom Taaffe (Ir) **Mrs Fitri Hay**

PLACINGS: 7319/7121015/F613-7 **RPR 167c**

Starts	1st	2nd	3rd	4th	Win & Pl
16	5	1	2	-	£96,440

2/14	Gowr	2m4f Gd2 Ch heavy	£21,667
4/13	Limk	3m Nov Gd2 Ch good	£19,817
12/12	Limk	2m3½f Nov Gd2 Ch heavy	£20,313
10/12	Limk	2m3½f Ch sft-hvy	£7,763
1/12	Thur	2m Mdn Hdl 4-5yo soft	£4,313

Has a patchy record but proved himself a high-class staying chaser when close third in Betfred Bowl behind Silviniaco Conti, relishing good ground; had previously won at Grade 2 level for third time at Gowran Park; has twice disappointed at Cheltenham.

Arnaud (Ire)

6 b g Chevalier - Jumbo Romance (Tagula)

Charles Byrnes (Ir) **Gigginstown House Stud**

PLACINGS: 5580/8325003/11129-P **RPR 152+c**

Starts	1st	2nd	3rd	4th	Win & Pl
19	4	2	2	1	£40,219

12/13	Dpat	2m2f Hdl good	£5,610
6/13	Rosc	2m Ch gd-fm	£8,976
5/13	Klny	2m1f Ch soft	£6,171
12/11	Limk	2m Mdn Hdl 3yo heavy	£6,246

Useful novice chaser last season, producing best performance when second to Valdez in a Grade

2 at Doncaster (was clear until tiring late); again raced too keenly subsequently but had been well backed for a big handicap at Aintree and could flourish if settling.

Art Of Logistics (Ire)

6 b g Exit To Nowhere - Sanadja (Slip Anchor)

Dessie Hughes (Ir) — **Munnelly Support Services Ltd**

PLACINGS: 4/11314/11540-21105 — RPR **146c**

Starts		1st	2nd	3rd	4th	Win & Pl
16		7	1	1	3	£75,292
	6/14	Punc	2m2f Ch gd-yld			£10,833
139	5/14	Punc	2m 119-145 Ch Hcap good			£12,188
	10/13	Punc	2m2f Nov Gd3 Ch good			£14,533
	10/13	Gowr	2m2f Ch good			£6,732
	2/13	Fair	2m Hdl soft			£5,610
	11/12	DRoy	2m Mdn Hdl 4-6yo yld-sft			£8,050
	10/12	Rosc	2m NHF 4yo heavy			£4,025

Slightly disappointing as a novice chaser last season, including when favourite for novice handicap at Cheltenham Festival, but flourished on preferred good ground at Punchestown in May and June; again below best in Galway Plate.

At Fishers Cross (Ire)

7 b g Oscar - Fermoy Supreme (Supreme Leader)

Rebecca Curtis — **John P McManus**

PLACINGS: 1125/111111/4U232-3 — RPR **166h**

Starts		1st	2nd	3rd	4th	Win & Pl
16		8	3	2	1	£265,446
	4/13	Aint	3m½f Cls1 Nov Gd1 Hdl gd-sft			£56,270
	3/13	Chel	3m Cls1 Nov Gd1 Hdl soft			£68,340
	1/13	Chel	2m4½f Cls1 Nov Gd2 Hdl heavy			£17,085
131	12/12	Chel	3m Cls2 122-145 Hdl Hcap heavy			£13,763
122	12/12	Newb	2m3f Cls2 122-138 Hdl Hcap soft			£12,996
	11/12	Ffos	2m Cls4 Nov Hdl soft			£3,249
	2/12	Ffos	2m Cls5 NHF 4-6yo soft			£1,754
	11/11	Cork	2m NHF 4-7yo sft-hvy			£5,948

Dominated a weak staying novice hurdle division two seasons ago and found things much harder in open company last term; still progressed well to finish placed in three Grade 1 races in the spring, going closest at Aintree despite jumping to his right.

At Fishers Cross: very talented staying hurdler

Attaglance

8 b g Passing Glance - Our Ethel (Be My Chief)

Malcolm Jefferson — **H Young, G Eifert & R Snyder**

PLACINGS: 5P111/P3338/P249520- **RPR 146+c**

Starts	1st	2nd	3rd	4th	Win & Pl
31	6	3	6	3	£98,305

144	4/12	Aint	2m4f Cls1 List 130-144 Hdl Hcap good	£22,780
139	3/12	Chel	2m4½f Cls2 132-145 Cond Hdl Hcap good	£28,152
130	2/12	MRas	2m3f Cls3 105-130 Hdl Hcap gd-sft	£4,549
121	10/11	Carl	2m1f Cls3 104-123 Hdl Hcap gd-sft	£4,549
	3/11	Hexm	2m½f Cls4 Nov Hdl gd-sft	£2,055
	11/10	MRas	2m3f Cls4 Nov Hdl gd-sft	£2,740

Without a win since achieving big handicap hurdle double at Cheltenham and Aintree three seasons ago but ran several fine races in defeat last season, including second in novice handicap chase at the festival and fourth in Paddy Power Gold Cup.

Aurore D'Estruval (Fr)

4 ch f Nickname - Option D'Estruval (Epervier Bleu)

John Quinn — **Carl Hinchy**

PLACINGS: 2125- **RPR 127+h**

Starts	1st	2nd	3rd	4th	Win & Pl
4	1	2	-	-	£15,441

	2/14	Weth	2m½f Cls4 Nov Hdl heavy	£3,285

Impressive 13-length winner on British debut in January before just being outstayed in a real slog at Haydock next time; did better when fifth in Grade 1 juvenile hurdle at Aintree and can improve again on softer ground; should win good races.

Azorian (Ire)

6 b g Westerner - Eliane Di Rupette (Cosmonaut)

Eoin Griffin (Ir) — **Gigginstown House Stud**

PLACINGS: 112/122363-0 **RPR 143h**

Starts	1st	2nd	3rd	4th	Win & Pl
9	2	3	2	-	£35,378

	11/13	Cork	2m4f Mdn Hdl soft	£7,293
	2/13	Leop	2m NHF 5-7yo soft	£4,768

Won a maiden hurdle and was placed four times at Graded level last season, though came up well short against the very best; always looked type to do better over fences (has already won a point-to-point) and should be a smart staying novice chaser.

Baby Mix (Fr)

6 gr g Al Namix - Douchka (Fijar Tango)

Warren Greatrex — **Gdm Partnership**

PLACINGS: 5/1619/350/012213- **RPR 143+c**

Starts	1st	2nd	3rd	4th	Win & Pl
14	4	2	2	-	£49,908

132	11/13	Kemp	2m4½f Cls3 Nov 130-133 Ch Hcap good	£6,410
	6/13	NAbb	2m½f Cls3 Nov Ch gd-fm	£7,596
	2/12	Kemp	2m Cls1 Gd2 Hdl 4yo good	£12,073
	12/11	Chel	2m1f Cls2 Hdl 3yo good	£10,010

Grade 2 winner over hurdles before badly losing his way but rejuvenated following switch to fences last summer; won again on second run for Warren Greatrex in good novice handicap chase at Ascot before suffering a setback; best on good ground.

Back In Focus (Ire)

9 ch g Bob Back - Dun Belle (Over The River)

Willie Mullins (Ir) — **Andrea & Graham Wylie**

PLACINGS: F/2118/211114/

Starts	1st	2nd	3rd	4th	Win & Pl
8	5	1	-	1	£136,243

	3/13	Chel	4m Cls2 Nov Am Ch gd-sft	£50,966
	12/12	Leop	3m Nov Gd1 Ch soft	£40,625
	11/12	Punc	2m6f Nov Gd2 Ch heavy	£20,313
	9/12	List	2m6f Ch heavy	£7,763
	2/11	Hayd	3m Cls1 Nov Gd2 Hdl heavy	£13,226

High-class chaser who has been unlucky to see career blighted by injury, missing second campaign through injury last season; had won National Hunt Chase at Cheltenham in 2013 to add to Grade 1 success over 3m and could do well in top staying handicaps.

Baily Green (Ire)

8 b g King's Theatre - Dream On Boys (Anshan)

Mouse Morris (Ir) — **R A Scott**

PLACINGS: 11111232P4/2528F2-41 **RPR 157c**

Starts	1st	2nd	3rd	4th	Win & Pl
34	9	5	5	4	£180,019

	5/14	Klny	2m4½f Ch yld-sft	£8,913
	11/12	Cork	2m4f Nov Gd3 Ch soft	£18,958
	10/12	Punc	2m2f Nov Gd3 Ch heavy	£14,896
	10/12	Rosc	2m Nov Gd3 Ch heavy	£20,313
121	9/12	Klny	2m1f 108-134 Hdl Hcap yld-sft	£15,438
	7/12	Limk	2m3½f Nov Ch good	£10,063
	6/12	Rosc	2m Nov Ch gd-sft	£7,188
	5/12	Rosc	2m Ch good	£4,600
	3/11	Cork	2m Mdn Hdl 5yo yield	£5,948

Prolific novice chaser two seasons ago when also finishing second to Simonsig in Racing Post Arkle; failed to win again until last May but had finished second in three Grade 2 contests last season; likely to be kept to lower level and can win more races.

Balder Succes (Fr)

6 b g Goldneyev - Frija Eria (Kadalko)

Alan King — **Masterson Holdings Limited**

PLACINGS: FU/31083U5/1F15111-3 **RPR 162+c**

Starts	1st	2nd	3rd	4th	Win & Pl
21	10	-	3	-	£210,258

	4/14	Aint	2m Cls1 Nov Gd1 Ch good	£61,897
	2/14	Kemp	2m4½f Cls1 Nov Gd2 Ch soft	£17,451
	2/14	Wwck	2m Cls1 Nov Gd2 Ch heavy	£22,780
	11/13	Wwck	2m Cls3 Nov Ch gd-sft	£7,148
	10/13	Chep	2m3½f Cls2 Nov Ch good	£12,996
	11/12	Hayd	2m Cls2 Hdl 4yo soft	£25,024
	2/12	Asct	2m Cls2 Nov Hdl gd-sft	£10,010
	1/12	Asct	2m Cls3 Hdl 4yo gd-sft	£5,630
	1/12	Plum	2m Cls4 Nov Hdl heavy	£2,669
	10/11	Autl	2m2f Hdl 3yo v soft	£22,759

Last season's leading two-mile novice chaser despite missing Cheltenham, instead going on to gain fifth win over fences in magnificent fashion at Aintree; did remarkably well to go close at Punchestown despite chasing suicidal gallop; leading Champion Chase hope.

Balgarry (Fr)

7 ch g Ballingarry - Marie De Motreff (Kendor)

David Pipe — **Brocade Racing**

PLACINGS: 2/1/17/

Starts	1st	2nd	3rd	4th	Win & Pl
4	2	1	-	-	£32,167

129	3/12	Newb	2m½f Cls3 115-131 Hdl Hcap gd-sft	£6,256
	8/10	Claf	2m2f Hdl 3yo v soft	£16,142

Hugely impressive winner on British debut in March 2012 and may have found Coral Cup coming too soon when sixth as joint-favourite; missed following season through injury and suffered freak jaw injury last term; remains a fine novice chase prospect.

Ballyalton (Ire)

7 b g Pierre - Almilto (Mandalus)

Ian Williams — **John Westwood**

PLACINGS: 111/2/11142- RPR **149h**

Starts	1st	2nd	3rd	4th	Win & Pl
8	5	2	-	1	£49,031

12/13	Chel	2m1f Cls3 Nov Hdl 4-6yo good	£7,507
11/13	Newc	2m6f Cls2 Nov Hdl good	£9,384
10/13	Uttx	2m Cls5 Mdn Hdl good	£2,209
2/12	Donc	2m½f Cls6 NHF 4-6yo good	£1,625
1/12	Wwck	2m Cls6 NHF 5-6yo gd-sft	£1,437

Dual bumper winner three seasons ago before missing nearly a year through injury; bounced back from poor run at Cheltenham (desperate ground) to finish second there in Neptune Novices' Hurdle; has won a point-to-point and likely to go novice chasing.

Ballybolley (Ire)

5 b g Kayf Tara - Gales Hill (Beau Sher)

Nigel Twiston-Davies — **Simon Munir & Isaac Souede**

PLACINGS: 2/F3111- RPR **129+b**

Starts	1st	2nd	3rd	4th	Win & Pl
3	3	-	-	-	£20,287

4/14	Aint	2m1f Cls1 Gd2 NHF 4-6yo gd-sft	£17,085
3/14	Towc	2m Cls6 NHF 4-6yo gd-sft	£1,560
12/13	Sthl	2m Cls6 NHF 4-6yo good	£1,643

Completed a hat-trick of bumper victories when narrowly landing Grade 2 contest at Aintree in April, looking sure to appreciate further; has already been placed in a couple of point-to-points and should do well when switched to hurdling.

ONE TO WATCH

Indian Castle Clocked a smart time on Festival Trials day in January at Cheltenham but was a beaten favourite in the Kim Muir at the festival. A mistake cost him dear, but he can exploit a favourable handicap mark.
[Dave Edwards, Topspeed]

Ballycasey (Ire)

7 gr g Presenting - Pink Mist (Montelimar)

Willie Mullins (Ir) — **Mrs S Ricci**

PLACINGS: 53/21/113/114F-2 RPR **156+c**

Starts	1st	2nd	3rd	4th	Win & Pl
9	5	1	1	1	£98,065

2/14	Leop	2m5f Nov Gd1 Ch sft-hvy	£43,438
11/13	Navn	2m1f Ch gd-yld	£8,415
1/13	Thur	2m6f Nov Hdl heavy	£7,854
12/12	Clon	2m4f Mdn Hdl heavy	£4,313
12/11	Leop	2m4f NHF 4-7yo gd-yld	£5,948

Won Grade 1 novice chase at Leopardstown last season and arguably unlucky not to win another when falling two out in Powers Gold Cup; twice beaten over 3m but had also disappointed on only run over that trip over hurdles and looks a doubtful stayer.

Ballynagour (Ire)

8 b g Shantou - Simply Deep (Simply Great)

David Pipe — **Allan Stennett**

PLACINGS: 27/412661/9P18/P13-2 RPR **157c**

Starts	1st	2nd	3rd	4th	Win & Pl
16	4	3	1	1	£193,359

140	3/14	Chel	2m4f Cls1 Gd3 131-157 Ch Hcap good	£51,255
123	2/13	Wwck	2m4½f Cls2 123-149 Ch Hcap soft	£18,768
	4/12	Engh	2m1½f Hdl v soft	£19,200
	6/11	Autl	2m5½f Ch 5yo v soft	£22,345

Flourished at end of last season having taken time to build on runaway win on British debut; hugely impressive winner of Byrne Group Plate at Cheltenham and went on to be placed twice at Grade 1 level over 2m and 2m4f; should have more to offer.

Balthazar King (Ire)

10 b g King's Theatre - Afdala (Hernando)

Philip Hobbs — **The Brushmakers**

PLACINGS: /15P0O1/120P/11112-F RPR **156c**

Starts	1st	2nd	3rd	4th	Win & Pl
43	14	8	1	4	£444,171

150	3/14	Chel	3m7f Cls2 130-150 Ch Hcap gd-sft	£31,280
	11/13	Chel	3m7f Cls2 Ch good	£15,640
139	10/13	Chel	3m½f Cls2 119-145 Ch Hcap good	£31,280
	9/13	Crao	3m6f List Ch gd-sft	£29,268
139	10/12	Chel	3m½f Cls2 128-147 Ch Hcap gd-sft	£31,280
139	3/12	Chel	3m7f Cls2 130-156 Ch Hcap gd-fm	£25,024
136	10/11	Chel	3m½f Cls2 124-150 Ch Hcap gd-fm	£15,698
	4/11	Chel	3m1½f Cls2 Nov Ch good	£9,480
	3/11	Hrfd	3m1½f Cls4 Nov Ch gd-sft	£3,253
	10/10	Chep	3m Cls3 Nov Ch gd-sft	£5,204
	9/10	Worc	2m7f Cls4 Ch good	£3,253
	10/09	Kemp	2m5f Cls4 Nov Hdl gd-fm	£3,253
	10/09	Ffos	2m4f Cls4 Mdn Hdl good	£3,253
	11/08	Plum	2m2f Cls6 Mdn NHF 4-6yo gd-sft	£1,713

Better than ever last season, winning four times and finishing a fine second in Grand National; underlined versatility when landing Cross Country Chase at Cheltenham Festival for second time; relishes running over extreme distances on good ground.

Baltimore Rock (Ire)

5 b g Tiger Hill - La Vita E Bella (Definite Article)

David Pipe **R S Brookhouse**

PLACINGS: 124/312114- RPR **138h**

Starts	1st	2nd	3rd	4th	Win & Pl
9	4	2	1	2	£60,051

125	3/14	Sand	2m½f Cls1 Gd3 118-139 Hdl Hcap soft	£39,865
116	2/14	Ludl	2m Cls3 104-125 Hdl Hcap heavy	£9,495
	1/14	Winc	2m Cls4 Nov Hdl heavy	£3,899
	11/12	Bang	2m1f Cls6 NHF 3-5yo gd-sft	£1,437

Progressed with each run last season and completed a hat-trick of handicap hurdle wins when landing Imperial Cup in impressive fashion; coped well with step up to Grade 1 level when fourth to Josses Hill at Aintree and unlucky not to finish closer.

Bear's Affair (Ire)

8 br g Presenting - Gladtogetit (Green Shoon)

Nicky Henderson **G B Barlow**

PLACINGS: 111/4U21/16P/2216-13 RPR **150+c**

Starts	1st	2nd	3rd	4th	Win & Pl
16	7	3	1	1	£61,613

137	5/14	Aint	3m1f Cls2 119-142 Ch Hcap good	£14,076
	11/13	Kemp	3m Cls4 Ch good	£5,198
140	12/12	Aint	2m4f Cls2 114-140 Hdl Hcap soft	£12,825
130	3/12	Kemp	2m5f Cls2 117-143 Hdl Hcap good	£9,812
	3/11	Bang	2m1f Cls4 Nov Hdl good	£2,602
	1/11	Sthl	2m Cls4 Nov Hdl gd-sft	£2,212
	10/10	Uttx	2m Cls6 NHF 4-6yo good	£1,301

Took a long time to get act together over fences but jumped much better and produced a terrific performance when winning at Aintree in May; best of those to race prominently when third in Summer Cup at Uttoxeter next time; prefers good ground.

Beat That (Ire)

6 b g Milan - Knotted Midge (Presenting)

Nicky Henderson **Michael Buckley**

PLACINGS: 26/121-1 RPR **159+h**

Starts	1st	2nd	3rd	4th	Win & Pl
6	3	2	-	-	£114,956

4/14	Punc	3m Nov Gd1 Hdl gd-yld	£46,500
4/14	Aint	3m½f Cls1 Nov Gd1 Hdl gd-sft	£56,270
11/13	Asct	2m3½f Cls3 Mdn Hdl gd-sft	£5,630

Arguably the leading staying novice hurdler of last season, winning at Aintree and Punchestown (did particularly well to battle past very smart Don Poli) having missed Cheltenham; disappointing favourite in a bumper on only start on soft ground.

Bellenos (Fr)

6 b g Apsis - Palmeria (Great Palm)

Dan Skelton — **Mr & Mrs J D Cotton**

PLACINGS: 1424/1235P/716221- RPR 147+c

Starts	1st	2nd	3rd	4th	Win & Pl
15	4	4	1	2	£68,161

	4/14	Strf	2m1½f Cls4 Nov Ch good	£4,549
122	12/13	Asct	2m1f Cls3 Nov 112-122 Ch Hcap soft	£6,882
	8/12	Buch	2m1f Hdl 4yo good	£7,600
	8/11	Vich	2m1½f Hdl 3yo v soft	£8,276

Smart French recruit who progressed well in novice chases last season apart from two below-par efforts at Doncaster; just beaten by Manyriverstocross in novice handicap chase at Ascot before making amends at Stratford; will be aimed at top 2m handicaps.

Benefit Cut (Ire)

8 b g Beneficial - I'm Maggy (Danseur Etoile)

Renee Robeson — **Howard Cooke & Terence Jenner**

PLACINGS: 12071/3221P1- RPR 142+c

Starts	1st	2nd	3rd	4th	Win & Pl
11	4	3	1	-	£24,775

	3/14	Asct	2m5½f Cls3 Nov Ch good	£7,577
122	2/14	MRas	2m4f Cls3 Nov 115-125 Ch Hcap soft	£6,498
	4/13	Kemp	2m Cls4 Nov Hdl gd-sft	£3,899
	6/12	MRas	2m1f Cls6 NHF 4-6yo good	£1,365

Won a bumper and novice hurdle two seasons ago before taking well to chasing last season; made all for wins at Market Rasen and Ascot, jumping notably well; still lightly raced and should have more to offer; has gained all his wins going right-handed.

Bennys Mist (Ire)

8 b g Beneficial - Dark Mist (Mister Lord)

Venetia Williams — **Mezzone Family**

PLACINGS: 1115351PF1P/6011302- RPR 143c

Starts	1st	2nd	3rd	4th	Win & Pl
25	7	2	3	1	£73,141

133	1/14	Winc	2m5f Cls3 115-140 Ch Hcap heavy	£15,640
127	1/14	Winc	2m5f Cls3 109-130 Ch Hcap heavy	£7,820
125	3/13	Newb	3m Cls3 Nov 106-125 Ch Hcap heavy	£6,498
119	1/13	Tntn	2m7½f Cls4 103-120 Ch Hcap heavy	£4,660
	10/12	Extr	3m Cls4 Ch heavy	£3,899
104	5/12	Uttx	3m Cls5 Nov 73-104 Hdl Hcap soft	£2,144
97	5/12	Extr	2m7½f Cls5 75-97 Hdl Hcap heavy	£1,949

Has gained last five wins on heavy ground, including twice last season over 2m5f at Wincanton; showed he could cope with higher mark when excellent second in Topham Chase on good ground and should do better back in more favourable conditions.

Benvolio (Ire)

7 b g Beneficial - Coumeenoole Lady (The Parson)

Paul Nicholls — **Dobson, Sutton & Woodhouse**

PLACINGS: P1/0311/F1132- RPR 147+c

Starts	1st	2nd	3rd	4th	Win & Pl
9	4	1	2	-	£39,013

	1/14	Hayd	2m5f Cls2 Ch heavy	£12,660
133	12/13	Newb	3m Cls3 Nov 124-138 Ch Hcap gd-sft	£6,498
126	2/13	Winc	2m6f Cls3 110-130 Hdl Hcap heavy	£7,798
	1/13	Winc	2m6f Cls4 Nov Hdl soft	£3,249

Tough and gritty performer whose four wins over last two seasons have all come by narrow margins; won two novice chases last season before disappointing when stepped up in class; looked best over 3m at Newbury and should appreciate further.

Big Occasion (Ire)

7 b g Sadler's Wells - Asnieres (Spend A Buck)

David Pipe — **The Old Betfairians**

PLACINGS: 14106/73343212/

Starts	1st	2nd	3rd	4th	Win & Pl
13	3	2	3	2	£94,322

126	3/13	Uttx	4m1½f Cls1 List 126-152 Ch Hcap heavy	£45,560
	2/12	Carl	2m4f Cls4 Nov Hdl soft	£2,599
	12/11	Chep	3m Cls4 Nov Hdl heavy	£2,274

Missed last season with a tendon injury; had excelled as a novice over extreme trips two seasons ago, winning Midlands National on heavy ground and finishing a fine second in Scottish National on good; should again be a force in top staying handicaps.

Baltimore Rock (9): progressive over hurdles last season and expected to do even better this term

Big Shu (Ire)

9 b g Milan - Straight 'n Furry (Furry Glen)

Peter Maher (Ir)
Hugh Duffy & Richard J Robinson & Miss Caroline M

PLACINGS: 532618B1/F74211/23F- **RPR 149c**

Starts	1st	2nd	3rd	4th	Win & Pl
17	3	3	1	2	£60,829

	4/13	Punc	4m1f Ch heavy	£15,854
136	3/13	Chel	3m7f Cls2 131-157 Ch Hcap gd-sft	£31,280
	4/12	Punc	3m Hunt Ch soft	£5,175

Has thrived in cross-country chases in last two seasons, winning major prizes at Cheltenham and Punchestown and placed three times; early faller when well fancied for last season's Grand National (hampered by loose horse) and may return to Aintree.

Black Hercules (Ire)

5 b g Heron Island - Annalecky (Bob's Return)

Willie Mullins (Ir) **Andrea & Graham Wylie**

PLACINGS: 1/114-0 **RPR 135B**

Starts	1st	2nd	3rd	4th	Win & Pl
4	2	-	-	1	£15,441

1/14	Gowr	2m NHF 5-7yo soft	£7,475
12/13	Punc	2m NHF 4yo gd-yld	£4,768

Dual bumper winner last season, looking particularly good on soft ground at Gowran; ran well in much quicker conditions when fourth in Champion Bumper at Cheltenham but flopped at Punchestown; good staying hurdler in the making.

Black Thunder (Fr)

7 bl g Malinas - Blackmika (Subotica)

Paul Nicholls **Donlon, Macdonald, Fulton & Webb**

PLACINGS: 4/1211/325F5/01112F- **RPR 157c**

Starts	1st	2nd	3rd	4th	Win & Pl
16	6	3	1	1	£60,372

12/13	Ling	3m Cls1 Nov Gd2 Ch soft	£17,370
11/13	Hayd	2m7f Cls2 Nov Ch soft	£16,245
10/13	Font	2m4f Cls4 Ch soft	£4,660
4/12	Chep	2m½f Cls4 Nov Hdl soft	£2,534
12/11	Tntn	2m3½f Cls4 Nov Hdl gd-sft	£3,080
5/11	NAbb	2m1f Cls6 NHF 4-6yo gd-fm	£1,494

Very smart novice chaser last season, suffering only defeat in four completions when second to Corrin Wood at Warwick (unsuited by heavy ground); had won all three previous starts and still in contention when falling in RSA Chase at Cheltenham.

Blakemount (Ire)

6 br g Presenting - Smashing Leader (Supreme Leader)

Sue Smith **Mrs Jacqueline Conroy**

PLACINGS: P51/31312- **RPR 140+h**

Starts	1st	2nd	3rd	4th	Win & Pl
5	2	1	2	-	£14,376

12/13	Newc	2m6f Cls4 Nov Hdl soft	£3,119
11/13	Weth	2m4f Cls4 Nov Hdl gd-sft	£3,422

Won soft novice hurdles at Wetherby and Newcastle last season before doing very well when stepped up in grade at Newcastle to finish a close second to Urban Hymn (first attempt over 3m); has won a point-to-point and should be a good novice chaser.

Blood Cotil (Fr)

5 b g Enrique - Move Along (Northern Crystal)

Willie Mullins (Ir) **Mrs S Ricci**

PLACINGS: 34/11462/1F0- **RPR 128+c**

Starts	1st	2nd	3rd	4th	Win & Pl
10	3	1	1	2	£103,076

5/13	Autl	2m3½f Gd3 Hdl 4yo v soft	£49,390
12/12	Leop	2m Gd2 Hdl 3yo soft	£23,021
11/12	Fair	2m Mdn Hdl 3yo soft	£4,313

Smart juvenile hurdler two seasons ago, finishing second to Diakali in a Grade 1 at Punchestown before reversing that form later at Auteuil; fell on chasing debut at Cork but in command jumping fluently to that point and could yet make a good novice chaser.

Blue Fashion (Ire)

5 b g Scorpion - Moon Glow (Solar One)

Nicky Henderson **Mr & Mrs J D Cotton**

PLACINGS: 5141/42- **RPR 150+h**

Starts	1st	2nd	3rd	4th	Win & Pl
6	2	1	-	2	£73,418

4/13	Autl	2m2f Hdl 4yo v soft	£27,317
12/12	Cagn	2m½f Hdl 3yo heavy	£12,800

Winning hurdler in France who moved to Nicky Henderson following fourth to Diakali in a Grade 1 at Auteuil; showed huge promise on sole start in Britain last season when second to More Of That in handicap hurdle at Haydock; looks exciting.

Bobs Worth (Ire)

9 b g Bob Back - Fashionista (King's Theatre)

Nicky Henderson — **The Not Afraid Partnership**

PLACINGS: 21/1111/1321/11/615- — **RPR 167c**

Starts	1st	2nd	3rd	4th	Win & Pl
15	10	2	1	-	£671,906

	12/13	Leop	3m Gd1 Ch yld-sft	£75,610
	3/13	Chel	3m2½f Cls1 Gd1 Ch soft	£313,225
160	12/12	Newb	3m2½f Cls1 Gd3 140-166 Ch Hcap gd-sft	£85,425
	3/12	Chel	3m½f Cls1 Gd1 Ch good	£74,035
	11/11	Newb	2m4f Cls1 Nov Gd2 Ch good	£13,668
	3/11	Chel	3m Cls1 Nov Gd1 Hdl good	£57,010
	1/11	Chel	2m4½f Cls1 Nov Gd2 Hdl gd-sft	£14,253
	1/11	Chel	2m4½f Cls3 Nov Hdl gd-sft	£6,262
	11/10	Kemp	2m Cls4 Nov Hdl 4-6yo good	£2,602
	4/10	Kemp	2m Cls6 NHF 4-6yo good	£1,370

Three-time Cheltenham Festival winner, most notably in 2013 Gold Cup, but only fifth in same race last season when less effective on quicker ground; had previously won Lexus Chase; likely to be lightly raced having run only three times in last two seasons.

Bog Warrior (Ire)

10 b g Strategic Choice - Kilmac Princess (King's Ride)

Tony Martin (Ir) — **Gigginstown House Stud**

PLACINGS: F1/11F13/F1115/U41-P — **RPR 156+c**

Starts	1st	2nd	3rd	4th	Win & Pl
17	9	-	1	1	£142,876

	3/14	Navn	2m4f Gd2 Ch heavy	£20,313
	1/13	Gowr	3m Gd2 Hdl heavy	£21,138
	12/12	Punc	2m4f Hdl heavy	£10,833
122	12/12	Fair	2m4f 92-122 Hdl Hcap soft	£8,625
	2/12	Naas	2m Nov Ch sft-hvy	£9,488
	12/11	Fair	2m4f Nov Gd1 Ch sft-hvy	£42,026
	11/11	Navn	2m Ch yld-sft	£9,517
	3/11	Cork	2m4f Mdn Hdl yield	£5,948
	1/11	Fair	2m NHF 5-7yo sft-hvy	£5,056

Won a hat-trick of hurdle races two seasons ago before incurring a leg injury when fifth in World Hurdle; reverted to fences when back from long absence last spring (had won a Grade 1 as a novice) and showed mixed form, though won a Grade 2 at Navan.

Bold Sir Brian (Ire)

8 b g Brian Boru - Black Queen (Bob Back)

Lucinda Russell — **A R Trotter**

PLACINGS: 12/417/221114/11FP6/

Starts	1st	2nd	3rd	4th	Win & Pl
16	7	3	-	2	£59,099

12/12	Sand	3m½f Cls1 List Ch soft	£10,251
11/12	Carl	2m4f Cls2 Ch heavy	£11,696
2/12	Muss	2m4f Cls3 Nov Ch gd-sft	£7,988
12/11	Kels	2m6½f Cls4 Nov Ch soft	£4,549
12/11	Hexm	2m½f Cls5 Ch heavy	£1,949
3/11	Kels	2m2f Cls1 Gd2 Hdl gd-sft	£17,103
12/09	Ayr	1m6f Cls5 NHF 3yo soft	£1,953

Suffered a fractured vertebrae when falling at Cheltenham two seasons ago (discovered only after two disappointing subsequent runs) and missed last season; had won five of last six races over fences prior to that and remains a high-class prospect.

Boston Bob (Ire)

9 b g Bob Back - Bavaway (Le Bavard)

Willie Mullins (Ir) — **Andrea & Graham Wylie**

PLACINGS: /31/1112/11FF/1661-1 — **RPR 165+c**

Starts	1st	2nd	3rd	4th	Win & Pl
15	9	1	1	-	£368,386

4/14	Punc	3m1f Gd1 Ch gd-yld	£100,000
4/14	Aint	2m4f Cls1 Gd1 Ch good	£112,540
12/13	Punc	2m4f Hdl heavy	£10,569
2/13	Leop	2m5f Nov Gd1 Ch sft-hvy	£39,675
12/12	Navn	2m4f Ch heavy	£8,913
1/12	Leop	2m4f Nov Gd2 Hdl heavy	£21,396
12/11	Navn	2m4f Nov Gd1 Hdl sft-hvy	£39,224
11/11	Navn	2m4f Mdn Hdl yld-sft	£8,328
3/11	Hexm	2m½f Cls5 Mdn NHF 4-6yo gd-sft	£1,370

Got career back on track after jumping problems with two superb victories at end of last season, winning Melling Chase and Punchestown Gold Cup, though both were modest contests for Grade 1 level; likely to be a big player in top staying chases in Ireland.

Briar Hill (Ire)

6 b g Shantou - Backaway (Bob Back)

Willie Mullins (Ir) — **Andrea & Graham Wylie**

PLACINGS: P111/111F- — **RPR 150+h**

Starts	1st	2nd	3rd	4th	Win & Pl
6	5	-	-	-	£99,608

1/14	Naas	2m4f Nov Gd2 Hdl soft	£20,313
12/13	Navn	2m4f Nov Gd1 Hdl yld-sft	£36,992
11/13	Wxfd	2m2f Mdn Hdl soft	£4,207
3/13	Chel	2m½f Cls1 Gd1 NHF 4-6yo gd-sft	£34,170
1/13	Thur	2m NHF 5-7yo sft-hvy	£3,927

Winner of 2013 Champion Bumper and took unbeaten run to five races when winning first three hurdles last season up to 2m4f; sure to stay further and sent off favourite for Albert Bartlett Hurdle but suffered heavy fall around halfway.

Brick Red

7 ch g Dubawi - Duchcov (Caerleon)

Venetia Williams — **Julian Taylor & Andrew Brooks**

PLACINGS: /21766111234/131273- — **RPR 153c**

Starts	1st	2nd	3rd	4th	Win & Pl
18	6	4	3	1	£71,304

135	1/14	Winc	2m Cls3 Nov 122-138 Ch Hcap heavy	£9,495
	1/14	Plum	2m1f Cls3 Nov Ch heavy	£7,148
137	2/13	Muss	2m Cls2 113-137 Hdl Hcap gd-sft	£12,512
125	1/13	Winc	2m Cls3 108-128 Hdl Hcap soft	£6,498
118	1/13	Ludl	2m Cls3 105-125 Hdl Hcap soft	£5,848
	5/12	Uttx	2m Cls5 Mdn Hdl soft	£2,144

Useful novice chaser last season; not beaten far when seventh in Racing Post Arkle despite being hampered two out; fine second to Balder Succes at Warwick and good third in novice handicap at Ascot either side of that; prefers cut in the ground.

Bright New Dawn (Ire)

7 br g Presenting - Shuil Dorcha (Bob Back)

Dessie Hughes (Ir) | **Gigginstown House Stud**

PLACINGS: **247/13213/152112-** | RPR **152+c**

Starts	1st	2nd	3rd	4th	Win & Pl
14	5	4	2	1	£114,387

	Date	Course	Race	Prize
	3/14	Naas	2m4f Nov Gd3 Ch soft	£16,250
	2/14	Navn	2m1f Nov Gd2 Ch heavy	£20,313
	12/13	Punc	2m4f Ch gd-yld	£7,293
	2/13	Thur	2m4f Nov Gd2 Hdl soft	£21,138
	12/12	Fair	2m2f Mdn Hdl soft	£5,750

Won three novice chases last season, most notably in a Grade 2 at Navan, though came up short in stronger races, including when 15-length second to Rebel Fitz in Powers Gold Cup; seemed not to stay 3m on only attempt when fifth to Carlingford Lough.

Brother Brian (Ire)

6 b g Millenary - Miner Detail (Presenting)

Hughie Morrison | **L A Garfield**

PLACINGS: **22/751341-** | RPR **135+h**

Starts	1st	2nd	3rd	4th	Win & Pl
8	2	2	1	1	£21,257

	Date	Course	Race	Prize
127	4/14	Chel	2m4½f Cls2 120-146 Hdl Hcap good	£12,512
	12/13	Newb	2m3f Cls4 Nov Hdl 4-6yo soft	£3,899

Progressed throughout last season and produced best performance on final start when encountering good ground for first time at Cheltenham; hadn't quite got home over similar trip when fourth at Sandown in EBF Final; should have more to offer.

Broughton (Ger)

4 b g Teofilo - Boccassini (Artan)

John Ferguson | **Bloomfields**

PLACINGS: **2180-** | RPR **131+h**

Starts	1st	2nd	3rd	4th	Win & Pl
4	1	1	-	-	£17,349

	Date	Course	Race	Prize
	2/14	Muss	2m Cls1 List Hdl 4yo soft	£11,390

Useful Flat horse (won a Glorious Goodwood handicap off 86 last year) who took well to hurdling and showed smart form to beat Clarcam at Musselburgh; struggled when stepped up to Grade 1 level at Cheltenham and Aintree but could do well in handicaps.

Buddy Bolero (Ire)

8 b g Accordion - Quinnsboro Ice (Glacial Storm)

David Pipe | **Malcolm C Denmark**

PLACINGS: **421/114/F2761F-** | RPR **152c**

Starts	1st	2nd	3rd	4th	Win & Pl
12	4	2	-	2	£33,675

	Date	Course	Race	Prize
135	2/14	Chep	3m Cls2 122-135 Hdl Hcap heavy	£12,512
129	1/13	Leic	2m7½f Cls3 112-138 Ch Hcap heavy	£6,963
	1/13	Extr	2m3½f Cls4 Ch heavy	£3,769
	12/11	Folk	2m6½f Cls4 Mdn Hdl soft	£1,779

Useful staying novice chaser two seasons ago (fourth in National Hunt Chase) but beaten favourite three times last term and reverted to hurdles for only win; beset by jumping problems and fell four out when in contention in Kim Muir; should do better.

Burton Port (Ire)

10 b g Bob Back - Despute (Be My Native)

Jonjo O'Neill | **Trevor Hemmings**

PLACINGS: **1121/2/242/509P82U2-** | RPR **149c**

Starts	1st	2nd	3rd	4th	Win & Pl
25	7	8	2	2	£298,814

	Date	Course	Race	Prize
	4/10	Aint	3m1f Cls1 Nov Gd2 Ch good	£45,608
	2/10	Asct	3m Cls1 Nov Gd2 Ch gd-sft	£16,899
	2/10	Sthl	3m½f Cls3 Nov Ch soft	£7,806
	12/09	Ling	3m Cls1 Nov Gd2 Ch heavy	£18,813
	11/09	Bang	2m4½f Cls4 Ch soft	£4,228
	1/09	Hrfd	2m1f Cls4 Nov Hdl soft	£2,927
	12/08	Hrfd	2m1f Cls6 NHF 4-6yo soft	£1,691

Formerly high-class chaser (fourth in 2012 Gold Cup) who finally exploited plummeting handicap mark to finish second in bet365 Gold Cup at end of last season; remains miles below peak mark so could take advantage now problems have been ironed out.

Bury Parade (Ire)

8 br g Overbury - Alexandra Parade (Mister Lord)

Paul Nicholls | **Highclerethoroughbredracing – Bury Parade**

PLACINGS: **6/12113/41523/1R12P-** | RPR **160+c**

Starts	1st	2nd	3rd	4th	Win & Pl
16	6	3	2	1	£82,616

	Date	Course	Race	Prize
143	1/14	Asct	2m5½f Cls2 127-149 Ch Hcap heavy	£31,280
	11/13	Kemp	2m4½f Cls2 Ch gd-sft	£12,628
	10/12	Carl	2m Cls4 Ch soft	£3,054
	12/11	Hexm	2m½f Cls4 Nov Hdl heavy	£2,534
	11/11	Hexm	2m½f Cls4 Nov Hdl 4-6yo soft	£2,534
	5/11	Prth	2m½f Cls6 NHF 4-6yo soft	£1,370

Blotted his copybook when refusing to race last season but twice won well either side of that and went on to finish second in BetBright Chase at Kempton; pulled up in bet365 Gold Cup (struggling not long after halfway but stepping into unknown with trip anyway).

Buywise (Ire)

7 b g Tikkanen - Greenogue Princess (Rainbows For Life)

Evan Williams | **T Hywel Jones**

PLACINGS: **21F/5811151-** | RPR **151+c**

Starts	1st	2nd	3rd	4th	Win & Pl
8	4	-	-	-	£51,951

	Date	Course	Race	Prize
134	4/14	Chel	2m5f Cls1 Gd2 129-146 Ch Hcap good	£28,475
120	2/14	Ludl	2m4f Cls3 107-133 Ch Hcap heavy	£12,660
109	1/14	Tntn	2m7½f Cls4 Nov 85-110 Ch Hcap heavy	£4,660
102	1/14	Ludl	2m4f Cls4 Nov 88-110 Ch Hcap heavy	£4,549

Began last season by finishing well beaten in two novice hurdles but improved immediately for switch to fences and went from strength to strength; unlucky fifth in novice handicap chase at Cheltenham Festival and won Grade 2 at same track next time.

Bury Parade: talented if inconsistent last season

Caid Du Berlais (Fr)

5 b g Westerner - Kenza Du Berlais (Kahyasi)

Paul Nicholls **Donlon, Doyle, Macdonald & C Barber**

PLACINGS: 883122292/21532-7 RPR 139c

Starts	1st	2nd	3rd	4th	Win & Pl
15	2	6	2	-	£104,660

	12/13	Extr	2m3½f Cls2 Nov Ch good	£12,974
	8/12	Claf	2m1f Hdl 3yo heavy	£13,600

Has run several big races in major handicap hurdles, twice finishing placed at Cheltenham Festival and again when second at Aintree; that followed aborted chasing campaign but returned to fences with fair seventh in Galway Plate and should improve.

Calipto (Fr)

4 b g Califet - Peutiot (Valanour)

Paul Nicholls **Ian Fogg & Chris Giles**

PLACINGS: 21143- RPR 139+h

Starts	1st	2nd	3rd	4th	Win & Pl
5	2	1	1	1	£42,684

	2/14	Newb	2m½f Cls3 Nov Hdl heavy	£6,498
	11/13	Newb	2m½f Cls3 Hdl 3yo gd-sft	£6,498

Won two juvenile hurdles last season and may be better than he showed when in the frame at Cheltenham and Aintree; particularly unlucky in Triumph Hurdle when going well until rider's stirrup leather broke two out; likely sort for big 2m handicap hurdles.

Cantlow (Ire)

9 b g Kayf Tara - Winnowing (Strong Gale)

Paul Webber **John P McManus**

PLACINGS: 40203/522110/912F08- RPR 158+c

Starts	1st	2nd	3rd	4th	Win & Pl
20	4	5	1	2	£104,885

140	11/13	Newb	2m4f Cls2 133-147 Ch Hcap gd-sft	£31,280
	1/13	Tntn	2m3f Cls3 Nov Ch heavy	£6,498
	12/12	Plum	2m1f Cls3 Nov Ch heavy	£5,848
	2/11	Ludl	3m Cls5 Mdn Hdl gd-sft	£2,277

Paid price for jumping errors when fast-finishing second in December Gold Cup last season having overcome similar problems to win at Newbury on previous start; fell next time at Cheltenham but capable of winning a big handicap if things go right.

Cape Tribulation

10 b g Hernando - Gay Fantastic (Ela-Mana-Mou)

Malcolm Jefferson **J David Abell**

PLACINGS: /5P50411/051155/P03- RPR 156+c

Starts	1st	2nd	3rd	4th	Win & Pl
31	9	3	2	3	£238,012

	1/13	Chel	3m1½f Cls1 Gd2 Ch heavy	£57,955
142	12/12	Weth	3m1f Cls1 Gd3 125-144 Ch Hcap heavy	£22,780
150	4/12	Aint	3m½f Cls1 Gd3 130-150 Hdl Hcap gd-sft	£25,628
142	3/12	Chel	3m Cls1 List 137-157 Hdl Hcap good	£39,865
	10/10	Hexm	3m1f Cls3 Nov Ch gd-sft	£6,337
	1/09	Donc	3m½f Cls1 Nov Gd2 Hdl soft	£17,850
	11/08	Uttx	2m4½f Cls4 Nov Hdl gd-sft	£3,903
	3/08	Uttx	2m Cls4 NHF 4-6yo gd-sft	£2,342
	3/08	MRas	2m1½f Cls6 NHF 4-6yo good	£1,370

Developed into a high-class staying chaser two seasons ago when winning Argento Chase and finishing fifth in Gold Cup; disappointing last season but still ran well when third in Rowland Meyrick Chase and fell to handicap mark 19lb below peak.

Capote (Ire)

6 b g Oscar - Kinsella's Rose (Roselier)

Jonjo O'Neill — **Trevor Hemmings**

PLACINGS: 1114- RPR 137+h

Starts	1st	2nd	3rd	4th	Win & Pl
3	2	-	-	1	£12,551

	3/14	Extr	2m7½f Cls4 Nov Hdl heavy	£3,488
	2/14	Catt	3m1½f Cls4 Nov Hdl heavy	£3,764

Looked a thorough stayer when winning two novice hurdles on heavy ground last season; not quite at that level in quicker conditions at Aintree but still ran a decent race to be fourth in a Grade 1 behind Beat That; should be a useful novice chaser.

Captain Chris (Ire)

10 b g King's Theatre - Function Dream (Strong Gale)

Philip Hobbs — **Mrs Diana L Whateley**

PLACINGS: 211/1U3P4/12264/311- RPR 176+c

Starts	1st	2nd	3rd	4th	Win & Pl
23	9	6	2	3	£427,368

	2/14	Asct	2m5½f Cls1 Gd1 Ch soft	£84,655
	1/14	Kemp	2m4½f Cls1 List Ch soft	£17,387
	11/12	Asct	2m3f Cls1 Gd2 Ch heavy	£28,475
	5/11	Punc	2m Nov Gd1 Ch good	£48,103
	3/11	Chel	2m Cls1 Gd1 Ch good	£74,113
	2/11	Kemp	2m4½f Cls1 Nov Gd2 Ch gd-sft	£13,340
	4/10	Chel	2m1f Cls2 Nov Hdl good	£8,454
	3/10	Kemp	2m Cls4 Nov Hdl good	£2,602
	3/10	Kemp	2m Cls4 Nov Hdl good	£3,253

Missed end of last season with a suspensory problem having earlier been ruled out of King George; looked better than ever when winning Ascot Chase (first Grade 1 since novice days) and should have top chases on his agenda if staying injury-free.

Captain Conan (Fr)

7 b g Kingsalsa - Lavandou (Sadler's Wells)

Nicky Henderson — **Triermore Stud**

PLACINGS: 3411622/11151/3P- RPR 162c

Starts	1st	2nd	3rd	4th	Win & Pl
14	6	2	2	1	£178,351

	4/13	Aint	2m4f Cls1 Nov Gd1 Ch good	£42,713
	2/13	Sand	2m4½f Cls1 Nov Gd1 Ch heavy	£22,780
	12/12	Sand	2m Cls1 Nov Gd1 Ch soft	£21,072
	11/12	Chel	2m Cls1 Nov Gd2 Ch soft	£14,238
	1/12	Sand	2m½f Cls1 Gd1 Hdl soft	£17,286
	6/11	Autl	2m2f Hdl 4yo v soft	£19,862

Has an outstanding record at Sandown, winning three Grade 1 races there as a novice over hurdles and fences before adding fourth at Aintree; ran only twice last season, needing first run before fracturing pelvis in Champion Chase.

Carlingford Lough (Ire)

8 b g King's Theatre - Baden (Furry Glen)

John Kiely (Ir) — **John P McManus**

PLACINGS: 61133574PP/21221U6-1 RPR 158+c

Starts	1st	2nd	3rd	4th	Win & Pl
21	7	3	2	1	£277,432

	4/14	Punc	3m1f Nov Gd1 Ch good	£46,500
	12/13	Leop	3m Nov Gd1 Ch yld-sft	£39,634
133	7/13	Gway	2m6f 133-147 Ch Hcap soft	£97,866
129	8/12	Gway	2m6f 114-142 Hdl Hcap sft-hvy	£21,667
119	7/12	Bell	2m4f 116-135 Hdl Hcap soft	£12,729
109	7/11	Gway	2m 95-116 Hdl Hcap good	£8,625
	7/11	Rosc	2m Mdn Hdl 4-5yo good	£4,461

Began chasing from a low level but won last season's Galway Plate off 133 and continued to go from strength to strength, emerging as Ireland's best staying novice with two Grade 1 wins; could improve again if ironing out jumping problems.

Carlingford Lough (right): improving chaser ended last season on a high with success in Punchestown Grade 1

Carole's Spirit

6 b m Hernando - Carole's Crusader (Faustus)

Robert Walford **Paul Murphy**

PLACINGS: 43/123/1112- RPR **146+h**

Starts	1st	2nd	3rd	4th	Win & Pl
9	4	2	2	1	£40,867

	12/13	Hayd	2m4f Cls1 Nov List Hdl soft	£11,888
	11/13	Newb	2m5f Cls3 Nov Hdl gd-sft	£6,498
	11/13	Plum	2m5f Cls4 Nov Hdl heavy	£3,249
	2/13	Wwck	2m Cls6 NHF 4-7yo soft	£1,884

Hugely progressive mare who built on smart bumper form (placed twice in Listed races) by winning three out of four over hurdles last season; suffered only loss when stepped up to Grade 2 level at Ascot, just outstayed by Highland Retreat over 3m on heavy ground.

Cause Of Causes (USA)

6 b g Dynaformer - Angel In My Heart (Rainbow Quest)

Gordon Elliott (Ir) **John P McManus**

PLACINGS: 26131107/6403372220- RPR **151+c**

Starts	1st	2nd	3rd	4th	Win & Pl
24	5	6	3	1	£217,075

	1/13	Navn	2m Hdl heavy	£10,569
142	12/12	Asct	2m Cls1 List 130-155 Hdl Hcap heavy	£84,405
	11/12	Fair	2m Hdl soft	£5,750
	7/12	Dpat	2m2f Hdl good	£5,750
	5/12	Kbgn	2m3f Mdn Hdl 4yo good	£4,313

Gave connections a frustrating time last season but improved throughout, finishing second in three major handicap chases (twice beaten in photos and may well have won Kim Muir but for mistake at final fence); should continue to excel in staying handicaps.

Ceasar Milan (Ire)

6 br g Milan - Standfast (Supreme Leader)

Paul Nicholls **The Stewart & Wylie Families**

PLACINGS: 2/111/7231153- RPR **133h**

Starts	1st	2nd	3rd	4th	Win & Pl
9	4	1	2	-	£23,565

124	2/14	Tntn	2m3½f Cls3 118-136 Hdl Hcap heavy	£5,523
117	2/14	Tntn	2m3½f Cls3 Nov 95-120 Hdl Hcap heavy	£6,330
	3/13	Ayr	2m Cls6 NHF 4-6yo soft	£1,560
	12/12	DRoy	2m NHF 4-7yo heavy	£4,025

Generally disappointing over hurdles last season (had been sent off 11-8 for Persian War Novices' Hurdle first time out) but improved to win twice at Taunton on heavy ground; looked in need of further when twice running well in good handicaps at Sandown.

Celestial Halo (Ire)

10 b g Galileo - Pay The Bank (High Top)

Paul Nicholls **The Stewart Family**

PLACINGS: 18/131129/426/16130- RPR **165+h**

Starts	1st	2nd	3rd	4th	Win & Pl
34	10	8	5	3	£651,417

	11/13	Newb	3m½f Cls1 Gd2 Hdl soft	£23,048
	5/13	Autl	2m5½f Gd2 Hdl v soft	£64,024
	1/12	Hayd	2m Cls1 Gd2 Hdl heavy	£28,475
160	12/11	Newb	2m½f Cls2 134-160 Hdl Hcap soft	£31,280
160	11/11	Winc	2m Cls1 Gd2 140-160 Hdl Hcap gd-sft	£28,810
	2/11	Font	2m4f Cls1 Gd2 Hdl soft	£18,528
165	11/09	Winc	2m Cls1 Gd2 145-165 Hdl Hcap gd-sft	£34,206
	1/09	Sand	2m½f Cls1 List Hdl soft	£17,103
	3/08	Chel	2m1f Cls1 Gd1 Hdl 4yo gd-sft	£68,424
	12/07	Newb	2m½f Cls3 Nov Hdl 3yo soft	£6,506

Former Champion Hurdle runner-up who filled same spot in 2013 World Hurdle on first attempt at 3m and cemented new status as a high-class stayer when winning Long Distance Hurdle at Newbury last season; below-par later and has something to prove. RETIRED AS BOOK WENT TO PRINT

Champagne Fever (Ire)

7 gr g Stowaway - Forever Bubbles (Roselier)

Willie Mullins (Ir) **Mrs S Ricci**

PLACINGS: 12111/123113/132-6 RPR **161c**

Starts	1st	2nd	3rd	4th	Win & Pl
14	7	3	3	-	£262,819

	11/13	Punc	2m4f Ch yield	£6,732
	3/13	Chel	2m½f Cls1 Nov Gd1 Hdl soft	£68,340
	2/13	Leop	2m2f Nov Gd1 Hdl soft	£42,276
	11/12	Cork	2m Mdn Hdl soft	£7,763
	4/12	Punc	2m Gd1 NHF 4-7yo heavy	£40,625
	3/12	Chel	2m½f Cls1 Gd1 NHF 4-6yo good	£31,323
	1/12	Fair	2m NHF 4-7yo soft	£4,600

Former winner of Champion Bumper and Supreme Novices' Hurdle who came within a head of Cheltenham Festival hat-trick when just beaten in Racing Post Arkle last season; otherwise failed to convince over fences but has looked type to benefit from step up in trip.

Champagne West (Ire)

6 b g Westerner - Wyndham Sweetmarie (Mister Lord)

Philip Hobbs **R S Brookhouse**

PLACINGS: 12/921114- RPR **143h**

Starts	1st	2nd	3rd	4th	Win & Pl
7	3	2	-	1	£29,626

	1/14	Asct	2m6f Cls3 Nov Hdl 4-7yo heavy	£5,630
123	12/13	Winc	2m6f Cls2 121-147 Hdl Hcap heavy	£11,711
	12/13	Wwck	2m5f Cls4 Mdn Hdl gd-sft	£3,769

Progressed well over hurdles last season, winning

a Pertemps qualifier at Wincanton in between two novice hurdle victories; relished step up to 3m when staying on well into fourth in Albert Bartlett Hurdle at Cheltenham; should make a fine staying chaser.

Champion Court (Ire)

9 b g Court Cave - Mooneys Hill (Supreme Leader)

Martin Keighley — **M Boothright**

PLACINGS: 23122/24251/72U2679- RPR **161+c**

Starts	1st	2nd	3rd	4th	Win & Pl
24	5	8	1	2	£165,535

155	4/13	Chel	2m5f Cls1 Gd2 149-169 Ch Hcap gd-sft	£28,475
	1/12	Chel	2m5f Cls1 Nov Gd2 Ch gd-sft	£14,238
	10/11	Aint	2m4f Cls3 Nov Ch good	£6,330
	11/10	Chel	2m5f Cls1 Nov Gd2 Hdl gd-sft	£14,253
	5/10	Kbgn	2m NHF 5yo yield	£4,274

Without a win last season but ran well in some top handicaps and was unlucky not to win Peterborough Chase (beaten half a length despite saddle slipping); has fallen to lowest handicap mark since novice days so should find more opportunuties.

Chartreux (Fr)

9 gr g Colonel Collins - Ruaha River (Villez)

Tom George — **R S Brookhouse**

PLACINGS: 30/F4/121022/00PF1-1 RPR **146+c**

Starts	1st	2nd	3rd	4th	Win & Pl
19	6	3	1	1	£75,385

131	5/14	Punc	3m1f 118-146 Ch Hcap gd-yld	£27,083
128	3/14	Sand	3m½f Cls3 113-135 Ch Hcap gd-sft	£11,261
127	1/13	Winc	3m3½f Cls3 103-127 Ch Hcap soft	£12,512
	12/12	Extr	2m3½f Cls2 Nov Ch heavy	£11,556
	1/10	Ffos	2m4f Cls4 Mdn Hdl gd-sft	£3,253
	12/09	Wwck	2m Cls6 NHF 4-6yo soft	£1,713

Out of sorts for first half of last season but would have won last three starts but for falling when in command at Kempton; gained biggest win at Punchestown in May, proving ability to cope with quicker ground, and can be a force in top staying handicaps.

Cheltenian (Fr)

8 b g Astarabad - Salamaite (Mansonnien)

Philip Hobbs — **R S Brookhouse**

PLACINGS: 211/20/14P4-3 RPR **142h**

Starts	1st	2nd	3rd	4th	Win & Pl
10	3	2	1	2	£50,756

12/13	Uttx	2m Cls5 Mdn Hdl heavy	£2,859
3/11	Chel	2m½f Cls1 Gd1 NHF 4-6yo good	£31,356
2/11	Kemp	2m Cls5 Mdn NHF 4-6yo gd-sft	£1,713

Won Champion Bumper at Cheltenham in 2011 before missing nearly two years through injury; back to form in top handicap hurdles last season, doing best when fourth in Betfair Hurdle and again over 2m4f at Aintree; could have another big race in him.

Chris Pea Green

5 b g Proclamation - Another Secret (Efisio)

Gary Moore — **C Green & Galloping On The South Downs**

PLACINGS: 11167/23473- RPR **145h**

Starts	1st	2nd	3rd	4th	Win & Pl
10	3	1	2	1	£41,169

2/13	Hntg	2m½f Cls2 Hdl 4yo gd-sft	£9,384
1/13	Ling	2m Cls5 Mdn Hdl 4yo heavy	£2,053
11/12	Hntg	1m6f Cls6 NHF 3yo soft	£1,625

Did himself no favours by going close in a big 2m handicap hurdle at Ascot first time out last season as he struggled to cope with subsequent rise despite running consistently well in similar races; handled step up to 2m4f on final start; should make a good chaser.

City Slicker (Ire)

6 b g King's Theatre - Donna's Princess (Supreme Leader)

Willie Mullins (Ir) — **John P McManus**

PLACINGS: 41423/11016P-2 RPR **150h**

Starts	1st	2nd	3rd	4th	Win & Pl
12	4	2	1	2	£39,985

	1/14	Punc	2m4f Hdl sft-hvy	£7,475
119	11/13	Punc	2m 112-137 Hdl Hcap yield	£11,890
	5/13	Punc	2m Mdn Hdl gd-yld	£5,610
	12/12	Fair	2m NHF 4yo heavy	£4,600

Has run to a consistently high level of form at Punchestown, winning three out of four at that track with only defeat coming when second under a big weight in handicap hurdle last April; below that level elsewhere, including when favourite for Ladbroke at Ascot.

Clarcam (Fr)

4 b g Califet - Rose Beryl (Lost World)

Gordon Elliott (Ir) — **Gigginstown House Stud**

PLACINGS: 221322F24- RPR **138h**

Starts	1st	2nd	3rd	4th	Win & Pl
9	1	5	1	1	£40,898

10/13	Thur	2m Mdn Hdl 3yo good	£4,207

Very busy last season and got better with experience, peaking when second in Grade 1 juvenile hurdle at Aintree having been in front when falling two out in Fred Winter at Cheltenham; had rare below-par run next time at Punchestown; could progress again.

Claret Cloak (Ire)

7 b g Vinnie Roe - Bewildered (Prince Sabo)

Emma Lavelle — **Hawksmoor Partnership**

PLACINGS: 12511/3001/12433-4 RPR **152c**

Starts	1st	2nd	3rd	4th	Win & Pl
15	5	2	3	2	£51,458

	10/13	Towc	2m½f Cls4 Nov Ch gd-fm	£4,549
133	4/13	Strf	2m½f Cls3 108-133 Hdl Hcap good	£6,498
	3/12	Newb	2m½f Cls4 Nov Hdl good	£2,924
	2/12	Sand	2m½f Cls4 Nov Hdl good	£2,599
	11/11	Winc	2m Cls6 NHF 4-6yo gd-sft	£1,560

Won well on chasing debut last season and

subsequently laid out for spring campaign due to preference for good ground; placed in major 2m handicaps at Cheltenham and Aintree when undone by habit of late mistakes; capable of winning good races.

Clondaw Court (Ire)

7 br g Court Cave - Secret Can't Say (Jurado)

Willie Mullins (Ir) — **Mrs S Ricci**

PLACINGS: **1/1/11-** — RPR **152+h**

Starts	1st	2nd	3rd	4th	Win & Pl
3	3	-	-	-	£17,670

	Date	Course	Race	Prize
	1/14	Thur	2m6f Nov Hdl soft	£6,900
	12/13	Leop	2m2f Mdn Hdl soft	£6,171
	11/12	Punc	2m NHF 5-7yo heavy	£4,600

Unbeaten in three runs under rules, winning sole bumper start by 27 lengths before twice successful in novice hurdles last season; looked particularly impressive when stepped up to 2m6f at Thurles; won a point-to-point in April 2012 and looks made for fences.

Clondaw Kaempfer (Ire)

6 b g Oscar - Gra-Bri (Rashar)

Donald McCain — **T Leslie & D Gorton**

PLACINGS: **321/11P/93014-** — RPR **145h**

Starts	1st	2nd	3rd	4th	Win & Pl
9	4	-	1	1	£99,378

	Date	Course	Race	Prize
137	4/14	Aint	2m4f Cls1 Gd3 128-145 Hdl Hcap gd-sft	£28,475
	11/12	Hayd	2m Cls1 Nov List Hdl soft	£11,888
	10/12	Aint	2m4f Cls4 Nov Hdl 4-6yo soft	£4,874
	4/12	Fair	2m NHF 4-5yo gd-sft	£49,167

Looked set to be a leading novice hurdler two seasons ago before being struck down by injury; steadily came back to form last season before winning a big handicap hurdle at Aintree in April over 2m4f; should stay further and could progress as a novice chaser.

Cloudy Too (Ire)

8 b g Cloudings - Curra Citizen (Phardante)

Sue Smith — **Formulated Polymer Products Ltd**

PLACINGS: **3416/14F1103/1012U6-** — RPR **161+c**

Starts	1st	2nd	3rd	4th	Win & Pl
25	7	1	3	2	£107,848

	Date	Course	Race	Prize
148	12/13	Weth	3m1f Cls1 Gd3 129-153 Ch Hcap soft	£22,887
	11/13	Carl	2m4f Cls1 List Ch heavy	£14,860
137	2/13	Hayd	2m4f Cls3 Nov 120-137 Ch Hcap heavy	£8,123
129	2/13	Weth	2m4½f Cls2 119-145 Ch Hcap soft	£11,574
	11/12	Carl	2m4f Cls3 Ch heavy	£5,653
121	3/12	Newc	3m Cls3 103-127 Hdl Hcap good	£3,639
	3/11	Sedg	2m4f Cls4 Nov Hdl gd-sft	£2,082

Progressed well last season, winning Rowland Meyrick Chase by ten lengths before finishing distant second to Captain Chris in Grade 1 Ascot Chase; out of his depth in Gold Cup next time and needs to improve again to justify stiff handicap mark.

Cloudy Too: progressed well in handicap chases last season

Cockney Sparrow

5 b m Cockney Rebel - Compose (Anabaa)

John Quinn **Mr & Mrs Paul Gaffney**

PLACINGS: 21211/12F51-5 RPR 153+h

Starts	1st	2nd	3rd	4th	Win & Pl
11	5	3	-	-	£116,046

148	4/14	Ayr	2m Cls1 Gd2 148-168 Hdl Hcap gd-sft	£39,865
	11/13	Weth	2m½f Cls1 List Hdl gd-sft	£12,814
130	4/13	Aint	2m½f Cls2 124-148 Cond Am Hdl Hcap gd-sft	£25,024
	3/13	Donc	2m½f Cls4 Nov Cond Hdl good	£3,899
	12/12	Donc	2m½f Cls5 Mdn Hdl 3yo soft	£3,899

High-class mare who gained biggest win in last season's Scottish Champion Hurdle; good fifth in Mares' Hurdle at Cheltenham behind Quevega despite being reportedly unsuited by undulating track and longer trip; best on good ground.

Cole Harden (Ire)

5 b g Westerner - Nosie Betty (Alphabatim)

Warren Greatrex **Mrs Jill Eynon & Robin Eynon**

PLACINGS: 1/1411272- RPR 152h

Starts	1st	2nd	3rd	4th	Win & Pl
8	4	2	-	1	£35,918

	1/14	Newb	2m3f Cls4 Nov Hdl soft	£3,574
	11/13	Font	2m4f Cls4 Mdn Hdl heavy	£3,119
	8/13	Worc	2m Cls6 NHF 4-6yo good	£1,560
	3/13	Sedg	2m1f Cls6 NHF 4-6yo heavy	£1,560

Won two bumpers and two novice hurdles to earn step up in class last spring and ran a huge race to finish second to Beat That at Aintree (first run over 3m) following fair seventh in Neptune Hurdle; needs to go left-handed judging by earlier run at Ascot.

Colour Squadron (Ire)

8 b g Old Vic - That's The Goose (Be My Native)

Philip Hobbs **John P McManus**

PLACINGS: 1212F0F2/2425/232- RPR 153c

Starts	1st	2nd	3rd	4th	Win & Pl
15	2	7	1	1	£94,913

	12/11	Newb	2m½f Cls4 Mdn Hdl soft	£2,599
	10/11	Chep	2m½f Cls5 NHF 4-6yo soft	£1,779

Yet to win in two seasons of chasing but has run a string of fine races in defeat and was placed in three major handicap chases at Cheltenham last term; unlucky to bump into handicap snip Ballynagour when clear second on final start; has a big race in him.

Commissioned (Ire)

4 b g Authorized - Zelda (Caerleon)

John Ferguson **Bloomfields**

PLACINGS: 324- RPR 135h

Starts	1st	2nd	3rd	4th	Win & Pl
3	-	1	1	1	£13,024

Had progressed rapidly on the Flat last summer (rated 102 after just three races) and did well in three starts over hurdles last season without winning; fine fourth in Grade 1 at Aintree behind Guitar Pete having raced keenly; still a novice and sure to win races.

Coneygree

7 b g Karinga Bay - Plaid Maid (Executive Perk)

Mark Bradstock **The Max Partnership**

PLACINGS: 18/1113/

Starts	1st	2nd	3rd	4th	Win & Pl
6	4	-	1	-	£35,583

	12/12	Chel	3m Cls1 Nov Gd2 Hdl heavy	£14,238
	11/12	Chel	2m5f Cls1 Nov Gd2 Hdl soft	£14,238
	11/12	Uttx	2m4½f Cls4 Nov Hdl soft	£2,534
	11/11	Uttx	2m Cls6 NHF 4-6yo gd-sft	£1,365

Missed last season after suffering a nasty cut to his leg; had been a smart novice hurdler two seasons ago, winning two Grade 2 novice hurdles at Cheltenham over 2m5f and 3m; won a bumper on good to soft but likely to prove best in more testing conditions.

Corrin Wood (Ire)

7 gr g Garuda - Allstar Rose (Fourstars Allstar)

Donald McCain **Dermot Hanafin**

PLACINGS: P1/3221332/1110- RPR 159+c

Starts	1st	2nd	3rd	4th	Win & Pl
11	4	3	3	-	£37,450

	1/14	Wwck	3m½f Cls2 Nov Ch heavy	£11,574
135	12/13	Catt	3m1½f Cls3 Nov 126-140 Ch Hcap good	£9,747
	11/13	MRas	2m6½f Cls4 Ch soft	£6,498
	12/12	Carl	2m3½f Cls4 Nov Hdl heavy	£3,249

Took to fences superbly last season and left hurdles form behind to win first three chase starts, making all and jumping superbly every time; bombed out when taken on in front in RSA Chase and may be best when dominating small fields; stays very well.

Court Minstrel (Ire)

7 b g Court Cave - Theatral (Orchestra)

Evan Williams **Mrs Janet Davies**

PLACINGS: 3/1214/13411/87412- RPR 154h

Starts	1st	2nd	3rd	4th	Win & Pl
15	6	2	2	3	£114,383

147	4/14	Aint	2m½f Cls2 126-147 Cond Am Hdl Hcap gd-sft	£25,024
141	4/13	Ayr	2m Cls1 Gd2 133-153 Hdl Hcap good	£34,170
131	3/13	Plum	2m Cls2 123-149 Hdl Hcap gd-sft	£16,245
	10/12	Chel	2m½f Cls3 Mdn Hdl gd-sft	£6,256
	3/12	Ludl	2m Cls5 NHF 4-6yo good	£1,949
	11/11	Ludl	2m Cls5 Mdn NHF 4-6yo good	£1,949

Has produced his best form during spring in last two seasons, coming close to landing second successive Scottish Champion Hurdle in April having defied top-weight to win strong 2m handicap at Aintree; has run only once on ground worse than good to soft.

ONE TO WATCH

Colour Squadron Nought from seven over fences but his turn will come. *[Dave Edwards, Topspeed]*

Cue Card

8 b g King's Theatre - Wicked Crack (King's Ride)

Colin Tizzard — **Mrs Jean R Bishop**

PLACINGS: **242/1U212/15112/312-** RPR **180+c**

Starts	1st	2nd	3rd	4th	Win & Pl
20	10	6	1	1	£638,516

RPR	Date	Course	Race	Prize
	11/13	Hayd	3m1f Cls1 Gd1 Ch soft	£112,637
	3/13	Chel	2m5f Cls1 Gd1 Ch gd-sft	£156,613
	2/13	Asct	2m5½f Cls1 Gd1 Ch soft	£84,405
157	11/12	Extr	2m1½f Cls1 Gd2 140-160 Ch Hcap gd-sft	£35,594
	12/11	Newb	2m2½f Cls3 Nov Ch soft	£7,323
	10/11	Chep	2m3½f Cls3 Nov Ch good	£7,148
	11/10	Chel	2m½f Cls1 Nov Gd2 Hdl good	£14,253
	10/10	Aint	2m4f Cls3 Nov Hdl 4-6yo gd-sft	£4,554
	3/10	Chel	2m½f Cls1 Gd1 NHF 4-6yo good	£34,206
	1/10	Font	1m6f Cls6 NHF 4-6yo soft	£1,431

Four-time Grade 1 winner who excelled over longer trips last season, winning Betfair Chase and finishing second in King George; missed Gold Cup after suffering minor pelvis fracture but should be a leading player again in top staying chases.

Cup Final (Ire)

5 ch g Presenting - Asian Maze (Anshan)

Nicky Henderson — **John P McManus**

PLACINGS: **4/230-** RPR **125h**

Starts	1st	2nd	3rd	4th	Win & Pl
4	-	1	1	1	£4,802

Without a win in four races under rules but showed plenty of ability last season when twice placed behind Irving; sent off just 16-1 for Neptune Hurdle but may have lacked sufficient experience for such a test; retains novice status and should begin to thrive.

Daneking

5 b g Dylan Thomas - Sadie Thompson (King's Best)

Willie Mullins (Ir) — **Mrs S Ricci**

PLACINGS: **23211-** RPR **141+h**

Starts	1st	2nd	3rd	4th	Win & Pl
5	2	2	1	-	£36,093

RPR	Date	Course	Race	Prize
128	4/14	Fair	2m 118-140 Hdl Hcap gd-yld	£27,083
	2/14	Navn	2m Mdn Hdl heavy	£5,750

Highly progressive novice hurdler last season, producing best performance on handicap debut at Fairyhouse on final start; had raced much too keenly initially (later helped by hood) and should continue to improve with experience; high-class prospect.

Dare To Endeavour

7 b g Alflora - Miss Chinchilla (Perpendicular)

Tom George — **J B Property Developments (Midlands) Ltd**

PLACINGS: **226075/5211P1-** RPR **142+c**

Starts	1st	2nd	3rd	4th	Win & Pl
12	3	3	-	-	£25,640

RPR	Date	Course	Race	Prize
133	4/14	Prth	2m4½f Cls3 Nov 123-133 Ch Hcap soft	£7,798
127	2/14	Extr	3m Cls3 Nov 116-134 Ch Hcap soft	£9,495
115	2/14	Hntg	3m Cls3 Nov 111-125 Ch Hcap heavy	£6,498

Began last season by maintaining moderate level of form over hurdles but improved instantly once switched to fences, winning three novice handicap chases before end of campaign; made all at Perth on final start and looks capable of ranking higher.

Dawalan (Fr)

4 gr g Azamour - Daltawa (Miswaki)

Nicky Henderson — **Simon Munir & Isaac Souede**

PLACINGS: **41100-** RPR **128+h**

Starts	1st	2nd	3rd	4th	Win & Pl
5	2	-	-	1	£6,975

RPR	Date	Course	Race	Prize
	1/14	Newb	2m½f Cls4 Hdl 4yo soft	£3,249
	12/13	Newb	2m½f Cls4 Hdl 3yo soft	£3,249

Won two juvenile hurdles at Newbury last season, doing particularly well to defy a penalty in January; beaten favourite in two valuable juvenile hurdles later, including Fred Winter Hurdle at Cheltenham, but had excuses and should do better over further.

Days Hotel (Ire)

9 b g Oscar - Call Catherine (Strong Gale)

Henry de Bromhead (Ir) — **James Treacy**

PLACINGS: **7414/11/14123/23410-** RPR **157c**

Starts	1st	2nd	3rd	4th	Win & Pl
17	6	2	2	4	£140,559

RPR	Date	Course	Race	Prize
	2/14	Naas	2m Gd2 Ch sft-hvy	£24,375
	2/13	Naas	2m Gd2 Ch sft-hvy	£24,573
	12/12	Cork	2m Gd2 Ch sft-hvy	£20,313
	11/11	Punc	2m Nov Gd2 Ch soft	£22,414
	10/11	Punc	2m Ch heavy	£7,138
	3/11	Clon	2m½f Mdn Hdl soft	£4,461

Four-time Grade 2 winner over fences, most recently when landing same February Grade 2 at Naas in each of last two seasons; disappointing on all three attempts at Grade 1 level; yet to win beyond 2m and unconvincing whenever tried over further.

De La Bech

7 ch g Karinga Bay - Vallis Vale (St Columbus)

Philip Hobbs — **B K Peppiatt**

PLACINGS: 51/3/5511021/716P37- RPR 136c

Starts	1st	2nd	3rd	4th	Win & Pl
14	4	1	2	-	£32,054

124	12/13	Chep	3m Cls2 123-145 Ch Hcap gd-sft	£12,996
	3/13	Extr	3m Cls4 Nov Ch good	£3,899
118	12/12	Asct	3m Cls4 Nov 99-118 Hdl Hcap heavy	£6,256
	11/12	Ling	2m3½f Cls4 Nov Hdl heavy	£2,669

Won a very strong handicap chase at Chepstow last December with Welsh National one-two in third and fourth; disappointed subsequently, including when twice favourite at Cheltenham, but dropped in handicap and remains a likely sort for Welsh National

Definitly Red (Ire)

5 ch g Definite Article - The Red Wench (Aahsaylad)

Steve Gollings — **P J Martin**

PLACINGS: 2P/1117- RPR 130b

Starts	1st	2nd	3rd	4th	Win & Pl
3	2	-	-	-	£13,339

2/14	Newb	2m½f Cls1 List NHF 4-6yo heavy	£11,390
12/13	Uttx	2m Cls6 Mdn NHF 4-6yo heavy	£1,949

Finished best of the British runners in last season's Champion Bumper at Cheltenham when seventh to Silver Concorde having won both previous bumpers, including a Listed contest at Newbury; acts on any ground and should make a fine novice hurdler.

Defy Logic (Ire)

7 ch g Flemensfirth - Osiery Girl (Phardante)

Paul Nolan (Ir) — **John P McManus**

PLACINGS: 2/1122/1215- RPR 154+c

Starts	1st	2nd	3rd	4th	Win & Pl
9	4	4	-	-	£80,762

12/13	Leop	2m1f Nov Gd1 Ch soft	£44,919
10/13	Naas	2m Ch yld-sft	£7,854
2/13	Fair	2m Mdn Hdl heavy	£4,207
11/12	Fair	2m2f NHF 4-7yo soft	£4,025

Smart novice chaser last season, winning on first run in Grade 1 company when beating Trifolium at Leopardstown over Christmas; broke blood vessel in only subsequent race; unproven on good ground and trainer has stated he prefers very soft conditions.

Dell' Arca (Ire)

5 b g Sholokhov - Daisy Belle (Acatenango)

David Pipe — **Prof Caroline Tisdall**

PLACINGS: 2121U253- RPR 145h

Starts	1st	2nd	3rd	4th	Win & Pl
8	2	3	1	-	£121,884

128	11/13	Chel	2m½f Cls1 Gd3 125-149 Hdl Hcap good	£56,950
	5/13	Comp	2m1f Hdl 4yo v soft	£8,585

Boasted strong form in France (beat Vukovar and lost by a nose to Un Temps Pour Tout) before winning Greatwood Hurdle on British debut; continued to run well in top handicaps, including second in Betfair Hurdle, and third at Grade 1 level at Aintree.

Deputy Dan (Ire)

6 b g Westerner - Louisas Dream (Supreme Leader)

Oliver Sherwood — **Tim Syder**

PLACINGS: 3/11/22112- RPR 151+h

Starts	1st	2nd	3rd	4th	Win & Pl
8	4	3	1	-	£50,580

1/14	Wwck	2m5f Cls1 Nov Gd2 Hdl heavy	£15,735
12/13	Chep	2m4f Cls4 Mdn Hdl heavy	£3,119
4/13	Extr	2m1f Cls6 NHF 4-6yo soft	£1,625
3/13	Uttx	2m Cls6 NHF 4-6yo heavy	£1,949

Dual bumper winner who improved with every run last season and proved his progress wasn't down to heavy ground when running well in quicker conditions to finish second in Albert Bartlett Hurdle at Cheltenham; top-class prospect with lots more to offer.

Desert Cry (Ire)

8 b/br g Desert Prince - Hataana (Robellino)

Donald McCain — **N.Y.P.D Racing**

PLACINGS: 2097/53112P3/P11242- RPR 160+c

Starts	1st	2nd	3rd	4th	Win & Pl
25	6	6	2	1	£92,128

139	1/14	Weth	2m Cls2 124-145 Ch Hcap soft	£11,711
	12/13	Extr	2m1½f Cls2 Ch soft	£12,820
134	1/13	Ayr	2m Cls3 120-134 Ch Hcap heavy	£7,798
127	12/12	Hayd	2m Cls3 122-133 Ch Hcap heavy	£9,747
135	11/11	Hayd	2m Cls3 109-135 Hdl Hcap good	£5,198
	2/11	Sedg	2m1f Cls4 Nov Hdl heavy	£3,253

Sharply progressive in good 2m handicap chases last season, winning well at Wetherby in January and then going close off increasingly tough marks when second at Sandown and Ayr; may be capable of competing at higher level.

Diakali (Fr)

5 gr g Sinndar - Diasilixa (Linamix)

Willie Mullins (Ir) — **Wicklow Bloodstock Limited**

PLACINGS: 11241/211343-34 RPR 165h

Starts	1st	2nd	3rd	4th	Win & Pl
13	5	2	3	3	£293,322

11/13	Naas	2m Gd3 Hdl 4yo yld-sft	£14,533
6/13	Autl	2m3½f Gd1 Hdl 4yo v soft	£98,780
4/13	Punc	2m Gd1 Hdl 4yo heavy	£40,325
1/13	Punc	2m Gd3 Hdl 4yo heavy	£14,533
11/12	Gowr	2m Mdn Hdl 3yo heavy	£5,750

Dual Grade 1 winner as a four-year-old in 2013 and ran several fine races in defeat last season from 2m to 2m4f, most notably behind The New One in Aintree Hurdle; may be capable of better over longer trips, though was only fourth in French Champion Hurdle.

Diamond King (Ire)

6 b g King's Theatre - Georgia On My Mind (Belmez)

Donald McCain — **Mrs Diana L Whateley**

PLACINGS: **11/131-** — RPR **136+h**

Starts	1st	2nd	3rd	4th	Win & Pl
5	4	-	1	-	£10,350

1/14	Donc	2m½f Cls4 Nov Hdl gd-sft	£3,119
11/13	Weth	2m½f Cls4 Nov Hdl gd-sft	£3,422
4/13	Bang	2m1f Cls6 Am NHF 4-6yo good	£1,643
2/13	Weth	2m½f Cls6 NHF 4-5yo soft	£1,643

Would be unbeaten in five races under rules but for blundering at the last when clear on second run over hurdles last season; all set for step up in class until missing end of season after a setback; should appreciate further than 2m; very smart prospect.

Djakadam (Fr)

5 b g Saint Des Saints - Rainbow Crest (Baryshnikov)

Willie Mullins (Ir) — **Mrs S Ricci**

PLACINGS: **2/U1124/11F-** — RPR **146+c**

Starts	1st	2nd	3rd	4th	Win & Pl
9	4	2	-	1	£52,895

1/14	Leop	2m5f Nov Gd2 Ch soft	£21,667
12/13	Leop	2m3f Ch yld-sft	£7,293
3/13	Limk	2m Hdl 4yo heavy	£7,293
2/13	Gowr	2m Mdn Hdl 4yo heavy	£5,890

Sent chasing as a four-year-old last season and looked a natural, most notably when comfortably beating Bright New Dawn in a Grade 2 at Leopardstown; going well when fell four out in JLT Novices' Chase at Cheltenham; top-class prospect.

Dell'Arca: landed the competitive Greatwood Hurdle at Cheltenham on his British debut last season

Doctor Harper (Ire)

6 b g Presenting - Supreme Dreamer (Supreme Leader)

David Pipe **The Johnson Family**

PLACINGS: **110/115131-** RPR **145+h**

Starts	1st	2nd	3rd	4th	Win & Pl
9	6	-	1	-	£54,451

138	4/14	Aint	3m½f Cls1 Gd3 135-147 Hdl Hcap good	£28,475
	2/14	Fknm	2m4f Cls3 Nov Hdl 4-7yo heavy	£5,848
	11/13	Extr	2m1f Cls4 Nov Hdl good	£3,249
	11/13	Extr	2m1f Cls3 Nov Hdl gd-sft	£5,523
	2/13	Sand	2m½f Cls5 NHF 4-6yo gd-sft	£2,599
	12/12	Tntn	2m1f Cls5 NHF 3-5yo soft	£2,060

Progressed steadily as he went up in trip last season, culminating with victory in a 3m handicap hurdle at Aintree in April when also appreciating quicker ground (though had previously won a weaker race on heavy); should make a smart staying novice chaser.

Dodging Bullets

6 b g Dubawi - Nova Cyngi (Kris S)

Paul Nicholls **Martin Broughton & Friends**

PLACINGS: **246/11397/111245-** RPR **161c**

Starts	1st	2nd	3rd	4th	Win & Pl
14	5	2	1	2	£117,361

12/13	Kemp	2m Cls1 Nov Gd2 Ch soft	£20,167
11/13	Chel	2m Cls1 Nov Gd2 Ch good	£18,224
10/13	Kemp	2m Cls4 Ch good	£4,549
11/12	Chel	2m½f Cls1 Nov Gd2 Hdl gd-sft	£14,238
10/12	Chel	2m½f Cls2 Hdl 4yo gd-sft	£18,768

Smart novice chaser last season, winning Grade 2 races at Cheltenham and Kempton before pushing Module close in Game Spirit Chase; seemed to have limitations exposed when only a fair fourth in Racing Post Arkle and may be hard to place.

Don Cossack (Ger)

7 br g Sholokhov - Depeche Toi (Konigsstuhl)

Gordon Elliott (Ir) **Gigginstown House Stud**

PLACINGS: 5111/1F23/1212F2-4 RPR **155c**

Starts	1st	2nd	3rd	4th	Win & Pl
15	6	4	1	1	£136,135

12/13	Fair	2m4f Nov Gd1 Ch gd-yld	£39,634
10/13	Gway	2m6f Ch heavy	£9,537
11/12	Navn	2m Mdn Hdl heavy	£7,763
4/12	Fair	2m NHF 4-7yo soft	£7,479
12/11	Navn	2m Gd2 NHF 4-7yo sft-hvy	£15,409
10/11	Naas	2m3f NHF 4-7yo heavy	£5,056

Long earmarked as a future star after outstanding bumper career and began to fulfil potential when sent novice chasing last season; won Grade 1 Drinmore over 2m4f at Fairyhouse and twice finished second at top level; may still have more to offer.

Don Poli (Ire)

5 b g Poliglote - Dalamine (Sillery)

Willie Mullins (Ir) **Gigginstown House Stud**

PLACINGS: 2/2111-2 RPR **153+h**

Starts	1st	2nd	3rd	4th	Win & Pl
6	3	3	-	-	£79,584

143	3/14	Chel	2m4½f Cls2 133-146 Cond Hdl Hcap good	£31,280
	2/14	Clon	3m Nov Gd3 Hdl heavy	£17,063
	1/14	Thur	2m6f Mdn Hdl sft-hvy	£6,325

Top-class staying novice hurdler last season who completed a hat-trick when winning the Martin Pipe Hurdle at Cheltenham, relishing the stiff test of stamina; narrowly beaten by Beat That at the Punchestown festival next time; effective on any ground; looks just the type to make a fine novice chaser.

Doctor Harper (leading on rail): smart in handicap hurdles last season and should do well in novice chases

Double Ross (Ire)

8 ch g Double Eclipse - Kinross (Nearly A Hand)

Nigel Twiston-Davies | **Options O Syndicate**

PLACINGS: 32F14453P/613211235- | **RPR 159c**

Starts	1st	2nd	3rd	4th	Win & Pl
27	5	5	7	2	£173,183

140	1/14	Chel	2m5f Cls1 Gd3 136-147 Ch Hcap soft	£28,978
133	12/13	Chel	2m5f Cls1 Gd3 130-151 Ch Hcap good	£56,950
	9/13	Prth	2m4½f Cls3 Nov Ch gd-sft	£7,148
130	11/12	Chel	2m5f Cls3 114-140 Hdl Hcap soft	£12,512
	12/11	Folk	2m1½f Cls4 Nov Hdl soft	£2,669

Ran several outstanding races at Cheltenham last season and won December Gold Cup on only fourth chase start; finished first and second in two more handicaps there before third in JLT Novices' Chase; should find more opportunities at the track.

Double Seven (Ire)

8 b g Milan - Bargante (Phardante)

Martin Brassil | **John P McManus**

PLACINGS: 62P8P47P0P/F1111163- | **RPR 155c**

Starts	1st	2nd	3rd	4th	Win & Pl
28	9	1	2	2	£256,605

	10/13	Wxfd	2m6f List Ch soft	£13,740
138	10/13	Limk	3m 129-141 Ch Hcap good	£48,780
126	8/13	Kbgn	2m4f 104-130 Ch Hcap good	£8,976
120	7/13	Kbgn	3m1f 118-138 Ch Hcap good	£26,423
111	6/13	Kbgn	2m4f 108-116 Ch Hcap gd-fm	£7,012
125	10/11	Tipp	2m4f 108-126 Hdl Hcap soft	£9,071
117	7/11	Gway	2m6f 112-140 Hdl Hcap good	£22,414
108	7/11	Tipp	2m 84-108 Hdl Hcap good	£7,435
	9/10	Slig	2m2f Mdn Hdl 4yo yield	£4,580

Ran a huge race when third in last season's Grand National on second run after a long break following a profitable summer when winning five successive chases; likely to return to Aintree and would be an even bigger threat on quicker ground.

Dynaste (Fr)

8 gr g Martaline - Bellissima De Mai (Pistolet Bleu)

David Pipe | **A J White**

PLACINGS: 216/1428/11121/2512- | **RPR 175c**

Starts	1st	2nd	3rd	4th	Win & Pl
20	7	5	1	3	£430,770

	3/14	Chel	2m5f Cls1 Gd1 Ch good	£156,613
	4/13	Aint	3m1f Cls1 Nov Gd2 Ch good	£42,914
	12/12	Kemp	3m Cls1 Nov Gd1 Ch heavy	£22,780
	11/12	Newb	2m4f Cls1 Nov Gd2 Ch gd-sft	£13,732
	11/12	Chel	2m4½f Cls2 Nov Ch gd-sft	£12,628
141	11/11	Hayd	3m Cls1 Gd3 131-151 Hdl Hcap gd-sft	£42,713
130	12/10	Tntn	2m3½f Cls2 122-147 Cond Hdl Hcap gd-sft	£12,674

Developed into a top-class staying chaser last season, winning Ryanair Chase at Cheltenham and finishing second in Betfair Chase and Betfred Bowl; disappointed in King George (pulled muscles) but should have that race as first big target again.

ONE TO WATCH

Red Sherlock Lost his unbeaten record in the Neptune at Cheltenham but had earlier won his first six. Has more to offer. *[Dave Edwards, Topspeed]*

Double Ross: developed into something of a Cheltenham specialist last season and should find further winning chances in handicap chases

Easter Day (Fr)

6 b g Malinas - Sainte Lea (Sirk)

Paul Nicholls **B Fulton & Broughton Thermal Insulation**

PLACINGS: 3/211217/411- **RPR 147c**

Starts	1st	2nd	3rd	4th	Win & Pl
10	5	2	1	1	£57,393

	12/13	Asct	2m5½f Cls2 Ch soft	£16,025
135	11/13	Newb	2m6½f Cls3 Nov 126-137 Ch Hcap gd-sft	£7,507
	2/13	Hntg	2m4½f Cls1 Nov List Hdl soft	£11,888
	11/12	Asct	2m6f Cls2 Nov Hdl soft	£10,010
	10/12	Font	2m2½f Cls4 Nov Hdl soft	£3,899

Missed second half of last season but earlier form in novice chases reads well having beaten subsequent RSA Chase winner O'Faolains Boy when last seen at Ascot; should progress on soft ground and could be a Hennessy Gold Cup type.

Eastlake (Ire)

8 b g Beneficial - Guigone (Esprit Du Nord)

Jonjo O'Neill **John P McManus**

PLACINGS: 120569712113/131463- **RPR 149c**

Starts	1st	2nd	3rd	4th	Win & Pl
26	10	3	3	2	£105,849

140	12/13	Chel	2m½f Cls2 126-152 Ch Hcap good	£18,768
135	10/13	Aint	2m Cls2 122-139 Ch Hcap good	£13,763
132	3/13	NAbb	2m½f Cls2 124-146 Ch Hcap soft	£15,784
125	2/13	Sand	2m Cls2 122-143 Ch Hcap heavy	£15,640
118	12/12	Asct	2m1f Cls4 Nov 104-120 Ch Hcap heavy	£6,882
	5/12	Weth	2m Cls4 Nov Ch good	£2,599
	5/12	Uttx	2m Cls5 Ch soft	£2,339
	8/11	Hrfd	2m1f Cls4 Nov Hdl gd-fm	£2,014
	4/11	Hrfd	2m1f Cls5 Mdn Hdl good	£1,399
	10/10	Worc	2m Cls6 NHF 4-6yo gd-sft	£1,370

Won good 2m handicap chases at Aintree and Cheltenham last season before struggling off much higher marks; did better when third in Topham at Aintree, taking well to National fences and proving stamina for longer trip to open up more options.

Edmund Kean (Ire)

7 b g Old Vic - Baliya (Robellino)

David Pipe **Walters Plant Hire & James & Jean Potter**

PLACINGS: 1/4113/0113P- **RRPR 144+c**

Starts	1st	2nd	3rd	4th	Win & Pl
9	4	-	2	1	£30,183

	2/14	Ludl	3m Cls4 Nov Ch heavy	£5,198
132	1/14	Leic	2m7½f Cls3 Nov 127-137 Ch Hcap soft	£6,498
	2/13	Tntn	2m1f Cls4 Nov Hdl heavy	£4,224
	2/13	Fknm	2m4f Cls3 Nov Hdl 4-7yo soft	£5,848

Identified as a future chasing prospect after good third in EBF Final at Sandown two seasons ago and duly won first two races over fences last season; disappointed next twice, including when pulled up in Scottish National, but likely to improve.

Eduard (Ire)

6 b g Morozov - Dinny Kenn (Phardante)

Nicky Richards **Kingdom Taverns Ltd**

PLACINGS: 1/213124/2111- **RPR 158+c**

Starts	1st	2nd	3rd	4th	Win & Pl
11	6	3	1	1	£58,634

4/14	Ayr	2m4f Cls1 Nov Gd2 Ch gd-sft	£26,748
3/14	Ayr	2m Cls4 Nov Ch heavy	£4,549
12/13	Carl	2m Cls3 Nov Ch gd-sft	£7,148
2/13	Carl	2m1f Cls4 Nov Hdl soft	£3,119
11/12	Newc	2m Cls4 Nov Hdl gd-sft	£2,859
3/12	Kels	2m½f Cls6 NHF 4-6yo good	£1,300

Campaigned very quietly last season (beat total of only nine rivals to gain three wins) but passed biggest test with flying colours when slamming Valdez by 20 lengths in 2m4f Grade 2 at Ayr; deserves to step up to higher level and could have lots more to offer.

Ely Brown (Ire)

9 b g Sunshine Street - Browneyed Daughter (Broken Hearted)

Charlie Longsdon **Countrywide Vehicle Rentals Taxi Hire**

PLACINGS: **U1U203P/13160/10115-** RRPR **148+c**

Starts	1st	2nd	3rd	4th	Win & Pl
24	7	3	3	1	£70,664

	2/14	Weth	3m1f Cls1 Nov Gd2 Ch heavy	£18,184
	12/13	Leic	2m7½f Cls3 Nov Ch gd-sft	£6,486
135	10/13	Aint	3m½f Cls2 127-150 Hdl Hcap good	£11,574
130	1/13	Wwck	3m1f Cls2 116-142 Hdl Hcap soft	£11,574
125	10/12	Aint	3m½f Cls2 125-150 Hdl Hcap soft	£10,010
	12/11	Donc	3m½f Cls4 Nov Hdl gd-sft	£2,534
	5/11	Worc	3m Cls4 Nov Hdl gd-fm	£1,952

Has begun last two seasons by winning same Pertemps qualifier at Aintree and went on to add two novice chases last season, including a soft Grade 2 at Wetherby; struck into himself when well beaten at Ascot next time; ideal sort for marathon staying chases.

Ericht (Ire)

8 b g Alderbrook - Lady Orla (Satco)

Nicky Henderson **Mrs Christopher Hanbury**

PLACINGS: **6/33200/17159/251P-6** RPR **146+c**

Starts	1st	2nd	3rd	4th	Win & Pl
19	5	3	2	-	£31,629

2/14	Muss	2m4f Cls3 Nov Ch soft	£7,798
2/13	Kemp	2m5f Cls4 Nov Hdl gd-sft	£3,249
1/13	Kemp	2m Cls4 NHF std-slw	£3,574
12/12	Fknm	2m4f Cls5 Mdn Hdl soft	£3,899
2/11	Newb	2m½f Cls1 Gd2 NHF 4-6yo soft	£5,701
1/11	Hntg	1m6f Cls6 NHF 4-6yo gd-sft	£1,370

Had a mixed campaign when sent chasing last season, looking a future star when winning well at Musselburgh but disappointing when well fancied for novice handicaps at Cheltenham and Punchestown; may be worth chancing to put that right.

Far West (Fr)

5 b g Poliglote - Far Away Girl (Cadoudal)

Paul Nicholls **Axom Xxxix**

PLACINGS: **3/11112/24F0-** RPR **153h**

Starts	1st	2nd	3rd	4th	Win & Pl
10	4	2	1	1	£87,662

2/13	Asct	2m Cls2 Nov Hdl soft	£10,010
12/12	Chel	2m1f Cls2 Hdl 3yo heavy	£13,436
11/12	Chel	2m½f Cls1 Gd2 Hdl 3yo soft	£14,238
10/12	Chep	2m½f Cls4 Hdl 3yo soft	£3,249

Won four times as a juvenile before coming second to Our Conor in 2013 Triumph Hurdle; showed mixed form last season but went close to winning Elite Hurdle and was running a big race when final-flight faller in Betfair Hurdle; likely to go novice chasing.

Faugheen (Ire)

6 b g Germany - Miss Pickering (Accordion)

Willie Mullins (Ir) **Mrs S Ricci**

PLACINGS: **1/11111-1** RPR **159+h**

Starts	1st	2nd	3rd	4th	Win & Pl
6	6	-	-	-	£148,974

4/14	Punc	2m Nov Gd1 Hdl gd-yld	£46,500
3/14	Chel	2m5f Cls1 Nov Gd1 Hdl good	£68,340
12/13	Limk	3m Nov Gd3 Hdl heavy	£15,061
12/13	Navn	2m4f Nov Hdl gd-yld	£7,293
11/13	Punc	2m6f Mdn Hdl yield	£7,293
5/13	Punc	2m NHF 5yo yield	£4,488

Unbeaten in six runs under rules, following stunning bumper victory with five wins over hurdles; easily won Neptune Hurdle at Cheltenham having won over 3m previously but looked even better when dropped to 2m at Punchestown; set to be a superstar over hurdles or fences.

Ericht (left): sparkled at Musselburgh last season and expected to get back on track this term

Felix Yonger (Ire)

8 b g Oscar - Marble Sound (Be My Native)

Willie Mullins (Ir) **Andrea & Graham Wylie**

PLACINGS: 210/21125/111224-4 RPR 160+c

Starts	1st	2nd	3rd	4th	Win & Pl
15	6	5	-	2	£125,012

12/13	Navn	2m1f Nov Ch gd-yld	£10,569
11/13	Punc	2m Nov Gd2 Ch yield	£20,874
5/13	Punc	2m4f Ch yield	£6,732
2/12	Naas	2m Nov Gd2 Hdl soft	£22,479
12/11	Dpat	2m2f Mdn Hdl 4-5yo sft-hvy	£6,841
1/11	Muss	2m Cls6 NHF 4-6yo good	£1,626

Made a striking return from more than a year out when winning first three novice chases last season; failed to live up to expectations after but could still be top-class over longer trips.

Festive Affair (Ire)

6 br g Presenting - Merry Batim (Alphabatim)

Jonjo O'Neill **John P McManus**

PLACINGS: 1F2P/P319- RPR 130+c

Starts	1st	2nd	3rd	4th	Win & Pl
6	1	1	1	-	£8,683

1/14	Newb	2m1f Cls3 Nov Ch soft	£6,498

Came from point-to-point arena in Ireland to go novice chasing for new yard last season and won well over 2m1f at Newbury having been too keen previously; may not have stayed in novice handicap chase at Cheltenham Festival having led three out.

Felix Yonger: could develop into a top-class chaser this season

Fingal Bay (Ire)

8 b g King's Theatre - Lady Marguerrite (Blakeney)

Philip Hobbs — **Mrs R J Skan**

PLACINGS: **1/11112/120/11-5** — RPR **154+h**

Starts	1st	2nd	3rd	4th	Win & Pl
12	8	2	-	-	£150,680

148	3/14	Chel	3m Cls1 List 135-148 Hdl Hcap good	£45,560
142	2/14	Extr	2m7½f Cls2 121-147 Hdl Hcap heavy	£12,512
	10/12	Chep	2m3½f Cls3 Nov Ch gd-sft	£7,323
	12/11	Newb	2m5f Cls1 Nov Gd1 Hdl soft	£17,085
	12/11	Sand	2m4f Cls1 Nov Gd2 Hdl gd-sft	£12,073
	11/11	Chel	2m5f Cls1 Nov Gd2 Hdl gd-sft	£12,244
	10/11	Chep	2m4f Cls1 Nov Gd2 Hdl good	£14,238
	2/11	Extr	2m1f Cls5 NHF 4-6yo heavy	£1,301

Former Grade 1-winning novice hurdler who returned from more than a year out in terrific form last season, following up comeback win with narrow victory in Pertemps Final at Cheltenham; beaten next time at higher level and may revert to fences.

Finian's Rainbow (Ire)

11 b g Tiraaz - Trinity Gale (Strong Gale)

Nicky Henderson — **Michael Buckley**

PLACINGS: **5/11121/1211/4642/P-**

Starts	1st	2nd	3rd	4th	Win & Pl
19	10	3	1	2	£498,641

4/12	Aint	2m4f Cls1 Gd1 Ch good	£98,558
3/12	Chel	2m Cls1 Gd1 Ch good	£182,240
12/11	Kemp	2m Cls1 Gd2 Ch good	£25,628
4/11	Aint	2m Cls1 Nov Gd1 Ch good	£56,632
2/11	Wwck	2m Cls1 Nov Gd2 Ch gd-sft	£17,637
1/11	Newb	2m1f Cls3 Nov Ch soft	£4,190
11/10	Newb	2m1f Cls3 Nov Ch gd-sft	£6,262
2/10	Asct	2m3½f Cls3 Nov Hdl gd-sft	£5,010
11/09	Newb	2m½f Cls3 Nov Hdl gd-sft	£6,262
3/09	Kemp	2m Cls6 NHF 4-6yo good	£1,713

Missed most of last season having been pulled up in Paddy Power Gold Cup; had won Champion Chase and Melling Chase in 2011 but failed to win in following campaign, though did well to be second to Sire De Grugy on final start; slipping down handicap.

First Lieutenant (Ire)

9 ch g Presenting - Fourstargale (Fourstars Allstar)

Mouse Morris (Ir) — **Gigginstown House Stud**

PLACINGS: **P223/4232213/34234-2** — RPR **165c**

Starts	1st	2nd	3rd	4th	Win & Pl
27	7	8	7	4	£505,943

4/13	Aint	3m1f Cls1 Gd1 Ch good	£84,478
11/11	Cork	2m4f Nov Gd3 Ch soft	£19,612
10/11	Tipp	2m4f Nov Gd3 Ch soft	£15,409
3/11	Chel	2m5f Cls1 Nov Gd1 Hdl good	£57,010
12/10	Leop	2m Nov Gd1 Hdl heavy	£46,018
10/10	Punc	2m4f Mdn Hdl good	£6,412
3/10	Gowr	2m2f NHF 4-7yo yld-sft	£5,190

Smart and consistent staying chaser whose second-place finishes in Lexus Chase and Punchestown Gold Cup last season brought total to seven in Grade 1 chases; sole win at that level over fences came on preferred good ground in 2013 Betfred Bowl.

Flaxen Flare (Ire)

5 ch g Windsor Knot - Golden Angel (Slew O'Gold)

Gordon Elliott (Ir) — **Mrs P Sloan**

PLACINGS: **12514/21343256-** — RPR **152h**

Starts	1st	2nd	3rd	4th	Win & Pl
13	3	3	2	2	£150,922

	8/13	Cork	2m Hdl 4yo good	£7,293
127	3/13	Chel	2m½f Cls1 Gd3 124-144 Hdl 4yo Hcap gd-sft	£42,713
	12/12	Leop	2m Mdn Hdl 3yo soft	£6,900

Won Fred Winter Hurdle at Cheltenham in 2013 and continued to thrive in major 2m handicaps last season despite rising mark, running well several times in defeat; may yet have another big handicap in him and worth a chance at higher level.

Flemenstar (Ire)

9 b g Flemensfirth - Different Dee (Beau Sher)

Tony Martin (Ir) — **Stephen Curran**

PLACINGS: **/41/4211111/11323/1-** — RPR **164+c**

Starts	1st	2nd	3rd	4th	Win & Pl
15	9	2	2	2	£280,380

11/13	Navn	2m Gd2 Ch yield	£21,138
12/12	Punc	2m4f Gd1 Ch heavy	£43,333
11/12	Navn	2m Gd2 Ch sft-hvy	£20,313
4/12	Fair	2m4f Gd1 Ch good	£48,750
3/12	Naas	2m4f Nov Gd3 Ch soft	£14,896
1/12	Leop	2m1f Nov Gd1 Ch sft-hvy	£43,333
1/12	Naas	2m Nov Ch sft-hvy	£11,917
11/11	Navn	2m1f Ch sft-hvy	£9,517
3/11	Navn	2m Mdn Hdl sft-hvy	£5,948

Looked a superstar in younger days, winning seven successive races including John Durkan Chase and Powers Gold Cup in 2012; ran only once for new trainer last season before suffering a tendon injury; could excel again from 2m to 2m4f having struggled over further.

Fox Appeal (Ire)

7 b g Brian Boru - Lady Appeal (Phardante)

Emma Lavelle — **The Hawk Inn Syndicate 3**

PLACINGS: **0/13119/013/5221334-** — RPR **155c**

Starts	1st	2nd	3rd	4th	Win & Pl
17	5	2	4	1	£64,559

	12/13	Asct	2m3f Cls1 Nov Gd2 Ch soft	£17,162
138	11/12	Kemp	2m5f Cls2 116-140 Hdl Hcap gd-sft	£10,010
130	1/12	Tntn	3m½f Cls3 112-130 Hdl Hcap gd-sft	£5,848
122	12/11	Tntn	3m½f Cls3 107-125 Hdl Hcap gd-sft	£4,549
	11/11	Font	2m4f Cls4 Mdn Hdl soft	£2,372

Consistent performer in several top novice chases last season; beat Raya Star by ten lengths in a Grade 2 at Ascot and twice went close under a penalty at that level behind Valdez and Balder Succes; raced only up to 2m5f but did well as a hurdler over further.

ONE TO WATCH

Dubawi Island Ran below expectations when third favourite for a hot Haydock handicap but will come on for that. *[Dave Edwards, Topspeed]*

Fox Norton (Fr)

4 b g Lando - Natt Musik (Kendor)

Nick Williams **B Dunn**

PLACINGS: 1/4216-3 **RPR 140h**

Starts	1st	2nd	3rd	4th	Win & Pl
6	2	1	1	1	£40,051

	12/13	Donc	2m½f Cls1 Gd2 Hdl 3yo good	£15,876
	4/13	Fntb	2m Hdl 3yo soft	£8,585

Among the better juvenile hurdlers early last season and won a Grade 2 at Doncaster; seemed to have limitations exposed when sixth at Aintree after a break but did better when third to Abbyssial at Punchestown; likely type for top 2m handicap hurdles.

Foxrock (Ire)

6 b g Flemensfirth - Midnight Light (Roselier)

Ted Walsh (Ir) **Barry Connell**

PLACINGS: 1U231/213119- **RPR 146+c**

Starts	1st	2nd	3rd	4th	Win & Pl
10	4	2	2	-	£63,227

	2/14	Navn	3m Nov Gd2 Ch heavy	£20,313
	1/14	Naas	3m Nov Gd2 Ch sft-hvy	£21,667
	11/13	Fair	2m5½f Ch gd-yld	£6,732
	3/13	Naas	3m Mdn Hdl soft	£5,610

Relished testing conditions when winning Grade 2 novice chases over 3m at Navan and Naas last season; major gamble for National Hunt Chase but jumped poorly on final circuit and managed only ninth, possibly finding much quicker ground against him.

Full Shift (Fr)

5 b g Ballingarry - Dansia (Lavirco)

Nicky Henderson **John P McManus**

PLACINGS: 1/1210- **RPR 139+h**

Starts	1st	2nd	3rd	4th	Win & Pl
4	2	1	-	-	£10,016

124	2/14	Kemp	2m5f Cls3 114-130 Hdl Hcap soft	£5,848
	11/13	Newc	2m Cls5 Mdn Hdl 4-6yo good	£3,119

Point-to-point recruit who shaped with great promise on first three runs over hurdles, winning twice, and was sent off favourite for Martin Pipe Hurdle only to find such a competitive race beyond him; should have much more to come, especially over fences.

Gaitway

4 b g Medicean - Milliegait (Tobougg)

Nicky Henderson **Mrs J K Powell**

PLACINGS: 1- **RPR 125+b**

Starts	1st	2nd	3rd	4th	Win & Pl
1	1	-	-	-	£29,505

	3/14	Newb	2m½f Cls2 NHF 4-5yo gd-sft	£29,505

Looked potentially smart when winning sole bumper start last season in a valuable sales race at Newbury in which first two pulled well clear; mainly Flat-bred but with winning hurdlers in his pedigree so should make a good novice.

Gallant Oscar (Ire)

8 b g Oscar - Park Wave (Supreme Leader)

Tony Martin (Ir) **G Kelly**

PLACINGS: **54/32/099041F/411U-** RPR **114+h**

Starts	1st	2nd	3rd	4th	Win & Pl
13	3	-	-	3	£38,167

119	3/14	Naas	3m 114-142 Ch Hcap soft	£27,083
93	1/14	Navn	2m4f 80-109 Hdl Hcap soft	£5,750
	3/13	Clon	2m4f Ch soft	£4,488

Joined Tony Martin last season and expertly laid out to win Leinster National in impressive fashion after a couple of prep runs over hurdles; unseated rider in Irish National next time; should progress again after just five runs over fences.

Garde La Victoire (Fr)

5 b g Kapgarde - Next Victory (Akarad)

Philip Hobbs **Mrs Diana L Whateley**

PLACINGS: **1/1124011-** RPR **140+h**

Starts	1st	2nd	3rd	4th	Win & Pl
8	5	1	-	1	£27,851

	4/14	Chel	2m4½f Cls2 Nov Hdl good	£10,010
	4/14	Tntn	2m3½f Cls4 Nov Hdl good	£4,106
	11/13	Wwck	2m Cls4 Nov Hdl gd-sft	£3,899
	10/13	Aint	2m½f Cls4 Mdn Hdl gd-sft	£4,549
	10/12	Extr	1m5f Cls6 NHF 3yo gd-sft	£1,365

Won four times in novice hurdles last season, though beaten three times in between when stepped up in class (came up well short twice at Grade 1 level including Supreme Novices' Hurdle); future lies over fences but could start off in handicap hurdles.

Gevrey Chambertin (Fr)

6 gr g Dom Alco - Fee Magic (Phantom Breeze)

David Pipe **Roger Stanley & Yvonne Reynolds III**

PLACINGS: **14/111P6/1P9-** RPR **149+h**

Starts	1st	2nd	3rd	4th	Win & Pl
10	5	-	-	1	£64,122

143	11/13	Hayd	3m Cls1 Gd3 125-148 Hdl Hcap soft	£45,560
130	1/13	Winc	2m4f Cls3 112-130 Hdl Hcap soft	£6,498
	11/12	Hayd	2m4f Cls4 Nov Hdl 4-7yo soft	£4,874
	10/12	Aint	2m½f Cls4 Mdn Hdl good	£3,899
	12/11	Ffos	2m Cls6 NHF 3-5yo heavy	£1,430

Long held in high regard and was a gutsy winner of Fixed Brush Hurdle at Haydock last season; jumped well on chasing debut but faded quickly after being too keen and showed little in RSA Chase; can do well in novice chase campaign.

Gilgamboa (Ire)

6 b g Westerner - Hi Native (Be My Native)

Enda Bolger (Ir) **John P McManus**

PLACINGS: **13110-** RPR **143+h**

Starts	1st	2nd	3rd	4th	Win & Pl
5	3	-	1	-	£65,073

128	1/14	Leop	2m 115-142 Hdl Hcap soft	£50,000
120	12/13	Punc	2m4f 106-128 Hdl Hcap heavy	£8,134
	10/13	Gway	2m Mdn Hdl 5yo heavy	£6,171

Won last season's valuable Boylesports Handicap Hurdle at Leopardstown just three months after making debut under rules in a maiden hurdle; still in with a chance when blundered two out in Supreme Novices' Hurdle; expected to be even better over fences.

Gevrey Chambertin: retains his novice status for chasing this season and can make his mark

Gitane Du Berlais (Fr)

4 b f Balko - Boheme Du Berlais (Simon Du Desert)

Willie Mullins (Ir) **Simon Munir & Isaac Souede**

PLACINGS: 64/13311-35 **RPR 130+h**

Starts	1st	2nd	3rd	4th	Win & Pl
9	3	-	3	1	£87,043

	1/14	Fair	2m2f Nov Gd3 Hdl soft	£16,250
	12/13	Aint	2m1f Cls1 List Hdl 3yo soft	£11,390
	5/13	Autl	2m1½f Hdl 3yo heavy	£18,732

Won Grade 3 and Listed hurdles last season before skipping big juvenile prizes due to need for further than 2m; twice headed to France instead last summer when fifth in Grade 1 contest at Auteuil; could be a smart stayer, especially over fences.

Glens Melody (Ire)

6 b m King's Theatre - Glens Music (Orchestra)

Willie Mullins (Ir) **Ms Fiona McStay**

PLACINGS: 1/112131121/13112-47 **RPR 146h**

Starts	1st	2nd	3rd	4th	Win & Pl
17	10	3	2	1	£201,673

	2/14	Wwck	2m5f Cls1 List Hdl heavy	£12,529
	1/14	Wwck	2m3f Cls1 List Hdl heavy	£11,390
	11/13	Punc	2m6f Hdl yield	£10,569
	4/13	Punc	2m2f Gd1 Hdl heavy	£50,407
	2/13	Fair	2m4f Nov Hdl 5-7yo soft	£13,211
	1/13	Leop	2m2f Nov List Hdl sft-hvy	£13,211
	12/12	Clon	2m4f Mdn Hdl heavy	£6,325
	6/12	Tipp	2m NHF 4yo soft	£5,750
	5/12	Slig	2m2f NHF 4yo good	£4,600
	4/12	Punc	2m1f NHF 4-6yo heavy	£24,500

High-class mare who came closer than any horse had ever done to breaking Quevega's dominance of Mares' Hurdle at Cheltenham when second in March and may find more opportunities with that superstar retired; had also won two Listed hurdles at Warwick.

God's Own (Ire)

6 b g Oscar - Dantes Term (Phardante)

Tom George **Crossed Fingers Partnership**

PLACINGS: 221313/U10242-1 **RPR 159c**

Starts	1st	2nd	3rd	4th	Win & Pl
12	4	3	2	1	£88,684

	5/14	Punc	2m Nov Gd1 Ch yield	£56,833
129	11/13	Kemp	2m5f Cls2 129-155 Hdl Hcap gd-sft	£11,574
	2/13	Muss	2m4f Cls4 Nov Hdl good	£3,899
	11/12	Donc	2m½f Cls4 Nov Hdl soft	£3,899

Pulled off surprise Grade 1 win at Punchestown last season (sat off overly strong gallop) after previous good placed efforts; had been deliberately held back for that meeting with its timing meaning he retains novice status for this season.

ONE TO WATCH

Wilde Blue Yonder Showed up well in Grade 1 company at Cheltenham and Aintree. Smart second-season hurdler who starts on a very fair mark. *[Steve Mason, Racing Post Ratings]*

Godsmejudge (Ire)

8 b g Witness Box - Eliza Everett (Meneval)

Alan King **Favourites Racing**

PLACINGS: 51271/2012131/5PP23- **RPR 153c**

Starts	1st	2nd	3rd	4th	Win & Pl
18	5	5	2	-	£205,379

139	4/13	Ayr	4m½f Cls1 Gd3 122-148 Ch Hcap good	£102,510
	2/13	Wwck	3m2f Cls3 Nov Ch heavy	£9,615
	12/12	Folk	3m1f Cls4 Ch good	£3,217
118	3/12	Uttx	3m Cls4 100-118 Hdl Hcap good	£2,989
	12/11	Hntg	3m2f Cls4 Nov Hdl gd-sft	£2,534

Very smart staying handicap chaser who finished second when defending Scottish National crown last season and was also placed in bet365 Gold Cup; likely to be aimed at Grand National having finished distressed in intended prep run last term.

Gold Bullet (Ire)

6 gr g Generous - Glenmoss Rosy (Zaffaran)

Tom Taaffe (Ir) **Mrs Fitri Hay**

PLACINGS: 132211/21- **RPR 135+c**

Starts	1st	2nd	3rd	4th	Win & Pl
8	4	3	1	-	£29,519

	11/13	DRoy	2m4f Ch yield	£7,012
123	4/13	Gowr	2m4f 100-130 Hdl Hcap good	£8,415
	3/13	Limk	2m3f Mdn Hdl 4-6yo heavy	£5,610
	6/12	Clon	2m NHF 4-7yo soft	£3,208

Made a big impression when winning well on chasing debut at Down Royal last season only to be struck down by injury; had previously won a bumper and a maiden hurdle but looks a natural over fences; smart prospect who seems to act on any going.

Golden Wonder (Ire)

8 b g Goldmark - Polyploid (Pollerton)

Dessie Hughes (Ir) **P M Cooney**

PLACINGS: 60/6544/423112542-6 **RPR 147c**

Starts	1st	2nd	3rd	4th	Win & Pl
14	2	3	1	2	£60,503

	8/13	Gway	2m6f Ch heavy	£7,854
	7/13	Bell	3m Mdn Hdl gd-fm	£4,488

Progressed rapidly last season, finishing second in Irish National on only fifth chase start just nine months after winning a maiden hurdle; fair sixth when unsuited by return to shorter in Galway Plate; won on heavy ground on chasing debut but prefers quicker.

Goonyella (Ire)

7 br g Presenting - Miss Fresher (Pampabird)

Jim Dreaper (Ir) **Ann & Alan Potts Partnership**

PLACINGS: /12/F211133P1/25827- **RPR 145+c**

Starts	1st	2nd	3rd	4th	Win & Pl
11	2	2	2	-	£30,484

127	4/13	Punc	3m6f 116-144 Ch Hcap heavy	£13,211
	12/12	Limk	2m6f Mdn Hunt Ch heavy	£4,888

Well fancied to win a big staying handicap

last season having landed a similar prize at Punchestown in April 2013 but proved a slight letdown in Welsh and Irish Nationals; showed engine is still intact with fine second in Grade 3 novice hurdle behind Don Poli.

Goulanes (Ire)

8 b g Mr Combustible - Rebolgiane (Red Sunset)

David Pipe — **R S Brookhouse**

PLACINGS: **211/1162/0P1-** RPR **152+c**

Starts	1st	2nd	3rd	4th	Win & Pl
8	4	1	-	-	£100,032

138	3/14	Uttx	4m1½f Cls1 List 135-161 Ch Hcap gd-sft	£56,950
	2/13	Weth	3m1f Cls1 Nov Gd2 Ch soft	£17,451
126	11/12	Chel	3m1½f Cls1 List 124-150 Hdl Hcap soft	£15,377
	3/12	Newb	2m5f Cls3 Mdn Hdl gd-sft	£4,549

Took time to build on impressive chasing debut win two seasons ago in a Grade 2 at Warwick but helped by a breathing operation before Midlands National and won well at Uttoxeter; clearly suited by extreme tests of stamina; could be a Grand National type.

Grand Jesture (Ire)

6 b g Gold Well - Four Moons (Cardinal Flower)

Henry de Bromhead (Ir) — **Alan & Ann Potts Partnership**

PLACINGS: **1/344/3522414-2** RPR **141+c**

Starts	1st	2nd	3rd	4th	Win & Pl
12	2	3	2	4	£26,009

	1/14	Fair	2m5½f Ch soft	£6,900
	4/12	Punc	2m NHF 4yo sft-hvy	£5,175

Mixed hurdling and chasing last season and proved far more adept over fences, running a cracker when second to Chartreux in a big handicap chase at Punchestown in May; should have plenty more to come after just four chase runs.

Grandouet (Fr)

7 b/br g Al Namix - Virginia River (Indian River)

Nicky Henderson — **Simon Munir**

PLACINGS: **113B/1F11/2F6/U2267-** RPR **157+c**

Starts	1st	2nd	3rd	4th	Win & Pl
21	6	4	3	-	£249,006

	12/11	Chel	2m1f Cls1 Gd2 Hdl good	£74,035
	11/11	Hayd	2m Cls2 Hdl 4yo gd-sft	£25,024
	5/11	Punc	2m Gd1 Hdl 4yo good	£42,759
	1/11	Asct	2m Cls3 Hdl 4yo gd-sft	£4,383
	12/10	Newb	2m½f Cls3 Hdl 3yo gd-sft	£4,879
	4/10	Engh	2m½f Hdl 3yo v soft	£19,540

Ruled out of year following win in 2011 International Hurdle and has failed to win since; unconvincing when sent novice chasing last season, though did well to finish a neck second to Hinterland in Sandown Grade 1; reverted to hurdles for final start.

Green Flag (Ire)

7 b g Milan - Erin Go Brea (Un Desperado)

Lucinda Russell — **John R Adam**

PLACINGS: **112/1211522/1112U46-** RPR **147+c**

Starts	1st	2nd	3rd	4th	Win & Pl
16	7	5	-	1	£66,521

138	11/13	Newc	3m Cls3 Nov 124-138 Ch Hcap good	£6,498
132	11/13	Ayr	3m1f Cls3 Nov 122-136 Ch Hcap soft	£7,988
	10/13	Kels	2m7½f Cls4 Nov Ch gd-sft	£4,549
	1/13	Ayr	2m4f Cls4 Nov Hdl 4-7yo heavy	£3,899
	12/12	Newc	2m6f Cls2 Nov Hdl heavy	£9,697
	10/12	Hexm	2m4½f Cls5 Mdn Hdl heavy	£2,144
	3/12	Hexm	2m½f Cls6 Mdn NHF 4-6yo good	£1,711

Took well to chasing last season, winning first

Green Flag: should do well in staying handicap chases

three races over fences and doing particularly well when staying on to be fourth to Holywell in very strong handicap chase at Cheltenham Festival; threatened for a long way before failing to stay in Scottish National.

Grey Gold (Ire)

9 gr g Strategic Choice - Grouse-N-Heather (Grey Desire)

Richard Lee **Mrs M A Boden**

PLACINGS: **4U3149/14/411/33212-** RPR **153c**

Starts	1st	2nd	3rd	4th	Win & Pl
17	5	2	3	5	£54,655

138	2/14	Sand	2m Cls2 135-148 Ch Hcap heavy	£15,640
	4/13	Punc	2m2f Nov Ch heavy	£9,817
	3/13	Carl	2m Cls3 Nov Ch heavy	£7,148
124	11/11	Bang	2m1f Cls3 116-130 Hdl Hcap gd-sft	£5,697
	1/11	Hrfd	2m1f Cls4 Nov Hdl heavy	£2,017

Performed consistently well last season and gained deserved win at Sandown on penultimate start on heavy ground; went close off much higher mark at Chepstow next time; should continue to run well in good 2m handicap chases in testing conditions.

Grumeti

6 b g Sakhee - Tetravella (Groom Dancer)

Alan King **Mcneill Family**

PLACINGS: **1F1131/4/35385-1** RPR **147h**

Starts	1st	2nd	3rd	4th	Win & Pl
13	5	-	3	1	£128,886

	5/14	Bang	2m1½f Cls4 Nov Ch good	£3,899
	4/12	Aint	2m½f Cls1 Gd1 Hdl 4yo gd-sft	£56,270
	2/12	Kemp	2m Cls1 Nov Gd2 Hdl good	£12,130
	1/12	Chel	2m1f Cls1 Gd2 Hdl 4yo gd-sft	£14,238
	12/11	Tntn	2m1f Cls4 Nov Hdl gd-sft	£3,422

Won a Grade 1 at Aintree as a juvenile hurdler three seasons ago but has since come up short at top level; impressed when winning easily on chasing debut at Bangor in May and should be capable of winning more novice chases; effective on any ground.

Guitar Pete (Ire)

4 br g Dark Angel - Innishmore (Lear Fan)

Dessie Hughes (Ir) **Mrs P Sloan**

PLACINGS: **12121131-6** RPR **141+h**

Starts	1st	2nd	3rd	4th	Win & Pl
9	5	2	1	-	£155,285

	4/14	Aint	2m1f Cls1 Gd1 Hdl 4yo good	£56,270
	2/14	Leop	2m Gd1 Hdl 4yo sft-hvy	£40,667
	12/13	Leop	2m Gd2 Hdl 3yo soft	£21,138
	11/13	DRoy	2m Hdl 3yo yld-sft	£7,854
	9/13	List	2m Hdl 3yo yield	£8,415

Proved a tough and classy juvenile during busy campaign last year, winning Grade 1 contests at Leopardstown (beat Triumph winner Tiger Roll) and Aintree; perhaps ridden too aggressively when only third in Triumph but well below best at Punchestown.

Grey Gold: smart performer at around 2m on testing ground

FRED
SANDOW

Gullinbursti (Ire)

8 b g Milan - D'Ygrande (Good Thyne)

Emma Lavelle — **Nicholas Mustoe**

PLACINGS: /11220/352F/153P332- — **RPR 150+c**

Starts	1st	2nd	3rd	4th	Win & Pl
19	4	5	4	-	£54,214

134	11/13	MRas	2m6½f Cls3 Nov 124-138 Ch Hcap soft	£9,747
	11/11	Hrfd	2m6½f Cls4 Nov Hdl gd-sft	£2,534
	11/11	Extr	2m5½f Cls4 Nov Hdl gd-sft	£2,274
	3/11	Cork	2m2f NHF 5-7yo yld-sft	£5,651

Failed to win when sent chasing two seasons ago but benefited from that experience to win novice handicap chase in terrific fashion first time out last season; unable to follow up after sharp rise but placed in several good races and should continue to pay his way.

Hadrian's Approach (Ire)

7 b g High Chaparral - Gifted Approach (Roselier)

Nicky Henderson — **Mr & Mrs R Kelvin-Hughes**

PLACINGS: 1/1F/1F2235/2U101- — **RPR 155c**

Starts	1st	2nd	3rd	4th	Win & Pl
13	4	3	1	-	£144,147

146	4/14	Sand	3m5½f Cls1 Gd3 134-158 Ch Hcap gd-sft	£85,425
	12/13	Newb	3m Cls2 Ch gd-sft	£12,021
	11/12	Asct	2m3f Cls3 Ch gd-sft	£6,882
	12/11	Asct	2m6f Cls3 Mdn Hdl soft	£5,005

Progress over fences hampered by jumping problems but finally put together a top-class performance in a big field when winning bet365 Gold Cup on final start last season; had shown huge promise in smaller fields previously and could continue to progress.

Harry Topper

7 b g Sir Harry Lewis - Indeed To Goodness (Welsh Term)

Kim Bailey — **D J Keyte**

PLACINGS: 1/51127/111UB/1331P- — **RPR 170+c**

Starts	1st	2nd	3rd	4th	Win & Pl
16	8	1	2	-	£141,725

	2/14	Newb	3m Cls1 Gd2 Ch heavy	£28,810
	11/13	Weth	3m1f Cls1 Gd2 Ch gd-sft	£57,218
	2/13	Extr	3m Cls2 Ch heavy	£12,512
	11/12	Newb	3m Cls1 Nov Gd2 Ch soft	£13,732
	10/12	Extr	3m Cls4 Ch gd-sft	£3,899
	1/12	Winc	2m6f Cls4 Nov Hdl soft	£3,249
	12/11	Uttx	2m4½f Cls5 Mdn Hdl soft	£1,689
	4/11	Hrfd	2m1f Cls6 NHF 4-6yo good	£1,431

Produced two outstanding performances on heavy ground last season, including runaway victory in Denman Chase; hasn't won on good ground since bumper debut (well below-par in such conditions twice) but hugely talented on softer ground.

Hawk High (Ire)

4 b g High Chaparral - Septembers Hawk (Machiavellian)

Tim Easterby — **Trevor Hemmings**

PLACINGS: 121610- — **RPR 128h**

Starts	1st	2nd	3rd	4th	Win & Pl
6	3	1	-	-	£51,425

130	3/14	Chel	2m½f Cls1 Gd3 127-139 Hdl 4yo Hcap good	£42,713
	1/14	Wwck	2m Cls4 Hdl 4yo soft	£3,249
	10/13	Aint	2m1f Cls4 Hdl 3yo good	£4,549

Progressed well last season until flopping on heavy ground at Haydock but relished return to quicker conditions (had won on good to firm on the Flat) when landing Fred Winter Hurdle at Cheltenham; found out at Grade 1 level when only tenth at Aintree.

Hidden Cyclone: accomplished chaser should be found plenty of winning opportunities

Hawkes Point

9 b g Kayf Tara - Mandys Native (Be My Native)

Paul Nicholls — **C G Roach**

PLACINGS: 135/125/212P/4260- RPR **146c**

Starts	1st	2nd	3rd	4th	Win & Pl
13	2	4	1	1	£42,416

	Date	Course	Race	Prize
	1/13	Extr	3m Cls3 Nov Ch heavy	£6,498
	1/12	Chep	3m Cls4 Mdn Hdl heavy	£2,274

Dour stayer who began last season with two fine runs at Chepstow, notably when beaten a head in Welsh National; out of sorts in two subsequent runs, possibly feeling effects of such a hard race; could be a leading contender in that contest again.

Hidden Cyclone (Ire)

9 b g Stowaway - Hurricane Debbie (Shahanndeh)

John Joseph Hanlon (Ir) — **Mrs A F Mee & David Mee**

PLACINGS: 11/13/1186F/213222-F RPR **166+c**

Starts	1st	2nd	3rd	4th	Win & Pl
21	10	4	3	-	£249,828

	Date	Course	Race	Prize
	9/13	List	2m4f Ch soft	£11,626
	11/12	Gowr	2m4f Ch heavy	£10,833
	10/12	Naas	2m Gd3 Ch soft	£14,896
	12/11	Leop	2m3f Ch gd-yld	£7,733
	3/11	Navn	2m7f Nov Hdl sft-hvy	£10,112
	2/11	Thur	2m4f Nov Gd2 Hdl soft	£21,013
	1/11	Leop	2m4f Nov Gd2 Hdl soft	£22,134
	11/10	Navn	2m Nov Gd3 Hdl soft	£16,394
	10/10	Tipp	2m Mdn Hdl 4-5yo yield	£3,186
	4/10	Gowr	2m NHF 4-7yo good	£5,190

Progressed well last season, finishing a fine third in Paddy Power Gold Cup and second three times at Grade 1 level from 2m to 2m5f on ground ranging from good to heavy; versatile and consistent so should find plenty of opportunities in good races.

Highland Lodge (Ire)

8 b g Flemensfirth - Supreme Von Pres (Presenting)

Emma Lavelle — **The Unusual Suspects**

PLACINGS: 1/114/131356/24P68- RPR **150+c**

Starts	1st	2nd	3rd	4th	Win & Pl
14	4	1	2	2	£45,401

	Date	Course	Race	Prize
	12/12	Chel	3m1½f Cls2 Nov Ch heavy	£12,512
	11/12	Towc	3m½f Cls3 Ch gd-sft	£5,507
	12/11	Hayd	2m4f Cls4 Nov Hdl heavy	£4,874
	11/11	Extr	2m5½f Cls4 Nov Hdl gd-sft	£2,274

Useful novice chaser two seasons ago and began last term in good form, most notably when fourth in Hennessy Gold Cup; favourite for Welsh National next time but out of sorts for rest of campaign; slipped down handicap and could win a big staying race.

Highland Retreat

7 b m Exit To Nowhere - St Kilda (Past Glories)

Harry Fry — **Richard Barber**

PLACINGS: 61/F1432313/1118- RPR **147+h**

Starts	1st	2nd	3rd	4th	Win & Pl
11	5	1	3	1	£66,593

	Date	Course	Race	Prize
	1/14	Asct	3m Cls1 Gd2 Hdl heavy	£22,780
	11/13	Kemp	3m½f Cls1 List Hdl good	£14,405
125	11/13	Winc	2m6f Cls2 111-137 Hdl Hcap gd-sft	£15,640
	2/13	Tntn	3m½f Cls3 Nov Hdl heavy	£6,498
	10/12	Extr	2m7½f Cls4 Nov Am Hdl gd-sft	£2,496

Progressive mare who won a Grade 2 hurdle at Ascot last season; had won previously on good ground but has produced best form on heavy and found conditions too quick when eighth in Mares' Hurdle at Cheltenham; set to go chasing and has won a point-to-point.

Hinterland (Fr)

6 b g Poliglote - Queen Place (Diamond Prospect)

Paul Nicholls — **Christopher Giles**

PLACINGS: 1123F/1222/11U7- RPR **157+c**

Starts	1st	2nd	3rd	4th	Win & Pl
13	5	4	1	-	£104,456

	Date	Course	Race	Prize
	12/13	Sand	2m Cls1 Nov Gd1 Ch good	£22,780
	11/13	Sand	2m Cls3 Ch soft	£6,657
141	10/12	Chep	2m½f Cls2 121-141 Hdl 4yo Hcap gd-sft	£14,296
	11/11	Chel	2m½f Cls1 Gd2 Hdl 3yo gd-sft	£12,244
	5/11	Autl	1m7f List Hdl 3yo v soft	£26,897

Failed to win in first novice chase campaign two seasons ago but put that experience to good use to land soft Grade 1 at Sandown early last season; going well when fell four out in Champion Chase but bitterly disappointing back in novice company at Aintree.

Holywell (Ire)

7 b g Gold Well - Hillcrest (Thatching)

Jonjo O'Neill — **Mrs Gay Smith**

PLACINGS: 131/2222124/32U1111- RPR **165+c**

Starts	1st	2nd	3rd	4th	Win & Pl
16	6	6	2	1	£215,991

	Date	Course	Race	Prize
	4/14	Aint	3m1f Cls1 Nov Gd1 Ch good	£50,643
145	3/14	Chel	3m½f Cls1 Gd3 129-151 Ch Hcap gd-sft	£51,255
	2/14	Donc	3m Cls4 Nov Ch gd-sft	£3,769
	1/14	Catt	2m3f Cls4 Ch soft	£4,660
140	3/13	Chel	3m Cls1 List 135-148 Hdl Hcap gd-sft	£45,560
	2/12	Chep	2m4f Cls4 Mdn Hdl soft	£2,274

Has made rapid progress during spring in each of last two seasons; developed into last season's leading staying novice chaser with victory in red-hot handicap at Cheltenham Festival and runaway win over Don Cossack at Aintree; top Gold Cup contender.

Horizontal Speed (Ire)

6 b g Vertical Speed - Rockababy (King's Ride)

Philip Hobbs **Favourites Racing**

PLACINGS: 2/21S2/1221101- RPR 138+h

Starts	1st	2nd	3rd	4th	Win & Pl
11	5	4	-	-	£25,774

132	4/14	Hayd	2m4f Cls3 Nov 117-132 Hdl 4-8yo Hcap good	£8,123
	1/14	Tntn	2m3½f Cls4 Nov Hdl 4-7yo heavy	£4,224
	12/13	Tntn	2m3½f Cls4 Nov Hdl heavy	£4,106
	10/13	Extr	2m1f Cls4 Nov Hdl gd-sft	£3,249
	12/12	Uttx	2m Cls6 Mdn NHF 4-6yo heavy	£1,430

Won four times as a novice hurdler last season, making steady progress throughout campaign and proving ability to handle all types of ground; may still be improving and has physique to make a good novice chaser.

Houblon Des Obeaux (Fr)

7 b g Panoramic - Harkosa (Nikos)

Venetia Williams **Mrs Julian Blackwell**

PLACINGS: 6/11423274/1614396U- RPR 166+c

Starts	1st	2nd	3rd	4th	Win & Pl
34	7	5	5	4	£196,065

152	12/13	Asct	3m Cls1 List 132-152 Ch Hcap soft	£24,525
144	11/13	Asct	3m Cls1 Gd3 133-153 Ch Hcap gd-sft	£56,270
	11/12	Winc	2m5f Cls1 Nov Gd2 Ch gd-sft	£14,238
	10/12	Worc	2m7f Cls4 Nov Ch gd-sft	£3,054
135	1/12	Chel	3m Cls2 134-160 Hdl Hcap gd-sft	£12,512
	2/11	Hayd	2m Cls2 Hdl 4yo heavy	£6,895
	5/10	Seno	1m7f Hdl 3yo good	£5,522

Smart staying chaser who won two good handicap chases at Ascot early last season before a fine third at same track off higher mark; subsequently came up short at top level, including ninth in Gold Cup, and may need help from handicapper to win again.

Hunt Ball (Ire)

9 b g Winged Love - La Fandango (Taufan)

Nicky Henderson **Atlantic Equine**

PLACINGS: 113/P23413/68693403- RPR 161c

Starts	1st	2nd	3rd	4th	Win & Pl
27	8	2	5	3	£166,997

155	4/13	Tntn	2m3f Cls2 130-155 Ch Hcap gd-fm	£21,896
142	3/12	Chel	2m4½f Cls1 Nov List 132-142 Ch Hcap good	£28,475
127	2/12	Kemp	2m4½f Cls3 108-128 Ch Hcap good	£7,148
117	2/12	Winc	2m5f Cls3 117-130 Ch Hcap soft	£7,148
108	1/12	Winc	2m5f Cls3 105-128 Ch Hcap gd-sft	£7,913
85	12/11	Folk	2m5f Cls5 76-95 Ch Hcap good	£1,916
75	12/11	Font	2m4f Cls5 68-94 Ch Hcap soft	£1,819
69	11/11	Folk	2m5f Cls5 Nov 69-95 Ch Hcap gd-fm	£1,916

Controversial chaser who has had a chequered career since staggering improvement three seasons ago but returned as good as ever following spell in USA last season, running a fine race to be fourth in Ryanair Chase; tends to struggle on soft ground.

Hurricane Fly (Ire)

10 b g Montjeu - Scandisk (Kenmare)

Willie Mullins (Ir) **George Creighton & Mrs Rose Boyd**

PLACINGS: 11/1131/11111/1114-2 RPR 170+h

Starts	1st	2nd	3rd	4th	Win & Pl
26	21	2	2	1	£1,637,556

1/14	Leop	2m Gd1 Hdl sft-hvy	£59,583
12/13	Leop	2m Gd1 Hdl soft	£48,780
11/13	Punc	2m Gd1 Hdl yield	£39,024
4/13	Punc	2m Gd1 Hdl heavy	£97,154
3/13	Chel	2m½f Cls1 Gd1 Hdl soft	£227,800
1/13	Leop	2m Gd1 Hdl sft-hvy	£58,130
12/12	Leop	2m Gd1 Hdl soft	£46,042
11/12	Punc	2m Gd1 Hdl heavy	£40,000
4/12	Punc	2m Gd1 Hdl heavy	£80,000
1/12	Leop	2m Gd1 Hdl heavy	£59,583
5/11	Punc	2m Gd1 Hdl good	£82,759
3/11	Chel	2m½f Cls1 Gd1 Hdl good	£210,937
1/11	Leop	2m Gd1 Hdl soft	£61,638
12/10	Leop	2m Gd1 Hdl heavy	£51,770
12/10	Fair	2m4f Gd1 Hdl soft	£48,894
4/10	Punc	2m Gd1 Hdl good	£90,265
4/09	Punc	2m Nov Gd1 Hdl soft	£60,194
12/08	Leop	2m Nov Gd1 Hdl yld-sft	£38,235
11/08	Fair	2m Nov Gd1 Hdl soft	£43,015
5/08	Autl	2m3½f Gd3 Hdl 4yo v soft	£43,015
5/08	Punc	2m Mdn Hdl 4-5yo gd-fm	£6,097

Dual Champion Hurdle winner who took Grade 1 haul to record 19 races last season; twice below best later in campaign, however, including when fourth at Cheltenham, and might not retain all his ability; trainer has mooted going up in distance.

I Need Gold (Ire)

6 b g Gold Well - Coola Cross (Be My Native)

Donald McCain **Deva Racing Golden Partnership**

PLACINGS: 431/23121- RPR 138+h

Starts	1st	2nd	3rd	4th	Win & Pl
5	2	2	1	-	£10,899

3/14	Ayr	3m½f Cls4 Nov Hdl heavy	£3,994
1/14	Catt	3m1½f Cls4 Nov Hdl soft	£4,874

Showed promise in staying novice hurdles last season and showed stamina to be a real forte when winning on heavy ground at Ayr; yet to be tested at a serious level but has already won a point-to-point and should have plenty more to offer as a novice chaser.

If In Doubt (Ire)

6 b g Heron Island - Catchers Day (Catcher In The Rye)

Philip Hobbs **John P McManus**

PLACINGS: 22163/1229- RPR 143h

Starts	1st	2nd	3rd	4th	Win & Pl
9	2	4	1	-	£23,694

124	11/13	Towc	2m3½f Cls3 102-124 Hdl Hcap gd-sft	£5,254
	1/13	Towc	2m Cls4 Nov Hdl heavy	£3,119

Progressive staying hurdler last season who was unlucky not to win good races having finished second to well-handicapped pair Saphir Du Rheu and Fingal Bay; below best when ninth in Pertemps Final; still lightly raced and should continue to improve.

Indian Castle (Ire)

6 b g Dr Massini - Indian Legend (Phardante)

Ian Williams **Askew, Dick, Hernon & Reynard**

PLACINGS: 4/31212/11217- **RPR 146+c**

Starts		1st	2nd	3rd	4th	Win & Pl
8		4	3	-	-	£29,188

135	1/14	Chel	2m5f Cls2 Nov 118-144 Ch Hcap heavy	£15,640
	11/13	Weth	3m1f Cls4 Ch gd-sft	£3,899
	5/13	Prth	3m½f Cls4 Nov Hdl good	£3,249
	3/13	Newc	2m4f Cls4 Nov Hdl soft	£3,119

Began 2013 in bumpers but quickly sent chasing last season and won twice, notably in a competitive novice handicap at Cheltenham in January; only seventh when favourite for Kim Muir and since left Donald McCain; should continue to improve.

Irish Saint (Fr)

5 b/br g Saint Des Saints - Minirose (Mansonnien)

Paul Nicholls **Mrs Johnny De La Hey**

PLACINGS: 11213/F0136- **RPR 152h**

Starts		1st	2nd	3rd	4th	Win & Pl
10		4	1	2	-	£106,287

140	1/14	Asct	2m3½f Cls1 Gd2 125-145 Hdl Hcap heavy	£22,780
	2/13	Kemp	2m Cls1 Gd2 Hdl 4yo good	£15,661
	12/12	Kemp	2m Cls3 Hdl 3yo heavy	£5,848
	9/12	Autl	2m2f List Hdl 3yo v soft	£26,000

Runaway winner of big handicap hurdle at Ascot last season, relishing step up to 2m3½f for first time; fair third when favourite for Betfair Hurdle next time but less effective on quicker ground at Aintree; should make a good novice chaser.

Irving

6 b g Singspiel - Indigo Girl (Sternkoenig)

Paul Nicholls **Axom XLIX**

PLACINGS: 11119- **RPR 149+h**

Starts		1st	2nd	3rd	4th	Win & Pl
5		4	-	-	-	£45,777

	2/14	Kemp	2m Cls1 Nov Gd2 Hdl soft	£15,661
	12/13	Asct	2m Cls1 Nov Gd2 Hdl soft	£17,387
	11/13	Asct	2m Cls3 Hdl gd-sft	£6,882
	11/13	Tntn	2m1f Cls3 Nov Hdl good	£5,848

Won first four races over hurdles, culminating in Grade 2s at Ascot and Kempton on soft ground; only ninth in Supreme Novices' Hurdle when perhaps unsuited by undulating track and quicker ground, though also looked to need further.

It's A Gimme (Ire)

7 b g Beneficial - Sorcera (Zilzal)

Jonjo O'Neill **John P McManus**

PLACINGS: 414/21218/2PP/2-2110 **RPR 140+c**

Starts		1st	2nd	3rd	4th	Win & Pl
16		5	5	-	2	£59,069

132	7/14	MRas	2m6½f Cls1 List 121-142 Ch Hcap gd-sft	£28,475
	6/14	Worc	2m4f Cls4 Nov Ch gd-fm	£3,769
	2/12	Sthl	2m4½f Cls4 Nov Hdl gd-sft	£2,534
	11/11	Newb	2m½f Cls3 Mdn Hdl gd-sft	£4,224
	12/10	Extr	1m5f Cls5 NHF 3yo gd-sft	£1,952

Has reportedly been hard to train and missed virtually all of last season; flourished on return from long absence this summer and won Summer Plate at Market Rasen on only fourth run over fences; should have more to offer in good novice and handicap chases.

Ivan Grozny (Fr)

4 b g Turtle Bowl - Behnesa (Suave Dancer)

Willie Mullins (Ir) **Andrea & Graham Wylie**

PLACINGS: 21401- **RPR 134h**

Starts		1st	2nd	3rd	4th	Win & Pl
5		2	1	-	1	£25,477

	4/14	Fair	2m Gd3 Hdl 4yo gd-yld	£16,250
	1/14	Naas	2m Mdn Hdl 4yo sft-hvy	£5,750

One-time ante-post favourite for Triumph Hurdle last season after winning by 12 lengths at Naas but twice found out in better company, racing too keenly; reinforced quality when settling slightly better to land a Grade 2 at Fairyhouse; can do more.

Jetson (Ire)

9 b g Oscar - La Noire (Phardante)

Jessica Harrington (Ir) **G McGrath & Mrs Moira McGrath**

PLACINGS: 3214632/2765003154-1 **RPR 158h**

Starts		1st	2nd	3rd	4th	Win & Pl
31		6	7	4	3	£196,771

	5/14	Punc	3m Gd1 Hdl yield	£100,000
136	2/14	Punc	3m 122-150 Hdl Hcap heavy	£13,000
	11/12	Dpat	2m7f Ch sft-hvy	£4,600
124	12/11	Leop	3m 111-139 Hdl Hcap soft	£13,448
	11/11	Cork	2m4f Mdn Hdl soft	£8,328
	2/10	Navn	2m NHF 5-7yo heavy	£5,190

Surprise winner of Grade 1 staying hurdle at Punchestown in May when holding off Quevega under clever tactical ride; had previously run well in many top handicaps (third and fifth in last two Pertemps Finals) but likely to be rated out of handicaps now.

Jezki (Ire)

6 b g Milan - La Noire (Phardante)

Jessica Harrington (Ir) **John P McManus**

PLACINGS: 118/111131/11241-1 **RPR 173+h**

Starts		1st	2nd	3rd	4th	Win & Pl
15		11	1	1	1	£593,066

	5/14	Punc	2m Gd1 Hdl gd-yld	£100,000
	3/14	Chel	2m½f Cls1 Gd1 Hdl gd-sft	£238,051
	12/13	Fair	2m4f Gd1 Hdl gd-yld	£42,276
	11/13	DRoy	2m Gd2 Hdl gd-yld	£26,423
	4/13	Punc	2m Nov Gd1 Hdl soft	£40,325
	12/12	Leop	2m Nov Gd1 Hdl soft	£43,333
	12/12	Fair	2m Nov Gd1 Hdl soft	£40,625
	11/12	Naas	2m Gd3 Hdl 4yo sft-hvy	£14,896
	10/12	Naas	2m Mdn Hdl 4yo soft	£5,750
	3/12	Leop	2m NHF 4yo good	£5,750
	1/12	Leop	2m NHF 4yo yield	£4,600

Gutsy winner of last season's Champion Hurdle and backed up that performance when easily beating Hurricane Fly at Punchestown; unlucky in running and then below best when twice behind that rival previously; has also won a Grade 1 over 2m4f.

Johns Spirit (Ire)

7 b g Gold Well - Gilt Ridden (Heron Island)

Jonjo O'Neill — **Christopher W T Johnston**

PLACINGS: 2361/58126733/11540- RPR **150+c**

Starts			1st	2nd	3rd	4th	Win & Pl
22			6	4	4	1	£171,276
139	11/13	Chel	2m4½f Cls1 Gd3 137-163 Ch Hcap good				£91,120
129	10/13	Chel	2m4f Cls2 127-152 Ch Hcap good				£31,280
125	12/12	Sand	2m4½f Cls3 Nov 109-125 Ch Hcap soft				£6,498
	4/12	MRas	2m1f Cls4 Nov Hdl soft				£2,534
	10/11	Strf	2m½f Cls3 Nov Hdl 4-6yo gd-sft				£4,431
	8/11	NAbb	2m1f Cls6 NHF 4-6yo gd-sft				£1,711

Big improver at start of last season when twice successful at Cheltenham, notably in Paddy Power Gold Cup, and again ran well there when fourth in very strong Byrne Group Plate; blundered at key stage on only run at 3m and worth another chance.

Josses Hill (Ire)

6 b g Winged Love - Credora Storm (Glacial Storm)

Nicky Henderson — **A D Spence**

PLACINGS: 211221- RPR **150h**

Starts			1st	2nd	3rd	4th	Win & Pl
6			3	3	-	-	£73,875
	4/14	Aint	2m½f Cls1 Nov Gd2 Hdl gd-sft				£34,170
	12/13	Newb	2m½f Cls4 Mdn Hdl soft				£3,899
	11/13	Asct	2m Cls5 NHF 4-6yo gd-sft				£2,283

High-class 2m novice hurdler last season, finishing second in Tolworth and Supreme Novices' Hurdle before gaining deserved victory at Aintree; grand chasing type who promises to improve with age and already a leading fancy for Racing Post Arkle.

Just A Par (Ire)

7 b g Island House - Thebrownhen (Henbit)

Paul Nicholls — **C G Roach & Paul K Barber**

PLACINGS: 21122/21476- RPR **155+c**

Starts			1st	2nd	3rd	4th	Win & Pl
8			2	3	-	1	£52,733
	11/13	Newb	3m Cls1 Nov Gd2 Ch gd-sft				£18,184
	11/12	Punc	2m4f Mdn Hdl heavy				£5,750

Second to At Fishers Cross at Grade 1 level as a hurdler and made bright start to chasing career with wide-margin win on second run last season; disappointing after, reportedly suffering breathing problems, but still a fair seventh in RSA Chase.

Kapga De Cerisy (Fr)

6 ch g Kapgarde - Non Liquet (Kendor)

Venetia Williams — **A Brooks**

PLACINGS: 54255410P/4F311PB/1- RPR **152+c**

Starts			1st	2nd	3rd	4th	Win & Pl
18			5	1	1	3	£105,385
139	11/13	Sand	2m4½f Cls2 123-147 Ch Hcap soft				£25,024
	2/13	Sand	2m Cls2 Nov Ch good				£11,574
128	2/13	Sand	2m4½f Cls3 Nov 102-128 Ch Hcap heavy				£9,384
	2/12	Sand	2m½f Cls4 Hdl 4yo gd-sft				£2,599
	5/11	Comp	2m Hdl 3yo v soft				£8,276

Restricted to just one run last season but made a big impression when winning a handicap chase by 12 lengths at Sandown (fourth win out of five at that track); has proved effective on any ground from 2m to 2m5f; could progress again.

Karinga Dancer

8 b g Karinga Bay - Miss Flora (Alflora)

Harry Fry — **H B Geddes**

PLACINGS: 342/2/011/15133-1 RRPR **151+c**

Starts			1st	2nd	3rd	4th	Win & Pl
13			5	2	3	1	£37,154
137	5/14	Extr	2m3½f Cls3 112-137 Ch Hcap good				£6,330
	12/13	Donc	2m3f Cls4 Nov Ch good				£4,660
135	10/13	Aint	2m1f Cls2 122-143 Hdl Hcap gd-sft				£12,512
	4/13	Tntn	2m3½f Cls4 Nov Hdl gd-fm				£4,549
	3/13	Winc	2m Cls4 Mdn Hdl gd-sft				£3,249
	1/13	Kemp	2m Cls5 NHF std-slw				£2,599

Prolific winner over hurdles during 2013 and expected to be a top novice chaser last season (sent off a short-priced favourite for all four starts over fences up to Exeter win in May); fell just short of that billing due to sloppy jumping but looks capable of better.

Katenko (Fr)

8 b g Laveron - Katiana (Villez)

Venetia Williams — **A Brooks**

PLACINGS: 6F2P874/F0211/F4430- RPR **163+c**

Starts			1st	2nd	3rd	4th	Win & Pl
27			7	3	2	4	£301,369
147	1/13	Chel	2m5f Cls1 Gd3 135-160 Ch Hcap heavy				£28,475
136	1/13	Sand	3m½f Cls2 130-156 Ch Hcap soft				£31,280
	11/10	Autl	2m5½f Gd3 Ch 4yo heavy				£59,735
	10/10	Autl	2m5½f List Ch 4yo heavy				£38,230
	9/10	Autl	2m1½f Ch 4yo v soft				£21,239
	4/10	Autl	2m2f Hdl 4yo v soft				£29,735
	4/10	Autl	2m1½f Hdl 4yo heavy				£18,690

Made rapid progress two seasons and looked a lively Gold Cup outsider until suffering from colic; generally disappointing last season but shaped with promise a couple of times, most notably when not beaten far in Peter Marsh Chase; something to prove.

Katgary (Fr)

4 b g Ballingarry - Kotkira (Subotica)

Paul Nicholls — **Andrea & Graham Wylie**

PLACINGS: 3/31126- RPR **130h**

Starts			1st	2nd	3rd	4th	Win & Pl
6			2	1	2	-	£46,182
	11/13	Engh	2m1½f Hdl 3yo heavy				£18,732
	10/13	Dax	2m1½f Hdl 3yo gd-sft				£6,634

Unlucky not to win last season's Fred Winter Hurdle at Cheltenham when twice hampered before finishing fast in second; had been well handicapped on strength of two wins in France, though only sixth when favourite after 7lb rise at Aintree.

Kayf Moss

6 b g Kayf Tara - Madam Mosso (Le Moss)

John Flint — L H & Mrs T Evans

PLACINGS: 220/5681118- — RPR **144h**

Starts		1st	2nd	3rd	4th	Win & Pl
10		3	2	-	-	£40,806
	2/14	Font	2m4f Cls1 Gd2 Hdl heavy			£28,475
110	2/14	Ffos	2m4f Cls3 110-128 Hdl Hcap heavy			£6,498
96	1/14	Leic	2m4½f Cls4 82-108 Hdl Hcap heavy			£4,549

Rapid improver midway through last season when winning three times on heavy ground including a Grade 2 at Fontwell; bound to find things tougher having gone up 47lb but better than he showed next time at Aintree when perhaps unsuited by quicker ground.

Kaylif Aramis

7 b g Kayf Tara - Ara (Birthright)

Nigel Twiston-Davies — The Grangers

PLACINGS: 25/3351315/3F651F2P- — RPR **141h**

Starts		1st	2nd	3rd	4th	Win & Pl
19		3	3	4	-	£59,954
131	2/14	Asct	2m3½f Cls2 124-143 Hdl Hcap soft			£24,760
122	3/13	Uttx	2m4½f Cls3 119-132 Hdl Hcap heavy			£7,507
112	2/13	Ffos	2m4f Cls3 105-130 Hdl Hcap heavy			£6,498

Progressive handicap hurdler last season and may well have done even better but for two falls when in contention at Cheltenham, most notably in Coral Cup; relished step up to 3m when second at Aintree next time but pulled up at Sandown on final start.

Killala Quay

7 b g Karinga Bay - Madam Bijou (Atraf)

Charlie Longsdon — Richard & Mrs Susan Perkins

PLACINGS: 15/1171P45- — RPR **149+h**

Starts		1st	2nd	3rd	4th	Win & Pl
9		4	-	-	1	£35,203
	12/13	Sand	2m4f Cls1 Nov Gd2 Hdl gd-sft			£15,946
	10/13	Chep	2m4f Cls4 Nov Hdl good			£3,899
	6/13	Aint	2m4f Cls4 Nov Hdl gd-sft			£4,549
	5/12	Uttx	2m Cls6 NHF 4-6yo good			£1,754

Patchy record in novice hurdles last season but proved very smart on his day, winning a Grade 2 at Sandown from Beat That and finishing fourth in Neptune Novices' Hurdle; flopped on only start on soft ground and failed to stay when stepped up to 3m at Aintree.

Killer Crow (Ire)

5 ch g Presenting - Rivervail (River Falls)

Willie Mullins (Ir) — Gigginstown House Stud

PLACINGS: 31-1 — RPR **122+b**

Starts		1st	2nd	3rd	4th	Win & Pl
3		2	-	1	-	£10,875
	6/14	List	2m4f NHF 4-7yo good			£5,750
	3/14	Cork	2m NHF 4-7yo heavy			£4,600

Won bumpers in March and June, making virtually all on both occasions and benefiting from stiff test of stamina (heavy ground for first win and stepped up to 2m4f on good next time); looks an excellent staying novice hurdler in the making.

Killultagh Vic (Ire)

5 b g Old Vic - Killultagh Dawn (Phardante)

Willie Mullins (Ir) — Mrs Rose Boyd & Mrs Marie J Armstrong & James Boyc

PLACINGS: 3/2116-5 — RPR **138+b**

Starts		1st	2nd	3rd	4th	Win & Pl
5		2	1	-	-	£14,207
	2/14	Naas	2m NHF 4-7yo sft-hvy			£7,763
	1/14	Naas	2m3f NHF 5-7yo sft-hvy			£4,600

Dual bumper winner last season who performed with great credit when stepped up to top level, most notably when beaten just five lengths in sixth at Cheltenham, despite twice finding ground quicker than ideal; novice hurdles await.

Kings Bandit (Ire)

6 b g King's Theatre - Gentle Lady (Strong Gale)

Donald McCain — Mrs Diana L Whateley

PLACINGS: 4/4111- — RPR **135+h**

Starts		1st	2nd	3rd	4th	Win & Pl
5		3	-	-	2	£11,656
	4/14	Tntn	2m3½f Cls4 Nov Hdl good			£3,422
	4/14	Weth	2m½f Cls4 Nov Hdl gd-sft			£4,106
	2/14	Ludl	2m Cls4 Nov Hdl soft			£3,899

Unbeaten in three novice hurdles last season, albeit at a modest level, doing best when defying a double penalty at Taunton despite looking green; looks type to improve with experience and should come into his own when sent novice chasing.

Kings Palace (Ire)

6 b g King's Theatre - Sarahs Quay (Witness Box)

David Pipe — Drew, George & Johnson Family

PLACINGS: 12F/111F- — RPR **154+h**

Starts		1st	2nd	3rd	4th	Win & Pl
7		4	1	-	-	£30,247
	12/13	Chel	3m Cls1 Nov Gd2 Hdl good			£17,085
	10/13	Chel	3m1½f Cls3 Nov Hdl good			£6,256
	10/13	Font	2m6½f Cls4 Mdn Hdl good			£3,119
	12/12	Plum	2m2f Cls6 NHF 4-5yo soft			£1,437

Hugely impressive when winning first three novice hurdles last season, including two runaway victories at Cheltenham on good ground; bitterly disappointing when only eighth in Albert Bartlett Hurdle; much better than that and could be a top stayer.

ONE TO WATCH

Le Bec One of last season's best staying novice chasers and was still very much in the mix when falling four out in the RSA. Better than his current mark of 149. *[Steve Mason, Racing Post Ratings]*

Kitten Rock (Fr)

4 b g Laverock - The Cat Eater (Tagel)

Edward OíGrady (Ir) | **Mrs E J O'Grady**

PLACINGS: 112-4 | **RPR 138h**

Starts	1st	2nd	3rd	4th	Win & Pl
4	2	1	-	1	£20,475

	3/14	Limk	2m Hdl 4yo heavy	£7,475
	3/14	Navn	2m Mdn Hdl 4yo sft-hvy	£5,750

Didn't make debut until last March before running four times in two months, winning two juvenile hurdles and twice doing well at higher level (beaten a head in a Grade 3 at Fairyhouse); should benefit from another summer and looks a useful prospect.

Knock A Hand (Ire)

9 br g Lend A Hand - Knockcross (Lake Coniston)

Richard Lee | **Alan Halsall**

PLACINGS: 1111P/44502/201P312- | **RPR 143c**

Starts	1st	2nd	3rd	4th	Win & Pl
18	6	4	1	2	£40,405

133	2/14	Leic	2m7½f Cls3 Nov 123-133 Ch Hcap soft	£6,330
133	12/13	Carl	2m5f Cls3 Nov 127-133 Ch Hcap heavy	£6,498
134	2/12	Newb	3m½f Cls2 119-145 Hdl Hcap gd-sft	£5,005
	12/11	Hayd	2m4f Cls4 Nov Hdl 4-7yo heavy	£3,249
	12/11	Chep	2m4f Cls4 Nov Hdl heavy	£2,274
	11/11	Chep	2m4f Cls5 Mdn Hdl heavy	£1,689

Won two novice handicap chases last season and progressed throughout campaign despite being knocked back when lacking experience for cauldron of Welsh National; should be more ready for similar races this term; needs soft ground.

L'Unique (Fr)

5 b m Reefscape - Sans Tune (Green Tune)

Alan King | **Denis J Barry**

PLACINGS: 41131/603321-5 | **RPR 147+h**

Starts	1st	2nd	3rd	4th	Win & Pl
12	4	1	3	1	£115,056

142	4/14	Sand	2m4f Cls2 116-142 Hdl Hcap gd-sft	£18,768
	4/13	Aint	2m½f Cls1 Gd1 Hdl 4yo good	£56,270
	1/13	Kemp	2m Cls4 Hdl 4yo soft	£3,899
	12/12	Aint	2m1f Cls1 List Hdl 3yo soft	£11,390

Very smart mare who has produced best form during spring in last two seasons when encountering quicker ground; won a Grade 1 at Aintree as a juvenile and finished close third to Quevega in Mares' Hurdle at Cheltenham last season; could go novice chasing.

Lac Fontana (Fr)

5 b g Shirocco - Fontaine Riant (Josr Algarhoud)

Paul Nicholls | **Potensis Limited**

PLACINGS: 238/14111-4 | **RPR 149+h**

Starts	1st	2nd	3rd	4th	Win & Pl
9	4	1	1	2	£118,963

	4/14	Aint	2m4f Cls1 Nov Gd1 Hdl gd-sft	£42,203
139	3/14	Chel	2m1f Cls1 Gd3 132-154 Hdl Hcap good	£45,560
127	1/14	Chel	2m1f Cls2 118-141 Hdl Hcap heavy	£16,245
	10/13	Chel	2m½f Cls3 Mdn Hdl good	£6,256

Won three times at Cheltenham last season, most notably when getting up late to land County Hurdle; equally effective when stepped up to 2m4f to win Grade 1 novice hurdle at Aintree and may have found subsequent trip to Punchestown one run too many.

Lamb Or Cod (Ire)

7 ch g Old Vic - Princess Lizzie (Homo Sapien)

Philip Hobbs — **Terry Warner**

PLACINGS: 93421/18P/2052331-11 — **RPR 146+c**

Starts	1st	2nd	3rd	4th	Win & Pl
17	5	3	3	1	£64,070

	8/14	NAbb	3m2½f Cls3 Nov Ch gd-fm	£9,177
	5/14	Fknm	3m½f Cls3 Nov Ch good	£7,214
128	4/14	Chel	3m1½f Cls3 Nov 110-130 Ch Hcap good	£6,279
124	10/12	Chep	2m4f Cls1 Gd3 119-145 Hdl Hcap gd-sft	£19,933
	2/12	Thur	2m Mdn Hdl sft-hvy	£4,313

Has finished first and second in Silver Trophy at Chepstow in last two seasons; later sent chasing last term and overcame initial jumping problems when winning by 18 lengths in a novice handicap at Cheltenham in April; should be a useful staying handicapper.

Le Bec (Fr)

6 ch g Smadoun - La Pelode (Dress Parade)

Emma Lavelle — **Tim Syder**

PLACINGS: 23/1264/112F- — **RPR 158+c**

Starts	1st	2nd	3rd	4th	Win & Pl
10	3	3	1	1	£33,280

11/13	Chel	3m½f Cls2 Nov Ch good	£12,512
10/13	Uttx	2m4f Cls4 Ch gd-sft	£6,256
10/12	Kemp	2m5f Cls4 Nov Hdl good	£3,249

Very smart staying novice chaser last season, running big races at Cheltenham when beating Shutthefrontdoor and finishing second to Sam Winner; still going well when falling four out in RSA Chase; looks an ideal type for Hennessy Gold Cup.

Le Rocher (Fr)

4 b g Saint Des Saints - Belle Du Roi (Adieu Au Roi)

Nick Williams — **John White & Anne Underhill**

PLACINGS: U/11711- — **RPR 149+h**

Starts	1st	2nd	3rd	4th	Win & Pl
6	4	-	-	-	£69,822

1/14	Chel	2m1f Cls1 Gd2 Hdl 4yo heavy	£17,085
12/13	Chep	2m½f Cls1 Gd1 Hdl 3yo heavy	£19,933
10/13	Autl	2m1½f Hdl 3yo v soft	£18,732
6/13	Diep	2m1f Hdl 3yo gd-sft	£8,585

Outstanding juvenile hurdler during first half of last season, winning top-class contests on heavy ground at Chepstow and Cheltenham with Kentucky Hyden in second both times; missed Triumph Hurdle with leg injury; needs to prove himself on quicker ground.

Le Vent D'Antan (Fr)

5 b g Martaline - Leeloo (Dr Devious)

Elizabeth Doyle (Ir) — **Goliath Syndicate**

PLACINGS: 17/3212-1 — **RPR 143h**

Starts	1st	2nd	3rd	4th	Win & Pl
7	3	2	1	-	£30,675

4/14	Punc	2m4f Hdl gd-yld	£12,188
3/14	Navn	2m4f Mdn Hdl yld-sft	£5,750
1/13	Leop	2m NHF 4yo heavy	£4,488

Initially disappointing over hurdles last season (beaten favourite three times) but improved with time and won a conditions hurdle comprehensively at Punchestown; held in very high regard and expected to develop into a high-class novice chaser.

Lamb Or Cod (right): should hold his own in handicap chases this season

Lieutenant Colonel

5 br g Kayf Tara - Agnese (Abou Zouz)

Dessie Hughes (Ir) — **Gigginstown House Stud**

PLACINGS: **121261-3** — RPR **151+h**

Starts	1st	2nd	3rd	4th	Win & Pl
7	3	2	1	-	£46,173

	4/14	Fair	2m4f Nov Gd2 Hdl soft	£21,667
	1/14	Fair	2m Mdn Hdl sft-hvy	£5,610
	11/13	Punc	2m NHF 4yo yield	£4,488

Impressive winner of Grade 2 novice hurdle over 2m4f at Fairyhouse but looked a weak stayer in two more strongly run Grade 1 races at that trip; set to make a fine chaser but may stick to hurdles for another season if thought capable of competing in top races.

Long Run (Fr)

9 b g Cadoudal - Libertina (Balsamo)

Nicky Henderson — **Robert Waley-Cohen**

PLACINGS: **1/2213/2132/54U1F-39** — RPR **162c**

Starts	1st	2nd	3rd	4th	Win & Pl
33	15	7	6	1	£1,542,715

	2/14	Kels	3m2f Cls2 Ch gd-sft	£12,512
	12/12	Kemp	3m Cls1 Gd1 Ch heavy	£113,900
	2/12	Newb	3m Cls1 Gd2 Ch gd-sft	£17,085
	3/11	Chel	3m2½f Cls1 Gd1 Ch good	£285,050
	1/11	Kemp	3m Cls1 Gd1 Ch gd-sft	£102,618
	2/10	Wwck	2m Cls1 Nov Gd2 Ch gd-sft	£17,103
	12/09	Kemp	3m Cls1 Nov Gd1 Ch gd-sft	£34,809
	11/09	Autl	2m6f Gd1 Ch 4yo holding	£152,913
	10/09	Autl	2m4½f Gd3 Ch 4yo v soft	£65,534
	5/09	Autl	2m4½f List Ch 4yo v soft	£41,942
	3/09	Autl	2m2f Gd3 Hdl 4yo holding	£56,796
	11/08	Autl	2m2f Gd1 Hdl 3yo v soft	£89,338
	10/08	Autl	2m2f Gd2 Hdl 3yo v soft	£57,904
	9/08	Autl	2m2f Hdl 3yo soft	£22,941
	5/08	Autl	2m2f List Hdl 3yo v soft	£30,000

Top-class staying chaser in his prime, winning two King Georges as well as 2011 Gold Cup; seemed past his best last season but still came third in Punchestown Gold Cup after falling in Grand National; injured after disappointing next time in France.

Lord Windermere (Ire)

8 b g Oscar - Satellite Dancer (Satco)

Jim Culloty (Ir) — **Dr R Lambe**

PLACINGS: **F11418/221231/8761-** — RPR **170c**

Starts	1st	2nd	3rd	4th	Win & Pl
16	6	3	1	1	£469,948

	3/14	Chel	3m2½f Cls1 Gd1 Ch good	£327,326
	3/13	Chel	3m½f Cls1 Gd1 Ch gd-sft	£85,425
	12/12	Leop	2m3f Ch soft	£7,475
	3/12	Naas	2m Nov Hdl yld-sft	£7,475
	12/11	Punc	2m Nov List Hdl heavy	£19,612
	11/11	Thur	2m Mdn Hdl 5yo sft-hvy	£4,461

Dramatic and surprising winner of Cheltenham Gold Cup last season, bouncing back to form for first win since RSA Chase 12 months earlier; yet to prove anywhere near as effective on flatter tracks but could still be a big player defending Gold Cup crown.

Lots Of Memories (Ire)

7 b g Jammaal - Remember Rob (Deep Society)

Paul Fahey (Ir) — **Mrs Siobhain Fahey & John A Breen**

PLACINGS: **222321/212143P1-3** — RPR **154+h**

Starts	1st	2nd	3rd	4th	Win & Pl
15	4	6	3	1	£85,978

129	4/14	Fair	3m Nov 107-135 Hdl Hcap gd-yld	£29,792
	11/13	Cork	3m Nov Gd3 Hdl soft	£18,496
	9/13	List	2m4f Nov Hdl soft	£11,890
	4/13	Punc	2m2f NHF 5-7yo soft	£5,049

Proved himself a top-class staying novice hurdler last spring when refreshed from a break having initially struggled to build on early promise; easily won novice handicap before unlucky third to Beat That at Punchestown; looks an exciting chasing prospect.

Lyreen Legend (Ire)

7 b g Saint Des Saints - Bint Bladi (Garde Royale)

Dessie Hughes (Ir) — **Lyreen Syndicate**

PLACINGS: **3122133/12F423/556-6** — RPR **165c**

Starts	1st	2nd	3rd	4th	Win & Pl
20	4	4	4	1	£127,512

	10/12	Gway	2m6f Ch heavy	£10,063
	3/12	Thur	2m4f Nov Gd2 Hdl sft-hvy	£21,667
	12/11	Navn	2m Nov Hdl 4-5yo heavy	£7,733
	10/11	Naas	2m Mdn Hdl 4yo soft	£5,948

Without a win since chasing debut two seasons ago but has twice run fine races in defeat since then at Cheltenham Festival when second in RSA Chase and close sixth in last season's Gold Cup; perhaps unsuited by generally softer ground in Ireland.

Ma Filleule (Fr)

6 gr m Turgeon - Kadaina (Kadalko)

Nicky Henderson — **Simon Munir**

PLACINGS: **3111P/5122102/3P121-** — RPR **164+c**

Starts	1st	2nd	3rd	4th	Win & Pl
20	7	4	4	1	£207,456

150	4/14	Aint	2m5½f Cls1 Gd3 129-155 Ch Hcap good	£67,524
137	12/13	Kemp	3m Cls2 118-139 Ch Hcap soft	£25,024
	2/13	Wwck	2m3f Cls1 Gd2 Hdl heavy	£17,085
	10/12	Hayd	2m Cls4 Nov Hdl gd-sft	£3,899
	3/12	Autl	2m1½f Ch 4yo v soft	£21,200
	2/12	Ange	2m2½f Ch 4yo gd-sft	£10,400
	12/11	Ange	2m2½f Ch 3yo v soft	£7,862

Winning chaser in France who went from strength to strength when switched to fences in Britain for first time last season; close second to Holywell at Cheltenham before gaining deserved compensation in Topham Chase at Aintree; could progress again.

ONE TO WATCH

Many Clouds His runs leading up to the festival mark him down as a very well handicapped second-season chaser and he looks an ideal sort for the Hennessy. *[Steve Mason, Racing Post Ratings]*

Magnifique Etoile

7 b g Kayf Tara - Star Diva (Toulon)

Charlie Longsdon — **Magnifique Etoile Partnership**

PLACINGS: 342/11130/1F0- RPR **152+h**

Starts	1st	2nd	3rd	4th	Win & Pl
11	4	1	2	1	£20,179

130	10/13	Strf	2m3f Cls3 109-130 Hdl Hcap soft	£6,330
	12/11	Bang	2m1f Cls4 Nov Hdl gd-sft	£2,274
	10/11	Strf	2m½f Cls4 Mdn Hdl gd-fm	£3,249
	9/11	MRas	2m1f Cls6 Am NHF 4-6yo good	£1,300

Finished third in 2012 Tolworth Hurdle as a novice but subsequently missed more than 18 months with a leg injury; showed class with 12-length win at Stratford on return last season but fell next time and disappointed in Coral Cup; set to go novice chasing.

Majala (Fr)

8 b g Lavirco - Majae (Dom Pasquini)

Tom George — **Sharon Nelson, Jayne Taylor & Darren Taylor**

PLACINGS: 2/2P32/11161/2FP571- RPR **146+c**

Starts	1st	2nd	3rd	4th	Win & Pl
22	6	4	2	-	£133,693

138	4/14	Prth	2m4½f Cls2 124-150 Ch Hcap soft	£16,245
	4/13	Autl	2m2f Hdl v soft	£18,732
	2/13	Wwck	2m Cls1 Nov Gd2 Ch heavy	£23,048
	12/12	Hayd	2m Cls2 Nov Ch heavy	£9,747
	11/12	Tntn	2m½f Cls3 Ch soft	£5,848
0	3/11	Autl	2m2f Hdl 5yo Hcap v soft	£20,690

Smart novice chaser two seasons ago (Grade 2 winner) but disappointed for much of last season; bounced back to form when winning at Perth in April and still rated well below peak mark even after subsequent 8lb rise so should win more races.

Mala Beach (Ire)

6 b g Beneficial - Peppardstown (Old Vic)

Gordon Elliott (Ir) — **C Jones**

PLACINGS: 90/930121/231- RPR **156+h**

Starts	1st	2nd	3rd	4th	Win & Pl
11	3	2	2	-	£67,770

	1/14	Gowr	3m Gd2 Hdl soft	£21,667
	3/13	Fair	2m4f Nov Gd2 Hdl soft	£21,138
	1/13	Leop	2m4f Mdn Hdl heavy	£6,171

Developed into a smart staying hurdler last season, easily winning a Grade 2 at Gowran having been unsuited by slow pace when first stepped up to 3m; missed Cheltenham as trainer had stated he would run only on very soft ground; could be a top novice chaser.

Mallowney (Ire)

8 br g Oscar - Silkaway (Buckskin)

Timothy Doyle (Ir) — **Glebeland Farm Partnership**

PLACINGS: 31572711F5/21F232-12 RPR **152+c**

Starts	1st	2nd	3rd	4th	Win & Pl
24	5	6	3	-	£85,182

139	5/14	Punc	2m 117-145 Ch Hcap yield	£27,083
	1/14	Naas	2m Nov Ch soft	£10,833
	3/13	Naas	2m Nov List Hdl soft	£13,211
119	2/13	Naas	2m 103-128 Hdl Hcap sft-hvy	£9,256
	7/12	Baln	2m Mdn Hdl heavy	£4,313

Ran consistently well in good novice chases last season but took form to another level when encountering quicker ground during spring, most notably when winning a big 2m handicap chase at Punchestown; ideally suited by a strong gallop.

Many Clouds (Ire)

7 br g Cloudings - Bobbing Back (Bob Back)

Oliver Sherwood — **Trevor Hemmings**

PLACINGS: 190/21212P/1212B4- RPR **157+c**

Starts	1st	2nd	3rd	4th	Win & Pl
15	5	5	-	1	£56,682

	12/13	Weth	2m4½f Cls3 Nov Ch soft	£6,498
	11/13	Carl	2m4f Cls4 Ch heavy	£6,498
	2/13	Extr	2m3f Cls4 Nov Hdl heavy	£4,549
	11/12	Asct	2m3½f Cls3 Mdn Hdl soft	£6,256
	2/12	Weth	2m½f Cls6 NHF 4-5yo gd-sft	£1,437

Long seen as a fine chasing prospect and did well as a novice last season, winning twice and finishing second in Reynoldstown Chase to subsequent RSA hero O'Faolains Boy; brought down when going well six out in that Cheltenham race; could progress again.

Manyriverstocross (Ire)

9 b g Cape Cross - Alexandra S (Sadler's Wells)

Alan King — **Mrs M C Sweeney**

PLACINGS: 131737/3/034/162715- RPR **148c**

Starts	1st	2nd	3rd	4th	Win & Pl
16	4	1	4	1	£106,751

138	3/14	Asct	2m1f Cls2 Nov 120-143 Ch Hcap good	£25,992
	11/13	Extr	2m1½f Cls2 Nov Ch gd-sft	£12,628
	12/09	Sand	2m4f Cls1 Nov Gd2 Hdl heavy	£17,103
	11/09	Chep	2m½f Cls4 Mdn Hdl soft	£2,927

Missed two and a half years through injury having once been a smart novice hurdler; took well to fences last season and won 2m novice handicap chase at Ascot having looked a weak stayer when seventh in similar race over 2m5f at Cheltenham Festival.

Mayfair Music (Ire)

5 br m Presenting - Native Bid (Be My Native)

Nicky Henderson **Mrs E Roberts**

PLACINGS: 1/511- RPR 136+h

Starts	1st	2nd	3rd	4th	Win & Pl
4	3	-	-	-	£17,726

	3/14	Donc	3m½f Cls1 Nov List Hdl good	£11,546
	12/13	Winc	2m6f Cls4 Mdn Hdl good	£3,249
	4/13	Fknm	2m Cls5 Mdn NHF 4-6yo good	£2,395

Won both runs over hurdles after finishing fifth in Listed bumper at Cheltenham last season; particularly impressive when landing Listed mares' novice hurdle at Doncaster; has size and scope to improve again and could make a fine chaser.

Medermit (Fr)

10 gr g Medaaly - Miss D'Hermite (Solicitor)

Alan King **The Dunkley & Reilly Partnership**

PLACINGS: /1R12142/132234/48-4 RPR 157c

Starts	1st	2nd	3rd	4th	Win & Pl
29	8	7	5	5	£320,013

154	11/11	Extr	2m1½f Cls1 Gd2 140-160 Ch Hcap good	£34,170
	2/11	Sand	2m4½f Cls1 Nov Gd1 Ch good	£21,094
	12/10	Plum	2m1f Cls3 Nov Ch gd-sft	£6,262
	10/10	Aint	2m Cls3 Nov Ch gd-sft	£6,983
	1/10	Hayd	2m½f Cls1 Gd2 Hdl soft	£25,655
	12/08	Asct	2m Cls1 Nov Gd2 Hdl gd-sft	£17,103
	11/08	Folk	2m1½f Cls4 Nov Hdl 4-6yo soft	£3,253
	5/08	Nant	2m1½f Hdl 4yo holding	£5,294

Formerly high-class hurdler and chaser but missed nearly two years through injury before comeback fourth in Ascot Chase last season; much closer fourth in Punchestown Gold Cup two runs later and may still have a future in good staying chases.

Medinas (Fr)

7 b/br g Malinas - Medicis (Sicyos)

Alan King **Mr & Mrs F D Bell**

PLACINGS: 1/23116/22411P/2275- RPR 156h

Starts	1st	2nd	3rd	4th	Win & Pl
17	5	6	1	1	£108,800

148	3/13	Chel	2m5f Cls1 Gd3 134-150 Hdl Hcap gd-sft	£45,560
140	2/13	Ffos	2m4f Cls2 134-154 Hdl Hcap heavy	£31,280
	4/12	Font	2m6½f Cls4 Nov Hdl good	£2,014
	3/12	Hrfd	2m4f Cls4 Nov Hdl 4-7yo soft	£2,534
	3/11	Newb	2m½f Cls5 NHF 4-6yo soft	£2,055

Won Coral Cup and Welsh Champion Hurdle two seasons ago but just came up short when forced into higher grade last season, doing best when second in Grade 2 staying hurdles to Tidal Bay and Celestial Halo; set to go novice chasing.

Melodic Rendezvous

8 ch g Where Or When - Vic Melody (Old Vic)

Jeremy Scott **Cash For Honours**

PLACINGS: 12/2111/151177- RPR 157+h

Starts	1st	2nd	3rd	4th	Win & Pl
12	7	2	-	-	£167,537

	2/14	Winc	2m Cls1 Gd2 Hdl heavy	£34,170
	1/14	Hayd	2m Cls1 Gd2 Hdl heavy	£42,914
150	11/13	Winc	2m Cls1 Gd2 130-150 Hdl Hcap gd-sft	£34,170
	2/13	Extr	2m1f Cls1 Nov List Hdl heavy	£11,390
	1/13	Sand	2m½f Cls1 Nov Gd1 Hdl heavy	£19,933
	12/12	Chel	2m1f Cls3 Nov Hdl 4-6yo heavy	£7,507
	3/12	Chep	2m½f Cls6 NHF 4-6yo gd-sft	£1,365

Won Haydock Champion Hurdle Trial and Kingwell Hurdle last season to add to earlier Tolworth victory, all three coming on heavy ground; badly outpaced when seventh in Champion Hurdle on good to soft; failed to stay on only run at 3m; set to go novice chasing.

Mendip Express (Ire)

8 b/br g King's Theatre - Mulberry (Denel)

Harry Fry — **The Mendip Syndicate**

PLACINGS: **31/FU1/11111/1113P-** — RPR **156+c**

Starts	1st	2nd	3rd	4th	Win & Pl
6	3	-	1	-	£24,703

139	1/14	Chel	3m2½f Cls2 117-139 Ch Hcap soft	£12,512
	11/13	Bang	3m½f Cls3 Nov Ch soft	£6,498
	11/13	Weth	3m1f Cls4 Nov Ch gd-sft	£4,549

Won first three chases last season, most notably from smart handicappers on desperate ground at Cheltenham; suspicion that may have left a mark when well beaten next time and finished distressed when pulled up in Scottish National; worth another chance.

Menorah (Ire)

9 b g King's Theatre - Maid For Adventure (Strong Gale)

Philip Hobbs — **Mrs Diana L Whateley**

PLACINGS: **411F314/313P22/P051-** — RPR **172+c**

Starts	1st	2nd	3rd	4th	Win & Pl
29	11	5	3	3	£440,063

	4/14	Sand	2m6f Cls1 List Ch gd-sft	£28,475
	12/12	Kemp	2m4½f Cls1 Gd2 Ch heavy	£22,780
	4/12	Aint	2m4f Cls1 Nov Gd1 Ch gd-sft	£42,713
	1/12	Kemp	2m Cls2 Nov Ch good	£13,436
	12/11	Tntn	2m3f Cls4 Nov Ch gd-sft	£3,764
	12/10	Chel	2m1f Cls1 Gd2 Hdl gd-sft	£85,515
151	11/10	Chel	2m½f Cls1 Gd3 127-151 Hdl Hcap gd-sft	£57,010
	3/10	Chel	2m½f Cls1 Nov Gd1 Hdl gd-sft	£57,010
	12/09	Kemp	2m Cls2 Nov Hdl gd-sft	£10,019
	11/09	Wwck	2m Cls4 Nov Hdl good	£2,927
	8/09	Naas	2m3f NHF 4-7yo soft	£5,702

Has a poor strike-rate over fences for horse of such ability and disappointed for much of last season until reinforcing class with runaway win in Listed chase at Sandown in April; won Peterborough Chase on heavy ground in 2012 but considered best on good.

Merry King (Ire)

7 ch g Old Vic - Merry Queen (Anshan)

Jonjo O'Neill — **F Gillespie**

PLACINGS: **661185/41220/2553P4-** — RPR **144c**

Starts	1st	2nd	3rd	4th	Win & Pl
18	3	3	1	2	£62,937

120	11/12	Bang	2m4½f Cls4 107-120 Ch Hcap gd-sft	£3,217
	2/12	Ffos	2m4f Cls4 Nov Hdl 4-7yo soft	£3,249
	1/12	Leic	2m4½f Cls4 Nov Hdl heavy	£3,249

Ran very well in succession of top staying handicaps last season, registering top-five finishes in Hennessy Gold Cup, Welsh National and Scottish National; likely to be a contender in similar races again and could be a Grand National type.

Midnight Prayer

9 b g Midnight Legend - Onawing Andaprayer (Energist)

Alan King — **The Legends Partnership**

PLACINGS: **241/9/1941/61U211-** — RPR **146+c**

Starts	1st	2nd	3rd	4th	Win & Pl
14	6	2	-	2	£79,033

	3/14	Chel	4m Cls1 Nov List Am Ch gd-sft	£50,966
	2/14	Wwck	3m2f Cls3 Nov Ch soft	£9,615
123	10/13	Strf	2m7f Cls3 Nov 111-125 Ch Hcap soft	£6,330
115	4/13	Winc	2m6f Cls3 104-125 Hdl Hcap good	£5,848
	12/12	Hrfd	2m4f Cls5 Mdn Hdl heavy	£2,144
	4/10	Extr	2m1f Cls6 NHF 4-6yo good	£1,301

Game winner of last season's National Hunt Chase, taking advantage of main rivals running below form; clearly appreciates a stiff test of stamina and seems to cope with all types of ground; likely to be a contender for top staying handicap chases.

Melodic Rendezvous: very smart hurdler who is set to tackle fences this season

Milsean (Ire)

5 b g Milan - Boro Supreme (Supreme Leader)

Willie Mullins (Ir) — **Gigginstown House Stud**

PLACINGS: 1/121- — **RPR 145+B**

Starts	1st	2nd	3rd	4th	Win & Pl
3	2	1	-	-	£11,683

	Date	Course	Race	Prize
	3/14	Limk	2m3f NHF 5-7yo heavy	£5,750
	1/14	Navn	2m NHF 5-7yo soft	£4,600

Galloped rivals into submission when winning a Limerick bumper in March by 25 lengths having finished second when ridden with more restraint previously; looks every inch a chaser (has won a point-to-point) and could go straight over fences.

Minella Foru (Ire)

5 b g King's Theatre - Shannon Rose (Topanoora)

Eddie Harty (Ir) — **John P McManus**

PLACINGS: 1/11736- — **RPR 142h**

Starts	1st	2nd	3rd	4th	Win & Pl
5	2	-	1	-	£25,717

	Date	Course	Race	Prize
	11/13	Navn	2m Nov Gd3 Hdl yield	£15,325
	9/13	List	2m Mdn Hdl 4yo yield	£6,171

Won first two races over hurdles last season and went on to run with credit in face of some stiff tasks, most notably when producing a terrific effort for one so inexperienced to finish sixth in County Hurdle; should have lots more to offer.

Module (Fr)

7 b g Panoramic - Before Royale (Dauphin Du Bourg)

Tom George — **Simon W Clarke**

PLACINGS: 1/5B1/F114/2413-P — **RPR 166c**

Starts	1st	2nd	3rd	4th	Win & Pl
13	5	1	1	2	£134,148

	Date	Course	Race	Prize
	2/14	Newb	2m1f Cls1 Gd2 Ch heavy	£28,475
	1/13	Leic	2m Cls4 Nov Ch heavy	£3,899
	12/12	Newb	2m2½f Cls3 Nov Ch heavy	£7,148
130	1/12	Chel	2m1f Cls2 119-145 Hdl Hcap gd-sft	£13,646
	4/11	Engh	2m1½f Hdl 4yo soft	£19,862

Developed into a high-class two-mile chaser last season, winning Game Spirit Chase in between near miss in Haldon Gold Cup and third in Champion Chase; has also run well up to 2m4f, though seemed not to stay similar trip in Peterborough Chase.

Mon Parrain (Fr)

8 b g Trempolino - Kadaina (Kadalko)

Paul Nicholls — **Mr & Mrs J D Cotton**

PLACINGS: 316112/5312/734/P81- — **RPR 145c**

Starts	1st	2nd	3rd	4th	Win & Pl
20	7	2	3	1	£129,657

	Date	Course	Race	Prize
137	4/14	Chel	3m1½f Cls2 123-145 Ch Hcap good	£12,512
133	3/11	Sand	3m½f Cls3 113-135 Ch Hcap good	£6,505
	12/09	Autl	2m1½f Ch 3yo heavy	£23,301
	11/09	Nanc	2m1f Ch v soft	£7,922
	10/09	Toul	2m1½f Ch 3yo gd-sft	£10,252
	8/09	Vich	2m½f Hdl 3yo	£7,922
	5/09	Roya	2m Hdl 3yo	£6,058

Out for 18 months before returning last season and bounced back to form on final start when getting up close home at Cheltenham; rated 8lb below peak even after subsequent rise and could be an Aintree type having impressed over National fences before.

Monbeg Dude (Ire)

9 b g Witness Box - Ten Dollar Bill (Accordion)

Michael Scudamore — **Oydunow**

PLACINGS: /45213P/U113P/34157- — **RPR 151+c**

Starts	1st	2nd	3rd	4th	Win & Pl
18	4	2	3	2	£129,044

	Date	Course	Race	Prize
138	12/13	Chel	3m1½f Cls1 Gd3 124-150 Ch Hcap good	£25,628
128	1/13	Chep	3m5½f Cls1 Gd3 127-153 Ch Hcap heavy	£51,255
121	11/12	Chel	3m3½f Cls1 Gd3 121-147 Ch Hcap soft	£28,475
107	11/11	Ling	3m Cls4 98-115 Ch Hcap good	£3,249

Smart stayer who won Welsh National in 2012 and added another big prize at Cheltenham last season; well fancied for Grand National but could manage only seventh after jumping errors; should continue to be a force in major staying handicaps.

Monksland (Ire)

7 b g Beneficial - Cush Jewel (Executive Perk)

Noel Meade (Ir) — **Mrs Patricia Hunt**

PLACINGS: 01113/121/

Starts	1st	2nd	3rd	4th	Win & Pl
7	5	1	1	-	£103,433

	Date	Course	Race	Prize
	12/12	Leop	3m Gd2 Hdl soft	£21,667
	11/12	DRoy	2m Gd2 Hdl yld-sft	£27,083
	1/12	Naas	2m4f Nov Gd2 Hdl sft-hvy	£20,313
	12/11	Navn	2m Mdn Hdl 4yo sft-hvy	£5,948
	11/11	DRoy	2m NHF 4-7yo soft	£5,056

Out through injury since landing a Grade 1 staying hurdle at Leopardstown at end of 2012; had looked a leading World Hurdle contender at that time having seemed unlucky (hampered when making headway) when third to Simonsig in Neptune Hurdle.

Montbazon (Fr)

7 b/br g Alberto Giacometti - Duchesse Pierji (Cadoudal)

Alan King — **David Sewell**

PLACINGS: 212/32114/037-44 — RPR **148h**

Starts	1st	2nd	3rd	4th	Win & Pl
13	3	3	2	3	£67,560

	2/12	Newb	2m½f Cls4 Nov Hdl gd-sft	£3,249
	1/12	Plum	2m Cls5 Mdn Hdl gd-sft	£1,916
	3/11	Donc	2m½f Cls2 NHF 4-5yo good	£34,585

Missed nearly two years through injury following fourth in 2012 Supreme Novices' Hurdle; ran a huge race on second run back last season when third in County Hurdle but disappointed on softer ground subsequently; could go novice chasing.

More Of That (Ire)

6 b g Beneficial - Guigone (Esprit Du Nord)

Jonjo O'Neill — **John P McManus**

PLACINGS: 1/1111- — RPR **172+h**

Starts	1st	2nd	3rd	4th	Win & Pl
5	5	-	-	-	£211,387

	3/14	Chel	3m Cls1 Gd1 Hdl good	£156,613
	12/13	Chel	2m4½f Cls1 Gd2 Hdl good	£22,780
137	11/13	Hayd	2m4f Cls2 121-147 Hdl Hcap soft	£24,692
130	11/13	Weth	2m4f Cls3 110-131 Hdl Hcap gd-sft	£5,523
	12/12	Folk	2m1½f Cls5 Mdn Hdl soft	£1,779

Sensational World Hurdle winner last season on only his fifth run, becoming first horse to ever beat Annie Power; still unexposed and should continue to progress; sets the standard in staying hurdle division but also has scope to make a top-class chaser.

Morning Assembly (Ire)

7 b g Shantou - Barrack Village (Montelimar)

Pat Fahy (Ir) — **Clipper Logistics Group Ltd**

PLACINGS: 13/21F1/1123-3 — RPR **156c**

Starts	1st	2nd	3rd	4th	Win & Pl
11	5	2	3	-	£117,165

	11/13	Punc	2m6f Nov Gd2 Ch yield	£20,874
	10/13	Punc	2m4f Ch yld-sft	£6,732
	4/13	Punc	3m Nov Gd1 Hdl soft	£40,325
	1/13	Naas	2m3f Mdn Hdl heavy	£7,854
	2/12	Punc	2m NHF 4-7yo heavy	£4,888

Among Ireland's leading staying novice chasers last season, though slightly disappointing he couldn't win a Grade 1 (placed three times) after impressive earlier win over Don Cossack at Punchestown; may be best sticking to right-handed tracks.

Moscow Mannon (Ire)

8 b g Moscow Society - Unfaithful Thought (Mind Games)

Henry de Bromhead (Ir) — **Jonathan Flanagan**

PLACINGS: 31114/1432/4124-2 — RPR **158c**

Starts	1st	2nd	3rd	4th	Win & Pl
14	5	3	2	4	£70,991

	2/14	Naas	2m Ch sft-hvy	£6,900
	12/12	Navn	2m Mdn Hdl heavy	£7,763
	1/12	Gowr	2m NHF 4-7yo sft-hvy	£7,479
	12/11	Fair	2m NHF 4-7yo sft-hvy	£6,246
	7/11	Gway	2m NHF 4-7yo good	£5,948

Hasn't quite lived up to big early expectations

***Monksland:* smart hurdler is due to return from injury**

but showed some smart form as a novice chaser last season and finished second to God's Own in a Grade 1 at Punchestown (benefited from sitting off overly strong gallop); needs to progress again.

Mount Benbulben (Ire)

9 b g Beneficial - Dramatic Dame (Buckskin)

Gordon Elliott (Ir) **Barry Connell**

PLACINGS: **S1127/3F1P24141/U42-** RPR **165+c**

Starts	1st	2nd	3rd	4th	Win & Pl
20	7	3	1	4	£132,182

4/13	Punc	3m1f Nov Gd1 Ch soft	£40,325
2/13	Thur	2m2f Ch soft	£12,154
12/12	Fair	2m5½f Ch soft	£6,900
11/11	Navn	2m4f Nov Gd2 Hdl sft-hvy	£21,013
11/11	Thur	2m2f Mdn Hdl 5-6yo sft-hvy	£4,461
3/11	Limk	2m3f NHF 5-7yo soft	£5,948
2/11	Thur	2m NHF 5-7yo soft	£4,759

Grade 1 winner as a novice chaser two seasons ago but has continued to be plagued by jumping errors and largely disappointed last season before missing end of term with a fractured splint bone; best going right-handed (kept to such tracks for last six runs).

Mountain Tunes (Ire)

5 br g Mountain High - Art Lover (Over The River)

Jonjo O'Neill **John P McManus**

PLACINGS: **31/11-** RPR **131+h**

Starts	1st	2nd	3rd	4th	Win & Pl
2	2	-	-	-	£6,238

12/13	Towc	2m5f Cls4 Nov Hdl soft	£3,119
11/13	Towc	2m5f Cls4 Nov Hdl gd-sft	£3,119

Won both novice hurdles last season over 2m5f at Towcester, doing particularly well to defy a penalty on second occasion; seems sure to appreciate further and should do well when sent novice chasing having already won a point-to-point; useful prospect.

Mountain Tunes: provided Tony McCoy with his 4,000th winner when scoring at Towcester last season

Mountainous (Ire)

9 b g Milan - Mullaghcloga (Glacial Storm)

Richard Lee — **Walters Plant Hire & James & Jean Potter**

PLACINGS: **2/31175/21241/3315F-** — RPR **147c**

Starts	1st	2nd	3rd	4th	Win & Pl
16	5	3	3	1	£90,115

137	12/13	Chep	3m5½f Cls1 Gd3 137-163 Ch Hcap heavy	£56,950
129	3/13	Ffos	3m Cls3 119-135 Ch Hcap heavy	£6,389
	12/12	Chep	3m Cls3 Ch heavy	£7,148
120	1/12	Ffos	2m4f Cls3 105-128 Hdl Hcap soft	£4,549
108	12/11	Ffos	2m Cls3 97-120 Hdl Hcap heavy	£4,549

Has won four out of six races on heavy ground, most notably when landing Welsh National at Chepstow last season from 5lb out of handicap; prominent when falling at Valentine's in Grand National; likely to be lined up for Welsh National repeat.

Moyle Park (Ire)

6 ch g Flemensfirth - Lovely Present (Presenting)

Willie Mullins (Ir) — **Mrs S Ricci**

PLACINGS: **11/13-** — RPR **137h**

Starts	1st	2nd	3rd	4th	Win & Pl
4	3	-	1	-	£66,288

	11/13	Navn	2m Mdn Hdl gd-yld	£7,293
	4/13	Punc	2m NHF 4-5yo soft	£47,967
	12/12	Leop	2m NHF 4yo soft	£5,175

Created a big impression with two bumper wins two seasons ago but wasn't as impressive in two runs over hurdles last term despite winning on debut, disappointing behind The Tullow Tank next time; should get better with time.

Mozoltov

8 b g Kayf Tara - Fairmead Princess (Rudimentary)

Willie Mullins (Ir) — **Gigginstown House Stud**

PLACINGS: **2/1213/11/131F1U-5** — RPR **154+c**

Starts	1st	2nd	3rd	4th	Win & Pl
14	7	2	2	-	£88,998

	3/14	Navn	2m1f Nov Ch heavy	£9,200
	2/14	Naas	2m4f Nov Gd2 Ch sft-hvy	£21,667
	12/13	Fair	2m Ch yld-sft	£6,171
	2/13	Punc	2m Nov Gd2 Hdl heavy	£20,874
	12/12	Gowr	2m2f Mdn Hdl soft	£5,750
	3/12	Limk	2m3f NHF 5-7yo heavy	£5,750
	1/12	Thur	2m NHF 5-7yo heavy	£4,025

Hugely talented horse who has won Grade 2 races as a novice over hurdles and fences; prevented from reaching higher level as a novice chaser last season by jumping issues, failing to complete in Grade 1 contests at Fairyhouse and Cheltenham.

Mr Mole (Ire)

6 br g Great Pretender - Emmylou Du Berlais (Kadalko)

Paul Nicholls — **John P McManus**

PLACINGS: **1/121P3/2132F1-** — RPR **144c**

Starts	1st	2nd	3rd	4th	Win & Pl
12	5	3	2	-	£43,619

	4/14	NAbb	2m5½f Cls3 Nov Ch gd-sft	£7,027
	12/13	Wwck	2m Cls4 Ch gd-sft	£5,198
126	2/13	Tntn	2m1f Cls3 Nov 110-126 Hdl Hcap heavy	£6,823
	10/12	Extr	2m1f Cls4 Nov Hdl gd-sft	£2,599
	4/12	Hrfd	2m1f Cls6 NHF 4-6yo soft	£1,365

Highly talented performer but has plenty of quirks and didn't always convince when sent chasing last season; has raced almost exclusively at 2m but successfully stepped up to 2m5½f at Newton Abbot on final start, though not extended by modest opposition.

Mullaghanoe River (Ire)

6 b g Beneficial - Wahiba Hall (Saddlers' Hall)

Noel Meade (Ir) — **Mrs Patricia Hunt**

PLACINGS: **B/12151/572F13UF-** — RPR **142+c**

Starts	1st	2nd	3rd	4th	Win & Pl
12	3	2	1	-	£25,960

	1/14	Punc	2m4f Ch sft-hvy	£6,900
	2/13	Navn	2m4f Mdn Hdl heavy	£7,293
	12/12	Leop	2m4f NHF 4-7yo soft	£5,750

Let down by jumping when sent chasing last season but did enough to suggest he is a fine prospect; gained only win over 2m4f at Punchestown but still going well when coming down five out in Irish National (third failure to get round in last five outings).

My Murphy (Ire)

8 b g Presenting - Fine De Claire (Teenoso)

Liam Burke (Ir) — **Hans Joerg Zindel**

PLACINGS: **331514/434FP/41421P-** — RPR **147c**

Starts	1st	2nd	3rd	4th	Win & Pl
18	5	1	3	5	£74,028

135	3/14	Navn	3m Nov 107-135 Ch Hcap soft	£27,083
	12/13	Fair	3m Ch soft	£4,488
	3/12	Navn	2m7f Nov Hdl soft	£9,200
	12/11	Limk	3m Nov Gd3 Hdl heavy	£15,409
	10/11	Wxfd	2m2f Mdn Hdl soft	£4,461

Failed to win during first season over fences but benefited from that experience when winning novice chases over 3m at Fairyhouse and Navan last season on soft ground; pulled up in Irish National when possibly finding conditions too quick.

My Tent Or Yours (Ire)

7 b g Desert Prince - Spartan Girl (Ela-Mana-Mou)

Nicky Henderson — **John P McManus**

PLACINGS: **122/121121/1123-** RPR **173+h**

Starts	1st	2nd	3rd	4th	Win & Pl
13	7	5	1	-	£386,031

	2/14	Kemp	2m Cls3 NHF std-slw	£6,330
	12/13	Kemp	2m Cls1 Gd1 Hdl soft	£56,950
	11/13	Newc	2m Cls1 Gd1 Hdl good	£56,270
	4/13	Aint	2m½f Cls1 Nov Gd2 Hdl gd-sft	£34,170
149	2/13	Newb	2m½f Cls1 Gd3 133-159 Hdl Hcap soft	£86,849
	1/13	Hntg	2m½f Cls4 Nov Hdl 4-7yo soft	£3,444
	11/12	Asct	2m Cls3 Nov Hdl gd-sft	£7,507
	12/11	Ludl	1m6f Cls5 NHF 4-5yo gd-sft	£2,274

Won Fighting Fifth and Christmas Hurdle last season but was just beaten in Champion Hurdle (second narrow defeat at Cheltenham having raced too keenly both times); could be even better if learning to settle.

My Wigwam Or Yours (Ire)

5 b g Beneficial - Midnight Pond (Long Pond)

Nicky Henderson — **The Happy Campers**

PLACINGS: **2342F314-** RPR **139+h**

Starts	1st	2nd	3rd	4th	Win & Pl
8	1	2	2	2	£9,649

	3/14	Newb	2m5f Cls3 Mdn Hdl good	£5,848

Has won just once in eight starts under rules, with six defeats at 2-1 or shorter, but remains held in high regard and underlined potential with runaway victory at Newbury when first stepped up to 2m5f; big horse who should make a good novice chaser.

Neck Or Nothing (Ger)

5 b g Intikhab - Nova (Winged Love)

Philip Hobbs — **R S Brookhouse**

PLACINGS: **1802-** RPR **123b**

Starts	1st	2nd	3rd	4th	Win & Pl
4	1	1	-	-	£4,964

	10/13	Punc	2m NHF 4-7yo good	£4,488

Cost 200,000gns after winning at Punchestown and finishing eighth in a Listed bumper at Cheltenham for Tom Hogan; pulled too hard in Champion Bumper on debut for Philip Hobbs before finding ground too quick when second next time; still a good prospect.

Ned Buntline

6 b g Refuse To Bend - Intrum Morshaan (Darshaan)

Noel Meade (Ir) — **John P McManus**

PLACINGS: **2/1213/3122-4** RPR **146c**

Starts	1st	2nd	3rd	4th	Win & Pl
10	3	4	2	1	£47,450

	12/13	Navn	2m1f Ch sft-hvy	£6,732
	12/12	Leop	2m Mdn Hdl 4yo soft	£6,325
	11/12	Naas	2m NHF 4yo sft-hvy	£4,600

Laid out for last season's Grand Annual Chase as a novice but just came up short when second to Savello and disappointed when favourite to make amends at Punchestown; should improve again after just five runs over fences and could stay further than 2m.

Never Enough Time (Ire)

6 b g Oscar - Ou La La (Be My Native)

Thomas Foley (Ir) — **John P McManus**

PLACINGS: **5310/P923110-** RPR **150+h**

Starts	1st	2nd	3rd	4th	Win & Pl
11	3	1	2	-	£32,302

130	2/14	Leop	2m 109-136 Hdl Hcap sft-hvy	£13,000
116	1/14	Gowr	2m1f 93-123 Hdl Hcap soft	£10,063
	3/13	Cork	2m Mdn Hdl 5yo heavy	£5,610

Sharply progressive handicap hurdler last season, romping to wide-margin wins at Gowran Park and Leopardstown before disappointing when 8-1 for County Hurdle; unable to carry big weights according to trainer so likely to go novice chasing.

Next Sensation (Ire)

7 b g Brian Boru - Road Trip (Anshan)

Michael Scudamore — **Mark Blandford**

PLACINGS: **P/31/236F6/311U145-** RPR **150+c**

Starts	1st	2nd	3rd	4th	Win & Pl
12	3	1	2	1	£22,808

133	12/13	Donc	2m½f Cls3 Nov 126-145 Ch Hcap gd-sft	£6,256
118	11/13	Newc	2m½f Cls4 94-120 Ch Hcap good	£3,769
105	10/13	Plum	2m1f Cls4 Nov 84-110 Ch Hcap soft	£3,899

Won first three completed starts over fences last season and looked unlucky when close fourth in Grand Annual, pulling into a massive lead yet still only giving best on run-in; suspicion that hard race had left its mark when disappointing fifth at Aintree next time.

Night In Milan (Ire)

8 b g Milan - Chione (Mandalus)

Keith Reveley — **Richard Collins**

PLACINGS: **22P/512323F1/2301P1-** RPR **149+c**

Starts	1st	2nd	3rd	4th	Win & Pl
29	7	6	4	1	£77,500

136	3/14	Donc	3m2f Cls2 129-150 Ch Hcap good	£32,490
130	12/13	Donc	3m Cls2 125-145 Ch Hcap good	£12,996
	4/13	Kels	2m7½f Cls4 Nov Ch gd-sft	£3,899
111	5/12	Kels	3m1f Cls3 99-125 Ch Hcap good	£7,798
107	1/12	Sthl	3m½f Cls4 95-114 Hdl Hcap gd-sft	£2,599
100	2/11	Newc	2m4f Cls4 77-100 Hdl Hcap heavy	£2,602
90	1/11	Sthl	2m4½f Cls5 70-90 Hdl Hcap gd-sft	£1,626

Progressive chaser who won twice over 3m at Doncaster last season, most notably in the Grimthorpe Chase when relishing forcing tactics; eliminated from Grand National but appeals as a likely Aintree type given sound jumping; needs good ground.

No Planning

7 b g Kayf Tara - Poor Celt (Impecunious)

Sue Smith **Mrs Jacqueline Conroy**

PLACINGS: /93412331F/31231461- RPR 148+c

Starts	1st	2nd	3rd	4th	Win & Pl
22	7	3	5	3	£82,837

137	4/14	Hayd	3m Cls2 131-157 Ch Hcap good	£31,280
132	2/14	Weth	2m4½f Cls2 125-143 Ch Hcap heavy	£11,734
127	11/13	Weth	3m1f Cls3 118-130 Ch Hcap gd-sft	£8,123
	3/13	Kels	2m1f Cls4 Nov Ch soft	£6,498
	10/12	Hexm	2m½f Cls4 Nov Ch heavy	£3,899
	10/11	Weth	2m½f Cls3 Nov Hdl good	£4,549
	5/11	Hexm	2m½f Cls6 NHF 4-6yo gd-fm	£1,370

Progressed throughout last season when winning three handicap chases, finishing off with comfortable win at Haydock on good ground; had previously won on heavy so effective in all conditions; could progress again but starts on much higher mark.

Noble Emperor (Ire)

6 b g Spadoun - Cherry Tops (Top Of The World)

Tony Martin (Ir) **John P McManus**

PLACINGS: 11- RPR 131+h

Starts	1st	2nd	3rd	4th	Win & Pl
2	2	-	-	-	£11,500

	4/14	Limk	2m3f Mdn Hdl sft-hvy	£6,900
	3/14	Navn	2m NHF 5-7yo yld-sft	£4,600

Bought by JP McManus after winning a Navan bumper in March and soon followed up in even more impressive fashion on hurdling debut by 13 lengths; looks sure to make a fine novice chaser.

O'Faolains Boy (Ire)

7 b g Oscar - Lisa's Storm (Glacial Storm)

Rebecca Curtis **Trembath, Hyde, Outhart & Hill**

PLACINGS: 2F1/31114/2P115- RPR 163+c

Starts	1st	2nd	3rd	4th	Win & Pl
10	5	1	1	1	£127,994

	3/14	Chel	3m½f Cls1 Gd1 Ch good	£85,425
	2/14	Asct	3m Cls1 Nov Gd2 Ch soft	£18,092
	2/13	Bang	3m Cls3 Nov Hdl heavy	£5,393
	1/13	Chep	2m4f Cls4 Mdn Hdl heavy	£3,249
	12/12	Chep	2m½f Cls6 NHF 4-6yo heavy	£1,754

Thorough stayer who won last season's RSA Chase in close finish from Smad Place (pair clear) having also landed Reynoldstown Chase; over the top when well beaten at Aintree next time; acts on any going; likely to be aimed at Gold Cup.

Off The Ground (Ire)

8 b g Oscar - Kaysel (Torus)

Emma Lavelle **Axom (XXVI)**

PLACINGS: /444210/346P/31180-P RPR 151+c

Starts	1st	2nd	3rd	4th	Win & Pl
16	3	1	2	4	£19,604

133	12/13	Donc	2m3f Cls3 120-140 Ch Hcap good	£7,148
118	11/13	Donc	2m3f Cls3 117-130 Ch Hcap good	£6,498
118	2/12	Sand	2m4f Cls4 Nov 100-120 Hdl Hcap gd-sft	£2,599

Took some time for penny to drop over fences but made rapid progress last winter when winning successive handicap chases at Doncaster, both on good ground; not disgracted when eighth in JLT Novices' Chase at Cheltenham but pulled up next time at Aintree.

On His Own (Ire)

10 b g Presenting - Shuil Na Mhuire (Roselier)

Willie Mullins (Ir) **Andrea & Graham Wylie**

PLACINGS: P1/B1F/1F5/1766112-8 RRPR 170c

Starts	1st	2nd	3rd	4th	Win & Pl
21	8	1	-	2	£296,932

	2/14	Fair	3m1f Gd2 Ch sft-hvy	£21,667
142	1/14	Gowr	3m1f 120-143 Ch Hcap soft	£50,000
	5/13	Slig	2m4f Hdl sft-hvy	£6,030
	2/13	Navn	2m5f Gd2 Hdl heavy	£21,138
125	1/12	Gowr	3m 123-144 Ch Hcap sft-hvy	£43,333
116	4/11	Ayr	3m1f Cls2 Nov 104-130 Ch Hcap good	£10,408
	1/11	Muss	3m Cls4 Ch gd-sft	£3,253
	12/09	Leop	2m4f NHF 4-7yo yield	£7,044

Blossomed last spring having spent previous two seasons being trained for unsuccessful attempts at Grand National; won second Thyestes Chase before 12-length win in Bobbyjo Chase and close second in Cheltenham Gold Cup; may still be improving.

One In A Milan (Ire)

9 b g Milan - Kitty Star (Montelimar)

Evan Williams **Paul Langford**

PLACINGS: 517233/3123/F3P465F- RPR 139c

Starts	1st	2nd	3rd	4th	Win & Pl
20	2	3	5	1	£32,220

	1/13	Ffos	3m Cls4 Nov Ch heavy	£3,769
	11/11	Naas	3m Mdn Hdl sft-hvy	£5,948

Highly tried last season considering lack of experience and was going well when falling at second Becher's in Grand National on only seventh run over fences; had been third in Midlands National as a novice and fourth in Welsh National last term.

Opening Batsman (Ire)

8 b g Morozov - Jolly Signal (Torus)

Harry Fry **The Twelfth Man Partnership**

PLACINGS: 23511/601211P/PF050- RPR 97c

Starts	1st	2nd	3rd	4th	Win & Pl
17	5	2	1	-	£78,442

140	2/13	Kemp	3m Cls1 Gd3 135-161 Ch Hcap good	£56,950
134	1/13	Winc	2m5f Cls3 Nov 121-135 Ch Hcap soft	£6,389
	12/12	Plum	2m4f Cls3 Ch soft	£5,848
	4/12	NAbb	2m3f Cls4 Nov Hdl gd-fm	£3,422
	3/12	Winc	2m4f Cls4 Nov Hdl gd-sft	£2,599

Won Racing Plus Chase as a novice in 2013; lost plot subsequently (failed to complete three times and then twice failed to beat a single rival) but showed much more promise in blinkers when leading to three out in bet365 Gold Cup; back to a very good mark.

Operating (Ire)

7 b g Milan - Seymourswift (Seymour Hicks)

Donald McCain | **Michael Buckley**

PLACINGS: 22/122314/3F343F31-1 | RPR 142c

Starts	1st	2nd	3rd	4th	Win & Pl
17	4	4	5	2	£78,578

128	5/14	Punc	2m5f Nov 124-145 Ch Hcap gd-yld	£50,000
	4/14	Cork	2m4f Ch yield	£6,900
	3/13	Leop	2m4f Mdn Hdl yield	£7,293
	5/12	Punc	2m1f NHF 4-7yo yield	£4,600

Expensive purchase out of Jessica Harrington's yard this summer; has gained all four wins on yielding ground or quicker and progressed well at end of last season granted favourable conditions, winning twice including novice handicap chase at Punchestown.

Oscar Hoof (Ire)

6 b g Oscar - New Legislation (Dominion Royale)

Nicky Henderson | **The Hoof Partnership**

PLACINGS: 131/211F- | RPR 135+h

Starts	1st	2nd	3rd	4th	Win & Pl
7	4	1	1	-	£15,394

3/14	Kemp	2m Cls4 Nov Hdl gd-sft	£3,899
12/13	Donc	2m3½f Cls4 Nov Hdl gd-sft	£3,249
4/13	MRas	2m1f Cls6 Am NHF 4-6yo good	£1,560
1/13	Ludl	1m6f Cls5 NHF 4-6yo soft	£1,949

Dual bumper winner who again progressed well when winning twice over hurdles last season; well backed for Grade 1 novice hurdle over 2m4f at Aintree and was still in contention when falling three out; should make an exciting novice chaser this season.

Oscar Whisky (Ire)

9 b g Oscar - Ash Baloo (Phardante)

Nicky Henderson | **Walters Plant Hire Ltd**

PLACINGS: /F1151/112P4/2111F2- | RPR 162+c

Starts	1st	2nd	3rd	4th	Win & Pl
25	15	3	1	2	£489,478

2/14	Sand	2m4½f Cls1 Nov Gd1 Ch heavy	£22,780
1/14	Chel	2m5f Cls1 Nov Gd2 Ch soft	£18,224
12/13	Chel	2m5f Cls2 Nov Ch good	£12,628
12/12	Chel	2m4½f Cls1 Gd2 Hdl heavy	£22,780
11/12	Asct	2m3½f Cls1 Gd2 Hdl heavy	£50,643
4/12	Aint	2m4f Cls1 Gd1 Hdl good	£91,096
2/12	Kemp	2m Cls6 NHF std-slw	£2,599
1/12	Chel	2m4½f Cls2 Hdl gd-sft	£12,512
12/11	Chel	2m4½f Cls1 Gd2 Hdl good	£17,085
4/11	Aint	2m4f Cls1 Gd1 Hdl good	£90,432
2/11	Ffos	2m Cls2 Hdl gd-sft	£28,179
1/11	Chel	2m4½f Cls2 Hdl gd-sft	£12,524
2/10	Sand	2m½f Cls3 Nov Hdl heavy	£5,204
12/09	Newb	2m½f Cls4 Mdn Hdl soft	£3,253
11/09	Newb	2m½f Cls5 NHF 4-6yo soft	£1,952
3/09	Newb	1m4½f Cls5 NHF 4yo good	£2,055

Dual Aintree Hurdle winner who took well to fences last season, though sole Grade 1 win at Sandown came in a soft three-runner affair; fell early at Cheltenham but finished a good second to Uxizandre at Aintree; chase mark still 8lb lower than hurdles rating.

Our Father (Ire)

8 gr g Shantou - Rosepan (Taipan)

David Pipe | **The Ives & Johnson Families**

PLACINGS: 122/10P/124/759U- | RPR 144c

Starts	1st	2nd	3rd	4th	Win & Pl
13	3	3	-	1	£29,028

	11/12	Chel	3m½f Cls2 Nov Ch soft	£12,512
129	12/11	Asct	2m6f Cls3 110-130 Hdl Hcap soft	£6,256
	1/11	Chep	2m4f Cls4 Mdn Hdl soft	£2,602

Seems best when fresh having produced high-class performances first time out in two seasons prior to last term; one-paced seventh when favourite for Hennessy Gold Cup last season and then bogged down in mud at Haydock; capable of winning a big handicap.

Outlander (Ire)

6 b g Stowaway - Western Whisper (Supreme Leader)

Willie Mullins | **Gigginstown House Stud**

PLACINGS: PP2/1116/

Starts	1st	2nd	3rd	4th	Win & Pl
4	3	-	-	-	£18,785

2/13	Naas	2m NHF 4-7yo sft-hvy	£7,573
12/12	Leop	2m NHF 4-7yo soft	£6,325
12/12	Fair	2m NHF 4yo soft	£4,888

Missed last season through injury; had looked a top-class prospect when winning first three bumpers during previous campaign, though managed only sixth when favourite for Grade 1 at Punchestown; should be an exciting novice hurdler.

Parsnip Pete

8 b g Pasternak - Bella Coola (Northern State)

Tom George | **The Parsnips**

PLACINGS: 253PF/41150/102461-U | RPR 145+c

Starts	1st	2nd	3rd	4th	Win & Pl
20	5	2	1	2	£69,093

134	4/14	Aint	2m Cls1 Gd3 126-150 Ch Hcap good	£45,560
	10/13	Sthl	2m Cls4 Nov Hdl gd-sft	£3,119
125	11/12	Newb	2m1f Cls3 Nov 119-132 Ch Hcap soft	£6,882
114	10/12	Hayd	2m Cls4 90-115 Ch Hcap soft	£3,249
	3/11	Ludl	2m Cls5 NHF 4-5yo good	£1,431

Realised long-term plan to win valuable 2m handicap chase at Aintree last season when relishing good ground and flat track; hasn't raced on ground worse than good to soft since disappointing in 2013 Grand Annual; may have more to offer.

Pearl Swan (Fr)

6 b g Gentlewave - Swanson (Diesis)

Paul Nicholls | **R J H Geffen**

PLACINGS: 11dF/0/

Starts	1st	2nd	3rd	4th	Win & Pl
4	1	1	-	-	£11,190

1/12	Tntn	2m1f Cls3 Nov Hdl gd-sft	£5,848

High-class juvenile hurdler three seasons ago

(likely to be placed in Triumph Hurdle until falling at last) but has run only once over hurdles since then in 2013 Betfair Hurdle and missed last season through injury; remains an interesting prospect.

Pendra (Ire)

6 ch g Old Vic - Mariah Rollins (Over The River)

Charlie Longsdon — **John P McManus**

PLACINGS: **1/1120/11730-** — RPR **143+c**

Starts	1st	2nd	3rd	4th	Win & Pl
10	5	1	1	-	£30,574

	11/13	Ling	2m Cls4 Nov Ch heavy	£3,769
	10/13	Carl	2m Cls4 Ch gd-sft	£4,549
	12/12	Plum	2m Cls4 Nov Hdl soft	£4,106
	11/12	Plum	2m Cls5 Mdn Hdl soft	£2,053
	3/12	Hntg	2m½f Cls6 NHF 4-6yo good	£1,365

Has threatened to land a big prize in each of last two seasons, disappointing when favourite for Coral Cup two seasons ago and then finishing third in novice handicap chase at Cheltenham Festival last term; likely to have more top handicaps on agenda.

Pepite Rose (Fr)

7 b/br m Bonbon Rose - Sambre (Turgeon)

Venetia Williams — **Falcon's Line Ltd**

PLACINGS: **114/35F23/74148162-3** — RPR **154c**

Starts	1st	2nd	3rd	4th	Win & Pl
32	8	2	7	8	£142,875

145	3/14	Newb	2m4f Cls2 120-145 Ch Hcap gd-sft	£12,660
140	12/13	Weth	2m Cls2 130-150 Ch Hcap soft	£14,427
135	3/12	Newb	2m6½f Cls1 Nov List 110-135 Ch Hcap good	£16,881
	3/12	Wwck	2m4½f Cls4 Nov Ch good	£3,899
118	3/12	Newb	2m2½f Cls3 Nov 109-127 Ch Hcap good	£7,148
111	2/12	Bang	2m1½f Cls4 Nov 93-115 Ch Hcap good	£3,054
	2/11	Wwck	2m Cls4 Hdl 4yo heavy	£2,602
	11/10	Folk	2m1½f Cls4 Hdl 3yo heavy	£2,602

Ideally suited by small fields and good ground, gaining all wins in fields of less than ten; proved she could compete at a higher level in such conditions when second to Sire De Grugy in Grade 1 at Sandown but subsequently raised to highest ever handicap mark.

Persian Snow (Ire)

8 b g Anshan - Alpine Message (Tirol)

Philip Hobbs — **D R Peppiatt**

PLACINGS: **/02127/38P/35212167-** — RPR **142+c**

Starts	1st	2nd	3rd	4th	Win & Pl
19	4	4	3	-	£43,578

132	2/14	Wwck	2m4½f Cls2 124-150 Ch Hcap soft	£18,768
	1/14	Wwck	2m4½f Cls3 Nov Ch soft	£6,498
	3/12	Hntg	2m4½f Cls4 Mdn Hdl heavy	£2,599
	10/10	Asct	2m Cls4 NHF 4-6yo good	£3,131

Steady improver over fences last season and won twice at Warwick, most notably when landing a handicap chase by eight lengths; good sixth next time in novice handicap chase at Cheltenham Festival but disappointed at same track following month.

Pineau De Re (Fr)

11 b g Maresca Sorrento - Elfe Du Perche (Abdonski)

Dr Richard Newland — **J A Provan**

PLACINGS: **0501621/60235F27131-** — RPR **157+c**

Starts	1st	2nd	3rd	4th	Win & Pl
34	7	6	4	1	£659,705

143	4/14	Aint	4m3½f Cls1 Gd3 138-161 Ch Hcap gd-sft	£561,300
133	1/14	Extr	3m Cls2 122-148 Ch Hcap soft	£11,574
125	4/13	Dpat	3m4f 102-130 Ch Hcap good	£13,211
	1/13	Thur	2m2f Ch sft-hvy	£4,488
	10/11	Thur	2m6f Hdl good	£8,922
	11/10	Limk	2m Mdn Hdl soft	£4,580
	2/08	Fair	2m NHF 4-6yo yield	£5,843

Comfortable winner of last season's Grand National to complete remarkable transformation after switch to current trainer; had also shown smart form over hurdles when close third in Pertemps Final; likely to be aimed at Aintree again.

Pont Alexandre (Ger)

6 b g Dai Jin - Panzella (Kahyasi)

Willie Mullins (Ir) — **Mrs S Ricci**

PLACINGS: **1113/**

Starts	1st	2nd	3rd	4th	Win & Pl
4	3	-	1	-	£78,830

	1/13	Leop	2m4f Nov Gd2 Hdl sft-hvy	£20,874
	12/12	Navn	2m4f Nov Gd1 Hdl heavy	£37,917
	5/12	Chol	2m1f Hdl 4yo gd-sft	£7,200

Missed last season through injury; had been a leading novice hurdler two seasons ago, winning a Grade 1 at Navan and easily defying a penalty next time at Leopardstown before finishing third to The New One in Neptune Hurdle; looks made for chasing.

Present View

6 b g Presenting - Carry Me (Lafontaine I)

Jamie Snowden — **Sir Chips Keswick**

PLACINGS: **F1/422/321211-** — RPR **146+c**

Starts	1st	2nd	3rd	4th	Win & Pl
9	3	4	1	1	£56,727

137	3/14	Chel	2m4½f Cls1 Nov List 131-140 Ch Hcap gd-sft	£34,170
126	2/14	Kemp	2m4½f Cls3 117-130 Ch Hcap soft	£6,498
118	11/13	MRas	2m6½f Cls3 107-118 Ch Hcap soft	£9,747

Progressed throughout last season and defied 11lb rise for impressive Kempton win by following up in novice handicap chase at Cheltenham Festival; suffered only chase defeats over 3m but was second both times and should have no problems returning to that trip.

ONE TO WATCH

Cup Final Finished down the field in the Neptune at Cheltenham, but showed enough when third to the smart Irving at Kempton to suggest he'll have no problem winning over hurdles. A handicap mark of 125 could prove lenient.
[Steve Mason, Racing Post Ratings]

Ptit Zig (Fr)

5 b g Great Pretender - Red Rym (Denham Red)

Paul Nicholls **Barry Fulton, Chris Giles & Richard Webb**

PLACINGS: **924131/212264-** RPR **160h**

Starts	1st	2nd	3rd	4th	Win & Pl
12	3	4	1	2	£251,616

	11/13	Autl	2m3½f Gd1 Hdl 4yo heavy	£98,780
134	4/13	Sand	2m Cls2 112-134 Hdl 4yo Hcap good	£15,640
	2/13	Ludl	2m Cls4 Mdn Hdl soft	£3,249

Very smart hurdler in testing conditions last season, winning a Grade 1 in France; was second in Haydock Champion Hurdle Trial and in the Ladbroke at Ascot under a big weight; ran well at Cheltenham and Aintree despite quicker ground; could be a top novice chaser.

Puffin Billy (Ire)

6 b g Heron Island - Downtown Train (Glacial Storm)

Oliver Sherwood **Tim Syder**

PLACINGS: **1/111255/5-** RPR **139h**

Starts	1st	2nd	3rd	4th	Win & Pl
8	4	1	-	-	£35,017

12/12	Asct	2m Cls1 Nov Gd2 Hdl heavy	£17,085
11/12	Newb	2m½f Cls3 Mdn Hdl soft	£4,549
11/12	Asct	2m Cls6 NHF 4-6yo gd-sft	£3,128
3/12	Font	2m2½f Cls6 NHF 4-6yo soft	£1,365

Very useful novice hurdler two seasons ago when winning three times (including a Grade 2 at Ascot) and in contention in red-hot Supreme Novices' Hurdle until blundering two out; suffered from colic last season but will go novice chasing.

Purple Bay (Ire)

5 b g Dubawi - Velvet Lady (Nashwan)

John Ferguson **Bloomfields**

PLACINGS: **154/211422-217** RPR **153h**

Starts	1st	2nd	3rd	4th	Win & Pl
12	4	4	-	2	£42,216

139	7/14	MRas	2m1f Cls1 List 121-147 Hdl Hcap gd-sft	£19,933
	11/13	Muss	2m Cls4 Nov Hdl good	£3,899
	10/13	Strf	2m½f Cls4 Mdn Hdl gd-sft	£3,249
	2/13	Donc	2m½f Cls6 NHF 4-6yo good	£1,560

Disappointing last season having finished fourth and fifth in championship bumpers at Cheltenham and Aintree in 2013 but came good when winning Summer Hurdle at Market Rasen by ten lengths; good seventh after 14lb rise in Galway Hurdle.

Quick Jack (Ire)

5 ch g Footstepsinthesand - Miss Polaris (Polar Falcon)

Tony Martin (Ir) **John Breslin**

PLACINGS: **500/113-** RPR **129+h**

Starts	1st	2nd	3rd	4th	Win & Pl
6	2	-	1	-	£20,897

113	11/13	Chel	2m½f Cls3 Nov 105-125 Hdl Hcap good	£7,507
95	9/13	List	2m 94-102 Hdl Hcap yield	£5,890

Very lightly raced over hurdles but very much caught the eye from limited opportunities last season, winning a novice handicap at Cheltenham before finishing third in valuable event at Leopardstown; has since done well on Flat and should have lots more to offer.

Rainbow Peak (Ire)

8 b g Hernando - Celtic Fling (Lion Cavern)

John Ferguson — **Bloomfields**

PLACINGS: **41202-** — RPR **140h**

Starts	1st	2nd	3rd	4th	Win & Pl
5	1	2	-	1	£10,637

	Date	Course	Race	Prize
	1/14	Donc	2m3½f Cls5 Mdn Hdl gd-sft	£2,053

Group 1 winner in Italy in 2010 but ran only once in next three years before emerging as a novice hurdler last season; progressed well and produced best run when second in competitive handicap hurdle at Aintree on final start; should do well in similar races.

Rajdhani Express

7 br g Presenting - Violet Express (Cadoudal)

Nicky Henderson — **Robert Waley-Cohen**

PLACINGS: **12P/P58P/2F1711/537-** — RPR **162c**

Starts	1st	2nd	3rd	4th	Win & Pl
18	5	2	1	-	£157,191

	Date	Course	Race	Prize
	4/13	Ayr	2m4f Cls1 Nov Gd2 Ch good	£23,776
140	3/13	Chel	2m4½f Cls1 Nov List 132-140 Ch Hcap soft	£34,170
129	12/12	Kemp	2m4½f Cls3 Nov 119-130 Ch Hcap heavy	£7,178
	10/10	Engh	2m1½f Hdl 3yo v soft	£20,389
	10/10	Fntb	2m2f Hdl 3yo v soft	£8,496

Has produced two best runs at Cheltenham Festival in last two seasons, winning novices' handicap chase and then finishing fourth in last season's Ryanair Chase; has lots of options over similar course and distance including Paddy Power Gold Cup (fifth last year).

Rathvinden (Ire)

6 b g Heron Island - Peggy Cullen (Presenting)

Willie Mullins (Ir) — **R A Bartlett**

PLACINGS: **F111F23-** — RPR **149+h**

Starts	1st	2nd	3rd	4th	Win & Pl
6	3	1	1	-	£34,477

Date	Course	Race	Prize
12/13	Cork	2m Mdn Hdl soft	£5,610
11/13	Cork	2m NHF 4-7yo sft-hvy	£5,610
6/13	Dpat	2m2f NHF 4-7yo gd-fm	£3,927

Progressed throughout last season despite failing to add to early bumper and maiden hurdle successes; good second to Red Sherlock at Cheltenham on heavy ground and reportedly better suited by that surface than when third in Neptune Hurdle on good.

Realt Mor (Ire)

9 b g Beneficial - Suez Canal (Exit To Nowhere)

Gordon Elliott (Ir) — **Mrs P Sloan**

PLACINGS: **1/F1/F2/33U11P/33-** — RPR **147c**

Starts	1st	2nd	3rd	4th	Win & Pl
12	3	1	4	-	£64,961

Date	Course	Race	Prize
3/13	Fair	2m4f Gd1 Ch soft	£47,561
3/13	Navn	2m4f Ch soft	£6,732
4/11	Kels	2m2f Cls4 Nov Hdl gd-sft	£1,952

Missed second half of last season having been slightly underwhelming when third on both starts over inadequate 2m; had been disappointing until switched to Gordon Elliott in 2013, soon winning Powers Gold Cup; should appreciate return to 2m4f.

Ptit Zig (left): could excel when sent over fences this season

Rebel Fitz (Fr)

9 b g Agent Bleu - Gesse Parade (Dress Parade)

Michael Winters (Ir) | **Brian Sweetnam**

PLACINGS: 24/111225/211111211- | **RPR 160+h**

Starts	1st	2nd	3rd	4th	Win & Pl
25	15	7	-	2	£356,504

	Date	Course	Race	Prize
	4/14	Fair	2m4f Gd1 Ch gd-yld	£48,750
	3/14	Cork	2m4f Hdl heavy	£10,833
	10/13	Tipp	2m4f Nov Gd3 Ch good	£14,533
	9/13	Gway	2m1f Nov Ch gd-fm	£11,626
	8/13	Gway	2m1f Nov Ch heavy	£12,154
	7/13	Klny	2m6f Nov Ch gd-fm	£8,695
	5/13	Baln	2m1f Ch sft-hvy	£6,171
	8/12	Cork	2m2f Hdl yld-sft	£11,917
145	8/12	Gway	2m 131-150 Hdl Hcap soft	£130,500
	7/12	Tipp	2m Gd3 Hdl soft	£33,854
	10/11	Cork	2m Nov Hdl yield	£10,112
	9/11	Clon	2m½f Nov Hdl good	£5,948
	8/11	Cork	2m Mdn Hdl good	£5,948
	10/10	Gway	2m NHF 4-7yo gd-yld	£7,022
	9/10	List	2m NHF 5yo good	£6,106

Equally smart over hurdles and fences and made Grade 1 breakthrough in last season's Powers Gold Cup, though would have faced close battle with Ballycasey had that one not fallen; long believed to be better on good ground but has won good races on heavy.

Red Devil Boys (Ire)

7 b g Oscar - Lohort Castle (Presenting)

John Ferguson | **Bloomfields**

PLACINGS: 1/2/11/

Starts	1st	2nd	3rd	4th	Win & Pl
3	2	1	-	-	£5,369

Date	Course	Race	Prize
12/12	Donc	2m3½f Cls4 Nov Hdl soft	£3,249
11/12	Donc	2m½f Cls6 NHF 4-6yo soft	£1,625

Missed last season through injury; had won a bumper and novice hurdle in impressive fashion during previous campaign; looks a fine chasing prospect (already a point-to-point winner) and described by trainer this summer as potentially his best ever horse.

Red Sherlock

5 ch g Shirocco - Lady Cricket (Cricket Ball)

David Pipe | **The Johnson Family**

PLACINGS: 11/11119- | **RPR 148+h**

Starts	1st	2nd	3rd	4th	Win & Pl
7	6	-	-	-	£39,082

Date	Course	Race	Prize
1/14	Chel	2m4½f Cls1 Nov Gd2 Hdl heavy	£17,165
1/14	Weth	2m4f Cls4 Nov Hdl 4-7yo soft	£3,769
12/13	Sthl	2m4½f Cls5 Mdn Hdl good	£1,949
11/13	Chel	2m½f Cls1 List NHF 4-6yo good	£11,390
2/13	Asct	2m Cls4 NHF 4-6yo soft	£3,249
1/13	Towc	2m Cls6 NHF 4-6yo heavy	£1,560

Unbeaten in first six races under rules comprising three bumpers and three novice hurdles, most notably when beating Rathvinden in a Grade 2 at Cheltenham; well below that form when only ninth in Neptune Novices' Hurdle; should bounce back.

Regal Encore (Ire)

6 b g King's Theatre - Go On Eileen (Bob Back)

Anthony Honeyball | **John P McManus**

PLACINGS: 12/2124-8 | **RPR 132+h**

Starts	1st	2nd	3rd	4th	Win & Pl
7	2	3	-	1	£23,807

Date	Course	Race	Prize
11/13	Plum	2m Cls4 Nov Hdl gd-sft	£3,249
10/12	Chep	2m½f Cls6 NHF 4-6yo gd-sft	£1,754
2/12	Sthl	2m Cls6 NHF 4-6yo std-slw	£1,437

Second to Briar Hill in Champion Bumper at Cheltenham in 2013 but subsequently

disappointed over hurdles; seemingly laid out to win a big handicap but only fourth in Imperial Cup and fifth at Punchestown (favourite both times); should do better.

Renneti (Fr)

5 b g Irish Wells - Caprice Meill (French Glory)

Willie Mullins (Ir) — **Mrs S Ricci**

PLACINGS: 12FR- — RPR **142+h**

Starts	1st	2nd	3rd	4th	Win & Pl
4	1	1	-	-	£15,792

	10/13	Dpat	2m2f Mdn Hdl 4yo yield	£4,207

Smart novice hurdler early last season, pushing The Tullow Tank close in Grade 1 Royal Bond; out for nearly four months after falling two out at Leopardstown over Christmas and refused to race on sole subsequent outing; talented if enthusiasm can be rekindled.

Restless Harry

10 b g Sir Harry Lewis - Restless Native (Be My Native)

Robin Dickin — **R G Whitehead**

PLACINGS: /6418503P/00UU15104- — RPR **154c**

Starts	1st	2nd	3rd	4th	Win & Pl
38	8	3	7	3	£165,386

141	2/14	Asct	3m Cls1 List 138-158 Ch Hcap soft	£22,780
122	1/14	Newb	3m Cls3 116-129 Ch Hcap soft	£6,498
	12/12	Newb	3m Cls2 Ch soft	£10,397
	2/12	Hayd	3m Cls1 Gd2 Hdl heavy	£18,509
	10/11	Weth	3m1f Cls1 Gd2 Hdl good	£18,310
	4/10	Chel	2m5½f Cls2 Nov Hdl good	£8,532
	1/10	Chel	2m4½f Cls1 Nov Gd2 Hdl soft	£15,393
	11/09	Towc	2m5f Cls3 Nov Hdl 4-6yo heavy	£6,337

Emerged from a year out of form with several good performances last spring, winning a Listed handicap chase at Ascot; not beaten far when fourth in bet365 Gold Cup despite ground being quicker than ideal; being aimed at Welsh National and should go well.

Reve De Sivola (Fr)

9 b g Assessor - Eva De Chalamont (Iron Duke)

Nick Williams — **Paul Duffy Diamond Partnership**

PLACINGS: /4753/21142/013148-7 — RPR **161h**

Starts	1st	2nd	3rd	4th	Win & Pl
32	8	5	7	4	£478,065

	12/13	Asct	3m1f Cls1 Gd1 Hdl soft	£42,701
	11/13	Autl	3m Gd1 Hdl heavy	£135,366
	1/13	Chel	3m Cls1 Gd2 Hdl heavy	£34,170
	12/12	Asct	3m1f Cls1 Gd1 Hdl heavy	£42,203
	12/10	Chel	2m5f Cls2 Nov Ch good	£9,798
	4/10	Punc	2m4f Nov Gd1 Hdl good	£46,637
	12/09	Newb	2m5f Cls1 Nov Gd1 Hdl heavy	£24,229
	10/09	Chep	2m4f Cls1 Nov Gd2 Hdl soft	£17,103

Confirmed mudlark who enjoyed ideal conditions when winning Long Walk Hurdle in each of last two seasons; also won Cleeve Hurdle and Grade 1 in France in 2013 but came unstuck in championship races last spring, including when finishing eighth in World Hurdle.

Rigadin De Beauchene (Fr)

9 b/br g Visionary - Chipie D'Angron (Grand Tresor)

Venetia Williams — **Andrew Wiles**

PLACINGS: FF1523U/23212PP/1PP- — RPR **150+c**

Starts	1st	2nd	3rd	4th	Win & Pl
25	3	5	2	1	£102,992

131	2/14	Hayd	3m5f Cls1 Gd3 127-149 Ch Hcap heavy	£42,713
122	1/13	Wwck	3m5f Cls1 Gd3 119-142 Ch Hcap soft	£34,170
104	12/11	Hrfd	2m5½f Cls4 104-120 Ch Hcap soft	£3,054

Hugely inconsistent but very capable on his day

Rebel Fitz: prolific winner who can land more valuable races in Ireland during the winter

and won last season's Grand National Trial at Haydock on heavy ground (only time he hasn't been pulled up in last five races); unsuited by much quicker ground subsequently and one to watch when mud is flying.

Rival D'Estruval (Fr)

9 b g Khalkevi - Kermesse D'Estruval (Cadoudal)

Pauline Robson **Mr & Mrs Raymond Anderson Green**

PLACINGS: 2/211045212/121FP/5- **RPR 127c**

Starts	1st	2nd	3rd	4th	Win & Pl
19	5	6	1	1	£44,279

	12/12	Kels	2m7½f Cls2 Nov Ch soft	£10,174
	10/12	Carl	2m4f Cls4 Nov Ch heavy	£3,054
	3/12	Hexm	3m Cls4 Nov Hdl good	£3,080
124	10/11	Aint	3m½f Cls2 124-150 Hdl Hcap good	£9,384
	5/11	Ctml	2m6f Cls4 Nov Hdl good	£3,253

High-class novice chaser two seasons ago and might have won National Hunt Chase at Cheltenham but for falling two out; needed an operation after only start last term but reportedly back to best this autumn; likely to start back over hurdles but could do well in good staying handicap chases.

Road To Riches (Ire)

7 b g Gamut - Bellora (Over The River)

Noel Meade (Ir) **Gigginstown House Stud**

PLACINGS: F/111186/13P41-21 **RPR 165+c**

Starts	1st	2nd	3rd	4th	Win & Pl
12	6	1	1	1	£167,601

149	7/14	Gway	2m6f 134-155 Ch Hcap good	£100,313
	4/14	Fair	2m1f Nov Ch gd-yld	£9,488
	11/13	Naas	2m3f Ch yld-sft	£6,732
	12/12	Cork	3m Nov Gd3 Hdl soft	£14,896
	11/12	Punc	2m4f Mdn Hdl heavy	£7,763
	10/12	Naas	2m3f NHF 4-7yo heavy	£5,750

Brilliant 11-length winner of Galway Plate in July, maintaining vast improvement on quicker ground having struggled in testing conditions in top novice chases last season (though had won a bumper and maiden hurdle on heavy); must now step up to Grade 1 level.

Roalco De Farges (Fr)

9 gr g Dom Alco - Vonaria (Vorias)

Philip Hobbs **The Brushmakers**

PLACINGS: 331/001362512/P31P7- **RPR 139+c**

Starts	1st	2nd	3rd	4th	Win & Pl
19	4	2	5	-	£66,573

127	3/14	Newb	3m2½f Cls3 122-137 Ch Hcap gd-sft	£12,512
	4/12	Chep	3m Cls3 Nov Ch gd-sft	£4,549
124	11/11	Newb	2m6½f Cls3 Nov 107-130 Ch Hcap good	£6,882
112	4/11	Chep	2m4f Cls3 109-132 Hdl Hcap gd-sft	£3,643

Returned last season after nearly two years out through injury (had been second in bet365 Gold Cup when last seen) and won well third time out; disappointed when co-favourite for Scottish National and bet365 Gold Cup but remains capable of better.

Rock On Ruby (Ire)

9 b g Oscar - Stony View (Tirol)

Harry Fry **The Festival Goers**

PLACINGS: 223/1213/3123/21182- **RPR 165h**

Starts	1st	2nd	3rd	4th	Win & Pl
21	9	6	4	1	£488,715

	2/14	Donc	2m½f Cls3 Nov Ch gd-sft	£6,498
	12/13	Plum	2m1f Cls3 Nov Ch soft	£6,975
	2/13	Donc	2m½f Cls1 List Hdl good	£10,571
	3/12	Chel	2m½f Cls1 Gd1 Hdl good	£210,715
145	11/11	Newb	2m½f Cls1 List 125-145 Hdl Hcap gd-sft	£11,390
	12/10	Newb	2m½f Cls3 Hdl gd-sft	£5,010
	11/10	Chel	2m½f Cls1 List NHF 4-6yo gd-sft	£6,841
	3/10	Newb	2m½f Cls5 NHF 4-6yo gd-sft	£2,055
	2/10	Tntn	2m1f Cls5 Mdn NHF 4-6yo gd-sft	£2,192

Former Champion Hurdle winner who never convinced when sent novice chasing last season despite winning twice; reverted to hurdles for final start at Aintree and ran a huge race to get to within a nose of The New One; could again be a force in top hurdle races.

Rocky Creek (Ire)

8 b g Dr Massini - Kissantell (Broken Hearted)

Paul Nicholls **The Johnson & Stewart Families**

PLACINGS: 1/218/21113/225- **RPR 164c**

Starts	1st	2nd	3rd	4th	Win & Pl
11	4	4	1	-	£145,033

2/13	Asct	3m Cls1 Nov Gd2 Ch soft	£18,855
1/13	Wwck	3m½f Cls2 Nov Ch soft	£12,001
12/12	Donc	3m Cls4 Nov Ch gd-sft	£3,899
1/12	Donc	3m½f Cls1 Nov Gd2 Hdl gd-sft	£14,305

Ran well in top races last season, most notably when second in Hennessy Gold Cup (would have preferred softer ground); looked a non-stayer when a fine fifth in Grand National having led two out; seems sure to win good staying chases.

Rogue Angel (Ire)

6 b g Presenting - Carrigeen Kohleria (Luso)

Mouse Morris (Ir) **Gigginstown House Stud**

PLACINGS: 11d/13P32/F34314740- **RPR 143+c**

Starts	1st	2nd	3rd	4th	Win & Pl
15	2	2	4	3	£31,198

12/13	Punc	3m Ch heavy	£6,732
10/12	Gway	2m Mdn Hdl 4yo yld-sft	£6,325

Inconsistent when sent chasing last season but showed smart form at his best, especially when granted a major stamina test; won over 3m on heavy ground at Punchestown and was a bold seventh in National Hunt Chase; should do well in marathon chases.

ONE TO WATCH

Vaniteux Progressive hurdler who finished an excellent third in the Supreme Novices' Hurdle. His trainer thinks he could be close to top class and, if that proves correct, a mark of 147 looks ripe for exploitation. *[Steve Mason, Racing Post Ratings]*

Roi Du Mee (Fr)

9 b g Lavirco - British Nellerie (Le Pontet)

Gordon Elliott (Ir) **Gigginstown House Stud**

PLACINGS: 8/51111211/F21P27P4- **RPR 164+c**

Starts	1st	2nd	3rd	4th	Win & Pl
41	13	8	3	2	£279,768

	11/13	DRoy	3m Gd1 Ch yld-sft	£68,293
	3/13	Cork	3m Gd3 Ch sft-hvy	£14,533
	2/13	Fair	3m1f Gd2 Ch soft	£21,138
	1/13	Tram	2m5f List Ch heavy	£15,854
118	12/12	Navn	2m7f 108-136 Hdl Hcap heavy	£14,896
	11/12	Thur	2m6f List Ch yld-sft	£14,896
	10/12	Punc	2m7f Gd3 Ch heavy	£16,250
	10/11	Punc	2m7f Gd3 Ch yld-sft	£16,810
	2/11	Naas	2m4f Nov Gd2 Ch sft-hvy	£22,414
	2/11	Punc	2m6f Nov Ch heavy	£9,517
	12/10	Limk	2m6f Ch sft-hvy	£8,243
	12/09	Gowr	2m Mdn Hdl 4yo heavy	£7,044
	9/09	Sabl	1m5½f NHF 4yo v soft	£10,680

Very prolific two seasons ago and maintained sharp upward curve when winning Grade 1 at Down Royal last November, making virtually all; subsequently lost his way in face of some stiff tasks but remains capable of much better and can win more good races.

Rolling Aces (Ire)

8 b g Whitmore's Conn - Pay Roll (Roselier)

Paul Nicholls **Paul Barber, Ian Fogg & David Martin**

PLACINGS: 21/120/43112/12P24- **RPR 157c**

Starts	1st	2nd	3rd	4th	Win & Pl
13	4	4	1	2	£117,504

	11/13	DRoy	2m4f Gd2 Ch soft	£26,423
	12/12	Winc	2m5f Cls3 Nov Ch heavy	£5,653
130	12/12	Newb	2m6½f Cls3 Nov 115-132 Ch Hcap gd-sft	£7,507
	11/11	Winc	2m6f Cls4 Nov Hdl gd-sft	£2,599

Showed high-class form last season to win a Grade 2 at Down Royal and finish second to Boston Bob in Melling Chase at Aintree; disappointing on three other runs (including defeat at odds-on) so has to prove his consistency but talented on his day.

Rolling Star (Fr)

5 b g Smadoun - Lyli Rose (Lyphard's Wish)

Nicky Henderson **Michael Buckley & The Vestey Family**

PLACINGS: 1165/100- **RPR 153+h**

Starts	1st	2nd	3rd	4th	Win & Pl
7	3	-	-	-	£68,377

11/13	Hayd	2m Cls2 Hdl soft	£25,024
1/13	Chel	2m1f Cls1 Gd2 Hdl 4yo heavy	£17,085
10/12	Autl	2m2f Hdl 3yo heavy	£22,000

Ultimately disappointing as a juvenile hurdler two seasons ago (only sixth when sent off favourite for Triumph Hurdle) but improved physically and made impressive winning return at Haydock; had nothing go right in two big handicaps subsequently; can do better.

Roudoudou Ville (Fr)

9 b/br g Winning Smile - Jadoudy Ville (Cadoudal)

Victor Dartnall **Mrs S De Wilde**

PLACINGS: 66834/P11/213/4PP42- **RPR 145+c**

Starts	1st	2nd	3rd	4th	Win & Pl
19	5	2	3	3	£46,346

137	11/11	Sand	2m4½f Cls3 124-137 Ch Hcap gd-sft	£7,507
114	3/11	Chep	2m3½f Cls4 99-114 Ch Hcap good	£3,253
102	3/11	Winc	2m Cls4 87-105 Ch Hcap gd-fm	£2,700
	5/09	Rost	1m3f NHF 4-5yo good	£3,884
	9/08	Chat	1m5f NHF 3yo gd-sft	£5,147

Looked to be going places in 2011 but missed two years through injury after close third in big handicap chase at Cheltenham; gradually returned to form last season, finishing with fine second at Perth; still young enough to make impact at high level.

Rival D'Estruval: on the comeback trail

Royal Boy (Fr)

7 b/br g Lavirco - Quintanilla (Royal Charter)

Nicky Henderson — **Michael Buckley**

PLACINGS: 1/23/311- — **RPR 150+h**

Starts	1st	2nd	3rd	4th	Win & Pl
5	2	1	2	-	£30,895

	Date	Course	Race	Prize
	1/14	Kemp	2m Cls1 Nov Gd1 Hdl soft	£18,224
	12/13	Asct	2m6f Cls3 Mdn Hdl soft	£5,630

Jumping fell apart on chasing debut last season but benefited from return to hurdles, winning well over 2m6f before outstaying Josses Hill to land Tolworth Hurdle at Kempton on sharp drop in trip; missed Cheltenham after setback; could return to fences.

Royal Irish Hussar (Ire)

4 b g Galileo - Adjalisa (Darshaan)

Nicky Henderson — **Triermore Stud**

PLACINGS: 11136-0 — **RPR 138+h**

Starts	1st	2nd	3rd	4th	Win & Pl
6	3	-	1	-	£41,755

	Date	Course	Race	Prize
	11/13	Chel	2m½f Cls1 Gd2 Hdl 3yo good	£17,085
	11/13	Weth	2m½f Cls1 List Hdl 3yo gd-sft	£9,682
	9/13	MRas	2m1f Cls2 Hdl 3yo good	£10,397

Quickly developed into a leading juvenile hurdler last season and claimed notable scalp of subsequent dual Grade 1 winner Guitar Pete at Cheltenham; below that form later, including when among favourites for Triumph Hurdle, but could easily bounce back.

Rule The World

7 b g Sulamani - Elaine Tully (Persian Bold)

Mouse Morris (Ir) — **Gigginstown House Stud**

PLACINGS: 1/12112P/14216- — **RPR 163+h**

Starts	1st	2nd	3rd	4th	Win & Pl
11	5	3	-	1	£109,832

	Date	Course	Race	Prize
	1/14	Naas	2m3f Gd3 Hdl sft-hvy	£16,250
	10/13	Naas	2m4f Hdl yld-sft	£10,569
	1/13	Naas	2m4f Nov Gd2 Hdl sft-hvy	£19,817
	12/12	Navn	2m4f Nov Hdl heavy	£7,475
	10/12	Punc	2m Mdn Hdl heavy	£5,750

Smart hurdler at around 2m4f, gaining all five hurdling wins up to that distance; has run well over further, though yet to win in three attempts, with best effort coming when sixth in World Hurdle; may go novice chasing and has already won a point-to-point.

ONE TO WATCH

Pearl Swan Has had his problems since falling at the last when set to place in the 2012 Triumph Hurdle, but his handicap mark has fallen from 146 to 138 as a result and he could be a very interesting contender for top handicap hurdles.
[Steve Mason, Racing Post Ratings]

Rum And Butter (Ire)

6 b g Milan - Silent Valley (Forzando)

Jonjo O'Neill — **John P McManus**

PLACINGS: 8/34451/4211220-1110 — **RPR 145+h**

Starts	1st	2nd	3rd	4th	Win & Pl
17	6	3	1	3	£47,280

	Date	Course	Race	Prize
	6/14	MRas	2m4f Cls4 Nov Ch good	£3,899
	5/14	Strf	2m4f Cls3 Nov Ch gd-sft	£6,498
	5/14	Kemp	2m4½f Cls3 Ch good	£6,498
122	8/13	NAbb	2m3f Cls2 114-135 Hdl Hcap gd-fm	£10,407
113	7/13	NAbb	2m3f Cls3 113-131 Hdl Hcap gd-fm	£7,121
102	4/13	NAbb	2m3f Cls4 Nov 79-105 Hdl Hcap gd-sft	£3,509

Useful hurdler (three-time winner in 2013) who took well to fences this summer when notching a hat-trick; worrying that he twice flopped in bigger fields either side of that and hasn't run on soft ground since 2012 but should have more to come.

Rutherglen

4 b g Tiger Hill - Hanella (Galileo)

John Quinn — **The Beer Swigging Strangers**

PLACINGS: 1115- — **RPR 132h**

Starts	1st	2nd	3rd	4th	Win & Pl
4	3	-	-	-	£16,351

	Date	Course	Race	Prize
	1/14	Muss	2m Cls3 Hdl 4yo soft	£7,798
	12/13	Bang	2m1f Cls4 Hdl 3yo soft	£3,285
	11/13	Weth	2m½f Cls5 Mdn Hdl 3yo gd-sft	£2,053

Won first three starts over hurdles last season (all at 5-4 or shorter) before coping well with huge rise in class to finish fifth in Triumph Hurdle at Cheltenham; found trip too sharp that day and should benefit from further; can win good races.

Sadler's Risk (Ire)

6 b g Sadler's Wells - Riskaverse (Dynaformer)

Henry de Bromhead (Ir) — **R S Brookhouse**

PLACINGS: 12632/02P0/70-61 — **RPR 150+c**

Starts	1st	2nd	3rd	4th	Win & Pl
13	2	3	1	-	£38,543

	Date	Course	Race	Prize
	5/14	Rosc	2m5f Ch soft	£5,175
	1/12	Kemp	2m Cls4 Hdl 4yo good	£3,249

Lost his way over hurdles having finished sixth in 2012 Triumph Hurdle, leading to unsuccessful return to Flat last summer; did slightly better this spring before looking rejuvenated by switch to fences on chasing debut in May; could be an exciting novice.

Salubrious (Ire)

7 b g Beneficial - Who Tells Jan (Royal Fountain)

Paul Nicholls — **The Johnson & Stewart Families**

PLACINGS: 171/425115/22295- — **RPR 156+h**

Starts	1st	2nd	3rd	4th	Win & Pl
14	4	4	-	1	£84,015

	Date	Course	Race	Prize
141	3/13	Chel	2m4½f Cls2 131-145 Cond Hdl Hcap soft	£31,280
133	2/13	Muss	2m4f Cls3 108-133 Cond Hdl Hcap gd-sft	£6,498
	12/11	Tntn	2m3½f Cls4 Nov Hdl gd-sft	£3,080
	9/11	Strf	2m½f Cls5 NHF 4-6yo gd-fm	£1,754

Ran away with Martin Pipe Hurdle two seasons

ago and ran two more fine races at Cheltenham in defeat last season when a short-head second in a strong handicap and chasing home More Of That; much better than he showed when ninth in World Hurdle.

Sam Winner (Fr)

7 b g Okawango - Noche (Night Shift)

Paul Nicholls — **Mrs Angela Yeoman**

PLACINGS: 211446/FF/503/3125P- RPR **153c**

Starts	1st	2nd	3rd	4th	Win & Pl
18	3	4	2	2	£87,699

	Date	Course	Race	Prize
	12/13	Chel	3m1½f Cls2 Nov Ch good	£12,512
	1/13	Kemp	2m Cls4 NHF std-slw	£3,574
	12/10	Chel	2m1f Cls2 Hdl 3yo gd-sft	£8,141
	11/10	Chel	2m½f Cls1 Gd2 Hdl 3yo gd-sft	£14,253

Took a long time to build on early promise (didn't run again over fences for nearly two years after falling on first two attempts in 2011) but did well in novice chases last season and finished good fifth in RSA Chase; should make his mark in good staying handicaps.

Samingarry (Fr)

7 ch g Ballingarry - Samansonnienne (Mansonnien)

Nigel Hawke — **D R Mead**

PLACINGS: 85224612/5713115P31- RPR **141+c**

Starts	1st	2nd	3rd	4th	Win & Pl
21	5	3	2	1	£35,885

	Date	Course	Race	Prize
127	4/14	Chep	3m Cls3 Nov 118-137 Ch Hcap soft	£7,148
121	12/13	Chep	3m Cls3 Nov 121-134 Ch Hcap gd-sft	£6,498
115	11/13	Extr	3m Cls3 115-125 Ch Hcap good	£7,913
106	10/13	Aint	3m1f Cls3 Nov 106-120 Ch Hcap good	£6,564
97	4/13	Sthl	2m4½f Cls4 Nov 95-105 Hdl Hcap good	£2,017

Progressive novice chaser last season, winning four times and producing best performance at Chepstow on final start; had jumped badly on only run on heavy ground before being out of his depth in RSA Chase; could run well in good staying handicaps.

Samstown

7 b g Kingsalsa - Red Peony (Montjeu)

Alistair Whillans — **Mrs Elizabeth Ferguson**

PLACINGS: /338/141740P/414221- RPR **136+c**

Starts	1st	2nd	3rd	4th	Win & Pl
17	4	2	2	5	£44,451

	Date	Course	Race	Prize
116	4/14	Ayr	3m1f Cls2 Nov 108-134 Ch Hcap gd-sft	£19,494
107	12/13	MRas	3m1f Cls3 Nov 107-120 Ch Hcap soft	£7,988
	6/12	Hexm	2m4½f Cls4 Nov Hdl heavy	£3,429
	5/12	Prth	3m½f Cls4 Nov Hdl good	£3,249

Runaway winner of novice handicap chase at Ayr on final start last season having reportedly not been right when running only adequately previously; raised 19lb in handicap so sure to face much stiffer tasks but could be on upgrade.

Saphir Du Rheu (Fr)

5 gr g Al Namix - Dona Du Rheu (Dom Pasquini)

Paul Nicholls — **The Stewart Family**

PLACINGS: 3310/541114- RPR **162+h**

Starts	1st	2nd	3rd	4th	Win & Pl
10	4	-	2	2	£86,430

	Date	Course	Race	Prize
158	2/14	Ffos	2m4f Cls2 130-158 Hdl Hcap heavy	£31,280
145	1/14	Kemp	2m5f Cls1 List 121-145 Hdl Hcap soft	£25,628
130	12/13	Sand	2m6f Cls2 120-142 Hdl Hcap gd-sft	£12,512
	1/13	Tntn	2m1f Cls4 Nov Hdl heavy	£4,106

Won a couple of valuable handicap hurdles last season, most notably when beating subsequent Grade 1 winner Whisper off 158 in Welsh Champion Hurdle; possibly over the top when beaten at 2-5 next time; has huge potential when sent chasing.

Samingarry: staying handicap chases will be his game this season

Sausalito Sunrise (Ire)

6 b g Gold Well - Villaflor (Religiously)

Philip Hobbs **Mrs Diana L Whateley**

PLACINGS: 1/223/3115611- RPR 143+h

Starts	1st	2nd	3rd	4th	Win & Pl
10	4	2	2	-	£33,265

	4/14	Prth	3m½f Cls2 Nov Hdl gd-sft	£9,747
	4/14	Bang	3m Cls4 Nov Hdl gd-sft	£3,899
129	12/13	Hayd	3m Cls3 120-140 Hdl Hcap soft	£9,495
	12/13	Chep	3m Cls4 Nov Hdl gd-sft	£3,119

Smart staying novice hurdler last season, winning four times at around 3m and finishing decent sixth in Albert Bartlett Hurdle at Cheltenham; has already won a point-to-point and should be even better over fences; has won on soft ground but best on quicker.

Savello (Ire)

8 ch g Anshan - Fontaine Frances (Lafontaine I)

Tony Martin (Ir) **Gigginstown House Stud**

PLACINGS: 11P00/754511/34391-3 RPR 157c

Starts	1st	2nd	3rd	4th	Win & Pl
23	5	1	4	3	£100,251

147	3/14	Chel	2m½f Cls1 Gd3 136-154 Ch Hcap good	£51,255
	3/13	Leop	2m1f Nov Ch yield	£10,569
	2/13	Clon	2m Ch heavy	£4,488
	11/11	Fair	2m Hdl soft	£7,733
	10/11	Wxfd	2m Mdn Hdl soft	£4,461

Won last season's Grand Annual Chase at Cheltenham having been backed from 33-1 to 16-1 so was clearly regarded as better than previously seen; fair third in Punchestown Grade 1 next time (made late blunders) and likely to be tested in top 2m chases.

Seeyouatmidnight

6 b g Midnight Legend - Morsky Baloo (Morpeth)

Sandy Thomson **Mrs A M Thomson**

PLACINGS: P3F/11113- RPR 154+h

Starts	1st	2nd	3rd	4th	Win & Pl
4	3	-	1	-	£47,511

2/14	Hayd	3m Cls1 Gd2 Hdl heavy	£20,787
2/14	Muss	3m½f Cls2 Hdl soft	£12,996
12/13	Hexm	2m½f Cls4 Nov Hdl soft	£3,119

Won first three hurdles last season, finishing off by stepping out of novice company to win 3m Grade 2 hurdle at Haydock on heavy ground; seemed less effective on good ground when distant third in Grade 1 at Aintree; should make a tremendous chaser.

Seven Nation Army (Ire)

5 gr g Rock Of Gibraltar - Crepe Ginger (Sadler's Wells)

David Pipe **R S Brookhouse**

PLACINGS: 31/15-0 RPR 125b

Starts	1st	2nd	3rd	4th	Win & Pl
5	2	-	1	-	£13,940

12/13	Asct	2m Cls1 List NHF 4-6yo soft	£11,390
4/13	Font	1m6f Cls6 NHF 4-6yo soft	£1,560

Smart bumper performer last season, winning a Listed race at Ascot from subsequent Champion

Seeyouatmidnight: smart hurdler should do well as a novice chaser this season

Bumper third Joshua Lane; much better than he showed at Newbury and Punchestown and should be a leading novice hurdler.

Sgt Reckless

7 b g Imperial Dancer - Lakaam (Danzero)

Mick Channon — **Mrs T P Radford**

PLACINGS: 100/31342-3 — RRPR **150+h**

Starts	1st	2nd	3rd	4th	Win & Pl
9	2	1	3	1	£33,636

	Date	Course	Race	Prize
	1/14	Kemp	2m Cls3 NHF std-slw	£6,330
	11/13	Kemp	2m Cls4 Nov Hdl 4-6yo good	£3,899
	1/13	Ling	2m Cls6 NHF 4-6yo stand	£1,643
	5/12	Winc	2m Cls6 NHF 4-6yo gd-sft	£1,430

Ran a remarkable race to finish fourth in last season's Supreme Novices' Hurdle having been last three out; proved that was no fluke with good second to Josses Hill at Aintree but below-par at Punchestown on final start; seems less effective on soft ground.

Shaneshill (Ire)

5 b g King's Theatre - Darabaka (Doyoun)

Willie Mullins (Ir) — **Andrea & Graham Wylie**

PLACINGS: 3/112-1 — RPR **137b**

Starts	1st	2nd	3rd	4th	Win & Pl
4	3	1	-	-	£71,669

	Date	Course	Race	Prize
	4/14	Punc	2m Gd1 NHF 4-7yo gd-yld	£48,750
	11/13	Fair	2m NHF 4-7yo gd-yld	£5,610
	11/13	Naas	2m NHF 4yo yld-sft	£4,488

Among last season's leading bumper performers, suffering only defeat when second to Silver Concorde at Cheltenham having been sent off favourite; reversed form with runner-up under more forceful ride at Punchestown; should excel at around 2m4f.

Shotavodka (Ire)

8 ch g Alderbrook - Another Vodka (Moscow Society)

David Pipe — **Mrs Jane Gerard-Pearse**

PLACINGS: 412/81117/92282132-1 — RPR **149c**

Starts	1st	2nd	3rd	4th	Win & Pl
17	6	5	1	1	£70,619

	Date	Course	Race	Prize
141	5/14	Hayd	2m6f Cls2 119-145 Ch Hcap soft	£19,494
	2/14	Hntg	2m½f Cls3 Nov Ch soft	£6,657
132	3/13	Newb	2m½f Cls2 113-132 Hdl Hcap heavy	£9,747
	2/13	Sand	2m½f Cls4 Nov Hdl gd-sft	£3,899
	2/13	Tntn	2m1f Cls4 Mdn Hdl heavy	£4,224
	10/11	Tram	2m NHF 5-7yo yield	£4,164

Finished second in two good handicap hurdles at around 2m4f last season before switching to fences; made steady progress and produced best performance to date when winning at Haydock in May; had also run well when stepped up to 3m previously.

Shotgun Paddy (Ire)

7 b g Brian Boru - Awesome Miracle (Supreme Leader)

Emma Lavelle — **Axom (XXXVI)**

PLACINGS: 8/81/1233/13212- — RPR **158+c**

Starts	1st	2nd	3rd	4th	Win & Pl
12	4	3	3	-	£76,955

	Date	Course	Race	Prize
145	1/14	Wwck	3m5f Cls1 Gd3 124-150 Ch Hcap soft	£34,170
	10/13	Chep	3m Cls4 Nov Ch soft	£4,549
	11/12	Chep	2m4f Cls5 Mdn Hdl soft	£3,899
	2/12	Thur	2m NHF 5-7yo heavy	£4,025

Impressive winner of Classic Chase at Warwick last season on only fourth run over fences; did well to go close in National Hunt Chase despite looking ill at ease on much quicker ground (jumped very badly); should be a force in top staying handicaps.

Shutthefrontdoor (Ire)

7 b/br g Accordion - Hurricane Girl (Strong Gale)

Jonjo O'Neill — **John P McManus**

PLACINGS: 111/31114/12461- — RPR **155+c**

Starts	1st	2nd	3rd	4th	Win & Pl
13	8	1	1	2	£166,845

	Date	Course	Race	Prize
142	4/14	Fair	3m5f 129-150 Ch Hcap gd-yld	£117,500
	10/13	Aint	2m4f Cls3 Nov Ch good	£7,507
135	2/13	Carl	3m1f Cls2 121-145 Hdl Hcap soft	£11,574
	1/13	Winc	2m Cls4 Nov Hdl soft	£3,899
	12/12	Uttx	2m Cls5 Mdn Hdl heavy	£1,689
	2/12	Newb	2m½f Cls1 List NHF 4-6yo gd-sft	£5,695
	12/11	Asct	2m Cls1 List NHF 4-6yo soft	£7,290
	11/11	Ffos	2m Cls6 NHF 4-5yo soft	£1,506

Thorough stayer who ended first season over fences with gutsy win in Irish National in April; had been given a wind operation after disappointing effort at Cheltenham earlier in campaign but jumped badly when sixth in National Hunt Chase next time.

Silsol (Ger)

5 b g Soldier Hollow - Silveria (Groom Dancer)

Paul Nicholls — **Michelle & Dan Macdonald**

PLACINGS: 42211- — RPR **140+h**

Starts	1st	2nd	3rd	4th	Win & Pl
5	2	2	-	1	£16,290

	Date	Course	Race	Prize
	4/14	NAbb	2m6f Cls4 Nov Hdl gd-sft	£3,509
124	4/14	Ayr	2m4f Cls3 102-128 Hdl Hcap gd-sft	£7,798

Made steady progress over hurdles last season and

won last two starts when fitted with cheekpieces, looking particularly impressive when winning by 14 lengths off 124 at Ayr; should continue to improve, especially when stepping up again in trip.

Silver Concorde

6 b g Dansili - Sacred Pearl (Daylami)

Dermot Weld (Ir) — **Dr R Lambe**

PLACINGS: 3/2/11-2 — **RPR 140+b**

Starts	1st	2nd	3rd	4th	Win & Pl
5	2	2	1	-	£55,002

	Date	Course	Race	Prize
	3/14	Chel	2m½f Cls1 Gd1 NHF 4-6yo good	£34,170
	12/13	Leop	2m NHF 4-6yo soft	£5,049

Won last season's Cheltenham Champion Bumper, making most of Flat pedigree when showing great speed on good ground; unable to confirm form with runner-up Shaneshill when second in slightly more testing conditions at Punchestown.

Silviniaco Conti (Fr)

8 ch g Dom Alco - Gazelle Lulu (Altayan)

Paul Nicholls — **Potensis Limited & Chris Giles**

PLACINGS: 34/31241/111F3/3141- — **RPR 179c**

Starts	1st	2nd	3rd	4th	Win & Pl
21	12	1	4	3	£643,304

	Date	Course	Race	Prize
	4/14	Aint	3m1f Cls1 Gd1 Ch good	£84,405
	12/13	Kemp	3m Cls1 Gd1 Ch soft	£114,436
	2/13	Newb	3m Cls1 Gd2 Ch soft	£25,628
	11/12	Hayd	3m Cls1 Gd1 Ch soft	£112,540
	11/12	Weth	3m1f Cls1 Gd2 Ch gd-sft	£56,950
	4/12	Aint	3m1f Cls1 Nov Gd2 Ch good	£42,713
	11/11	Winc	2m5f Cls1 Nov Gd2 Ch gd-sft	£20,093
	11/10	Asct	2m3½f Cls1 Gd2 Hdl gd-sft	£50,697
	10/10	Chep	2m4f Cls1 Nov Gd2 Hdl soft	£14,253
	10/10	Bang	2m1f Cls3 Nov Hdl good	£4,879
	4/10	Nanc	2m1f Hdl 4yo good	£12,743
	3/10	Seno	2m2f Hdl 4yo gd-sft	£5,097

Has done superbly in top staying chases and added King George and Betfred Bowl victories to his CV last season; fell when going well in 2013 Gold Cup and led at the last before finishing fourth there in March; will have third attempt as his priority.

Simonsig

8 gr g Fair Mix - Dusty Too (Terimon)

Nicky Henderson — **R A Bartlett**

PLACINGS: 1F1/112111/111/

Starts	1st	2nd	3rd	4th	Win & Pl
9	8	1	-	-	£248,771

	Date	Course	Race	Prize
	3/13	Chel	2m Cls1 Gd1 Ch soft	£85,425
	12/12	Kemp	2m Cls1 Nov Gd2 Ch heavy	£13,326
	12/12	Asct	2m3f Cls1 Nov Gd2 Ch heavy	£19,667
	4/12	Aint	2m4f Cls1 Nov Gd2 Hdl good	£28,475
	3/12	Chel	2m5f Cls1 Nov Gd1 Hdl good	£56,950
	2/12	Kels	2m2f Cls2 Hdl gd-sft	£9,747
	11/11	Asct	2m3½f Cls3 Nov Hdl good	£5,005
	4/11	Fair	2m2f NHF 4-6yo good	£25,647

Missed last season after suffering a splint on near-fore; had taken record under rules to eight wins out of nine during unbeaten novice chase campaign, including victory in Racing Post Arkle; has also won Neptune Hurdle and likely to return to longer trips.

Simply Ned (Ire)

7 ch g Fruits Of Love - Bishops Lass (Marju)

Nicky Richards — **David & Nicky Robinson**

PLACINGS: /1114/4731P/F122132- — **RPR 157c**

Starts	1st	2nd	3rd	4th	Win & Pl
17	6	4	2	2	£71,633

	Date	Course	Race	Prize
138	1/14	Donc	2m½f Cls2 130-153 Ch Hcap gd-sft	£14,076
130	11/13	Ayr	2m Cls3 109-130 Ch Hcap soft	£7,798
127	2/13	Ayr	2m Cls3 112-133 Hdl Hcap soft	£5,523
117	12/11	Muss	2m Cls3 95-121 Hdl Hcap gd-sft	£6,498
	11/11	Sedg	2m1f Cls4 Nov Hdl 4-6yo good	£2,534
	10/11	Kels	2m½f Cls5 Mdn Hdl gd-sft	£1,819

Moved straight into handicaps when sent chasing last season and made steady progress with two wins coming off 130 and 138; took another big step forward when second to Balder Succes in Grade 1 novice chase at Aintree; looks a very exciting prospect.

Sir Des Champs (Fr)

8 b g Robin Des Champs - Liste En Tete (Video Rock)

Willie Mullins (Ir) — **Gigginstown House Stud**

PLACINGS: 1/11/11111/24121/F4- — **RPR 158+c**

Starts	1st	2nd	3rd	4th	Win & Pl
15	10	2	-	2	£482,585

	Date	Course	Race	Prize
	4/13	Punc	3m1f Gd1 Ch soft	£73,171
	2/13	Leop	3m Gd1 Ch sft-hvy	£74,797
	4/12	Punc	3m1f Nov Gd1 Ch sft-hvy	£41,333
	3/12	Chel	2m4f Cls1 Nov Gd2 Ch good	£51,255
	1/12	Leop	2m5f Nov Gd2 Ch yield	£21,667
	12/11	Limk	2m3½f Nov Gd2 Ch heavy	£21,013
	12/11	Fair	2m5½f Ch sft-hvy	£7,138
134	3/11	Chel	2m4½f Cls2 127-140 Cond Hdl Hcap good	£28,179
	1/11	Navn	2m Hdl soft	£7,733
	3/10	Autl	2m1½f Hdl 4yo v soft	£18,690

Top staying chaser who had last season cut short by tendon injury after fourth in Lexus Chase; previous three seasons had seen him win twice at Cheltenham Festival before chasing home Bobs Worth in 2013 Gold Cup; should have that race on agenda again.

Sire De Grugy (Fr)

8 ch g My Risk - Hirlish (Passing Sale)

Gary Moore — **The Preston Family & Friends Ltd**

PLACINGS: 4138/121411/1211111- — **RPR 174+c**

Starts	1st	2nd	3rd	4th	Win & Pl
24	14	4	2	2	£613,804

	Date	Course	Race	Prize
	4/14	Sand	2m Cls1 Gd1 Ch gd-sft	£71,188
	3/14	Chel	2m Cls1 Gd1 Ch good	£199,325
	1/14	Asct	2m1f Cls1 Gd1 Ch heavy	£59,199
	12/13	Kemp	2m Cls1 Gd2 Ch soft	£45,774
	12/13	Sand	2m Cls1 Gd1 Ch good	£76,883
161	10/13	Chep	2m½f Cls2 135-161 Ch Hcap soft	£16,245
	4/13	Sand	2m Cls1 Gd2 Ch good	£56,950
	4/13	Strf	2m1½f Cls4 Nov Ch good	£4,549
	11/12	Ling	2m Cls4 Nov Ch heavy	£3,217
	10/12	Kemp	2m Cls4 Ch good	£3,899
141	2/12	Tntn	2m1f Cls2 121-147 Hdl Hcap gd-sft	£12,660
	2/11	Kemp	2m Cls1 Nov Gd2 Hdl gd-sft	£12,086
	2/11	Folk	2m1½f Cls4 Nov Hdl soft	£1,918
	1/11	Fknm	2m Cls5 Mdn Hdl soft	£1,713

Outstanding two-mile chaser of last season in Sprinter Sacre's absence, winning four Grade 1 races and dispelling doubts that he was less effective at Cheltenham and on quicker ground with easy win in Champion Chase; sets high standard in that division.

Sizing Europe (Ire)

12 b g Pistolet Bleu - Jennie Dun (Mandalus)

Henry de Bromhead (Ir) — **Ann & Alan Potts Partnership**

PLACINGS: 121121/111122/1244-1 — **RPR 163c**

Starts	1st	2nd	3rd	4th	Win & Pl
42	21	10	3	3	£1,294,122

	Date	Course	Race	Prize
	4/14	Punc	2m Gd1 Ch good	£103,333
	10/13	Gowr	2m4f Gd2 Ch good	£20,610
	2/13	Punc	2m Gd2 Ch heavy	£21,138
	12/12	Leop	2m1f Gd1 Ch soft	£54,167
	11/12	Clon	2m4f Gd2 Ch soft	£24,375
	10/12	Gowr	2m4f Gd2 Ch good	£21,125
	4/12	Punc	2m Gd1 Ch sft-hvy	£72,333
	2/12	Punc	2m Gd2 Ch heavy	£21,667
	12/11	Sand	2m Cls1 Gd1 Ch gd-sft	£68,340
	10/11	Gowr	2m4f Gd2 Ch soft	£21,853
	3/11	Chel	2m Cls1 Gd1 Ch good	£182,432
	3/10	Chel	2m Cls1 Gd1 Ch gd-sft	£85,515
	12/09	Leop	2m1f Nov Gd1 Ch yield	£56,796
	11/09	Punc	2m Nov Gd2 Ch heavy	£25,282
	10/09	Punc	2m2f Nov Gd3 Ch gd-yld	£18,013
	5/09	Punc	2m4f Ch heavy	£9,057
	1/08	Leop	2m Gd1 Hdl yield	£73,529
137	11/07	Chel	2m½f Cls1 Gd3 124-143 Hdl Hcap soft	£57,020
	4/07	Punc	2m Nov Hdl good	£13,196
	11/06	Newb	2m½f Cls3 Mdn Hdl gd-sft	£6,506
	10/06	Naas	2m NHF 4yo soft	£4,289

Outstanding chaser who won Champion Chase in 2011 and was unbeaten against Irish chasers short of 3m for nearly three years subsequently; remained a force last season and famously won Grade 1 at Punchestown in May having been fourth at Cheltenham.

Sizing Gold (Ire)

7 b g Flemensfirth - Mandys Gold (Mandalus)

Henry de Bromhead (Ir) — **Alan & Ann Potts Partnership**

PLACINGS: 21/22125/126-0 — **RPR 145+c**

Starts	1st	2nd	3rd	4th	Win & Pl
11	3	5	-	-	£38,019

Date	Course	Race	Prize
12/13	Navn	2m4f Ch yld-sft	£8,415
12/12	Leop	2m4f Mdn Hdl soft	£6,325
2/12	Navn	2m NHF 4-7yo soft	£4,600

Made a big impression on chasing debut last season before being outstayed by Foxrock over 3m; returned to more suitable trip next twice but still disappointed at Cheltenham and Punchestown, possibly finding ground too quick; should do better.

ONE TO WATCH

Cantlow Failed to build on his good early season form last term, but his official mark has dipped back into the 140s and the form of his second to the smart Double Ross at Cheltenham in December suggests he could land a big handicap off his current rating.
[Steve Mason, Racing Post Ratings]

Smad Place (Fr)

7 gr g Smadoun - Bienna Star (Village Star)

Alan King — **Mrs Peter Andrews**

PLACINGS: 1310/123U/3233/U112- — **RPR 163+c**

Starts	1st	2nd	3rd	4th	Win & Pl
18	5	4	5	-	£182,981

	Date	Course	Race	Prize
	2/14	Newb	3m Cls3 Nov Ch heavy	£7,798
	11/13	Extr	3m Cls3 Nov Ch gd-sft	£6,330
144	1/12	Asct	2m3½f Cls1 Gd2 125-145 Hdl Hcap gd-sft	£22,780
	2/11	Winc	2m Cls4 Nov Hdl gd-sft	£2,439
	11/10	Newb	2m½f Cls3 Hdl 3yo gd-sft	£6,505

Dual World Hurdle third who took well to fences last season and quickly reached a similar level, finishing close second to O'Faolains Boy in RSA Chase (pair clear); hasn't finished out of first three since 2011 when completing and should run well in top chases.

Solwhit (Fr)

10 b g Solon - Toowhit Towhee (Lucky North)

Charles Byrnes (Ir) — **Top Of The Hill Syndicate**

PLACINGS: 1131162/1222/2111/2-

Starts	1st	2nd	3rd	4th	Win & Pl
23	13	7	1	-	£924,680

	Date	Course	Race	Prize
	4/13	Aint	3m½f Cls1 Gd1 Hdl gd-sft	£67,524
	3/13	Chel	3m Cls1 Gd1 Hdl gd-sft	£156,613
	1/13	Naas	2m3f Gd3 Hdl heavy	£14,533
	11/10	Punc	2m Gd1 Hdl sft-hvy	£48,894
	1/10	Leop	2m Gd1 Hdl sft-hvy	£63,274
	12/09	Leop	2m Gd1 Hdl soft	£56,796
	11/09	Punc	2m Gd1 Hdl heavy	£53,641
	5/09	Punc	2m Gd1 Hdl sft-hvy	£116,505
	4/09	Aint	2m4f Cls1 Gd1 Hdl gd-sft	£96,917
	2/09	Gowr	2m Gd2 Hdl soft	£36,342
127	11/08	Fair	2m 117-145 Hdl Hcap soft	£19,147
	4/08	Punc	2m Hdl 4yo gd-yld	£14,360
	11/07	Engh	2m½f Hdl 3yo heavy	£14,270

Missed nearly all of last season with a fetlock injury having finished second in 2013 French Champion Hurdle; had returned from similar absence when reinvented as a staying hurdler two seasons ago, winning World Hurdle and following up at Aintree.

Somersby (Ire)

10 b g Second Empire - Back To Roost (Presenting)

Mick Channon — **Mrs T P Radford**

PLACINGS: 3/1224172/34U/12U2-5 — **RPR 167c**

Starts	1st	2nd	3rd	4th	Win & Pl
30	7	8	7	3	£443,581

	Date	Course	Race	Prize
155	11/13	Extr	2m1½f Cls1 Gd2 152-172 Ch Hcap gd-sft	£35,594
	1/12	Asct	2m1f Cls1 Gd1 Ch gd-sft	£59,135
	10/11	Kemp	2m4½f Cls2 Ch good	£12,512
	12/09	Sand	2m Cls1 Nov Gd2 Ch soft	£18,813
	11/09	Wwck	2m Cls3 Nov Ch good	£6,505
	11/08	Kemp	2m Cls4 Nov Hdl 4-6yo good	£4,554
	3/08	Hntg	2m½f Cls5 NHF 4-6yo soft	£1,713

High-class two-mile chaser whose career had stalled due to attempts to step him up in distance but bounced back to form over minimum trip last season; won Haldon Gold Cup before finishing second to Sire De Grugy in Tingle Creek and Champion Chase.

Southfield Theatre (Ire)

6 b g King's Theatre - Chamoss Royale (Garde Royale)

Paul Nicholls **Mrs Angela Yeoman**

PLACINGS: 34/1311/134321- **RPR 152h**

Starts	1st	2nd	3rd	4th	Win & Pl
12	5	1	4	2	£68,907

	Date	Course	Race	Prize
	4/14	Sand	2m6f Cls1 List Hdl gd-sft	£28,475
	10/13	Winc	2m6f Cls4 Nov Hdl good	£3,249
	4/13	Winc	2m4f Cls4 Nov Hdl soft	£3,249
	3/13	Extr	2m7½f Cls4 Nov Hdl good	£3,249
	10/12	Chel	2m½f Cls4 NHF 4-6yo gd-sft	£4,549

Ran consistently well in good staying handicap hurdles last season, most notably when beaten a nose in Pertemps Final at Cheltenham; deserved subsequent narrow win at Sandown; will go novice chasing and identified by trainer as RSA type.

Special Tiara

7 b g Kayf Tara - Special Choice (Bob Back)

Henry de Bromhead (Ir) **Mrs S Rowley-Williams**

PLACINGS: 2/22112513/U3463-53 **RPR 161c**

Starts	1st	2nd	3rd	4th	Win & Pl
15	3	3	4	1	£112,232

	Date	Course	Race	Prize
	4/13	Aint	2m Cls1 Nov Gd1 Ch good	£62,190
	9/12	Baln	2m1f Ch yld-sft	£4,600
	7/12	Kbgn	2m Mdn Hdl 4-5yo yield	£4,313

Has produced all his best form on good ground, most notably when winning a Grade 1 novice chase at Aintree two seasons ago; without a win since then but ran well for a long way when sixth in Champion Chase, paying price for going too quickly in front.

Splash Of Ginge

6 b g Oscar - Land Of Honour (Supreme Leader)

Nigel Twiston-Davies **J D Neild**

PLACINGS: 464/424133102- **RPR 146h**

Starts	1st	2nd	3rd	4th	Win & Pl
12	2	2	2	4	£117,205

	Date	Course	Race	Prize
134	2/14	Newb	2m½f Cls1 Gd3 124-150 Hdl Hcap heavy	£86,849
	12/13	Aint	2m1f Cls4 Mdn Hdl soft	£5,198

Won last season's Betfair Hurdle at 33-1 and showed that was no fluke when finishing second in Grade 1 novice hurdle over 2m4f at Aintree to Lac Fontana; can continue to thrive in good handicaps.

Spring Heeled (Ire)

7 b g Old Vic - Central Arch (Dilum)

Jim Culloty (Ir) **Dr R Lambe**

PLACINGS: 481P/5334/21328015-4 **RPR 151c**

Starts	1st	2nd	3rd	4th	Win & Pl
18	4	2	3	3	£91,035

	Date	Course	Race	Prize
140	3/14	Chel	3m1½f Cls2 131-144 Am Ch Hcap good	£35,976
	8/13	Klny	2m4½f Nov Ch good	£6,451
	4/12	Limk	2m4f Nov Hdl good	£7,475
	10/11	Gway	2m Mdn Hdl 4yo heavy	£6,543

Won last season's Kim Muir Chase at Cheltenham,

improving on earlier second in Munster National; did well to be fifth in bet365 Gold Cup (jumped badly) and fourth in Galway Plate (trip too short); needs good ground; could be a Grand National horse.

Sprinter Sacre (Fr)

8 b/br g Network - Fatima III (Bayolidaan)

Nicky Henderson **Mrs Caroline Mould**

PLACINGS: /2113/11111/11111/P-

Starts	1st	2nd	3rd	4th	Win & Pl
17	14	1	1	-	£724,886

4/13	Punc	2m Gd1 Ch soft	£100,813
4/13	Aint	2m4f Cls1 Gd1 Ch good	£113,072
3/13	Chel	2m Cls1 Gd1 Ch gd-sft	£208,300
1/13	Chel	2m½f Cls1 Gd1 Ch heavy	£39,389
12/12	Sand	2m Cls1 Gd1 Ch soft	£68,340
4/12	Aint	2m Cls1 Nov Gd1 Ch good	£56,270
3/12	Chel	2m Cls1 Gd1 Ch good	£74,035
2/12	Newb	2m1f Cls1 Gd2 Ch gd-sft	£17,085
12/11	Kemp	2m Cls1 Nov Gd2 Ch good	£13,326
12/11	Donc	2m½f Cls4 Nov Ch good	£3,444
2/11	Asct	2m Cls2 Nov Hdl soft	£6,262
2/11	Ffos	2m Cls4 Nov Hdl gd-sft	£2,602
4/10	Ayr	2m Cls4 NHF 4-6yo good	£4,554
2/10	Asct	2m Cls3 NHF 4-6yo gd-sft	£5,204

Took unbeaten record over fences to ten races with five Grade 1 wins two seasons ago, including when stepped up to 2m4f for first time; suffered heart problems on only run last term so has plenty to prove but remains a league above rivals if back to his best.

Stonebrook (Ire)

6 b g Flemensfirth - Boberelle (Bob Back)

Donald McCain **John P McManus**

PLACINGS: 3113110- **RPR 127+h**

Starts	1st	2nd	3rd	4th	Win & Pl
7	4	-	2	-	£9,620

3/14	Newc	2m Cls4 Nov Hdl soft	£3,119
2/14	Ayr	2m Cls5 Mdn Hdl heavy	£2,079
12/13	Carl	2m1f Cls6 NHF 4-6yo soft	£1,560
11/13	Carl	2m1f Cls6 NHF 4-6yo heavy	£1,949

Progressed rapidly last season to win two bumpers and two novice hurdles, defying a 7lb penalty with ease at Newcastle; sent off favourite on handicap debut at Aintree and running a fair race, albeit beaten, when badly hampered; should improve.

Stuccodor (Ire)

5 b g Modigliani - Armilina (Linamix)

Dermot Weld (Ir) **Dominick Glennane**

PLACINGS: 52- **RPR 133h**

Starts	1st	2nd	3rd	4th	Win & Pl
2	-	1	-	-	£1,333

Has progressed into a smart Flat horse (won Irish Lincoln off 102 in March) and had previously shaped with promise in a couple of runs over hurdles; seems sure to win novice hurdles and may be suited by hurly-burly of big-field handicaps.

Splash Of Ginge leads the way before winning the Betfair Hurdle

Tanerko Emery (Fr)

8 b g Lavirco - Frequence (Panoramic)

David Pipe — **Walters Plant Hire Ltd & Egan Waste Ltd**

PLACINGS: 2/F5/1211325/25F- — **RPR 148+h**

Starts	1st	2nd	3rd	4th	Win & Pl
13	3	4	1	-	£51,418

124	12/12	Ling	2m Cls4 105-124 Hdl Hcap heavy	£5,848
117	12/12	Sand	2m½f Cls4 Nov 99-118 Hdl Hcap heavy	£3,249
	10/12	Strf	2m½f Cls5 Mdn Hdl gd-sft	£2,274

Missed most of last season after falling at Wincanton on second run over fences having looked unlucky to be touched off by Raya Star on chasing debut; had progressed into a smart 2m handicap hurdler (second in Imperial Cup) and retains novice chase status.

Tap Night (USA)

7 ch g Pleasant Tap - Day Mate (Dayjur)

Lucinda Russell — **John P McManus**

PLACINGS: 116/1141522/2883P49- — **RPR 141c**

Starts	1st	2nd	3rd	4th	Win & Pl
21	6	5	2	2	£81,776

	2/13	Ayr	2m5f Cls4 Nov Ch heavy	£3,899
	1/13	Ayr	2m Cls4 Nov Ch heavy	£3,899
140	11/12	Ayr	2m Cls3 121-140 Hdl Hcap soft	£7,798
	3/12	Kels	2m2f Cls1 Gd2 Hdl good	£17,085
	2/12	Newc	2m4f Cls4 Nov Hdl soft	£2,014
110	11/11	Carl	2m3½f Cls4 Nov 84-110 Hdl Hcap gd-sft	£2,738

Smart novice chaser two seasons ago (second to Captain Conan in Grade 1 at Aintree) but failed to win last season; eyecatching third at Cheltenham in January but couldn't build on that; ended campaign 12lb lower than at start and should take advantage.

Taquin Du Seuil (Fr)

7 b/br g Voix Du Nord - Sweet Laly (Marchand De Sable)

Jonjo O'Neill — **Martin Broughton & Friends 1**

PLACINGS: 12116/113211- — **RPR 164+c**

Starts	1st	2nd	3rd	4th	Win & Pl
11	7	2	1	-	£150,242

	3/14	Chel	2m4f Cls1 Nov Gd1 Ch good	£68,340
	1/14	Hayd	2m5f Cls1 Nov Gd2 Ch heavy	£17,912
	11/13	Chel	2m4½f Cls2 Nov Ch good	£12,512
	10/13	Ffos	2m Cls4 Nov Ch heavy	£4,549
	12/12	Newb	2m5f Cls1 Nov Gd1 Hdl heavy	£17,165
	12/12	Sand	2m4f Cls1 Nov Gd2 Hdl heavy	£12,676
	10/12	Uttx	2m Cls5 Mdn Hdl gd-sft	£2,144

Grade 1 winner as a novice over hurdles and fences in last two seasons; took form to another level with latest victory in JLT Novices' Chase, quickening up well to prove effectiveness on quicker ground (best form previously on heavy); could stay further.

Teaforthree (Ire)

10 b g Oscar - Ethel's Bay (Strong Gale)

Rebecca Curtis — **Conyers, O'Reilly, Roddis & Zeffman**

PLACINGS: 8/321P11/86203/928U- — **RPR 158c**

Starts	1st	2nd	3rd	4th	Win & Pl
22	4	5	4	1	£196,607

	3/12	Chel	4m Cls2 Nov Am Ch good	£44,970
	2/12	Chep	3m Cls4 Nov Ch soft	£2,599
	12/11	Chep	3m Cls3 Nov Ch heavy	£4,549
	11/10	Ffos	3m Cls4 Nov Hdl gd-sft	£2,602

Without a win since 2012 National Hunt Chase but was placed in Grand National and Welsh National two seasons ago and a Listed handicap chase at Ascot last season; unseated rider when favourite for the National and may be trained for Aintree again.

Ted Veale (Ire)

7 b g Revoque - Rose Tanner (Roselier)

Tony Martin (Ir) — **John Breslin**

PLACINGS: 4/3192312/8354F6-781 — **RPR 153c**

Starts	1st	2nd	3rd	4th	Win & Pl
20	4	4	3	2	£99,558

	8/14	Gway	2m1f Ch yld-sft	£8,050
134	3/13	Chel	2m1f Cls1 Gd3 132-154 Hdl Hcap gd-sft	£45,560
	9/12	List	2m Mdn Hdl 5yo heavy	£6,900
	1/12	Leop	2m NHF 5-7yo heavy	£4,600

Gained first win over jumps since 2013 County Hurdle when winning beginners' chase at Galway this summer having largely struggled over fences last season; should be a threat in good novice and handicap chases over 2m.

Texas Jack (Ire)

8 b g Curtain Time - Sailors Run (Roselier)

Noel Meade (Ir) — **Robert Watson**

PLACINGS: 146476/2133127/3314- — **RPR 159c**

Starts	1st	2nd	3rd	4th	Win & Pl
19	6	2	4	3	£152,489

	1/14	Thur	2m4f Gd2 Ch soft	£20,313
	1/13	Leop	2m5f Nov Gd2 Ch heavy	£21,138
	11/12	Naas	2m3f Ch sft-hvy	£6,900
	11/11	Clon	2m4f Nov Hdl soft	£8,328
	10/11	Fair	2m4f Mdn Hdl good	£5,948
	5/11	Punc	2m NHF 4-5yo gd-yld	£50,862

Dual Grade 2 winner over fences, most notably when landing 2m4f Kinloch Brae Chase at Thurles last season; has shown all his best form over that sort of trip and didn't quite seem to stay on both attempts at 3m, though highly tried at Grade 1 level both times.

The Giant Bolster

9 b g Black Sam Bellamy - Divisa (Lomitas)

David Bridgwater — **Simon Hunt & Gary Lambton**

PLACINGS: 4U72142/3P247/7U513- **RPR 170c**

Starts	1st	2nd	3rd	4th	Win & Pl
30	5	5	3	3	£344,669

	1/14	Chel	3m1½f Cls1 Gd2 Ch heavy	£56,950
145	1/12	Chel	2m5f Cls1 Gd3 142-168 Ch Hcap gd-sft	£22,780
140	1/11	Chel	2m5f Cls2 Nov 121-140 Ch Hcap gd-sft	£12,524
	10/10	Worc	2m7f Cls3 Nov Ch good	£4,861
	11/09	MRas	2m3f Cls4 Nov Hdl soft	£2,797

Has a superb record at Cheltenham and has made the frame in last three runnings of Gold Cup, coming closest when beaten three-quarters of a length in third last season; had been out of sorts earlier in campaign until winning Argento Chase.

The Italian Yob (Ire)

6 b g Milan - The Rebel Lady (Mister Lord)

Nick Williams — **The Macaroni Beach Society**

PLACINGS: 84/U3126/221PPP- **RPR 139+c**

Starts	1st	2nd	3rd	4th	Win & Pl
13	2	3	1	1	£19,232

125	12/13	Sand	2m4½f Cls3 Nov 113-125 Ch Hcap good	£6,498
	12/12	Extr	2m1f Cls4 Nov Hdl 4-6yo heavy	£3,249

Bitterly disappointing at end of last season when pulled up three times, breaking a blood vessel on first occasion and appearing to lose confidence; had looked a smart prospect previously and said to possess a huge amount of scope by his trainer.

The Last Samuri (Ire)

6 ch g Flemensfirth - Howaboutthis (Oscar)

Donald McCain — **Paul & Clare Rooney**

PLACINGS: FU2/121119- **RPR 132+h**

Starts	1st	2nd	3rd	4th	Win & Pl
5	3	1	-	-	£10,873

	1/14	Catt	3m1½f Cls4 Nov Hdl soft	£3,249
	11/13	Bang	2m4f Cls4 Nov Hdl soft	£3,249
	11/13	Kels	2m6½f Cls4 Nov Hdl gd-sft	£3,899

Looked a fine prospect when winning three novice hurdles last season; found step up in class beyond him at Aintree (trainer had feared he may be too immature) but has always been seen as a chaser in the making and should continue to progress over fences.

The Liquidator

6 b g Overbury - Alikat (Alhaarth)

David Pipe — **R S Brookhouse**

PLACINGS: 2/2141/1150-4 **RPR 145h**

Starts	1st	2nd	3rd	4th	Win & Pl
10	4	2	-	2	£89,588

	11/13	Chel	2m½f Cls1 Nov Gd2 Hdl good	£17,085
	10/13	Carl	2m1f Cls4 Nov Hdl soft	£3,899
	4/13	Punc	2m Gd1 NHF 4-7yo soft	£42,276
	2/13	Extr	2m1f Cls6 NHF 4-6yo heavy	£1,625

Won a Grade 1 bumper at Punchestown two seasons ago and made a bright start to hurdling career when winning first two races last season, most notably in a Grade 2 at Cheltenham by 15 lengths; disappointed subsequently but worth another chance.

The New One (Ire)

6 b g King's Theatre - Thuringe (Turgeon)

Nigel Twiston-Davies — **Mrs S Such**

PLACINGS: 1161/111212/11231- **RPR 173+h**

Starts	1st	2nd	3rd	4th	Win & Pl
15	10	3	1	-	£437,514

	4/14	Aint	2m4f Cls1 Gd1 Hdl good	£112,540
	12/13	Chel	2m1f Cls1 Gd2 Hdl good	£74,035
	10/13	Kemp	2m Cls1 List Hdl gd-sft	£14,238
	3/13	Chel	2m5f Cls1 Nov Gd1 Hdl gd-sft	£68,340
	1/13	Wwck	2m5f Cls1 Nov Gd2 Hdl soft	£15,735
	10/12	Chel	2m5f Cls2 Nov Hdl gd-sft	£10,635
	10/12	NAbb	2m3f Cls4 Nov Hdl soft	£2,924
	4/12	Aint	2m1f Cls1 Gd2 NHF 4-6yo good	£14,238
	1/12	Chel	1m6½f Cls1 List NHF 4yo gd-sft	£7,133
	11/11	Wwck	1m6f Cls6 NHF 3yo good	£2,053

Suffered a frustrating campaign last year when just beaten in Christmas Hurdle after late blunder and badly hampered in Champion Hurdle before finishing fast in third; still won International and Aintree Hurdle and should be big player in Champion Hurdle again.

The Paparrazi Kid (Ire)

7 b g Milan - Banbury Cross (Supreme Leader)

Willie Mullins (Ir) — **Byerley Thoroughbred Racing**

PLACINGS: 12/2221031/131- **RPR 146c**

Starts	1st	2nd	3rd	4th	Win & Pl
12	5	4	2	-	£91,555

	12/13	Limk	2m3½f Nov Gd2 Ch soft	£19,817
	11/13	Limk	2m3½f Ch sft-hvy	£7,012
125	4/13	Punc	2m4f 114-139 Hdl Hcap heavy	£40,325
	1/13	Limk	2m3f Mdn Hdl heavy	£7,854
	12/11	Navn	2m NHF 4-7yo heavy	£4,759

Missed second half of last season but had proved himself a smart novice chaser with two wins from three runs over fences, claiming notable scalp of Felix Yonger when coping with soft ground far better than runner-up at Limerick; should stay 3m.

The Rainbow Hunter

10 b g Rainbow High - Sobranie (High Top)

Kim Bailey — **May We Never Be Found Out Partnership**

PLACINGS: /FF204/311P4UP/261U- **RPR 148c**

Starts	1st	2nd	3rd	4th	Win & Pl
31	5	6	3	5	£86,339

136	1/14	Donc	3m Cls1 List 127-153 Ch Hcap soft	£42,713
135	11/12	Asct	3m Cls3 118-135 Ch Hcap soft	£12,512
131	5/12	Sthl	3m½f Cls3 118-131 Ch Hcap good	£5,558
114	11/10	Ffos	2m5f Cls4 Nov 96-115 Ch Hcap gd-sft	£3,253
112	1/10	Winc	2m Cls3 91-116 Hdl Hcap heavy	£6,337

Apparently much improved for undergoing a breathing operation midway through last season, winning Sky Bet Chase at Doncaster on first subsequent outing; unseated rider on first circuit in Grand National; likely to be a contender in top staying handicaps.

The Romford Pele (Ire)

7 b g Accordion - Back And Fore (Bob Back)

Rebecca Curtis — **Trembath, Hill, Outhart & Fletcher**

PLACINGS: 7/2211488/233246-311 — **RPR 154+c**

Starts		1st	2nd	3rd	4th	Win & Pl
20		5	6	3	2	£78,386
139	6/14	Uttx	3m2f Cls1 List 127-146 Ch Hcap good			£34,170
128	6/14	Worc	2m4f Cls3 111-132 Ch Hcap gd-sft			£7,666
	12/12	Chep	2m4f Cls4 Nov Hdl heavy			£3,249
	11/12	Tntn	2m1f Cls3 Nov Hdl good			£5,198
	2/12	Bang	2m1f Cls6 NHF 4-6yo good			£1,437

Has always shown lots of ability but initially dogged by jumping problems when sent novice chasing last season; came good this summer when two wins included Summer Cup at Uttoxeter and can improve again, though raised 22lb for those successes.

The Tullow Tank (Ire)

6 b g Oscar - Bobbing Back (Bob Back)

Dessie Hughes (Ir) — **Barry Connell**

PLACINGS: 2/451/1112- — **RPR 148+h**

Starts		1st	2nd	3rd	4th	Win & Pl
7		4	1	-	1	£105,577
	12/13	Leop	2m Nov Gd1 Hdl soft			£42,276
	12/13	Fair	2m Nov Gd1 Hdl gd-yld			£39,634
	11/13	Naas	2m Mdn Hdl yld-sft			£5,610
	3/13	Fair	2m NHF 4-7yo soft			£5,049

Won two Grade 1 novice hurdles last season and ran another fine race in Deloitte Hurdle when second to Vautour; missed Cheltenham at owner's request due to problems concerning Philip Fenton and later removed from yard; good chasing prospect who should stay well.

The Westener Boy (Ire)

7 b g Westerner - Designer Lady (Buckskin)

Colm Murphy (Ir) — **John P McManus**

PLACINGS: 5F11/2231PF/32- — **RPR 133+h**

Starts		1st	2nd	3rd	4th	Win & Pl
10		2	3	2	-	£19,769
	12/12	Navn	3m Ch sft-hvy			£6,900
	1/12	Fair	2m NHF 5-7yo sft-hvy			£4,600

Promising novice chaser two seasons ago but fell when joint-favourite for Thyestes Chase that year and picked up a knock which ruled him out for 13 months; twice shaped well over hurdles at end of last term; should be a force in top staying handicaps.

Theatre Guide (Ire)

7 b g King's Theatre - Erintante (Denel)

Colin Tizzard — **Mrs Jean R Bishop**

PLACINGS: 41/2617/13PFP1/332- — **RPR 158+c**

Starts		1st	2nd	3rd	4th	Win & Pl
15		4	2	3	1	£72,867
	4/13	NAbb	2m5½f Cls3 Nov Ch gd-sft			£8,578
	11/12	Extr	2m1½f Cls2 Nov Ch gd-sft			£9,902
	2/12	Winc	2m Cls4 Nov Hdl soft			£3,249
	4/11	Chep	2m½f Cls6 NHF 4-6yo gd-sft			£1,821

Missed second half of last season having gone close in two major staying handicap chases, finishing third in Hennessy Gold Cup and second at Cheltenham just two weeks later (both times clear of remainder); should again be a contender in similar races.

Third Intention (left): consistent in smart novice chase company and should make smooth transition to decent staying handicaps

Third Intention (Ire)

7 b g Azamour - Third Dimension (Suave Dancer)

Colin Tizzard — **Robert & Sarah Tizzard**

PLACINGS: 0184/2333262/132335- — **RPR 149c**

Starts	1st	2nd	3rd	4th	Win & Pl
25	4	7	6	1	£124,762

	Date	Course	Race	Prize
	10/13	Chel	2m4f Cls2 Nov Ch good	£12,512
	2/12	Font	2m4f Cls1 Gd2 Hdl gd-sft	£16,800
	4/11	Chel	2m1f Cls2 Nov Hdl good	£6,262
	12/10	Newb	2m½f Cls4 Hdl 3yo good	£3,903

Has spent last two seasons racing in top novice chases having won only once at Cheltenham last term; has run several fine races in defeat, getting placed four times at Grade 1 level and five at Grade 2; should be a smart handicapper from 2m4f to 3m.

Thomas Brown

5 b g Sir Harry Lewis - Tentsmuir (Arctic Lord)

Harry Fry — **The Corse Lawners**

PLACINGS: 11/4181- — **RPR 122b**

Starts	1st	2nd	3rd	4th	Win & Pl
4	2	-	-	1	£5,445

	Date	Course	Race	Prize
	3/14	Bang	2m1f Cls5 NHF 4-6yo gd-sft	£2,053
	11/13	Newb	2m½f Cls4 NHF 4-6yo gd-sft	£3,249

Progressed well in bumpers last season apart from one poor run when unsuited by heavy ground; clearly held in high regard having been sent off 5-4 for a Listed contest that day and redeemed reputation by winning at Bangor; should make a good staying novice.

Thousand Stars (Fr)

10 gr g Grey Risk - Livaniana (Saint Estephe)

Willie Mullins (Ir) — **Hammer & Trowel Syndicate**

PLACINGS: 3/11432632/495231-19 — **RPR 158+h**

Starts	1st	2nd	3rd	4th	Win & Pl
46	10	8	8	7	£901,078

	Date	Course	Race	Prize
	5/14	Autl	2m5½f Gd2 Hdl v soft	£65,625
	4/14	Fair	2m4f Gd2 Hdl gd-yld	£27,083
	6/12	Autl	3m1½f Gd1 Hdl v soft	£138,750
	5/12	Autl	2m5½f Gd2 Hdl v soft	£65,625
	11/11	Punc	2m Gd1 Hdl soft	£41,379
	6/11	Autl	3m1½f Gd1 Hdl v soft	£143,534
134	3/10	Chel	2m1f Cls1 Gd3 129-152 Hdl Hcap good	£42,758
125	11/09	Fair	2m 121-149 Hdl Hcap heavy	£18,645
107	10/09	Naas	2m3f 103-130 Hdl Hcap good	£16,433
	5/08	Klny	2m1f Mdn Hdl 4yo good	£4,827

High-class hurdler who has been a regular competitor at top level ever since winning 2010 County Hurdle, adding two French Champion Hurdles; had gone nearly two years without a win until landing Grade 2 races at Fairyhouse and Auteuil last spring.

Three Kingdoms (Ire)

5 ch g Street Cry - Chan Tong (Hampstead)

John Ferguson — **Bloomfields**

PLACINGS: 2340/13110- — **RPR 144h**

Starts	1st	2nd	3rd	4th	Win & Pl
9	3	1	2	1	£22,874

	Date	Course	Race	Prize
131	12/13	Kemp	2m Cls3 116-132 Hdl Hcap soft	£12,996
	12/13	Leic	2m Cls4 Nov Hdl gd-sft	£3,899
	10/13	Weth	2m4f Cls4 Nov Hdl gd-sft	£3,249

Failed to win during first season over hurdles but did much better last season when winning three times from 2m to 2m4f, most notably in a

handicap hurdle at Kempton; not disgraced when 12th in Supreme Novices' Hurdle; interesting handicapper.

Tiger Roll (Ire)

4 b g Authorized - Swiss Roll (Entrepreneur)

Gordon Elliott (Ir) **Gigginstown House Stud**

PLACINGS: 121-7 **RPR 144+h**

Starts	1st	2nd	3rd	4th	Win & Pl
4	2	1	-	-	£84,155

	Date	Course	Race	Prize
	3/14	Chel	2m1f Cls1 Gd1 Hdl 4yo good	£68,340
	11/13	MRas	2m1f Cls4 Hdl 3yo soft	£3,899

Impressive winner of last season's Triumph Hurdle when quickening clear of Kentucky Hyden before running well below that form at Punchestown; had run only twice previously (unraced on Flat) so likely to have plenty of improvement to come.

Timesremembered (Ire)

6 b/br g Akbar - Native Hope (Be My Native)

Emma Lavelle **Tim Syder & Sarah Prior**

PLACINGS: 2213/112266- **RPR 146h**

Starts	1st	2nd	3rd	4th	Win & Pl
7	2	2	1	-	£35,231

	Date	Course	Race	Prize
	10/13	Chep	2m4f Cls1 Nov Gd2 Hdl soft	£17,085
	10/13	Uttx	2m Cls5 Mdn Hdl good	£2,209

Won first two hurdle races last October, including Persian War Novices' Hurdle, and ran well in defeat subsequently; sixth in Coral Cup on good ground having had previous best run on heavy when second in Challow Hurdle; likely to go novice chasing.

Toner D'Oudairies (Fr)

7 b g Polish Summer - Iroise D'Oudairies (Passing Sale)

Gordon Elliott (Ir) **Gigginstown House Stud**

PLACINGS: 1/2F4431P1112212241- **RPR 154c**

Starts	1st	2nd	3rd	4th	Win & Pl
37	10	8	2	6	£175,937

	Date	Course	Race	Prize
	4/14	Cork	3m Gd3 Ch yield	£16,250
	1/14	Thur	2m2f List Ch heavy	£14,300
	10/13	Punc	2m7f Gd3 Ch good	£15,589
	10/13	Slig	2m4f Ch heavy	£8,835
	9/13	List	2m4f Nov Ch soft	£11,626
	8/13	Tram	2m6f Ch good	£7,012
	4/13	Fair	2m1f Ch yield	£6,732
	12/10	Fair	2m Gd3 Hdl 3yo soft	£17,257
	11/10	DRoy	2m Mdn Hdl 3yo soft	£8,549
	7/10	Le L	1m3½f NHF 3yo gd-sft	£11,504

Wonderfully consistent during busy campaign last season, finishing out of first two only once in last ten races when close fourth to Boston Bob in Grade 1 at Punchestown; won twice at Grade 3 level and was second in four Grade 2s; effective from 2m to 3m.

Tour Des Champs (Fr)

7 b/br g Robin Des Champs - Massada I (Kashtan)

Nigel Twiston-Davies **H R Mould**

PLACINGS: 06/1F81F13874/26P35- **RPR 137c**

Starts	1st	2nd	3rd	4th	Win & Pl
22	4	2	3	1	£62,269

	Date	Course	Race	Prize
	2/13	Ffos	3m Cls3 Nov Ch heavy	£7,214
127	12/12	Ludl	3m Cls3 115-129 Ch Hcap soft	£9,583
	5/12	Uttx	2m6½f Cls4 Nov Ch gd-sft	£3,249
	10/11	Strf	2m6½f Cls4 Mdn Hdl gd-sft	£2,599

Big eyecatcher when fourth in 2013 Scottish National as a novice and expected to land a similar

Trifolium: smart performer can score at around 2m over fences this season

prize last season (sent off favourite for two major handicaps) but just came up short; still ran well several times and has continued to slip to a very good mark.

Trifolium (Fr)

7 b g Goldneyev - Opium Des Mottes (April Night)

Charles Byrnes (Ir) **Gigginstown House Stud**

PLACINGS: 23112132/24/122133-5 RPR **158c**

Starts	1st	2nd	3rd	4th	Win & Pl
24	7	8	5	1	£200,724

	1/14	Leop	2m1f Nov Gd1 Ch heavy	£43,333
	11/13	Thur	2m2f Ch yield	£4,488
	2/12	Punc	2m Nov Gd2 Hdl heavy	£21,396
	12/11	Limk	2m Hdl 4yo heavy	£11,487
	12/11	Cork	2m Mdn Hdl 4-5yo sft-hvy	£5,948
	5/11	Fntb	1m4½f NHF 4yo soft	£12,069
	11/10	Ange	1m6½f NHF 3yo v soft	£7,522

Won last season's Arkle at Leopardstown but otherwise tends to come up short at top level (beaten in all other seven Grade 1 races); still ran well to finish third at Cheltenham and Aintree and could find plenty of opportunities in good 2m chases in Ireland.

Triolo D'Alene (Fr)

7 ch g Epalo - Joliette D'Alene (Garde Royale)

Nicky Henderson **Mr & Mrs Sandy Orr**

PLACINGS: 4541110/2P381/1310P- RPR **164+c**

Starts	1st	2nd	3rd	4th	Win & Pl
17	6	1	2	2	£230,295

147	11/13	Newb	3m2½f Cls1 Gd3 132-158 Ch Hcap good	£99,663
139	4/13	Hntg	3m Cls2 130-156 Ch Hcap good	£14,076
132	4/13	Aint	2m5½f Cls1 Gd3 125 151 Ch Hcap gd-sft	£67,524
127	1/12	Asct	2m3f Cls3 Nov 120-134 Ch Hcap gd-sft	£9,495
	11/11	Fntb	2m2f Ch 4yo v soft	£9,103
	10/11	Mlns	2m2f Ch 4yo soft	£6,621

Slow learner following arrival with big reputation from France three seasons ago but proved himself a high-class chaser when winning Hennessy Gold Cup last season; pulled up in Grand National despite winning over fences previously; needs good ground.

Trustan Times (Ire)

8 b g Heron Island - Ballytrustan Maid (Orchestra)

Tim Easterby **Mrs M E Armitage & Peter Armitage**

PLACINGS: 1233236/1132/483343- RPR **150h**

Starts	1st	2nd	3rd	4th	Win & Pl
19	4	4	7	2	£112,697

142	11/12	Hayd	3m Cls1 Gd3 124-142 Hdl Hcap soft	£45,560
134	11/12	Weth	2m4f Cls3 108-134 Hdl Hcap gd-sft	£5,198
	11/11	Sedg	2m4f Cls5 Ch good	£2,079
	1/11	Weth	2m4f Cls4 Nov Hdl 4-7yo soft	£2,602

Without a win since 2012 Fixed Brush Hurdle at Haydock but has run several fine races in defeat; good third in last season's Scottish National on only second run over fences since novice campaign three seasons ago and should have more to offer in that sphere.

Turban (Fr)

7 b g Dom Alco - Indianabelle (Useful)

Willie Mullins (Ir) **Edward O'Connell**

PLACINGS: 152402/221/4212F- RRPR **155+c**

Starts	1st	2nd	3rd	4th	Win & Pl
14	3	6	-	2	£78,058

140	1/14	Fair	2m1f 127-148 Ch Hcap soft	£50,000
	4/13	Cork	2m Ch heavy	£6,732
	11/11	Thur	2m Mdn Hdl 4yo sft-hvy	£4,461

Lightly raced over fences in last two seasons and gained biggest win in a strong handicap chase at Fairyhouse in January; outstayed over 2m4f on heavy ground and may be best over 2m in similar conditions; should progress after just six chase starts.

Turn Over Sivola (Fr)

7 b g Assessor - Notting Hill (Garde Royale)

Alan King **International Plywood (Importers) Ltd**

PLACINGS: 4/1219301/0222322-21 RPR **144+c**

Starts	1st	2nd	3rd	4th	Win & Pl
20	4	7	3	2	£48,655

	5/14	Hntg	2m½f Cls4 Nov Ch gd-sft	£3,769
119	4/13	Winc	2m Cls3 114-130 Hdl Hcap good	£5,254
	11/12	Plum	2m Cls4 Nov Hdl gd-sft	£2,669
	5/12	Plum	2m Cls5 Mdn Hdl soft	£1,916

Had been placed in all seven runs over fences before finally breaking duck at 2-9 in May, meaning he retains novice status; had produced best effort when second in Red Rum Handicap Chase at Aintree and should do well in more top 2m handicaps.

Twinlight (Fr)

7 b g Muhtathir - Fairlight (Big Shuffle)

Willie Mullins (Ir) **M L Bloodstock Ltd**

PLACINGS: 135F/3111241/11332-6 RPR **161+c**

Starts	1st	2nd	3rd	4th	Win & Pl
26	8	3	8	1	£258,008

	12/13	Cork	2m Gd2 Ch soft	£23,780
	10/13	Naas	2m Gd3 Ch yld-sft	£14,533
146	4/13	Punc	2m 118-146 Ch Hcap heavy	£13,211
	11/12	Punc	2m Nov Gd2 Ch heavy	£21,688
	10/12	Gway	2m1f Nov Gd3 Ch soft	£16,250
	9/12	List	2m1f Ch heavy	£8,050
	4/11	Fair	2m Gd3 Hdl 4yo good	£16,250
	5/10	Autl	2m1½f List Hdl 3yo v soft	£36,106

Has a good record in good 2m chases, winning two Graded chases in each of last two seasons, but disappointed at Punchestown when sixth in first Grade 1; doesn't seem to stay much beyond 2m (well beaten on all four attempts at around 2m4f).

ONE TO WATCH

Next Sensation Springheeled trailblazer. Temper his enthusiasm and the sky's the limit. *[Dave Edwards, Topspeed]*

Ubak (Fr)

6 b g Kapgarde - Gesse Parade (Dress Parade)

Gary Moore — **Nick Peacock**

PLACINGS: **3P4/234712/**

Starts	1st	2nd	3rd	4th	Win & Pl
9	1	2	2	2	£63,025

	Date	Course	Race	Prize
	4/13	Aint	2m4f Cls1 Nov Gd2 Hdl gd-sft	£34,170

Missed last season through injury; had come good at end of previous campaign when running away with a Grade 2 novice hurdle at Aintree by 16 lengths and proving that was no fluke by running Un Atout close at Punchestown; likely to go novice chasing.

Un Ace (Fr)

6 b g Voix Du Nord - First Ball (Beyssac)

Kim Bailey — **Ace In The Pack Partnership**

PLACINGS: **30/18P-** RPR **145h**

Starts	1st	2nd	3rd	4th	Win & Pl
5	1	-	1	-	£4,127

	Date	Course	Race	Prize
	2/14	Donc	2m½f Cls4 Nov Hdl 4-7yo gd-sft	£3,899
	1/13	Ling	2m Cls6 NHF 4-6yo std-slw	£1,625

Restricted to just three runs last season having waited for quicker ground before winning on good to soft on hurdling debut at Doncaster; did very well to finish eighth in Supreme Novices' Hurdle next time but broke blood vessels at Aintree; sure to improve.

Un Atout (Fr)

6 br g Robin Des Champs - Badrapette (Bad Conduct)

Willie Mullins (Ir) — **Gigginstown House Stud**

PLACINGS: **1/1141/**

Starts	1st	2nd	3rd	4th	Win & Pl
5	4	-	-	1	£67,729

	Date	Course	Race	Prize
	4/13	Punc	2m4f Nov Gd1 Hdl heavy	£40,325
	1/13	Naas	2m Nov Hdl heavy	£10,659
	12/12	Navn	2m Mdn Hdl 4yo heavy	£5,750
	1/12	Naas	2m NHF 4yo sft-hvy	£4,600

Missed last season through injury; had suffered only one defeat two seasons ago in novice hurdles when fourth in red-hot Supreme Novices' Hurdle; benefited from step up in trip when winning Grade 1 at Punchestown and built to be a chaser.

ONE TO WATCH

Brother Brian Lightly raced six-year-old who improved his Racing Post Rating with each run last season, rounding off with a win in a competitive handicap at Cheltenham in April. Looks sure to rate higher and win more races.
[Steve Mason, Racing Post Ratings]

Un De Sceaux (Fr)

6 b g Denham Red - Hotesse De Sceaux (April Night)

Willie Mullins (Ir) — **E O'Connell**

PLACINGS: **1/111/11111-** RPR **164+h**

Starts	1st	2nd	3rd	4th	Win & Pl
9	9	-	-	-	£181,876

	Date	Course	Race	Prize
	4/14	Autl	2m3½f Gd2 Hdl heavy	£65,625
	3/14	Autl	2m3½f Gd3 Hdl v soft	£50,625
	2/14	Gowr	2m Gd2 Hdl heavy	£21,667
	1/14	Navn	2m Hdl soft	£10,833
	12/13	Thur	2m Hdl soft	£8,695
	4/13	Punc	2m Nov Hdl heavy	£11,890
	2/13	Punc	2m Mdn Hdl sft-hvy	£4,207
	10/12	Sbri	1m4f NHF 4yo v soft	£4,167
	2/12	Mchl	1m4f NHF 4yo gd-sft	£4,167

Unbeaten in nine bumpers and hurdle races, gaining all three victories in Ireland last season by wide margins; avoided big spring festivals to win twice at Auteuil, though looked less impressive when stepped up to 2m4f; deserves to be tested at higher level.

Un Temps Pour Tout (Ire)

5 b g Robin Des Champs - Rougedespoir (Bonnet Rouge)

David Pipe — **Professor Caroline Tisdall & Bryan Drew**

PLACINGS: **333/11331321-3** RPR **156+h**

Starts	1st	2nd	3rd	4th	Win & Pl
12	4	1	7	-	£179,784

	Date	Course	Race	Prize
	2/14	Asct	2m3½f Cls2 Nov Hdl heavy	£15,640
	9/13	Autl	2m2f Gd3 Hdl 4yo v soft	£49,390
0	5/13	Autl	2m3½f List Hdl 4yo Hcap heavy	£34,756
	5/13	Bord	2m2½f Hdl 4yo gd-sft	£8,585

Record jumps purchase after finishing third to Ptit Zig in Grade 1 hurdle at Auteuil last season; showed lots of promise in three runs for David Pipe, winning well on heavy ground but coping with quicker when third at Punchestown; should go novice chasing.

Une Artiste (Fr)

6 b m Alberto Giacometti - Castagnette III (Tin Soldier)

Nicky Henderson — **Simon Munir**

PLACINGS: **1411R/119P/7212181-3** RPR **138+c**

Starts	1st	2nd	3rd	4th	Win & Pl
22	11	2	2	1	£159,915

	Date	Course	Race	Prize
	4/14	Fair	2m4f Gd3 Ch gd-yld	£18,958
	2/14	Kemp	2m4½f Cls2 Ch heavy	£12,512
	12/13	Hntg	2m4½f Cls4 Nov Ch gd-sft	£4,874
	1/13	Sand	2m4f Cls1 List Hdl heavy	£11,390
	11/12	Weth	2m½f Cls1 List Hdl gd-sft	£11,390
	4/12	Chel	2m1f Cls1 Nov List Hdl soft	£11,888
127	3/12	Chel	2m½f Cls1 Gd3 125-138 Hdl 4yo Hcap good	£34,170
	2/12	Hayd	2m Cls2 Hdl 4yo soft	£10,072
	1/12	Pau	2m1½f Hdl 4yo heavy	£12,800
	12/11	Pau	1m4f NHF 3yo v soft	£6,466
	10/11	Fntb	1m4½f NHF 3yo v soft	£6,034

Smart mare who won Fred Winter Hurdle at Cheltenham in 2012 and adapted well to fences last season, winning three times including a Grade 3 mares' contest at Fairyhouse; better than bare form of third at Punchestown in May (lost ground at start).

Union Dues (Fr)

6 b g Malinas - Royale Dorothy (Smadoun)

Willie Mullins (Ir) | **Allan McLuckie**

PLACINGS: **118/**

Starts	1st	2nd	3rd	4th	Win & Pl
3	2	-	-	-	£19,208

	Date	Course	Race	Prize
	12/12	Navn	2m Gd2 NHF 4-7yo heavy	£14,896
	7/12	Klny	2m1f NHF 4yo gd-yld	£4,313

Missed last season through injury; had been a leading bumper performer two seasons ago, winning twice including a Grade 2 at Navan, though disappointed in Champion Bumper at Cheltenham; should be a leading novice hurdler.

Unioniste (Fr)

6 gr g Dom Alco - Gleep Will (Laniste)

Paul Nicholls | **J Hales**

PLACINGS: **422165/113114/31838-** RPR **161+c**

Starts	1st	2nd	3rd	4th	Win & Pl
18	6	3	3	2	£175,005

	Date	Course	Race	Prize
	12/13	Aint	3m1f Cls1 List Ch gd-sft	£17,387
	2/13	Newb	3m Cls3 Nov Ch soft	£8,123
143	12/12	Chel	2m5f Cls1 Gd3 136-157 Ch Hcap heavy	£56,950
	10/12	Aint	2m4f Cls3 Nov Ch good	£6,963
	5/12	Autl	2m1½f Ch 4yo heavy	£21,200
	2/12	Pau	2m3f Hdl soft	£13,600

Struggled to build on excellent novice campaign last season, coming up short in top staying chases and finding stiff marks beyond him in handicaps; regarded as a long-term Grand National type and may do better when granted stiffer tests of stamina.

Urban Hymn (Fr)

6 b g Robin Des Champs - Betty Brune (Dark Stone)

Malcolm Jefferson | **Mr & Mrs G Calder**

PLACINGS: **FU1/12117-** RPR **141+h**

Starts	1st	2nd	3rd	4th	Win & Pl
5	3	1	-	-	£23,092

Date	Course	Race	Prize
1/14	Donc	3m½f Cls1 Nov Gd2 Hdl soft	£15,661
12/13	Hayd	2m4f Cls4 Nov Hdl 4-7yo heavy	£3,899
11/13	Hntg	2m½f Cls6 NHF 4-6yo gd-sft	£1,625

Looked very smart when winning two novice hurdles last season, romping home at Newbury over 2m4f before just edging home in a Grade 2 at Doncaster when stepped up to 3m; only seventh in Albert Bartlett Hurdle but always likely to be better over fences.

Utopie Des Bordes (Fr)

6 b m Antarctique - Miss Berry (Cadoudal)

Nicky Henderson | **Simon Munir & Isaac Souede**

PLACINGS: **3214111521/4254505-8** RPR **143h**

Starts	1st	2nd	3rd	4th	Win & Pl
30	7	6	3	3	£386,060

Date	Course	Race	Prize
4/13	Prth	3m½f Cls2 Nov Hdl gd-sft	£9,747
2/13	Sand	2m4f Cls1 Nov List Hdl heavy	£11,444
2/13	Donc	2m½f Cls4 Nov Hdl good	£3,249
11/12	Autl	2m6f Gd1 Ch 4yo heavy	£131,250
9/12	Autl	2m5½f Gd3 Ch 4yo v soft	£58,125
12/11	Cagn	2m3f Ch gd-sft	£17,379
12/11	Cagn	2m2½f Ch gd-sft	£14,069

Grade 1 winner over fences in France in 2012; largely unsuccessful when spending subsequent

Utopie Des Bordes (left): ran over hurdles last season but could be switched back to fences

two seasons over hurdles despite some fair runs in defeat; could do better returned to fences despite disappointing when favourite for handicap chase at Punchestown in May.

Uxizandre (Fr)

6 ch g Fragrant Mix - Jolisandre (Dear Doctor)

Alan King **John P McManus**

PLACINGS: 2312315/11521- RPR 162+c

Starts	1st	2nd	3rd	4th	Win & Pl
12	5	3	2	-	£108,251

	4/14	Aint	2m4f Cls1 Nov Gd1 Ch good	£50,643
	11/13	Plum	2m4f Cls3 Nov Ch gd-sft	£6,498
135	10/13	Plum	2m4f Cls3 Nov 123-137 Ch Hcap soft	£8,123
	3/13	Wwck	3m1f Cls4 Nov Hdl soft	£3,899
	12/12	Newb	2m3f Cls4 Nov Hdl 4-6yo soft	£3,899

Excelled in novice chases last season and beat Oscar Whisky to gain deserved Grade 1 win at Aintree having just been touched off by Taquin Du Seuil at Cheltenham; has won over 3m over hurdles so could step up in trip but set to be aimed at Ryanair Chase.

Valdez

7 ch g Doyen - Skew (Niniski)

Alan King **Riverdee Stable**

PLACINGS: 1/4/2171302/11152- RPR 159+c

Starts	1st	2nd	3rd	4th	Win & Pl
14	6	3	1	1	£59,827

	1/14	Donc	2m½f Cls1 Nov Gd2 Ch gd-sft	£17,370
135	11/13	Newb	2m1f Cls3 Nov 125-135 Ch Hcap good	£9,471
	11/13	Extr	2m1½f Cls4 Ch gd-sft	£4,549
	1/13	Plum	2m Cls4 Nov Hdl soft	£3,422
	11/12	Hntg	2m½f Cls4 Nov Hdl soft	£2,534
	2/12	Kemp	2m Cls6 NHF 4-6yo std-slw	£1,437
	3/11	Wwck	2m Cls6 NHF 4-6yo good	£1,507

Smart novice chaser last season, winning a Grade 2 at Doncaster and finishing fifth in Racing Post

Arkle; may have more to offer over further (close second to Whisper over 2m4f as a hurdler) despite disappointing when thrashed by Eduard at Ayr last time.

Valseur Lido (Fr)

5 b g Anzillero - Libido Rock (Video Rock)

Willie Mullins (Ir) **Gigginstown House Stud**

PLACINGS: 61/1101-2 **RPR 145h**

Starts	1st	2nd	3rd	4th	Win & Pl
7	4	1	-	-	£61,319

4/14	Fair	2m Nov Gd2 Hdl soft	£21,667
12/13	Navn	2m Nov Hdl sft-hvy	£7,293
11/13	Cork	2m Mdn Hdl 4yo sft-hvy	£5,610
11/12	Pari	1m4f NHF 3yo v soft	£12,500

Won first two novice hurdles but was outpaced in Supreme Novices' Hurdle and again at Punchestown; won a Grade 2 at Fairyhouse in between, relishing softer ground in race that turned into stiff test of stamina; should appreciate further, especially over fences.

Vaniteux (Fr)

5 br g Voix Du Nord - Expoville (Video Rock)

Nicky Henderson **Mr & Mrs R Kelvin-Hughes**

PLACINGS: 34/1413- **RPR 150h**

Starts	1st	2nd	3rd	4th	Win & Pl
4	2	-	1	1	£23,604

2/14	Donc	2m3½f Cls4 Nov Hdl 4-7yo gd-sft	£3,574
12/13	Sand	2m½f Cls3 Nov Hdl gd-sft	£6,498

Good third in last season's Supreme Novices' Hurdle having been unlucky when suffering only previous hurdling defeat (challenging when slipped at last); won over 2m3f in between and should appreciate return to further; could go novice chasing.

Valdez: bold jumper did well in novice company last season and could do well if upped in trip in handicaps

Vautour (Fr)

5 b g Robin Des Champs - Gazelle De Mai (Dom Pasquini)

Willie Mullins (Ir) — **Mrs S Ricci**

PLACINGS: 22/1111-1 — **RPR 158+h**

Starts	1st	2nd	3rd	4th	Win & Pl
7	5	2	-	-	£200,261

	Date	Course	Race	Prize
	5/14	Punc	2m4f Nov Gd1 Hdl gd-yld	£46,500
	3/14	Chel	2m½f Cls1 Nov Gd1 Hdl gd-sft	£68,340
	2/14	Leop	2m2f Nov Gd1 Hdl sft-hvy	£43,333
	1/14	Punc	2m Nov Gd2 Hdl sft-hvy	£20,313
	12/13	Navn	2m Mdn Hdl 4yo gd-yld	£5,610

Brilliant winner of last season's Supreme Novices' Hurdle at Cheltenham, destroying a strong field by six lengths; less impressive at Punchestown next time over 2m4f but still took unbeaten record for Willie Mullins to five; has world at his feet over hurdles or fences.

Very Wood (Fr)

5 b g Martaline - Ball Of Wood (Cadoudal)

Noel Meade (Ir) — **Gigginstown House Stud**

PLACINGS: 211/12531-6 — **RPR 153+h**

Starts	1st	2nd	3rd	4th	Win & Pl
7	3	1	1	-	£86,851

	Date	Course	Race	Prize
	3/14	Chel	3m Cls1 Nov Gd1 Hdl good	£68,340
	10/13	Gway	2m Mdn Hdl 4yo heavy	£6,171
	4/13	Punc	2m NHF 4yo soft	£5,049

Surprise winner of Albert Bartlett Hurdle at Cheltenham last season, leaving previous form behind when running over 3m for first time; unsuited by much slower gallop when sixth at Punchestown next time; has won a point-to-point and looks made for fences.

Via Sundown (Fr)

6 ch g Until Sundown - Via Fratina (Mansonnien)

Gary Moore — **The Old Brokers**

PLACINGS: 32326/F1141- — **RPR 144c**

Starts	1st	2nd	3rd	4th	Win & Pl
10	3	2	2	1	£33,602

	Date	Course	Race	Prize
	2/14	Font	2m6f Cls2 Nov Ch heavy	£12,972
125	12/13	Ling	3m Cls3 105-128 Ch Hcap soft	£6,498
112	11/13	Ling	3m Cls4 101-114 Ch Hcap heavy	£3,769

Won three out of five novice chases last season; came up short in two toughest tests but progressed well throughout and finished off with gutsy defeat of useful Benvolio at Fontwell; should be capable of running well in good staying handicap chases.

Vibrato Valtat (Fr)

5 gr g Voix Du Nord - La Tosca Valtat (Dom Alco)

Paul Nicholls — **Axom XLIII**

PLACINGS: 2/122/2522131-3 — **RPR 140+h**

Starts	1st	2nd	3rd	4th	Win & Pl
12	3	6	2	-	£46,443

	Date	Course	Race	Prize
	4/14	Ayr	2m Cls3 Nov Hdl gd-sft	£6,657
	2/14	Extr	2m1f Cls1 Nov List Hdl heavy	£11,390
	9/12	Angl	1m5f NHF 3yo good	£4,167

Useful novice hurdler last season who should have landed a big handicap prize by now, finding much less than looked likely when third in Swinton Hurdle in May having filled same spot in Imperial Cup; still on a good mark if trainer can work his magic.

Victor Hewgo

9 b g Old Vic - Pennys Pride (Pips Pride)

Keith Reveley — **Sir Ian Good**

PLACINGS: /905443/16121/2121P- — **RPR 143+c**

Starts	1st	2nd	3rd	4th	Win & Pl
18	5	5	1	2	£21,316

	Date	Course	Race	Prize
	3/14	Donc	3m Cls4 Nov Ch good	£3,899
	1/14	Donc	3m Cls4 Nov Ch gd-sft	£3,769
	4/13	Newc	2m4f Cls4 Nov Hdl gd-sft	£3,119
118	11/12	Donc	3m½f Cls4 105-119 Hdl Hcap soft	£2,534
103	7/12	Uttx	3m Cls4 98-110 Hdl Hcap soft	£2,534

Novice chase form last season worked out exceptionally well with two victories plus narrow defeats to Cheltenham Festival winners Western Warhorse and Holywell, with all four runs coming at Doncaster; pulled up next time at Aintree but worth another chance.

Vieux Lion Rouge (Fr)

5 ch g Sabiango - Indecise (Cyborg)

David Pipe — **Prof Caroline Tisdall & John Gent**

PLACINGS: 1110/11103- — **RPR 141+h**

Starts	1st	2nd	3rd	4th	Win & Pl
9	6	-	1	-	£18,976

	Date	Course	Race	Prize
	2/14	Sedg	2m1f Cls4 Nov Hdl heavy	£3,379
	1/14	Winc	2m Cls3 Nov Hdl heavy	£5,523
	1/14	Winc	2m Cls4 Nov Hdl heavy	£3,899
	2/13	Extr	2m1f Cls6 NHF 4-6yo heavy	£1,625
	1/13	Newb	1m4½f Cls6 NHF 4yo soft	£1,643
	12/12	Ffos	2m Cls6 NHF 3-5yo heavy	£1,430

Has won all six races in bumpers and novice hurdles away from Cheltenham but beaten when stepped up in class at that track three times; still ran well when third over 2m4f on final start, looking in need of further; has plenty of size and should be an exciting chaser.

Vigil (Ire)

5 b g Dansili - Magnolia Lane (Sadler's Wells)

Dermot Weld (Ir) — **Martin Bourke**

PLACINGS: 215- — **RPR 134b**

Starts	1st	2nd	3rd	4th	Win & Pl
3	1	1	-	-	£7,536

	Date	Course	Race	Prize
	2/14	Leop	2m NHF 5-7yo sft-hvy	£4,888

Impressive when winning a Leopardstown bumper last season and well backed for Champion Bumper at Cheltenham (strongly preferred in market to victorious stablemate Silver Concorde) before finishing creditable fifth; should be a smart novice hurdler.

Vino Griego (Fr)

9 b g Kahyasi - Vie De Reine (Mansonnien)

Gary Moore — **C E Stedman**

PLACINGS: 8/442F21125/UF1PP02- RPR 158c

Starts	1st	2nd	3rd	4th	Win & Pl
37	5	7	4	4	£127,340

	12/13	Sand	3m½f Cls1 List Ch good	£17,085
138	2/13	Asct	3m Cls1 List 133-145 Ch Hcap soft	£22,780
128	1/13	Chel	2m5f Cls2 Nov 120-142 Ch Hcap heavy	£15,640
	1/10	Winc	2m Cls4 Nov Hdl heavy	£2,927
	2/09	Asct	2m Cls3 NHF 4-6yo heavy	£5,204

Smart staying chaser who easily won a strong Listed chase at Sandown last season; later came within a head of winning at Aintree on Grand National day and still starts campaign lower than previous highest mark having badly lost his way in between.

Vintage Star (Ire)

8 b g Presenting - Rare Vintage (Germany)

Sue Smith — **Trevor Hemmings**

PLACINGS: 38213P/2212P/1262FP- RPR 148+c

Starts	1st	2nd	3rd	4th	Win & Pl
22	4	8	3	-	£54,084

	11/13	Carl	3m½f Cls2 Ch heavy	£12,512
	1/13	Catt	3m1½f Cls4 Nov Ch soft	£4,549
121	3/12	MRas	3m Cls3 105-123 Hdl Hcap good	£4,549
	11/11	Carl	2m1f Cls4 Nov Hdl gd-sft	£4,061

Developed into a smart staying handicapper last season and unlucky not to land a big-race win, just getting touched off in Rehearsal Chase and Peter Marsh Chase; early faller at Cheltenham Festival and again jumped poorly when pulled up in Grand National.

Virak (Fr)

5 b g Bernebeau - Nosika D'Airy (Oblat)

Paul Nicholls — **Hills Of Ledbury (aga)**

PLACINGS: 211/031164- RPR 149+h

Starts	1st	2nd	3rd	4th	Win & Pl
9	4	1	1	1	£43,072

140	2/14	Tntn	2m1f Cls2 114-140 Hdl Hcap heavy	£11,819
130	1/14	Tntn	2m3½f Cls3 118-130 Hdl Hcap heavy	£5,848
	3/13	NAbb	2m3f Cls4 Nov Hdl soft	£4,061
	1/13	Pau	2m1½f Hdl 4yo heavy	£12,488

Hacked up in two heavy-ground handicap hurdles at Taunton last season before twice running well in quicker conditions at Cheltenham; had flopped on chasing debut but was having problems at that time (reportedly choked) and should do better back over fences.

Volnay De Thaix (Fr)

5 ch g Secret Singer - Mange De Thaix (Mont Basile)

Nicky Henderson — **Mrs Judy Wilson**

PLACINGS: 4111215- RPR 143h

Starts	1st	2nd	3rd	4th	Win & Pl
7	4	1	-	1	£38,117

138	3/14	Newb	2m½f Cls2 123-138 Hdl Hcap good	£9,747
	11/13	Newb	2m½f Cls3 Nov Hdl gd-sft	£6,256
	11/13	Kemp	2m Cls4 Nov Hdl gd-sft	£3,899
	6/13	Sabl	2m1f Hdl 4yo soft	£8,195

Buzz horse for much of last season and sent off at odds-on for a Grade 2 novice hurdle at Ascot in December when managing only third; made amends impressively next time before fair fifth in a Grade 1 at Aintree; likely to go novice chasing.

Vukovar (Fr)

5 b g Voix Du Nord - Noraland (Homme De Loi)

Harry Fry — **Gdm Partnership**

PLACINGS: 1F1/11217- RPR 148+c

Starts	1st	2nd	3rd	4th	Win & Pl
8	5	1	-	-	£50,917

12/13	Newb	2m2½f Cls3 Nov Ch soft	£7,798
6/13	Autl	2m1½f Hdl 4yo v soft	£18,732
5/13	Ange	2m1f Hdl 4yo heavy	£7,415
4/13	MsnL	1m4½f NHF 4yo soft	£11,382
3/13	Saum	2m NHF 4yo	£4,065

Prolific winner in France before running three times in Britain for Harry Fry last season; stepped up on chasing debut when making all second time out at Newbury but seemingly unsuited by switch to hold-up tactics at Cheltenham; capable of much better.

Walkon (Fr)

9 gr g Take Risks - La Tirana (Akarad)

Alan King — **Mcneill Family**

PLACINGS: 207/1345P/22P52/U4P- RPR 74c

Starts	1st	2nd	3rd	4th	Win & Pl
22	5	6	1	2	£271,292

12/11	Extr	2m3½f Cls2 Nov Ch gd-sft	£10,860
4/09	Aint	2m½f Cls1 Nov Gd1 Hdl 4yo good	£74,113
1/09	Chel	2m1f Cls1 Nov Gd2 Hdl 4yo heavy	£17,103
12/08	Chep	2m½f Cls1 Gd1 Hdl 3yo soft	£28,505
11/08	Hntg	2m½f Cls2 Nov Hdl 3yo good	£13,010

Ran several fine races in top handicap chases two seasons ago, finishing second in Paddy Power Gold Cup, December Gold Cup and Topham Chase; laid out for Grand National last term but looked a clear non-stayer; should do better back over shorter.

West Wizard (Fr)

5 b/br g King's Theatre - Queen's Diamond (Konigsstuhl)

Nicky Henderson **Walters Plant Hire Ltd**

PLACINGS: 1/2- RPR **134+h**

	Starts	1st	2nd	3rd	4th	Win & Pl
	2	1	1	-	-	£4,133
3/13	Kemp	2m Cls4 Mdn NHF 4-6yo soft				£2,989

Expected to figure among last season's novice hurdlers after impressive bumper win but was rubbed off for year after losing at 1-6 on hurdling debut (reportedly had growing issues); remains a high-class prospect and should benefit from connections' patience.

Western Boy (Ire)

5 b g Antonius Pius - Skala (Hernando)

Pat Fahy (Ir) **Ballyclare Syndicate**

PLACINGS: 24/21127-5 RPR **146h**

	Starts	1st	2nd	3rd	4th	Win & Pl
	8	2	3	-	1	£23,087
12/13	Leop	2m Mdn Hdl 4yo soft				£6,171
11/13	Thur	2m NHF 4-7yo yield				£3,927

Smart bumper performer who did well over hurdles last season in top company, finishing seventh in Supreme Novices' Hurdle having pushed Vautour much closer in testing conditions previously; should have more to offer, especially over fences.

Whisper (Fr)

6 b g Astarabad - Belle Yepa (Mansonnien)

Nicky Henderson **Walters Plant Hire Ltd**

PLACINGS: 1/14141/331211- RPR **159h**

		Starts	1st	2nd	3rd	4th	Win & Pl
		12	7	1	2	2	£160,421
	4/14	Aint	3m½f Cls1 Gd1 Hdl gd-sft				£67,524
153	3/14	Chel	2m5f Cls1 Gd3 135-154 Hdl Hcap good				£45,560
140	12/13	Newb	2m5f Cls2 134-144 Hdl Hcap heavy				£11,574
	4/13	Chel	2m4½f Cls2 Nov Hdl gd-sft				£10,010
	2/13	Ffos	2m4f Cls4 Nov Hdl 4-7yo heavy				£3,574
	12/12	Ffos	2m4f Cls4 Nov Hdl heavy				£2,599
	4/12	Ffos	2m Cls6 NHF 4-5yo good				£1,848

Progressed throughout last season and won Coral Cup at Cheltenham under a big weight before confirming quality of that effort by following up at Grade 1 level with win over At Fishers Cross at Aintree (first run over 3m); likely to go novice chasing.

Wicklow Brave

5 b g Beat Hollow - Moraine (Rainbow Quest)

Willie Mullins (Ir) **Wicklow Bloodstock Limited**

PLACINGS: 9/21111166-F RPR **149+h**

	Starts	1st	2nd	3rd	4th	Win & Pl
	10	5	1	-	-	£43,308
2/14	Punc	2m Nov List Hdl heavy				£16,250
1/14	Cork	2m Mdn Hdl 4-5yo heavy				£6,038
10/13	Tipp	2m NHF 4-7yo good				£6,030
9/13	List	2m NHF 4-7yo soft				£7,854
7/13	Gway	2m NHF 4-7yo good				£4,488

Followed three bumper victories by winning first two races over hurdles but finished last season badly; only sixth in Supreme Novices' Hurdle and ran a shocker next time, though doing better until falling two out at Punchestown.

Wilde Blue Yonder (Ire)

5 b g Oscar - Blue Gallery (Bluebird)

Alan King **Maybe Only Fools Have Horses**

PLACINGS: 20/11FF54- RPR **148+h**

	Starts	1st	2nd	3rd	4th	Win & Pl
	8	2	1	-	1	£15,706
11/13	Newb	2m½f Cls3 Mdn Hdl gd-sft				£6,498
11/13	Uttx	2m Cls6 NHF 4-6yo soft				£1,560

Let down by jumping last season, twice falling when in a winning position and making mistakes when fourth in Grade 1 novice hurdle at Aintree; still underlined rich potential that day, building on good fifth in Supreme Novices' Hurdle.

William's Wishes (Ire)

9 b g Oscar - Strong Wishes (Strong Gale)

Evan Williams **Mrs D E Cheshire**

PLACINGS: 3/2312211/7111/11/5- RPR **145c**

		Starts	1st	2nd	3rd	4th	Win & Pl
		15	8	3	2	-	£78,338
144	1/13	Sand	2m Cls2 120-145 Ch Hcap soft				£18,768
135	11/12	Asct	2m1f Cls2 135-155 Ch Hcap heavy				£30,998
	1/11	Hrfd	2m Cls3 Nov Ch soft				£4,554
	11/10	Leic	2m Cls3 Nov Ch good				£4,816
	10/10	Ludl	2m Cls4 Ch good				£3,757
	4/10	Sthl	2m Cls4 Nov Hdl good				£3,426
	3/10	Hrfd	2m1f Cls4 Nov Cond Hdl gd-sft				£3,253
	9/09	Worc	2m4f Cls4 Mdn Hdl good				£2,602

Hugely talented but fragile chaser; missed rest of season after finishing fifth on return in Haldon Gold Cup last term; had been unbeaten in five runs over fences previously so still interesting when fully fit.

Willow's Saviour

7 ch g Septieme Ciel - Willow Gale (Strong Gale)

Dan Skelton — **Triple F Partnership**

PLACINGS: 33/4576/2052P/111- RPR **142+h**

Starts	1st	2nd	3rd	4th	Win & Pl
14	3	2	2	1	£105,469

130	12/13	Asct	2m Cls1 Gd3 130-151 Hdl Hcap soft	£84,405
121	11/13	Muss	2m Cls2 119-145 Hdl Hcap good	£12,996
115	11/13	Asct	2m3½f Cls4 Nov 100-118 Hdl Hcap gd-sft	£5,630

Went from strength to strength for new trainer last season, culminating in the Ladbroke Hurdle at Ascot; missed end of season through injury but should have plenty more to offer.

Wishfull Thinking

11 ch g Alflora - Poussetiere Deux (Garde Royale)

Philip Hobbs — **Mrs Diana L Whateley**

PLACINGS: 26F25/214133/662158- RPR **162+c**

Starts	1st	2nd	3rd	4th	Win & Pl
32	10	7	2	1	£386,177

156	1/14	Chel	2m5f Cls1 Gd3 130-156 Ch Hcap heavy	£28,475
	2/13	Newb	2m1f Cls1 Gd2 Ch soft	£25,628
	11/12	Chel	2m Cls2 Ch soft	£31,280
159	5/11	Punc	2m5f Nov 138-159 Ch Hcap yield	£40,086
	4/11	Aint	2m4f Cls1 Nov Gd2 Ch gd-sft	£42,959
148	1/11	Chel	2m5f Cls1 Gd3 131-157 Ch Hcap gd-sft	£22,804
	11/10	Winc	2m5f Cls1 Nov Gd2 Ch good	£18,458
	2/10	Extr	2m3f Cls4 Nov Hdl gd-sft	£2,927
	1/10	Tntn	2m3½f Cls3 Nov Hdl 4-7yo soft	£5,529
	12/09	Hrfd	2m4f Cls4 Mdn Hdl soft	£3,578

As good as ever last season despite advancing years, winning a big handicap at Cheltenham in January and finishing fifth in Champion Chase; last three wins have come on soft or heavy ground with just one defeat in such conditions during that time.

Wonderful Charm (Fr)

6 b g Poliglote - Victoria Royale (Garde Royale)

Paul Nicholls — **R J H Geffen**

PLACINGS: 442512/18/111253- RPR **159+c**

Starts	1st	2nd	3rd	4th	Win & Pl
14	5	3	1	2	£152,270

	11/13	Newb	2m4f Cls1 Nov Gd2 Ch gd-sft	£17,912
	11/13	Winc	2m5f Cls1 Nov Gd2 Ch gd-sft	£17,912
	10/13	Fknm	2m5½f Cls3 Nov Ch good	£6,990
	10/12	Chep	2m4f Cls1 Nov Gd2 Hdl gd-sft	£12,073
	3/12	Autl	2m2f Hdl 4yo v soft	£28,000

Won two Grade 2 contests and narrowly failedto concede 8lb to Oscar Whisky early last season; well beaten at Cheltenham and Aintree, though, failing to improve for step up to 3m; could do better.

Wychwoods Brook

8 b g Midnight Legend - Miss Millbrook (Meadowbrook)

Evan Williams — **Kevin & Anne Glastonbury**

PLACINGS: 2/12277/2F11F- RPR **149+c**

Starts	1st	2nd	3rd	4th	Win & Pl
11	3	4	-	-	£39,555

137	1/14	Hayd	3m1f Cls1 Gd2 137-157 Ch Hcap heavy	£28,475
119	12/13	Ling	2m4f Cls4 98-119 Ch Hcap soft	£3,769
	11/12	Sand	2m½f Cls6 NHF 4-6yo soft	£2,599

Progressed rapidly when sent chasing last season and did remarkably well to win Peter Marsh Chase on only fourth run over fences, relishing tough slog on heavy ground; exhausted when taking heavy fall next time; could be a Welsh National type.

Wyck Hill (Ire)

10 b g Pierre - Willow Rose (Roselier)

David Bridgwater — **John P McManus**

PLACINGS: 493/11F2/1103/99P16- RPR **148+c**

Starts	1st	2nd	3rd	4th	Win & Pl
21	5	1	3	2	£87,887

133	2/14	Newc	4m1f Cls2 119-145 Ch Hcap heavy	£37,140
135	12/12	Asct	3m Cls1 List 135-161 Ch Hcap heavy	£25,825
122	11/12	Weth	3m1f Cls3 115-130 Ch Hcap soft	£6,498
115	11/11	MRas	2m6½f Cls3 Nov 115-128 Ch Hcap good	£6,368
106	10/11	Chep	2m3½f Cls4 Nov 100-114 Ch Hcap good	£3,899

Finally came good when outstaying rivals to win last season's Eider Chase at Newcastle; had struggled since winning on heavy ground at Ascot in 2012 but relished similar conditions and should again do well given a severe stamina test; being trained for Grand National.

Zaidpour (Fr)

8 b g Red Ransom - Zainta (Kahyasi)

Willie Mullins (Ir) — **Mrs S Ricci**

PLACINGS: /251222P23/732162-56 RPR **160+h**

Starts	1st	2nd	3rd	4th	Win & Pl
28	8	10	2	-	£424,467

	12/13	Leop	3m Gd1 Hdl soft	£42,276
	12/12	Fair	2m4f Gd1 Hdl soft	£43,333
	2/12	Gowr	2m Gd2 Hdl soft	£21,667
	1/12	Gowr	3m Gd2 Hdl sft-hvy	£21,667
	12/11	Navn	2m4f Gd2 Hdl sft-hvy	£21,013
	11/11	Thur	2m6½f Hdl heavy	£5,948
	12/10	Fair	2m Nov Gd1 Hdl soft	£46,018
	11/10	Punc	2m4f Mdn Hdl 4yo soft	£6,412

Smart staying hurdler who has won Grade 1 races in each of last two seasons over 2m4f and 3m, comfortably beating Rule The World at Leopardstown last Christmas; disappointing subsequently (beaten favourite twice) and something to prove.

Zarkandar (Ire)

7 b g Azamour - Zarkasha (Kahyasi)

Paul Nicholls — **Chris Giles & Potensis Limited**

PLACINGS: /15F/11141/222244-63 RPR **165h**

Starts	1st	2nd	3rd	4th	Win & Pl
19	8	4	1	3	£629,401

	4/13	Aint	2m4f Cls1 Gd1 Hdl good	£112,540
	2/13	Winc	2m Cls1 Gd2 Hdl heavy	£34,170
	12/12	Chel	2m1f Cls1 Gd2 Hdl heavy	£74,035
163	11/12	Winc	2m Cls1 Gd2 143-163 Hdl Hcap gd-sft	£32,746
151	2/12	Newb	2m½f Cls1 Gd3 136-162 Hdl Hcap gd-sft	£86,849
	4/11	Aint	2m½f Cls1 Gd1 Hdl 4yo gd-sft	£56,632
	3/11	Chel	2m1f Cls1 Gd1 Hdl 4yo good	£57,010
	2/11	Kemp	2m Cls1 Gd2 Hdl 4yo gd-sft	£12,086

Without a win last season, though never disgraced in face of several stiff tasks; stepped up to longer trips on most recent outings but never threatened when twice held up and looked a non-stayer when ridden more forcefully; probably best at around 2m4f.

THIS SEASON'S LEADING CONTENDERS LISTED BY TRAINER

Kim Bailey
Harry Topper
The Rainbow Hunter
Un Ace (Fr)

Enda Bolger
Gilgamboa (Ire)

Peter Bowen
Al Co (Fr)

Mark Bradstock
Coneygree

Martin Brassil
Double Seven (Ire)

David Bridgwater
The Giant Bolster
Wyck Hill (Ire)

Liam Burke
My Murphy (Ire)

Charles Byrnes
Arnaud (Ire)
Solwhit (Fr)
Trifolium (Fr)

Mick Channon
Sgt Reckless
Somersby (Ire)

Jim Culloty
Lord Windermere (Ire)
Spring Heeled (Ire)

Rebecca Curtis
At Fishers Cross (Ire)
O'Faolains Boy (Ire)
Teaforthree (Ire)
The Romford Pele (Ire)

Victor Dartnall
Roudoudou Ville (Fr)

Henry de Bromhead
Days Hotel (Ire)
Grand Jesture (Ire)
Moscow Mannon (Ire)
Sadler's Risk (Ire)
Sizing Europe (Ire)
Sizing Gold (Ire)
Special Tiara

Robin Dickin
Restless Harry

Elizabeth Doyle
Le Vent D'Antan (Fr)

Timothy Doyle
Mallowney (Ire)

Jim Dreaper
Goonyella (Ire)

Tim Easterby
Hawk High (Ire)
Trustan Times (Ire)

Gordon Elliott
Cause Of Causes (USA)
Clarcam (Fr)
Don Cossack (Ger)
Flaxen Flare (Ire)
Mala Beach (Ire)
Mount Benbulben (Ire)
Realt Mor (Ire)
Roi Du Mee (Fr)
Tiger Roll (Ire)
Toner D'Oudairies (Fr)

Paul Fahey
Lots Of Memories (Ire)

Pat Fahy
Morning Assembly (Ire)
Western Boy (Ire)

Philip Fenton
The Tullow Tank (Ire)

John Ferguson
Broughton (Ger)
Commissioned (Ire)
Purple Bay (Ire)
Rainbow Peak (Ire)
Red Devil Boys (Ire)
Three Kingdoms (Ire)

John Flint
Kayf Moss

Tom Foley
Never Enough Time (Ire)

Harry Fry
Activial (Fr)
Highland Retreat
Karinga Dancer
Mendip Express (Ire)
Opening Batsman (Ire)
Rock On Ruby (Ire)
Thomas Brown
Vukovar (Fr)

Tom George
Chartreux (Fr)
Dare To Endeavour
God's Own (Ire)
Majala (Fr)
Module (Fr)
Parsnip Pete

Steve Gollings
Definitly Red (Ire)

Warren Greatrex
Baby Mix (Fr)
Cole Harden (Ire)

Eoin Griffin
Azorian (Ire)

John Hanlon
Hidden Cyclone (Ire)

Jessica Harrington
Jetson (Ire)
Jezki (Ire)
Operating (Ire)

Eddie Harty
Minella Foru (Ire)

Nigel Hawke
Samingarry (Fr)

Nicky Henderson
Bear's Affair (Ire)
Beat That (Ire)
Blue Fashion (Ire)
Bobs Worth (Ire)
Captain Conan (Fr)
Cup Final (Ire)
Dawalan (Fr)
Ericht (Ire)
Finian's Rainbow (Ire)
Full Shift (Fr)
Gaitway
Grandouet (Fr)
Hadrian's Approach (Ire)
Hunt Ball (Ire)
Josses Hill (Ire)
Long Run (Fr)
Ma Filleule (Fr)
Mayfair Music (Ire)
My Tent Or Yours (Ire)
My Wigwam Or Yours (Ire)
Oscar Hoof (Ire)
Oscar Whisky (Ire)
Rajdhani Express
Rolling Star (Fr)
Royal Boy (Fr)
Royal Irish Hussar (Ire)
Simonsig
Sprinter Sacre (Fr)
Triolo D'Alene (Fr)
Une Artiste (Fr)
Utopie Des Bordes (Fr)
Vaniteux (Fr)
Volnay De Thaix (Fr)
West Wizard (Fr)
Whisper (Fr)

Philip Hobbs
Balthazar King (Ire)
Captain Chris (Ire)
Champagne West (Ire)
Cheltenian (Fr)
Colour Squadron (Ire)
De La Bech
Fingal Bay (Ire)
Garde La Victoire (Fr)
Horizontal Speed (Ire)
If In Doubt (Ire)
Lamb Or Cod (Ire)
Menorah (Ire)
Neck Or Nothing (Ger)
Persian Snow (Ire)
Roalco De Farges (Fr)
Sausalito Sunrise (Ire)
Wishfull Thinking

Anthony Honeyball
Regal Encore (Ire)

Dessie Hughes
Apache Jack (Ire)
Art Of Logistics (Ire)
Bright New Dawn (Ire)
Golden Wonder (Ire)
Guitar Pete (Ire)
Lieutenant Colonel
Lyreen Legend (Ire)

Malcolm Jefferson
Attaglance
Cape Tribulation
Urban Hymn (Fr)

Martin Keighley
Annacotty (Ire)
Champion Court (Ire)

John Kiely
Carlingford Lough (Ire)

Alan King
Balder Succes (Fr)
Godsmejudge (Ire)
Grumeti
L'Unique (Fr)
Manyriverstocross (Ire)
Medermit (Fr)
Medinas (Fr)
Midnight Prayer
Montbazon (Fr)
Smad Place (Fr)
Turn Over Sivola (Fr)
Uxizandre (Fr)
Valdez
Walkon (Fr)
Wilde Blue Yonder (Ire)

Emma Lavelle
Claret Cloak (Ire)
Fox Appeal (Ire)
Gullinbursti (Ire)
Highland Lodge (Ire)
Le Bec (Fr)
Off The Ground (Ire)
Shotgun Paddy (Ire)
Timesremembered (Ire)

Richard Lee
Grey Gold (Ire)
Knock A Hand (Ire)
Mountainous (Ire)

Charlie Longsdon
Ely Brown (Ire)
Killala Quay
Magnifique Etoile
Pendra (Ire)

Peter Maher
Big Shu (Ire)

Tony Martin
Bog Warrior (Ire)
Flemenstar (Ire)
Gallant Oscar (Ire)
Noble Emperor (Ire)
Quick Jack (Ire)
Savello (Ire)
Ted Veale (Ire)

Donald McCain
Clondaw Kaempfer (Ire)
Corrin Wood (Ire)
Desert Cry (Ire)
Diamond King (Ire)
I Need Gold (Ire)

Indian Castle (Ire)
Kings Bandit (Ire)
Stonebrook (Ire)
The Last Samuri (Ire)

Noel Meade
Apache Stronghold (Ire)
Monksland (Ire)
Mullaghanoe River (Ire)
Ned Buntline
Road To Riches (Ire)
Texas Jack (Ire)
Very Wood (Fr)

Gary Moore
Chris Pea Green
Sire De Grugy (Fr)
Ubak (Fr)
Via Sundown (Fr)
Vino Griego (Fr)

Mouse Morris
Baily Green (Ire)
First Lieutenant (Ire)
Rogue Angel (Ire)
Rule The World

Hughie Morrison
Brother Brian (Ire)

Tom Mullins
Alderwood (Ire)

Willie Mullins
Abbyssial (Ire)
Adriana Des Mottes (Fr)
Alelchi Inois (Fr)
Analifet (Fr)
Annie Power (Ire)
Arctic Fire (Ger)
Back In Focus (Ire)
Ballycasey (Ire)
Black Hercules (Ire)
Blood Cotil (Fr)
Boston Bob (Ire)
Briar Hill (Ire)
Champagne Fever (Ire)
City Slicker (Ire)
Clondaw Court (Ire)
Daneking
Diakali (Fr)
Djakadam (Fr)
Don Poli (Ire)
Faugheen (Ire)
Felix Yonger (Ire)
Gitane Du Berlais (Fr)
Glens Melody (Ire)
Hurricane Fly (Ire)
Ivan Grozny (Fr)
Killer Crow (Ire)
Killultagh Vic (Ire)
Milsean (Ire)
Moyle Park (Ire)
Mozoltov
On His Own (Ire)
Outlander (Ire)
Pont Alexandre (Ger)
Rathvinden (Ire)
Renneti (Fr)
Shaneshill (Ire)
Sir Des Champs (Fr)
The Paparrazi Kid (Ire)
Thousand Stars (Fr)
Turban (Fr)
Twinlight (Fr)
Un Atout (Fr)
Un De Sceaux (Fr)
Union Dues (Fr)
Valseur Lido (Fr)
Vautour (Fr)
Wicklow Brave
Zaidpour (Fr)

Colm Murphy
The Westener Boy (Ire)

Richard Newland
Ahyaknowyerself (Ire)
Ardkilly Witness (Ire)
Pineau De Re (Fr)

Paul Nicholls
Al Ferof (Fr)
Aldopicgros (Fr)
Benvolio (Ire)
Black Thunder (Fr)
Bury Parade (Ire)
Caid Du Berlais (Fr)
Calipto (Fr)
Ceasar Milan (Ire)
Dodging Bullets
Easter Day (Fr)
Far West (Fr)
Hawkes Point
Hinterland (Fr)
Irish Saint (Fr)
Irving
Just A Par (Ire)
Katgary (Fr)
Lac Fontana (Fr)
Mon Parrain (Fr)
Mr Mole (Ire)
Pearl Swan (Fr)
Ptit Zig (Fr)
Rocky Creek (Ire)
Rolling Aces (Ire)
Salubrious (Ire)
Sam Winner (Fr)
Saphir Du Rheu (Fr)
Silsol (Ger)
Silviniaco Conti (Fr)
Southfield Theatre (Ire)
Unioniste (Fr)
Vibrato Valtat (Fr)
Virak (Fr)
Wonderful Charm (Fr)
Zarkandar (Ire)

Paul Nolan
Defy Logic (Ire)

Edward O'Grady
Kitten Rock (Fr)

Jonjo O'Neill
Burton Port (Ire)
Capote (Ire)
Eastlake (Ire)
Festive Affair (Ire)
Holywell (Ire)
It's A Gimme (Ire)
Johns Spirit (Ire)
Merry King (Ire)
More Of That (Ire)
Mountain Tunes (Ire)
Rum And Butter (Ire)
Shutthefrontdoor (Ire)
Taquin Du Seuil (Fr)

Andy Oliver
All Set To Go (Ire)

David Pipe
Balgarry (Fr)
Ballynagour (Ire)
Baltimore Rock (Ire)
Big Occasion (Ire)
Buddy Bolero (Ire)
Dell' Arca (Ire)
Doctor Harper (Ire)
Dynaste (Fr)
Edmund Kean (Ire)
Gevrey Chambertin (Fr)
Goulanes (Ire)
Kings Palace (Ire)
Our Father (Ire)
Red Sherlock
Seven Nation Army (Ire)
Shotavodka (Ire)
Tanerko Emery (Fr)
The Liquidator
Un Temps Pour Tout (Ire)
Vieux Lion Rouge (Fr)

John Quinn
Aurore D'Estruval (Fr)
Cockney Sparrow
Rutherglen

Keith Reveley
Night In Milan (Ire)
Victor Hewgo

Nicky Richards
Eduard (Ire)
Simply Ned (Ire)

Renee Robeson
Benefit Cut (Ire)

Pauline Robson
Rival D'Estruval (Fr)

Lucinda Russell
Bold Sir Brian (Ire)
Green Flag (Ire)
Tap Night (USA)

Jeremy Scott
Melodic Rendezvous

Michael Scudamore
Monbeg Dude (Ire)
Next Sensation (Ire)

Oliver Sherwood
Deputy Dan (Ire)
Many Clouds (Ire)
Puffin Billy (Ire)

Dan Skelton
Bellenos (Fr)
Willow's Saviour

Sue Smith
Blakemount (Ire)
Cloudy Too (Ire)
No Planning
Vintage Star (Ire)

Jamie Snowden
Present View

Tom Taaffe
Argocat (Ire)
Gold Bullet (Ire)

Sandy Thomson
Seeyouatmidnight

Colin Tizzard
Cue Card
Theatre Guide (Ire)
Third Intention (Ire)

Nigel Twiston-Davies
Ballybolley (Ire)
Double Ross (Ire)
Kaylif Aramis
Splash Of Ginge
The New One (Ire)
Tour Des Champs (Fr)

Tim Vaughan
Ackertac (Ire)

Robert Walford
Carole's Spirit

Ted Walsh
Foxrock (Ire)

Paul Webber
Cantlow (Ire)

Dermot Weld
Silver Concorde
Stuccodor (Ire)
Vigil (Ire)

Alistair Whillans
Samstown

Evan Williams
Buywise (Ire)
Court Minstrel (Ire)
One In A Milan (Ire)
William's Wishes (Ire)
Wychwoods Brook

Ian Williams
Ballyalton (Ire)
Indian Castle (Ire)

Nick Williams
Amore Alato
Fox Norton (Fr)
Le Rocher (Fr)
Reve De Sivola (Fr)
The Italian Yob (Ire)

Venetia Williams
Bennys Mist (Ire)
Brick Red
Houblon Des Obeaux (Fr)
Kapga De Cerisy (Fr)
Katenko (Fr)
Pepite Rose (Fr)
Rigadin De Beauchene (Fr)

Michael Winters
Rebel Fitz (Fr)

RACING POST RATINGS: LAST SEASON'S LEADING CHASERS

KEY: Horse name, best RPR figure, finishing position when earning figure, (details of race where figure was earned)

Abbey Lane (IRE) 135 4 (2m 1f, Fair, Sft, Apr 6)
According To Trev (IRE) 138 3 (3m 110y, Chel, Gd, Oct 18)
Ace High 136 3 (3m 5f, Hayd, Sft, Nov 23)
Ackertac (IRE) 147 2 (2m 4f 110y, Sand, Sft, Nov 9)
Across The Bay (IRE) 152 1 (3m 4f, Hayd, Hvy, Dec 30)
Adrenalin Flight (IRE) 136 4 (4m, Chel, GS, Mar 11)
African Gold (IRE) 140 (3m, Utto, Sft, Dec 10)
Ahyaknowyerself (IRE) 139 4 (2m 4f 110y, Chel, GS, Mar 11)
Al Co (FR) 151 1 (4m 110y, Ayr, GS, Apr 12)
Al Ferof (FR) 168 1 (2m 3f, Asco, GS, Nov 23)
Alasi 142 5 (2m 4f 110y, Hunt, GS, Dec 12)
Alfie Sherrin 135 8 (3m 110y, Chel, GS, Mar 11)
Alfie Spinner (IRE) 136 2 (3m 2f 110y, Chel, Sft, Jan 1)
Alpha Victor (IRE) 146 2 (4m 1f 110y, Utto, GS, Mar 15)
Alvarado (IRE) 140 1 (3m 3f 110y, Chel, Gd, Nov 16)
Anay Turge (FR) 138 1 (2m, Chel, Gd, Nov 15)
Annacotty (IRE) 155 1 (3m, Kemp, Sft, Dec 26)
Anquetta (IRE) 147 (2m 5f 110y, Stra, GF, Jun 8)
Any Currency (IRE) 139 3 (3m 7f, Chel, Gd, Nov 15)
Ardkilly Witness (IRE) 141 5 (3m, Kemp, Sft, Feb 22)
Argocat (IRE) 167 3 (3m 1f, Live, Gd, Apr 3)
Arnaud (IRE) 152 2 (2m 110y, Donc, GS, Jan 25)
Art Of Logistics (IRE) 138 5 (2m 4f, Fair, Yld, Dec 1)
Arvika Ligeonniere (FR) 166 1 (2m 1f, Fair, Sft, Apr 6)
Astracad (FR) 146 2 (2m 5f, Chel, Gd, Apr 16)
Attaglance 146 2 (2m 4f 110y, Chel, GS, Mar 11)
Aupcharlie (IRE) 149 (2m 2f, Punc, Hvy, Apr 27)
Australia Day (IRE) 154 1 (2m 110y, Taun, GF, May 2)
Avondhu Lady (IRE) 140 1 (2m, Naas, Hvy, Feb 8)
Baby Mix (FR) 143 1 (2m 4f 110y, Kemp, Gd, Nov 25)
Baby Run (FR) 148 2 (3m 2f, Live, Sft, Dec 7)
Baby Shine (IRE) 139 1 (2m 4f, Newb, Sft, Jan 15)
Baile Anrai (IRE) 138 2 (3m, Donc, Sft, Jan 25)
Baily Green (IRE) 157 2 (2m 4f, Nava, Hvy, Mar 29)
Balder Succes (FR) 162 1 (2m, Live, Gd, Apr 5)
Bally Legend 146 4 (2m 5f, Chel, Gd, Apr 16)
Ballybough Gorta (IRE) 135 4 (3m 2f, Live, Sft, Dec 7)
Ballycasey (IRE) 156 (2m 4f, Fair, Yld, Apr 20)
Ballygarvey (FR) 144 4 (2m, Chel, Gd, Nov 15)
Ballynagour (IRE) 156 3 (2m 4f, Live, Gd, Apr 4)
Balnaslow (IRE) 142 4 (3m 1f, Gowr, Sft, Jan 23)
Balthazar King (IRE) 156 2 (4m 3f 110y, Live, GS, Apr 5)
Bar De Ligne (FR) 138 2 (2m 4f 110y, Pert, Sft, Apr 25)
Baresi (IRE) 142 1 (2m 3f 110y, Lime, Gd, Apr 27)
Barrakilla (IRE) 137 1 (2m 4f 110y, Warw, Sft, Dec 31)
Beachdale Lad (IRE) 144 1 (2m 4f, Kilb, GF, Jun 24)
Bear's Affair (IRE) 142 2 (2m 5f 110y, Fake, Gd, Oct 25)
Beeves (IRE) 138 2 (2m 7f 110y, Leic, GS, Dec 27)
Beforeall (IRE) 135 1 (3m 1f 110y, Ffos, Hvy, Apr 6)
Bellenos (FR) 147 1 (2m 1f 110y, Stra, Gd, Apr 13)
Benbens (IRE) 137 1 (2m 4f, Ludl, Sft, Feb 27)
Benefficient (IRE) 166 1 (2m 1f, Leop, Sft, Dec 27)
Benefit Cut (IRE) 142 1 (2m 4f, Mark, Sft, Feb 4)
Bennys Mist (IRE) 143 2 (2m 5f 110y, Live, Gd, Apr 4)
Benvolio (IRE) 147 1 (3m, Newb, GS, Dec 18)
Big Fella Thanks 143 5 (3m, Donc, GS, Feb 19)
Big Shu (IRE) 149 3 (3m 7f, Chel, GS, Mar 12)
Billie Magern 145 4 (2m 5f 110y, Newt, Gd, Aug 31)
Bit Of A Jig (IRE) 138 1 (3m 1f 110y, Catt, GS, Feb 25)
Black Benny (IRE) 135 4 (2m 4f 120y, Kill, Gd, Aug 29)
Black Thunder (FR) 157 2 (3m 110y, Warw, Hvy, Jan 11)
Bless The Wings (IRE) 147 6 (3m, Asco, GS, Nov 2)
Bobowen (IRE) 145 1 (2m 6f 110y, Mark, GF, Jul 20)
Bobs Worth (IRE) 167 5 (3m 2f 110y, Chel, Gd, Mar 14)
Bocciani (GER) 143 1 (2m 4f, Mark, Gd, May 10)
Bog Warrior (IRE) 156 1 (2m 4f, Nava, Hvy, Mar 29)
Bold Chief (IRE) 149 4 (3m, Hayd, Gd, Apr 19)
Bonisland 136 1 (2m 4f, Punc, Gd, Oct 16)
Boston Bob (IRE) 163 1 (2m 4f, Live, Gd, Apr 4)
Bouggler 151 1 (2m 6f 110y, Mark, Gd, Sep 28)
Bradley 139 1 (3m 110y, Sand, Sft, Mar 7)
Brass Tax (IRE) 138 2 (3m, Kemp, Gd, Apr 15)
Brick Red 153 7 (2m, Chel, GS, Mar 11)
Bright New Dawn (IRE) 152 1 (2m 4f, Naas, Sft, Mar 9)
Buck Mulligan 137 2 (3m, Pert, GF, Jun 9)
Buckers Bridge (IRE) 152 3 (3m 1f, Fair, Hvy, Feb 22)
Bucking The Trend 135 2 (3m, Newc, Hvy, Feb 22)
Buddy Bolero (IRE) 152 2 (3m 110y, Carl, Hvy, Nov 11)
Burn And Turn (IRE) 135 1 (2m 1f, Lime, Yld, May 4)
Burton Port (IRE) 149 2 (3m 5f 110y, Sand, GS, Apr 26)
Bury Parade (IRE) 160 2 (3m, Kemp, Sft, Feb 22)
Buywise (IRE) 151 1 (2m 5f, Chel, Gd, Apr 16)
Byerley Babe (IRE) 141 2 (2m, Naas, Hvy, Feb 8)
Bygones Of Brid (IRE) 137 1 (2m 110y, Hexh, Gd, Jun 23)
Caid Du Berlais (FR) 139 5 (2m 110y, Donc, GS, Jan 25)
Caim Hill (IRE) 136 2 (3m, Lime, Hvy, Nov 10)
Canaly (IRE) 146 2 (2m 6f, Punc, Yld, Dec 8)
Cantlow (IRE) 158 2 (2m 5f, Chel, Gd, Dec 14)
Caoimhe's Delight (IRE) 136 3 (2m 4f, Thur, Sft, Jan 16)
Cape Tribulation 156 3 (3m 1f, Weth, Sft, Dec 26)
Captain Chris (IRE) 176 1 (2m 5f 110y, Asco, Sft, Feb 15)
Captain Conan (FR) 162 3 (2m, Sand, Gd, Dec 7)
Carlingford Lough (IRE) 154 6 (3m 110y, Chel, Gd, Mar 12)
Carlito Brigante (IRE) 140 1 (2m 4f, Carl, Gd, Apr 19)
Carrickboy (IRE) 136 3 (2m 5f, Winc, Hvy, Jan 30)
Carrigmorna King (IRE) 135 2 (2m 6f 110y, Newb, Gd, Nov 30)
Carruthers 157 2 (3m 5f, Warw, Sft, Jan 11)
Carsonstown Boy (IRE) 136 2 (3m 2f 110y, Chel, Gd, Mar 14)
Cause Of Causes (USA) 151 2 (3m 1f 110y, Chel, Gd, Mar 13)
Cedre Bleu (FR) 144 2 (3m, Asco, Sft, Dec 21)
Champagne Fever (IRE) 161 2 (2m, Chel, GS, Mar 11)
Champion Court (IRE) 161 2 (2m 4f 110y, Hunt, GS, Dec 12)
Chance Du Roy (FR) 148 1 (3m 2f, Live, Sft, Dec 7)
Changing The Guard 149 1 (2m 110y, Newt, Gd, Apr 19)
Chapoturgeon (FR) 147 1 (2m 5f 110y, Newt, GF, May 20)
Charingworth (IRE) 135 2 (3m 110y, Chel, Gd, Nov 15)
Chartreux (FR) 138 1 (3m 110y, Sand, GS, Mar 8)
Chicago Grey (IRE) 139 5 (3m 7f, Chel, Gd, Nov 15)
Clar Na Mionn (IRE) 139 3 (3m, Nava, Hvy, Feb 16)
Claret Cloak (IRE) 152 3 (2m, Live, Gd, Apr 3)
Clonbanan Lad (IRE) 139 3 (2m 6f, Punc, Yld, Nov 17)
Cloudy Too (IRE) 161 1 (3m 1f, Weth, Sft, Dec 26)
Colbert Station (IRE) 159 3 (3m, Nava, Yld, Nov 24)
Colour Squadron (IRE) 153 2 (2m 4f, Chel, Gd, Mar 13)
Come To The Party (IRE) 138 1 (3m, Lime, Hvy, Nov 10)
Competitive Edge (IRE) 144 2 (2m 1f, Fair, Sft, Jan 19)
Conquisto 156 1 (2m 4f, Live, Gd, Oct 26)
Consigliere (FR) 147 1 (2m 3f 110y, Chep, Sft, Mar 8)
Cootamundra (IRE) 141 1 (3m, Nava, Yld, Nov 24)
Corbally Ghost (IRE) 136 2 (2m 4f, Punc, Yld, Nov 16)
Corrin Wood (IRE) 159 1 (3m 110y, Warw, Hvy, Jan 11)
Count Salazar (IRE) 143 1 (2m 6f, Galw, Hvy, Oct 28)
Court By Surprise (IRE) 135 2 (3m 5f 110y, Sand, Gd, Dec 7)
Coverholder (IRE) 143 1 (2m 7f 110y, Kels, GS, Dec 8)
Cowards Close (IRE) 136 1 (2m 7f 110y, Taun, Gd, Apr 23)
Croco Bay (IRE) 138 2 (2m 1f, Kels, GS, Feb 13)
Cue Card 180 1 (3m 1f, Hayd, Sft, Nov 23)
Current Event (FR) 141 1 (2m 4f 110y, Pert, GF, Jun 9)
Dan Breen (IRE) 149 7 (2m, Sand, Gd, Apr 27)
Dantes King (IRE) 138 1 (3m, Pert, GF, Jul 3)
Dare Me (IRE) 147 3 (2m 4f 110y, Pert, Sft, Apr 24)
Dare To Endeavour 142 1 (2m 4f 110y, Pert, Sft, Apr 25)
Daring Article (IRE) 137 2 (2m 5f, Leop, Sft, Jan 25)
Dark Lover (GER) 141 2 (2m 1f, Newb, Sft, Jan 15)
Darroun (IRE) 136 3 (2m 4f, Cork, Gd, Oct 20)
Darwins Fox (FR) 142 1 (2m, Rosc, GF, Sep 30)
Days Hotel (IRE) 157 1 (2m, Naas, Hvy, Feb 23)
De Boitron (FR) 152 2 (3m, Donc, Gd, Dec 14)
De La Bech 136 1 (3m, Chep, GS, Dec 7)
Defy Logic (IRE) 154 1 (2m 1f, Leop, Sft, Dec 26)
Desert Cry (IRE) 160 2 (2m, Ayr, GS, Apr 12)
Diamond Harry 136 (3m 6f, Catt, Hvy, Jan 9)
Dick Dundee 139 3 (2m 3f 120y, Lime, Hvy, Dec 27)

Dineur (FR) 142 3 (2m, Ffos, Gd, Aug 22)
Diocles (IRE) 135 1 (2m 4f 110y, Weth, GS, Apr 13)
Djakadam (FR) 146 1 (2m 5f, Leop, Sft, Jan 25)
Dodging Bullets 161 2 (2m 1f, Newb, Hvy, Feb 8)
Doeslessthanme (IRE) 148 1 (2m 110y, Donc, Gd, Mar 1)
Dolatulo (FR) 139 1 (2m 7f, Stra, GS, Mar 29)
Domtaline (FR) 146 2 (2m 3f 110y, Devo, Gd, Dec 6)
Don Cossack (GER) 155 2 (3m 1f, Live, Gd, Apr 4)
Double Ross (IRE) 159 3 (2m 4f, Chel, Gd, Mar 13)
Double Seven (IRE) 155 3 (4m 3f 110y, Live, GS, Apr 5)
Drumshambo (USA) 152 3 (2m 1f, Asco, GS, Nov 23)
Duke Of Lucca (IRE) 147 1 (3m 1f, Live, Gd, Apr 5)
Dursey Sound (IRE) 141 (2m 5f 110y, Fake, GS, Nov 19)
Dylan Ross (IRE) 145 2 (2m, Naas, Sft, Nov 9)
Dynaste (FR) 175 2 (3m 1f, Hayd, Sft, Nov 23)
Easter Day (FR) 147 1 (2m 5f 110y, Asco, Sft, Dec 21)
Easter Meteor 151 2 (2m 4f, Newb, GS, Nov 29)
Eastlake (IRE) 149 3 (2m 5f 110y, Live, Gd, Apr 4)
Edgardo Sol (FR) 139 7 (2m 4f, Live, Gd, Oct 26)
Edmund Kean (IRE) 144 1 (3m, Ludl, Hvy, Feb 5)
Eduard (IRE) 158 1 (2m 4f, Ayr, GS, Apr 12)
Ely Brown (IRE) 148 1 (3m 1f, Weth, Hvy, Feb 1)
Emperor's Choice (IRE) 140 1 (3m 4f, Ffos, Hvy, Feb 1)
Ericht (IRE) 146 1 (2m 4f, Muss, Sft, Feb 2)
Fago (FR) 155 1 (2m 1f, Hayd, Sft, Nov 22)
Far Away So Close (IRE) 140 2 (2m, Punc, Yld, May 11)
Farrells Fancy (IRE) 143 (2m, Cork, Gd, Oct 20)
Felix Yonger (IRE) 160 1 (2m 1f, Nava, Yld, Dec 7)
Fentara 135 3 (3m 4f, Hayd, Gd, Apr 19)
Fiendish Flame (IRE) 150 2 (2m 4f, Mark, Gd, May 10)
Filbert (IRE) 140 4 (2m, Weth, Sft, Jan 11)
Fill The Power (IRE) 144 1 (3m 1f, Weth, Hvy, Feb 18)
Financial Climate (IRE) 138 1 (3m 1f, Weth, GS, Apr 22)
Fine Parchment (IRE) 137 1 (3m 110y, Sand, Gd, Dec 6)
Finger Onthe Pulse (IRE) 135 2 (2m 4f 110y, Sout, Gd, Aug 18)
Finian's Rainbow (IRE) 164 2 (2m, Sand, Gd, Apr 27)
Firebird Flyer (IRE) 136 3 (3m, Hayd, Gd, Apr 19)
Firm Order (IRE) 135 3 (3m, Donc, GS, Feb 19)
First Lieutenant (IRE) 165 4 (3m 1f, Live, Gd, Apr 3)
Firth Of The Clyde 139 3 (2m 1f, Kels, GS, Feb 13)
Flaming Gorge (IRE) 137 1 (3m, Hunt, Gd, Apr 21)
Flemenstar (IRE) 164 1 (2m, Nava, Yld, Nov 10)
Flying Award (IRE) 137 1 (3m 6f 110y, Devo, Hvy, Mar 4)
Foildubh (IRE) 154 6 (3m, Leop, Sft, Dec 28)
Followmeuptocarlow (IRE) 136 2 (2m 2f, Gowr, Sft, Mar 8)
Folsom Blue (IRE) 145 1 (3m 4f, Punc, Hvy, Feb 2)
Forgotten Gold (IRE) 145 2 (3m 1f 110y, Chel, Gd, Apr 17)
Forpadydeplasterer (IRE) 144 2 (2m 4f, List, Sft, Sep 20)
Fosters Cross (IRE) 144 2 (2m, Cork, Gd, Oct 20)
Foundry Square (IRE) 135 2 (2m 4f 110y, Bang, GS, Oct 3)
Fox Appeal (IRE) 155 3 (2m 4f 110y, Kemp, Sft, Feb 22)
Foxrock (IRE) 146 1 (3m, Nava, Hvy, Feb 16)
Freckle Face 136 1 (2m 3f 110y, Devo, Gd, Mar 18)
French Opera 160 5 (2m 110y, Chel, Gd, Mar 14)
Fruity O'rooney 139 1 (2m 6f, Font, Gd, Apr 11)
Funny Star (FR) 144 1 (2m 110y, Taun, Gd, Dec 12)
Galway Jack (IRE) 139 1 (2m 4f, Newc, Sft, Mar 28)
Gansey (IRE) 136 2 (2m 5f, Hayd, Sft, Dec 30)
Garleton (IRE) 145 4 (2m 7f 110y, Kels, Gd, May 8)
Gas Line Boy (IRE) 137 3 (3m 1f, Hayd, Sft, Nov 23)
Gauvain (GER) 141 4 (3m, Asco, Gd, Mar 30)
General Miller 137 1 (2m 6f 110y, Mark, GF, Jul 20)
Gentleman Anshan (IRE) 137 3 (2m 6f 110y, Mark, GF, Jul 7)
Get It On (IRE) 135 1 (2m 3f 110y, Ffos, Hvy, Oct 29)
Ghizao (GER) 151 6 (2m 4f 110y, Hunt, GS, Dec 12)
Giorgio Quercus (FR) 141 1 (2m 4f 110y, Kemp, Gd, Nov 25)
Go All The Way (IRE) 147 3 (2m 1f, Kill, GF, Jul 15)
God's Own (IRE) 149 2 (2m 4f 110y, Kemp, Sft, Feb 22)
Godsmejudge (IRE) 153 2 (4m 110y, Ayr, GS, Apr 12)
Golan Way 135 1 (3m 2f, Warw, Sft, Mar 9)
Golanbrook (IRE) 141 3 (2m 1f, Fair, Yld, Apr 20)
Gold Bullet (IRE) 135 1 (2m 4f, Dowr, Yld, Nov 1)
Golden Call (IRE) 139 1 (3m, Donc, GS, Feb 6)
Golden Chieftain (IRE) 142 5 (3m 1f, Live, Gd, Apr 5)
Golden Kite (IRE) 137 1 (3m 100y, Rosc, GF, Jun 10)
Golden Wonder (IRE) 147 2 (3m 5f, Fair, Yld, Apr 21)
Goonyella (IRE) 145 2 (2m 6f, Galw, Hvy, Oct 28)
Goulanes (IRE) 152 1 (4m 1f 110y, Utto, GS, Mar 15)
Grandads Horse 141 1 (2m 4f, Mark, Gd, May 31)
Grandioso (IRE) 155 2 (2m 5f 110y, Asco, Hvy, Jan 18)
Grandouet (FR) 157 2 (2m, Sand, Gd, Dec 7)
Green Flag (IRE) 147 1 (3m, Newc, Gd, Nov 30)
Grey Gold (IRE) 153 2 (2m 110y, Chep, Hvy, Feb 22)
Gullible Gordon (IRE) 136 1 (3m 1f, Live, GS, Jun 14)
Gullinbursti (IRE) 150 1 (2m 6f 110y, Mark, Sft, Nov 10)
Gus Macrae (IRE) 135 2 (2m 1f, Asco, Sft, Dec 21)
Hadrian's Approach (IRE) 155 1 (3m 5f 110y, Sand, GS, Apr 26)
Hansupfordetroit (IRE) 138 2 (2m 5f, Winc, Hvy, Jan 16)
Harry The Viking 139 3 (3m, Donc, GS, Feb 6)
Harry Topper 170 1 (3m, Newb, Hvy, Feb 8)
Hawkes Point 146 2 (3m 5f 110y, Chep, Hvy, Dec 28)
Hazy Tom (IRE) 142 1 (2m 4f 110y, Bang, GS, Oct 3)
He'llberemembered (IRE) 147 1 (2m 5f, Leop, Sft, Jan 25)
Headly's Bridge (IRE) 136 3 (2m 4f, Ayr, GS, Apr 11)
Heaney (IRE) 135 5 (3m, Lime, Gd, Oct 13)
Hector's Choice (FR) 138 1 (2m 5f, Winc, GS, Apr 2)
Herdsman (IRE) 138 1 (3m 1f 110y, Catt, Hvy, Feb 10)
Hey Big Spender (IRE) 149 1 (3m, Asco, Gd, Mar 30)
Hidden Cyclone (IRE) 166 2 (2m 5f, Chel, Gd, Mar 13)
Highland Lodge (IRE) 150 2 (3m 3f 110y, Winc, Gd, Oct 27)
Hinterland (FR) 157 1 (2m, Sand, Gd, Dec 7)
His Excellency (IRE) 146 2 (2m, Muss, Sft, Feb 2)
Holywell (IRE) 165 1 (3m 1f, Live, Gd, Apr 4)
Home Farm (IRE) 149 5 (3m 100y, Leop, Sft, Dec 27)
Houblon Des Obeaux (FR) 166 3 (3m, Asco, Sft, Feb 15)
Howard's Legacy (IRE) 136 2 (3m, Chep, Gd, Apr 21)
Hunt Ball (IRE) 161 4 (2m 5f, Chel, Gd, Mar 13)
Ifyousayso (IRE) 136 2 (3m, Newb, Gd, Mar 21)
Ikorodu Road 143 1 (2m 4f, Stra, Sft, Oct 26)
Immediate Response (IRE) 143 (2m 3f 120y, Lime, Hvy, Dec 27)
Imperial Vic (IRE) 140 3 (3m 110y, Carl, Hvy, Nov 11)
Indian Castle (IRE) 146 1 (2m 5f, Chel, Hvy, Jan 25)
Invictus (IRE) 139 (3m 2f 110y, Newb, Gd, Nov 30)
Ipsos Du Berlais (FR) 144 3 (3m 100y, Leop, Sft, Dec 27)
Irish Thistle (IRE) 140 2 (2m 1f, Nava, Hvy, Mar 29)
Italian Master (IRE) 135 1 (3m 1f, Mark, Sft, Nov 10)
Ivor's King (IRE) 135 1 (2m 110y, Newt, GS, Sep 30)
Jacksonslady (IRE) 142 3 (2m 6f, Galw, Sft, Jul 31)
Jamsie Hall (IRE) 143 4 (3m 5f, Fair, Yld, Apr 21)
Jet Master (IRE) 139 1 (2m 1f, Kels, Gd, Mar 22)
Johannisberger (IRE) 139 1 (2m 4f, Dowr, Gd, May 6)
Johns Spirit (IRE) 150 1 (2m 4f 110y, Chel, Gd, Nov 16)
Jump City (FR) 139 3 (2m 4f 110y, Kemp, Gd, Nov 25)
Junior 159 2 (3m, Hunt, Gd, Apr 28)
Jupitor (IRE) 135 1 (3m 1f, Fair, Sft, Apr 6)
Just A Par (IRE) 155 1 (3m, Newb, GS, Nov 28)
Kapga De Cerisy (FR) 152 1 (2m 4f 110y, Sand, Sft, Nov 9)
Karinga Dancer 141 3 (2m 3f, Donc, GS, Jan 8)
Kasbadali (FR) 136 2 (3m 110y, Sand, GS, Mar 8)
Katenko (FR) 163 4 (3m 1f, Hayd, Hvy, Jan 18)
Kauto Stone (FR) 156 5 (2m, Sand, Gd, Dec 7)
Keki Buku (FR) 136 1 (2m 110y, Worc, GF, Jun 26)
Kid Cassidy (IRE) 162 1 (2m, Chel, Gd, Nov 17)
Kie (IRE) 141 1 (2m, Winc, Gd, Apr 13)
King Edmund 144 1 (2m 4f 110y, Kemp, Sft, Jan 11)
King's Grace 135 1 (2m 4f 110y, Bang, GS, Apr 12)
Kings Grey (IRE) 139 1 (2m, Sout, Gd, Apr 23)
Klepht (IRE) 138 6 (2m 6f, Galw, Sft, Jul 31)
Knock A Hand (IRE) 143 2 (3m, Utto, GS, Mar 15)
Knockara Beau (IRE) 154 7 (3m 2f 110y, Chel, Gd, Mar 14)
Kruzhlinin (GER) 153 1 (2m 7f 110y, Kels, GS, Dec 8)
Kumbeshwar 149 4 (2m 1f 110y, Devo, GS, Nov 5)
Laganbank (IRE) 147 4 (2m 4f, Gowr, Gd, Oct 5)
Lamb Or Cod (IRE) 146 1 (3m 1f 110y, Chel, Gd, Apr 17)
Lancetto (FR) 150 4 (2m, Sand, GS, Apr 26)
Last Instalment (IRE) 168 1 (3m, Leop, Hvy, Feb 9)
Last Shot (FR) 135 2 (2m, Winc, Hvy, Dec 26)
Lastoftheleaders (IRE) 146 3 (2m 1f, Fair, Sft, Jan 19)
Le Bacardy (FR) 137 1 (2m, Ayr, GS, Apr 12)
Le Bec (FR) 158 2 (3m 1f 110y, Chel, Gd, Dec 14)
Lead Kindly Light (IRE) 137 2 (2m, Cork, Sft, Dec 8)
Letter Of Credit (IRE) 145 2 (3m, Lime, Hvy, Mar 30)

Lidar (FR) 144 2 (2m 1f 110y, Devo, Sft, Dec 19)
Lion Na Bearnai (IRE) 141 1 (2m 5f 100y, Fair, Hvy, Feb 1)
Loch Ba (IRE) 140 2 (3m, Hayd, Sft, Dec 21)
Long Run (FR) 162 (3m, Kemp, Sft, Dec 26)
Loose Chips 144 1 (3m, Hunt, Hvy, Jan 24)
Lord Of House (GER) 140 1 (2m, Ludl, Hvy, Jan 16)
Lord Windermere (IRE) 170 1 (3m 2f 110y, Chel, Gd, Mar 14)
Los Amigos (IRE) 137 3 (3m, Naas, Sft, Mar 9)
Lost Glory (NZ) 145 3 (3m 2f, Utto, Gd, Jun 30)
Lost Legend (IRE) 137 1 (2m 4f 110y, Kemp, GS, Mar 15)
Lyreen Legend (IRE) 165 6 (3m 2f 110y, Chel, Gd, Mar 14)
Ma Filleule (FR) 164 1 (2m 5f 110y, Live, Gd, Apr 4)
Mad Brian (IRE) 150 2 (3m, Nava, Yld, Nov 24)
Madam Bovary (IRE) 137 1 (2m 5f, Punc, Hvy, Apr 26)
Maggio (FR) 144 1 (2m 7f 110y, Kels, GS, Mar 1)
Mail De Bievre (FR) 139 3 (2m 3f 110y, Chep, Hvy, Dec 28)
Majala (FR) 146 1 (2m 4f 110y, Pert, Sft, Apr 24)
Make A Track (IRE) 156 1 (2m 3f 120y, Lime, Hvy, Dec 27)
Mallowney (IRE) 146 3 (2m 1f, Leop, Sft, Mar 2)
Many Clouds (IRE) 157 1 (2m 4f 110y, Weth, Sft, Dec 27)
Manyriverstocross (IRE) 148 1 (2m 1f, Asco, Gd, Mar 30)
Marito (GER) 156 1 (2m 5f 50y, Tram, Hvy, Jan 1)
Mart Lane (IRE) 146 1 (3m, Donc, GS, Dec 29)
Massena (IRE) 143 1 (2m, Weth, Hvy, Feb 18)
Mcmurrough (IRE) 144 3 (3m, Donc, GS, Feb 19)
Medermit (FR) 146 8 (2m 5f, Chel, Gd, Mar 13)
Meister Eckhart (IRE) 139 (2m 5f, Winc, GS, Nov 9)
Mendip Express (IRE) 156 1 (3m 2f 110y, Chel, Sft, Jan 1)
Menorah (IRE) 172 1 (2m 6f, Sand, GS, Apr 26)
Merrion Square (IRE) 137 2 (3m 110y, Sand, Gd, Dec 6)
Merry King (IRE) 144 3 (3m 1f, Hayd, Hvy, Jan 18)
Micheal Flips (IRE) 144 6 (2m 4f, Mark, Gd, May 10)
Midnight Appeal 146 2 (3m, Kemp, Hvy, Feb 7)
Midnight Prayer 146 1 (3m 2f, Warw, Sft, Feb 8)
Midnight Sail 141 1 (2m 4f 110y, Sand, GS, Mar 8)
Mikael D'haguenet (FR) 145 5 (2m 4f, Clon, Yld, Nov 14)
Milborough (IRE) 136 2 (3m 1f, Mark, Gd, Apr 6)
Miley Shah (IRE) 139 2 (2m 4f, Clon, Hvy, Apr 3)
Minella For Value (IRE) 138 1 (3m 1f, Gowr, Gd, Oct 5)
Mister Marker (IRE) 143 1 (2m 7f 110y, Kels, GS, Feb 13)
Module (FR) 166 3 (2m, Chel, Gd, Mar 12)
Mon Parrain (FR) 145 1 (3m 1f 110y, Chel, Gd, Apr 17)
Monbeg Dude (IRE) 151 1 (3m 1f 110y, Chel, Gd, Dec 13)
Morning Assembly (IRE) 156 3 (3m 110y, Chel, Gd, Mar 12)
Moscow Mannon (IRE) 151 4 (2m, Live, Gd, Apr 5)
Mossey Joe (IRE) 159 1 (3m 4f, Stra, Gd, Jun 7)
Mount Benbulben (IRE) 165 4 (3m, Kemp, Sft, Dec 26)
Mount Colah (IRE) 151 1 (2m 1f, Leop, Sft, Mar 2)
Mountainous (IRE) 147 1 (3m 5f 110y, Chep, Hvy, Dec 28)
Mozoltov 154 1 (2m 4f, Naas, Hvy, Feb 23)
Mr Cracker (IRE) 141 1 (2m 3f, List, Gd, Jun 3)
Mr Mole (IRE) 144 (2m 110y, Chel, Gd, Mar 14)
Mr Moonshine (IRE) 156 1 (2m 4f 110y, Warw, Hvy, Feb 8)
Muirhead (IRE) 139 3 (3m, List, Sft, Sep 18)
Muldoon's Picnic (IRE) 140 1 (3m, Hunt, Sft, Oct 15)
Mullaghanoe River (IRE) 142 (2m 4f, Naas, Sft, Mar 9)
Mumbles Head (IRE) 139 1 (3m, Pert, GS, Jul 30)
Mwaleshi 143 1 (2m, Hayd, Sft, Dec 21)
My Brother Sylvest 138 1 (2m 110y, Hunt, Gd, Oct 6)
My Murphy (IRE) 147 1 (3m, Nava, Sft, Mar 16)
Nadiya De La Vega (FR) 141 3 (2m 3f, Donc, Gd, Dec 14)
Nearest The Pin (IRE) 146 2 (2m 4f 110y, Kemp, GS, Mar 15)
Ned Buntline 146 2 (2m 110y, Chel, Gd, Mar 14)
Next Sensation (IRE) 150 1 (2m 110y, Donc, GS, Dec 29)
Niceonefrankie 150 1 (2m 3f, Asco, GS, Nov 22)
Night Alliance (IRE) 139 1 (3m, Hayd, Sft, Dec 21)
Night In Milan (IRE) 149 1 (3m 2f, Donc, Gd, Mar 1)
No Buts 137 2 (2m 4f 110y, Warw, Sft, Jan 23)
No Loose Change (IRE) 153 1 (3m 2f 110y, Newt, GF, Jul 8)
No Planning 148 1 (3m, Hayd, Gd, Apr 19)
No Secrets (IRE) 137 2 (3m 2f 110y, Newb, GS, Mar 22)
Noble Legend 139 2 (2m 4f 110y, Leic, Sft, Feb 13)
Noble Prince (GER) 144 2 (3m, Cork, Yld, Apr 20)
Nuts N Bolts 145 1 (3m 5f, Hayd, Sft, Nov 23)
O'faolains Boy (IRE) 163 1 (3m 110y, Chel, Gd, Mar 12)
Off The Ground (IRE) 151 1 (2m 3f, Donc, Gd, Dec 14)
Ohio Gold (IRE) 138 2 (3m, Chep, Sft, Apr 5)
Oiseau De Nuit (FR) 155 2 (2m, Kemp, Sft, Dec 27)
On His Own (IRE) 170 2 (3m 2f 110y, Chel, Gd, Mar 14)
On The Bridge (IRE) 143 2 (2m 4f, Worc, Gd, Jul 10)
On The Fringe (IRE) 137 1 (2m 7f, Dowr, Sft, Dec 26)
One In A Milan (IRE) 139 4 (3m 5f 110y, Chep, Hvy, Dec 28)
Original Option (IRE) 137 2 (3m, Lime, GF, Jul 7)
Orpheus Valley (IRE) 139 2 (2m 4f, Nava, Sft, Jan 12)
Oscar Hill (IRE) 147 1 (2m, Ludl, Gd, Dec 4)
Oscar Whisky (IRE) 162 2 (2m 4f, Live, Gd, Apr 3)
Oscars Well (IRE) 149 2 (2m 4f, Gowr, Yld, Nov 23)
Our Father (IRE) 144 7 (3m 2f 110y, Newb, Gd, Nov 30)
Our Mick 138 6 (3m 1f, Live, Gd, Apr 5)
Owega Star (IRE) 140 1 (2m 6f, List, Sft, Sep 19)
Owen Glendower (IRE) 138 2 (2m 6f 110y, Mark, GF, Jul 7)
Pacha Du Polder (FR) 148 (3m 110y, Chel, GS, Mar 11)
Page Turner (IRE) 138 1 (2m 1f, Lime, Hvy, Mar 30)
Paint The Clouds 139 1 (2m 7f, Stra, Gd, Apr 13)
Pantxoa (FR) 146 1 (2m 5f, Chel, Gd, Apr 16)
Parsnip Pete 145 1 (2m, Live, Gd, Apr 3)
Passage Vendome (FR) 137 (2m 1f, Ball, Gd, Sep 24)
Pearlysteps 140 1 (3m 110y, Towc, Hvy, Jan 19)
Pendra (IRE) 143 3 (2m 4f 110y, Chel, GS, Mar 11)
Pepite Rose (FR) 154 1 (2m 4f, Newb, GS, Mar 22)
Perfect Smile (IRE) 137 3 (2m 1f, Fair, Yld, Nov 30)
Persian Snow (IRE) 142 1 (2m 4f 110y, Warw, Sft, Feb 21)
Pete The Feat (IRE) 148 1 (3m 2f 110y, Font, GS, Dec 10)
Pickamus (FR) 139 1 (3m 1f 110y, Ludl, Gd, Dec 4)
Pigeon Island 136 2 (3m 1f, Live, Gd, Oct 26)
Pineau De Re (FR) 157 1 (4m 3f 110y, Live, GS, Apr 5)
Pinerolo 136 1 (3m, Newc, Hvy, Feb 22)
Planet Of Sound 152 1 (3m, Kemp, Sft, Jan 11)
Poole Master 147 1 (2m 110y, Chep, Hvy, Feb 22)
Portrait King (IRE) 139 4 (3m 4f, Punc, Hvy, Feb 2)
Poungach (FR) 144 2 (3m 5f, Taun, Sft, Mar 10)
Present View 146 1 (2m 4f 110y, Chel, GS, Mar 11)
Prince De Beauchene (FR) 149 4 (2m 4f, Thur, Sft, Jan 16)
Prince Of Dreams 136 1 (2m 1f, Newb, GS, Mar 22)
Prince Of Fire (GER) 137 1 (2m 1f, Kill, GF, Jul 15)
Problema Tic (FR) 140 1 (3m, Pert, GF, Jun 9)
Prospect Wells (FR) 142 2 (2m 7f, Stra, Gd, Jul 2)
Pure Faith (IRE) 142 2 (3m 2f, Utto, Gd, Jun 30)
Quantitativeeasing (IRE) 149 2 (2m 6f, Galw, Sft, Jul 31)
Quentin Collonges (FR) 143 1 (3m 5f 110y, Sand, Gd, Apr 27)
Quincy Des Pictons (FR) 137 2 (2m 3f 110y, Chep, Sft, Mar 8)
Quito De La Roque (FR) 154 5 (3m 4f, Punc, Hvy, Feb 2)
Rajdhani Express 162 3 (2m 5f, Chel, Gd, Mar 13)
Rajnagan (IRE) 141 3 (2m 1f 110y, Stra, GF, Jul 14)
Rathlin 158 1 (2m 6f, Galw, Gd, Jul 30)
Raya Star (IRE) 154 3 (2m 1f, Newb, Hvy, Feb 8)
Realt Mor (IRE) 147 3 (2m, Nava, Yld, Nov 10)
Rebel Fitz (FR) 157 1 (2m 4f, Fair, Yld, Apr 20)
Rebel Rebellion (IRE) 153 2 (2m 4f, Newb, Hvy, Mar 1)
Relax (FR) 144 1 (3m 110y, Sand, Hvy, Feb 1)
Renard (FR) 148 3 (3m 2f, Donc, Gd, Mar 1)
Restless Harry 154 4 (3m 5f 110y, Sand, GS, Apr 26)
Rigadin De Beauchene (FR) 150 1 (3m 5f, Hayd, Hvy, Feb 15)
Riverside Theatre 156 1 (2m 4f 110y, Hunt, GS, Dec 12)
Road To Riches (IRE) 149 1 (2m 1f, Fair, Yld, Apr 20)
Roalco De Farges (FR) 139 1 (3m 2f 110y, Newb, GS, Mar 22)
Rob Conti (FR) 136 2 (2m 4f, Chel, Gd, Oct 19)
Roberto Goldback (IRE) 156 4 (3m, Asco, GS, Nov 2)
Rock On Ruby (IRE) 152 1 (2m 110y, Donc, GS, Feb 6)
Rockiteer (IRE) 140 1 (3m, Ludl, Gd, Apr 10)
Rocky Creek (IRE) 164 2 (3m 2f 110y, Newb, Gd, Nov 30)
Rockyaboya (IRE) 137 1 (3m 100y, Leop, Sft, Dec 27)
Rody (FR) 143 4 (2m 1f, Newb, Gd, Nov 30)
Rogue Angel (IRE) 143 1 (3m, Punc, Hvy, Dec 31)
Roi Du Mee (FR) 164 1 (3m, Dowr, Sft, Nov 2)
Rolling Aces (IRE) 157 2 (2m 4f, Live, Gd, Apr 4)
Rose Of The Moon (IRE) 142 1 (3m 1f, Weth, Sft, Jan 21)
Roudoudou Ville (FR) 145 2 (2m 4f 110y, Pert, Sft, Apr 24)
Royale's Charter 137 2 (2m 110y, Worc, Gd, Sep 27)
Ruben Cotter (IRE) 136 3 (2m 6f 110y, Newb, Gd, Nov 30)
Rubi Ball (FR) 162 3 (3m, Leop, Sft, Dec 28)
Rubi Light (FR) 158 3 (2m 4f, Gowr, Gd, Oct 5)

Rupert Lamb 148 1 (2m, Naas, Sft, Nov 9)
Saint Are (FR) 138 4 (3m 1f, Hayd, Sft, Nov 23)
Saint Roque (FR) 137 2 (2m 5f, Chel, Gd, Apr 16)
Salsify (IRE) 152 1 (3m 1f, Punc, Hvy, Apr 26)
Sam Winner (FR) 153 5 (3m 110y, Chel, Gd, Mar 12)
Same Difference (IRE) 151 2 (3m 5f 110y, Sand, Gd, Apr 27)
Samingarry (FR) 141 1 (3m, Chep, Sft, Apr 5)
Samstown 136 1 (3m 1f, Ayr, GS, Apr 12)
Sanctuaire (FR) 155 6 (2m, Sand, Gd, Apr 27)
Saoirse Dun (IRE) 141 3 (3m 5f, Fair, Yld, Apr 21)
Saved By John (IRE) 138 2 (2m 1f, Asco, GS, Nov 23)
Savello (IRE) 157 1 (2m 110y, Chel, Gd, Mar 14)
Seebright 138 1 (3m, Pert, Sft, Apr 24)
Sew On Target (IRE) 136 1 (2m, Sand, Hvy, Feb 1)
Shangani (USA) 144 2 (2m 4f 110y, Kemp, Hvy, Feb 7)
Shanpallas (IRE) 142 6 (2m 1f, Leop, Sft, Dec 26)
Shoegazer (IRE) 149 3 (2m 5f 110y, Newt, Gd, Aug 31)
Shot From The Hip (GER) 145 1 (2m 4f 120y, Kill, Gd, Aug 30)
Shotavodka (IRE) 142 2 (3m, Hayd, Gd, Apr 19)
Shotgun Paddy (IRE) 158 1 (3m 5f, Warw, Sft, Jan 11)
Shrapnel (IRE) 140 3 (2m 5f 100y, Fair, Hvy, Feb 1)
Shutthefrontdoor (IRE) 155 1 (3m 5f, Fair, Yld, Apr 21)
Si C'etait Vrai (FR) 140 (3m 1f, Fair, Hvy, Feb 1)
Silver By Nature 152 2 (3m 1f, Hayd, Sft, Nov 23)
Silver Roque (FR) 148 1 (2m 4f, Sedg, Sft, Nov 12)
Silviniaco Conti (FR) 179 1 (3m, Kemp, Sft, Dec 26)
Simply Ned (IRE) 157 2 (2m, Live, Gd, Apr 5)
Sir Des Champs (FR) 158 4 (3m, Leop, Sft, Dec 28)
Sir Du Bearn (FR) 137 2 (3m 1f 110y, Ffos, Hvy, Dec 16)
Sire Collonges (FR) 149 1 (3m 7f, Chel, Gd, Dec 13)
Sire De Grugy (FR) 174 1 (2m 1f, Asco, Hvy, Jan 18)
Sivola De Sivola (FR) 139 1 (3m, Ffos, GS, Oct 13)
Sixty Something (FR) 140 1 (3m 110y, Bang, GS, Mar 22)
Sizing Europe (IRE) 162 4 (2m, Chel, Gd, Mar 12)
Sizing Gold (IRE) 145 1 (2m 4f, Nava, Sft, Dec 15)
Sizing Italy (IRE) 140 1 (2m 1f, Kill, GF, Jul 17)
Sizing Rio (IRE) 148 1 (2m 4f, Cork, Sft, Nov 3)
Slieveardagh (IRE) 137 1 (2m 4f, Tipp, GF, Jul 21)
Smad Place (FR) 163 2 (3m 110y, Chel, Gd, Mar 12)
Smoking Aces (IRE) 136 2 (4m 1f, Newc, Hvy, Feb 22)
Sole Witness (IRE) 138 2 (3m 4f, Punc, Hvy, Feb 2)
Soll 138 5 (3m 5f 110y, Sand, Gd, Dec 7)
Some Tikket (IRE) 146 1 (2m 1f, Fair, Sft, Apr 6)
Somersby (IRE) 167 2 (2m, Chel, Gd, Mar 12)
Sonofvic (IRE) 147 1 (3m, Devo, GS, Oct 22)
Sound Investment (IRE) 145 1 (2m, Sand, GS, Mar 8)
Special Tiara 161 3 (2m, Chel, Gd, Nov 17)
Speed Master (IRE) 136 2 (2m 4f, Ludl, Gd, Apr 10)
Spring Heeled (IRE) 151 1 (3m 1f 110y, Chel, Gd, Mar 13)
Sraid Padraig (IRE) 139 8 (2m 4f, Chel, Gd, Mar 13)
Stagecoach Pearl 136 2 (2m, Weth, Gd, Oct 16)
Standing Ovation (IRE) 136 1 (3m 1f 110y, Winc, GS, Nov 9)
Steps To Freedom (IRE) 138 2 (2m 1f, Kill, GF, Jul 17)
Stonemaster (IRE) 141 2 (3m, Punc, Yld, May 11)
Storm Survivor (IRE) 136 2 (3m 2f, Donc, Gd, Mar 1)
Summery Justice (IRE) 137 1 (3m 2f 110y, Newb, Hvy, Mar 1)
Sun Cloud (IRE) 140 1 (3m 6f, Catt, Hvy, Jan 9)
Suntiep (FR) 138 3 (4m, Chel, GS, Mar 11)
Super Duty (IRE) 155 2 (3m, Newb, GS, Dec 18)
Supreme Doc (IRE) 138 3 (2m 6f, Lime, GF, Jul 7)
Sweeney Tunes 146 6 (3m 100y, Leop, Sft, Dec 27)
Swift Arrow (IRE) 138 1 (2m, Muss, Sft, Feb 2)
Swincombe Rock 139 3 (3m 4f, Font, Hvy, Nov 17)
Swing Bill (FR) 137 5 (3m 2f, Live, Sft, Dec 7)
Sydney Paget (IRE) 149 1 (3m 1f, Hayd, Sft, Nov 23)
Tahiti Pearl (IRE) 140 1 (2m 4f, Sedg, Hvy, Jan 26)
Tammys Hill (IRE) 141 1 (3m 2f 110y, Chel, Gd, Mar 14)
Tanks For That (IRE) 141 8 (2m, Sand, Gd, Apr 27)
Tap Night (USA) 141 3 (2m 5f, Chel, Hvy, Jan 25)
Taquin Du Seuil (FR) 164 1 (2m 4f, Chel, Gd, Mar 13)
Tarla (FR) 140 1 (2m 3f 110y, Lime, Hvy, May 19)
Tataniano (FR) 140 5 (2m, Chel, Gd, Nov 17)
Tatenen (FR) 142 4 (2m 5f 110y, Live, Gd, Apr 4)
Teaforthree (IRE) 158 2 (3m, Asco, Sft, Feb 15)
Ted Veale (IRE) 153 (2m, Chel, GS, Mar 11)
Terminal (FR) 139 9 (3m 2f 110y, Newb, Gd, Nov 30)
Texas Jack (IRE) 159 4 (3m, Leop, Hvy, Feb 9)
Thanks For Coming 137 1 (3m, Newb, Gd, Mar 21)
That's Rhythm (FR) 137 1 (3m 110y, Bang, Gd, May 18)
The Cockney Mackem (IRE) 136 4 (2m, Chel, Gd, Nov 17)
The Disengager (IRE) 155 1 (2m 5f 110y, Newt, Gd, Aug 31)
The Druids Nephew (IRE) 143 2 (3m, Chep, GS, Dec 7)
The Giant Bolster 170 3 (3m 2f 110y, Chel, Gd, Mar 14)
The Italian Yob (IRE) 139 1 (2m 4f 110y, Sand, Gd, Dec 6)
The Package 148 3 (3m 110y, Chel, GS, Mar 11)
The Paparrazi Kid (IRE) 146 1 (2m 3f 120y, Lime, Sft, Dec 26)
The Rainbow Hunter 148 1 (3m, Donc, Sft, Jan 25)
The Real Article (IRE) 146 1 (2m 4f, List, Yld, Sep 15)
The Romford Pele (IRE) 144 2 (2m 3f 110y, Chep, Gd, Oct 12)
Theatre Guide (IRE) 158 2 (3m 1f 110y, Chel, Gd, Dec 13)
Theatrical Star 140 3 (3m 110y, Sand, Hvy, Feb 1)
Third Intention (IRE) 149 3 (3m, Asco, Sft, Feb 15)
Tidal Bay (IRE) 172 3 (3m 5f 110y, Chep, Hvy, Dec 28)
Time For Rupert (IRE) 143 2 (3m, Asco, Gd, Mar 30)
Tindaro (FR) 140 2 (2m 1f 110y, Stra, GF, Jul 14)
Tofino Bay (IRE) 142 (2m 4f, Dowr, Sft, Nov 2)
Toner D'oudairies (FR) 154 4 (2m 4f, Live, Gd, Apr 4)
Tony Star (FR) 142 3 (2m 4f, Hayd, Gd, May 11)
Toon River (IRE) 139 1 (2m 4f, Gowr, Sft, Mar 8)
Torphichen 148 3 (2m 5f 50y, Tram, Hvy, Jan 1)
Toubab (FR) 142 4 (2m, Ffos, Gd, Aug 22)
Touch The Eden (FR) 149 1 (3m, Lime, Hvy, Mar 30)
Tour Des Champs (FR) 137 2 (3m 110y, Chel, Gd, Oct 19)
Tranquil Sea (IRE) 146 1 (3m, Donc, GS, Feb 19)
Tribes And Banner (IRE) 142 2 (2m 1f, Ball, Gd, Aug 27)
Trifolium (FR) 158 3 (2m, Live, Gd, Apr 5)
Triolo D'alene (FR) 164 1 (3m 2f 110y, Newb, Gd, Nov 30)
Trustan Times (IRE) 148 3 (4m 110y, Ayr, GS, Apr 12)
Turban (FR) 155 1 (2m 1f, Fair, Sft, Jan 19)
Turn Over Sivola (FR) 142 2 (2m, Live, Gd, Apr 3)
Twinlight (FR) 161 1 (2m, Cork, Sft, Dec 8)
Twirling Magnet (IRE) 147 1 (3m 110y, Chel, Gd, Oct 18)
Ulck Du Lin (FR) 137 5 (2m 1f, Asco, Sft, Dec 21)
Ultimate 144 1 (2m 4f 110y, Weth, GS, Nov 1)
Umberto D'olivate (FR) 136 1 (2m 2f, Font, GS, Mar 15)
Uncle Junior (IRE) 148 2 (3m 7f, Chel, Gd, Nov 15)
Uncle Tom Cobley (IRE) 136 2 (2m 3f, List, Gd, Jun 3)
Une Artiste (FR) 138 1 (2m 4f 110y, Hunt, GS, Dec 12)
Unioniste (FR) 161 1 (3m 1f, Live, GS, Dec 7)
Up To Something (FR) 142 2 (2m 4f, Newb, GS, Nov 29)
Upsilon Bleu (FR) 145 2 (2m 110y, Donc, GS, Jan 25)
Urbain De Sivola (FR) 142 3 (2m 4f 110y, Kemp, Sft, Dec 26)
Usuel Smurfer (FR) 136 1 (2m 6f 100y, Fair, Yld, Apr 21)
Uxizandre (FR) 162 1 (2m 4f, Live, Gd, Apr 3)
Valdez 159 1 (2m 1f, Newb, Gd, Nov 30)
Vesper Bell (IRE) 148 2 (3m 6f, Punc, Hvy, Apr 26)
Via Sundown (FR) 144 1 (2m 6f, Font, Hvy, Feb 23)
Victor Hewgo 143 1 (3m, Donc, Gd, Mar 1)
Vino Griego (FR) 158 2 (3m 1f, Live, Gd, Apr 5)
Vintage Star (IRE) 148 2 (3m, Newc, Gd, Nov 30)
Viva Colonia (IRE) 147 2 (2m 4f, Muss, Sft, Jan 1)
Vukovar (FR) 148 1 (2m 2f 110y, Newb, Sft, Dec 28)
Warne (IRE) 138 1 (2m 5f 110y, Live, GS, Apr 3)
Wayward Prince 156 2 (3m 1f, Weth, GS, Nov 2)
Well Refreshed 144 3 (3m 5f 110y, Sand, Gd, Dec 7)
West End Rocker (IRE) 136 3 (4m 1f 110y, Utto, GS, Mar 15)
West With The Wind 148 1 (2m 3f 110y, Devo, GF, May 7)
Western Warhorse (IRE) 161 1 (2m, Chel, GS, Mar 11)
What A Warrior (IRE) 136 3 (3m, Asco, Sft, Dec 21)
Whats Happening (IRE) 141 2 (2m 7f 110y, Leic, Sft, Jan 7)
White Star Line (IRE) 141 1 (3m, List, Sft, Sep 18)
Wiesentraum (GER) 137 2 (3m 110y, Fake, Gd, Mar 14)
William's Wishes (IRE) 145 5 (2m 1f 110y, Devo, GS, Nov 5)
Wishfull Thinking 162 1 (2m 5f, Chel, Hvy, Jan 25)
Witness In Court (IRE) 145 1 (2m, Hayd, Gd, Apr 19)
Wonderful Charm (FR) 159 2 (2m 5f, Chel, Gd, Dec 13)
Woolcombe Folly (IRE) 158 2 (2m 6f 110y, Mark, GF, Jul 20)
Wychwoods Brook 149 1 (3m 1f, Hayd, Hvy, Jan 18)
Wyck Hill (IRE) 148 1 (4m 1f, Newc, Hvy, Feb 22)
Yes Tom (IRE) 143 1 (3m 2f, Dowr, Sft, Mar 17)
Yesyoucan (IRE) 142 2 (3m, Hunt, Hvy, Jan 24)
You Must Know Me (IRE) 145 3 (2m 5f 110y, Live, Sft, Dec 7)
Zaru (FR) 137 2 (2m 4f, Newc, Sft, Dec 21)

RACING POST RATINGS: LAST SEASON'S LEADING HURDLERS

KEY: Horse name, best RPR figure, finishing position when earning figure, (details of race where figure was earned)

Abbyssial (IRE) 134 1 (2m, Fair, Hvy, Feb 22)
Act Of Kalanisi (IRE) 143 1 (2m, Leic, Sft, Dec 27)
Aegean Dawn 132 3 (3m, Hayd, Sft, Dec 21)
Aerlite Supreme (IRE) 135 1 (2m 4f, Lime, Hvy, Mar 30)
Ahyaknowyerself (IRE) 148 3 (2m, Winc, GS, Nov 9)
Akatara (IRE) 133 5 (2m, Punc, Yld, Nov 17)
Alaivan (IRE) 135 2 (2m, Winc, Hvy, Jan 16)
Aldopicgros (FR) 135 1 (2m 3f, Newb, GS, Mar 22)
Alelchi Inois (FR) 137 1 (2m 4f, Fair, Sft, Nov 6)
Alfie Sherrin 134 4 (3m, Hayd, Sft, Nov 23)
Ally Cascade (IRE) 141 4 (2m 4f, Nava, Sft, Dec 15)
Alonso (SPA) 137 4 (2m, Fair, Yld, Dec 1)
Alpha Victor (IRE) 144 1 (3m, Bang, Hvy, Feb 26)
Amore Alato 139 2 (2m, Kemp, Sft, Feb 22)
Analifet (FR) 137 1 (2m, Fair, Yld, Dec 1)
Ancient Sands (IRE) 132 1 (2m, Ball, Gd, Sep 24)
Andy Kelly (IRE) 132 2 (2m 6f, Asco, Sft, Dec 20)
Annie Power (IRE) 164 2 (3m, Chel, Gd, Mar 13)
Another Rebel (IRE) 135 1 (2m 6f, Kill, Gd, Aug 30)
Anshan Dreams 136 1 (2m, Cork, GF, Aug 5)
Apache Jack (IRE) 149 3 (3m, Chel, Gd, Mar 14)
Apache Stronghold (IRE) 149 1 (2m 4f, Nava, Yld, Nov 24)
Araldur (FR) 144 4 (3m, Hayd, Gd, May 11)
Archie Meade (IRE) 137 5 (2m 6f, Thur, Gd, Oct 24)
Arctic Fire (GER) 150 2 (2m 1f, Chel, Gd, Mar 14)
Art Of Payroll (GER) 143 1 (2m, Leop, Sft, Mar 2)
Art Professor (IRE) 134 2 (2m 3f 110y, Asco, Sft, Feb 15)
As I Am (IRE) 140 1 (2m 1f, Chel, Gd, Apr 17)
At Fishers Cross (IRE) 166 3 (3m, Chel, Gd, Mar 13)
Attaglance 141 5 (3m 110y, Muss, Sft, Feb 2)
Aubusson (FR) 137 1 (2m 4f 110y, Chel, Sft, Jan 1)
Aughnacurraveel (IRE) 140 2 (3m, Gowr, Yld, Oct 5)
Australia Day (IRE) 138 4 (2m, Muss, Gd, Nov 8)
Awaywiththegreys (IRE) 135 1 (3m, Chep, Hvy, Dec 28)
Azorian (IRE) 143 2 (2m 4f, Nava, Sft, Dec 15)
Bally Legend 137 1 (2m 6f 110y, Font, Sft, Oct 23)
Ballyadam Brook (IRE) 132 4 (2m, Dowr, Sft, Nov 2)
Ballyalton (IRE) 149 2 (2m 5f, Chel, Gd, Mar 12)
Ballyculla (IRE) 136 2 (3m, Chel, Gd, Apr 17)
Ballyrock (IRE) 133 5 (3m 110y, Live, Gd, May 17)
Balnagon Boy (IRE) 132 4 (2m, Nava, Sft, Dec 15)
Balnaslow (IRE) 136 2 (2m 6f, Kill, Gd, Aug 30)
Baltimore Rock (IRE) 138 4 (2m 110y, Live, GS, Apr 4)
Band Of Blood (IRE) 135 2 (3m, Cork, Sft, Dec 8)
Baresi (IRE) 138 1 (2m 3f, Naas, Yld, Oct 20)
Barizan (IRE) 135 (2m 1f, Chel, Gd, Mar 14)
Battle Group 151 1 (3m, Hayd, Gd, May 11)
Bayan (IRE) 142 3 (2m 5f, Chel, Gd, Mar 12)
Beat That (IRE) 159 1 (3m 110y, Live, GS, Apr 4)
Beluckyagain (IRE) 132 2 (2m 4f, Fair, Sft, Apr 6)
Benbane Head (USA) 136 2 (3m, Chel, Gd, Oct 18)
Berea Boru (IRE) 136 2 (3m, Ffos, Sft, Nov 22)
Berkeley Barron (IRE) 135 1 (2m 6f, Sand, Sft, Mar 7)
Big Buck's (FR) 160 5 (3m, Chel, Gd, Mar 13)
Big Easy (GER) 135 6 (3m 110y, Live, Gd, Apr 3)
Big Hands Harry 132 2 (2m 4f, Bang, GS, Mar 22)
Big Time Billy (IRE) 145 1 (3m, Ffos, Gd, Jun 20)
Billfromthebar (IRE) 132 1 (3m, Hexh, GS, Oct 4)
Black Benny (IRE) 132 4 (2m 6f, Kill, GF, Jul 17)
Black Thunder (FR) 136 5 (2m 3f 110y, Sand, Gd, Apr 27)
Blacklough (IRE) 143 1 (2m 3f, Cork, Sft, Apr 20)
Blackmail (FR) 144 1 (2m 1f, Bell, Gd, Aug 22)
Blackwell Synergy (FR) 138 1 (3m, List, Sft, Sep 19)
Blakemount (IRE) 140 2 (3m 110y, Donc, Sft, Jan 25)
Blood Cotil (FR) 144 2 (2m, Punc, Hvy, Apr 27)
Blossom Gate (IRE) 136 1 (2m 5f, Lime, GF, Jul 7)
Blue Fashion (IRE) 150 2 (2m 4f, Hayd, Sft, Nov 23)
Bob Le Beau (IRE) 136 1 (2m, Dowr, GF, Aug 30)
Bondage (IRE) 144 1 (2m 4f, Kill, Sft, May 13)
Bonzo Bing (IRE) 134 1 (2m, Gowr, Hvy, Mar 22)
Boston Bob (IRE) 148 1 (2m 4f, Punc, Hvy, Dec 31)
Brave Vic (IRE) 134 1 (2m 4f, Sand, Sft, Mar 8)
Briar Hill (IRE) 150 1 (2m 4f, Naas, Sft, Jan 5)
Broadway Buffalo (IRE) 139 4 (2m 4f, Chep, Sft, Oct 26)
Brother Brian (IRE) 135 1 (2m 4f 110y, Chel, Gd, Apr 16)
Brother Du Berlais (FR) 137 1 (2m 5f 110y, Ayr, GS, Apr 12)
Buddy Bolero (IRE) 148 1 (3m, Chep, Hvy, Feb 22)
Busty Brown (IRE) 142 3 (2m 2f, Leop, Sft, Mar 2)
Bygones Of Brid (IRE) 135 1 (2m, Newc, Sft, Mar 28)
Caid Du Berlais (FR) 152 2 (2m 4f, Live, GS, Apr 4)
Cailin Annamh (IRE) 142 1 (2m 2f, Punc, Gd, Oct 17)
Caim Hill (IRE) 141 2 (2m 5f 190y, Galw, Hvy, Oct 28)
Calculated Risk 137 1 (2m 4f, Sedg, Sft, Dec 26)
Calipto (FR) 139 4 (2m 1f, Chel, Gd, Mar 14)
Call Me Bubbles (FR) 150 2 (2m, List, Sft, Sep 17)
Call The Cops (IRE) 132 1 (2m 5f, Ludl, Gd, Apr 22)
Caoimhe's Delight (IRE) 132 2 (2m 4f, Leop, Sft, Dec 29)
Cape Express (IRE) 134 (2m 3f, Mark, GF, Jul 7)
Capote (IRE) 137 1 (2m 7f 110y, Devo, Hvy, Mar 4)
Captain Arceus (IRE) 149 1 (2m 4f, Galw, GF, Sep 11)
Captain Cee Bee (IRE) 160 5 (2m 110y, Chel, GS, Mar 11)
Captain Cutter (IRE) 150 1 (2m 5f, Newb, Hvy, Dec 28)
Captain Sunshine 142 3 (3m 1f, Weth, GS, Nov 2)
Cara's Oscar (IRE) 140 1 (2m 6f, Fair, Yld, Apr 21)
Carole's Destrier 133 1 (2m 5f, Kemp, GS, Mar 15)
Carole's Spirit 146 2 (3m, Asco, Hvy, Jan 18)
Carraig Mor (IRE) 145 1 (2m 4f 110y, Utto, Sft, Nov 1)
Carriganog (IRE) 136 1 (2m, Wexf, Sft, Oct 27)
Cash And Go (IRE) 141 3 (2m 4f, Live, GS, Apr 4)
Ceasar Milan (IRE) 133 5 (2m 4f, Sand, Sft, Mar 8)
Celestial Halo (IRE) 165 1 (3m 110y, Newb, Sft, Nov 30)
Champagne West (IRE) 143 4 (3m, Chel, Gd, Mar 14)
Chatterbox (IRE) 144 2 (2m 110y, Newb, GS, Nov 28)
Cheltenian (FR) 142 4 (2m 4f, Live, GS, Apr 4)
Chris Pea Green 145 3 (2m 4f, Font, Hvy, Feb 23)
Citizenship 138 1 (2m 1f, Devo, Sft, Dec 19)
City Slicker (IRE) 144 1 (2m 4f, Punc, Hvy, Jan 11)
Clarcam (FR) 138 2 (2m 1f, Live, Gd, Apr 3)
Clerk's Choice (IRE) 145 3 (2m 6f, Sand, GS, Apr 26)
Clever Cookie 145 1 (2m 2f, Kels, GS, Mar 1)
Clondaw Court (IRE) 152 1 (2m 6f, Thur, Sft, Jan 16)
Clondaw Draft (IRE) 136 3 (2m 5f, Chel, Gd, Oct 18)
Clondaw Kaempfer (IRE) 145 4 (2m 6f, Sand, GS, Apr 26)
Close House 132 9 (3m 1f 110y, Chel, Gd, Nov 16)
Cockney Sparrow 153 1 (2m, Ayr, GS, Apr 12)
Cocktails At Dawn 133 1 (2m 5f, Kemp, Gd, Apr 15)
Coffee (IRE) 136 2 (2m 1f, Mark, Gd, Jul 20)
Cole Harden (IRE) 152 2 (3m 110y, Live, GS, Apr 4)
Commissioned (IRE) 135 4 (2m 1f, Live, Gd, Apr 3)
Connectivity (IRE) 134 1 (3m 110y, Sout, Sft, Nov 11)
Cool Macavity (IRE) 134 1 (2m 1f, Bang, Gd, Aug 2)
Coolmill (IRE) 134 1 (2m 4f, Cork, Hvy, Nov 17)
Cops And Robbers 137 3 (2m, Punc, Hvy, Apr 26)
Cotton Mill 146 4 (2m, Newc, Gd, Nov 30)
Courage (IRE) 134 1 (3m, Leop, Sft, Dec 28)
Court Minstrel (IRE) 154 2 (2m, Ayr, GS, Apr 12)
Courtncatcher (IRE) 134 3 (3m, Cork, Sft, Nov 3)
Creepy (IRE) 137 1 (2m 5f, Chel, Gd, Nov 16)
Cross Kennon (IRE) 143 4 (3m 1f 110y, Chel, Gd, Nov 16)
Crowning Jewel 137 1 (2m 4f, Live, Gd, Oct 27)
Cry Of Freedom (USA) 132 1 (2m 1f, Taun, GF, May 2)
Curley Bill (IRE) 142 1 (2m, List, Yld, Sep 15)
Dancing Tornado (IRE) 141 4 (2m, Cork, Gd, May 24)
Daneking 141 1 (2m, Fair, Yld, Apr 20)
Darwins Fox (FR) 140 2 (2m, Fair, Yld, Apr 20)
Dawn Commander (GER) 133 1 (3m 110y, Donc, Gd, Mar 1)
Dedigout (IRE) 155 1 (2m 4f, Nava, Yld, Nov 10)
Deep Trouble (IRE) 141 2 (2m, Kemp, Sft, Jan 11)
Dell' Arca (IRE) 145 3 (2m 4f, Live, GS, Apr 5)
Deputy Dan (IRE) 151 2 (3m, Chel, Gd, Mar 14)
Desertmore Stream (IRE) 137 2 (2m, Fair, Yld, Apr 20)
Diakali (FR) 165 3 (2m 4f, Live, Gd, Apr 3)
Diamond King (IRE) 136 1 (2m 110y, Donc, GS, Jan 8)

Dildar (IRE) 133 3 (2m, Asco, GS, Nov 2)
Discovery Bay 133 2 (2m, Hayd, Gd, Mar 19)
Djakadam (FR) 135 4 (2m, Punc, Hvy, Apr 27)
Doctor Harper (IRE) 145 1 (3m 110y, Live, Gd, Apr 3)
Dogora (FR) 135 3 (2m, Punc, Hvy, Apr 27)
Dolatulo (FR) 140 1 (2m 3f 110y, Ling, Sft, Dec 14)
Domination 154 1 (2m 2f, Cork, Gd, Aug 25)
Don Poli (IRE) 153 1 (2m 4f 110y, Chel, Gd, Mar 14)
Double Irish (IRE) 139 1 (2m, Leop, Sft, Dec 27)
Double Ross (IRE) 139 6 (3m, Hayd, Gd, May 11)
Doyly Carte 141 2 (2m, Hayd, Sft, Nov 23)
Drive Time (USA) 157 4 (2m, Galw, Hvy, Aug 1)
Drum Valley 132 4 (3m 110y, Donc, GS, Dec 29)
Duke Of Navan (IRE) 137 6 (2m, Newc, Gd, Nov 30)
Dunguib (IRE) 156 1 (2m 5f, Nava, Hvy, Feb 16)
Dunraven Storm (IRE) 141 1 (2m 3f 110y, Taun, Gd, Apr 3)
Dushybeag (IRE) 135 2 (2m 6f, Punc, Yld, Nov 16)
Dysios (IRE) 134 1 (2m, Leop, Sft, Dec 28)
Edeymi (IRE) 135 2 (3m, Cork, GF, Aug 5)
Edgardo Sol (FR) 148 6 (2m 4f, Hayd, Sft, Nov 23)
Elegant Statesman (IRE) 133 4 (2m, Galw, Gd, Jul 30)
Ely Brown (IRE) 144 1 (3m 110y, Live, Gd, Oct 27)
Empire Of Dirt (IRE) 144 2 (2m 4f, Leop, Sft, Jan 25)
False Economy (IRE) 145 1 (2m, Lime, Yld, Nov 10)
Far West (FR) 153 (2m 110y, Newb, Hvy, Feb 8)
Faugheen (IRE) 155 1 (2m 5f, Chel, Gd, Mar 12)
Fergall (IRE) 140 1 (2m, Plum, GS, Apr 20)
Festive Felon (IRE) 140 4 (3m, Punc, Hvy, Feb 2)
Fiery Oscar (IRE) 140 1 (2m, List, Sft, Sep 19)
Fine Rightly (IRE) 135 1 (2m 4f, Weth, Hvy, Feb 18)
Fingal Bay (IRE) 154 1 (3m, Chel, Gd, Mar 13)
First In The Queue (IRE) 143 1 (2m 110y, Chel, Gd, Oct 18)
Fisher 133 2 (2m, Newc, Gd, Mar 15)
Flaming Dawn (IRE) 136 4 (2m 7f, Nava, Sft, Mar 16)
Flat Out (FR) 140 6 (2m, Fair, Yld, Nov 30)
Flaxen Flare (IRE) 152 5 (2m 1f, Chel, Gd, Mar 14)
Flemenson (IRE) 132 1 (2m 6f, Weth, Hvy, Feb 1)
Flicka Williams (IRE) 133 2 (2m 4f 110y, Utto, Hvy, Dec 31)
Foildubh (IRE) 151 1 (2m 6f 110y, Thur, Gd, Nov 28)
Followmeuptocarlow (IRE) 132 1 (2m 4f, Fair, Yld, Nov 30)
Fosters Cross (IRE) 139 3 (2m, Tipp, GF, Jul 21)
Fox Appeal (IRE) 152 5 (3m, Hayd, Gd, May 11)
Fox Norton (FR) 137 1 (2m 110y, Donc, Gd, Dec 14)
Foxcub (IRE) 134 1 (2m 4f 110y, Leic, GS, Dec 11)
Franciscan 137 1 (2m 1f, Chel, Gd, Apr 16)
Free To Dream (IRE) 140 1 (3m, Mark, Sft, Nov 21)
Full Shift (FR) 139 1 (2m 5f, Kemp, Sft, Feb 22)
Gallant Tipp (IRE) 137 5 (2m 4f, Leop, Hvy, Jan 26)
Garde La Victoire (FR) 140 1 (2m 4f 110y, Chel, Gd, Apr 16)
Gauvain (GER) 138 6 (3m 1f 110y, Chel, Gd, Nov 16)
General Miller 140 1 (3m, Bang, Gd, Sep 13)
Get Me Out Of Here (IRE) 154 2 (2m 5f, Chel, Gd, Mar 12)
Getoutwhenyoucan (IRE) 136 1 (2m, Lime, Hvy, Mar 30)
Gevrey Chambertin (FR) 149 1 (3m, Hayd, Sft, Nov 23)
Giant's Quest (AUS) 139 1 (2m 4f, Bell, Gd, Aug 22)
Giantofaman (IRE) 140 1 (2m 4f, Thur, Hvy, Feb 27)
Gibb River (IRE) 141 5 (2m, Asco, GS, Nov 2)
Gilgamboa (IRE) 143 (2m 110y, Chel, GS, Mar 11)
Gilt Shadow (IRE) 138 3 (2m 4f, Leop, Hvy, Jan 26)
Gimli's Rock (IRE) 139 3 (3m, Cork, GF, Aug 5)
Glam Gerry (IRE) 133 4 (2m 4f, Cork, Hvy, Nov 17)
Glens Melody (IRE) 144 2 (2m 4f, Chel, GS, Mar 11)
God's Own (IRE) 135 1 (2m 5f, Kemp, GS, Nov 4)
Gold Bullet (IRE) 141 2 (2m 6f, Dowr, Gd, May 6)
Gold Patrol (IRE) 133 2 (3m, Thur, Hvy, Mar 20)
Goonyella (IRE) 145 2 (3m, Clon, Hvy, Feb 20)
Grand Vision (IRE) 143 2 (3m 1f, Warw, Hvy, Jan 11)
Grands Crus (FR) 152 5 (2m 5f, Kemp, GS, Nov 4)
Grange (IRE) 133 (2m 4f, Thur, Sft, Jan 16)
Grumeti 147 3 (2m, Newc, Gd, Nov 30)
Guitar Pete (IRE) 141 1 (2m 1f, Live, Gd, Apr 3)
Gullinbursti (IRE) 140 5 (3m, Hayd, Sft, Nov 23)
Hada Men (USA) 132 2 (3m, Mark, Gd, May 10)
Hammersly Lake (FR) 133 (2m, Asco, GS, Nov 22)
Handazan (IRE) 135 1 (2m 110y, Chep, Gd, Oct 12)
Hannibal The Great (IRE) 134 1 (2m 4f 110y, Sout, Gd, Dec 3)
Hazariban (IRE) 137 2 (2m 3f, Naas, Sft, Mar 9)
He'llberemembered (IRE) 149 2 (2m 4f, Nava, Sft, Dec 15)
Heronry (IRE) 137 1 (3m, Asco, Gd, Mar 30)
Hi Note 132 2 (2m 2f 110y, Font, Gd, Oct 4)
Hidden Identity (IRE) 139 1 (2m 4f 110y, Hunt, Sft, Nov 12)
Highland Retreat 147 1 (3m, Asco, Hvy, Jan 18)
Hint Of Mint 135 1 (2m 1f, Taun, Gd, Apr 10)
Hisaabaat (IRE) 139 5 (2m, Galw, Hvy, Aug 1)
Home Run (GER) 135 2 (2m 6f, Sand, GS, Dec 7)
Horatio Hornblower (IRE) 132 2 (2m 4f, Hayd, Gd, Apr 19)
Horendus Hulabaloo (IRE) 134 2 (2m 4f, Wexf, Sft, Apr 11)
Horizontal Speed (IRE) 138 1 (2m 4f, Hayd, Gd, Apr 19)
Hunting Party (IRE) 136 1 (2m 4f, Ball, Sft, May 28)
Hunting Tower 133 2 (2m 4f, Worc, Gd, Aug 13)
Hurricane Fly (IRE) 171 1 (2m, Punc, Hvy, Apr 26)
I Need Gold (IRE) 138 1 (3m 110y, Ayr, Hvy, Mar 8)
If In Doubt (IRE) 143 2 (2m 7f 110y, Devo, Hvy, Feb 9)
Ifandbutwhynot (IRE) 142 5 (2m, Ayr, GS, Apr 12)
Il Fenomeno (ITY) 141 7 (2m 4f, Punc, Hvy, Apr 27)
Indevan 143 1 (2m 5f, Lime, Gd, Oct 13)
Indian File (IRE) 133 1 (2m, Lime, Hvy, Dec 27)
Inis Meain (USA) 142 1 (2m 7f, Nava, Hvy, Feb 16)
Irish Cavalier (IRE) 133 1 (2m 1f, Bang, GS, Mar 22)
Irish Saint (FR) 152 3 (2m 110y, Newb, Hvy, Feb 8)
Irving 149 1 (2m, Kemp, Sft, Feb 22)
Ivan Grozny (FR) 134 1 (2m, Fair, Yld, Apr 21)
Jennies Jewel (IRE) 143 2 (2m 3f, Naas, Hvy, Jan 18)
Jetson (IRE) 148 5 (3m, Chel, Gd, Mar 13)
Jezki (IRE) 173 1 (2m 110y, Chel, GS, Mar 11)
Join The Clan (IRE) 134 2 (2m 7f 110y, Devo, Gd, Apr 15)
Josses Hill (IRE) 150 2 (2m 110y, Chel, GS, Mar 11)
Jubilee Year (IRE) 133 1 (2m 4f, Tipp, Hvy, May 16)
Jumps Road 138 3 (2m 1f, Chel, Gd, Dec 14)
Junction Fourteen (IRE) 137 1 (2m 5f, Kemp, Sft, Dec 26)
Kaki De La Pree (FR) 135 2 (3m, Hayd, Hvy, Feb 15)
Kangaroo Court (IRE) 143 1 (2m 6f, Newt, Gd, Oct 11)
Karinga Dancer 143 1 (2m 1f, Live, GS, Oct 26)
Katachenko (IRE) 132 1 (2m 2f, Kels, Sft, Apr 7)
Kayf Moss 144 1 (2m 4f, Font, Hvy, Feb 23)
Kaylif Aramis 141 2 (3m 110y, Live, Gd, Apr 3)
Kaysersberg (FR) 133 1 (3m, Mark, GS, Mar 9)
Kentucky Hyden (IRE) 141 2 (2m 1f, Chel, Gd, Mar 14)
Kerrieonvic (IRE) 134 1 (3m, Cork, Yld, Apr 21)
Killala Quay 149 4 (2m 5f, Chel, Gd, Mar 12)
King Ali (IRE) 134 5 (3m, Galw, Sft, Jul 31)
King Of The Picts (IRE) 138 3 (2m 110y, Live, GS, Apr 4)
King Shabra (IRE) 137 2 (2m 4f, Naas, Sft, Oct 28)
Kings Bandit (IRE) 135 1 (2m 3f 110y, Taun, Gd, Apr 23)
Kings Palace (IRE) 154 1 (3m, Chel, Gd, Dec 14)
Kingsmere 133 1 (3m, Chel, Gd, Apr 17)
Kitten Rock (FR) 138 2 (2m, Fair, Yld, Apr 21)
Knight Of Noir (IRE) 135 1 (2m 4f, Winc, Hvy, Feb 15)
Knight Of Pleasure 134 1 (2m 2f 110y, Font, Hvy, Nov 17)
Knockara Beau (IRE) 154 1 (3m, Chel, Hvy, Jan 25)
Kris Spin (IRE) 142 2 (3m, Asco, Gd, Mar 30)
L'unique (FR) 147 1 (2m 4f, Sand, GS, Apr 26)
Lac Fontana (FR) 149 1 (2m 4f, Live, GS, Apr 5)
Land Of Vic 133 1 (3m 110y, Ayr, GS, Apr 11)
Landero 137 1 (3m, Rosc, GF, Jul 9)
Lastoftheleaders (IRE) 136 2 (2m, Leop, Sft, Dec 27)
Laudatory 135 1 (2m 110y, Stra, GF, Sep 7)
Layla Joan (IRE) 140 1 (2m 5f 110y, Ayr, Hvy, Feb 11)
Le Rocher (FR) 149 1 (2m 1f, Chel, Hvy, Jan 25)
Le Vent D'antan (FR) 141 2 (2m 4f, Fair, Sft, Apr 6)
Leah Claire (IRE) 136 2 (2m, Leop, Sft, Dec 28)
Leavethelighton (IRE) 136 2 (2m 4f, Gowr, Hvy, Mar 22)
Legacy Gold (IRE) 138 4 (2m 5f, Kemp, GS, Mar 15)
Leo Luna 133 3 (2m 3f 110y, Asco, Sft, Feb 15)
Letsby Avenue 138 1 (2m 6f 110y, Stra, GS, Sep 17)
Lexi's Boy (IRE) 133 3 (2m, Kemp, Sft, Jan 11)
Liberty's Gift (IRE) 133 1 (2m, Tipp, Gd, Oct 6)
Lie Forrit (IRE) 141 1 (3m 3f, Kels, Gd, Mar 22)
Lienosus (IRE) 140 1 (3m 110y, Taun, Hvy, Jan 18)
Lieutenant Colonel 151 1 (2m 4f, Fair, Sft, Apr 6)
Life And Soul (IRE) 132 2 (2m, Kemp, GS, Oct 20)
Like Minded 140 3 (2m 5f, Kemp, Sft, Jan 11)

Lindenhurst (IRE) 135 3 (2m, Fair, Yld, Apr 21)
Local Hero (GER) 143 2 (2m, Muss, Sft, Feb 2)
Lookoutnow (IRE) 139 5 (3m, Clon, Sft, Nov 14)
Lots Of Memories (IRE) 154 1 (3m, Fair, Yld, Apr 20)
Lovcen (GER) 134 3 (3m 110y, Live, Gd, Oct 27)
Loyaute (FR) 134 3 (2m 5f 110y, Chel, Gd, Apr 17)
Lughnasa (IRE) 133 1 (2m 2f, Leop, Hvy, Feb 9)
Luska Lad (IRE) 137 3 (2m, Lime, Yld, Nov 10)
Lyvius 140 4 (2m, Muss, Sft, Feb 2)
Magnifique Etoile 152 1 (2m 3f, Stra, Sft, Oct 26)
Makari 136 1 (2m 110y, Donc, Gd, Dec 14)
Make Your Mark (IRE) 151 3 (2m, Galw, Hvy, Aug 1)
Mala Beach (IRE) 156 1 (3m, Gowr, Sft, Jan 23)
Maller Tree 135 1 (2m 4f, Fake, Sft, Jan 1)
Man Of Leisure 139 1 (2m 7f, Worc, Gd, Jul 30)
Man With Van (IRE) 136 2 (2m 4f, Ayr, Hvy, Mar 8)
Marcilhac (FR) 134 2 (2m 5f, Kemp, GS, Mar 15)
Marito (GER) 153 2 (2m, Punc, Yld, Nov 17)
Massini's Trap (IRE) 134 4 (2m, Asco, Sft, Dec 20)
Master Of The Game (IRE) 138 1 (2m 3f 110y, Donc, GS, Jan 25)
Masters Hill (IRE) 136 2 (2m 5f, Warw, Hvy, Jan 11)
Maxim Gorky (IRE) 137 2 (2m, Fair, Yld, Nov 30)
Mayfair Music (IRE) 136 1 (3m 110y, Donc, Gd, Mar 1)
Mazuri Cowboy (IRE) 136 1 (2m 3f, Lime, Hvy, Dec 27)
Medinas (FR) 156 7 (3m, Chel, Gd, Mar 13)
Meister Eckhart (IRE) 150 3 (3m 110y, Live, Gd, Apr 3)
Melodic Rendezvous 157 1 (2m, Winc, Hvy, Feb 15)
Mickie 146 1 (3m 110y, Kemp, Sft, Dec 27)
Midnight Game 147 4 (2m, Punc, Yld, Nov 17)
Midnight Oil 135 2 (2m 4f, Kill, Sft, May 13)
Mijhaar 136 5 (2m 110y, Live, GS, Apr 4)
Mikael D'haguenet (FR) 152 3 (2m, Punc, Yld, Nov 17)
Milan Bound (IRE) 132 1 (3m, Utto, GS, Nov 28)
Miley Shah (IRE) 144 2 (2m 1f, Kill, Sft, May 12)
Milo Man (IRE) 133 1 (2m 1f, Taun, Hvy, Jan 28)
Minella Forfitness (IRE) 147 2 (2m 3f 110y, Sand, Gd, Apr 27)
Minella Foru (IRE) 142 6 (2m 1f, Chel, Gd, Mar 14)
Mischievous Milly (IRE) 140 2 (2m 5f, Warw, Hvy, Feb 8)
Missunited (IRE) 149 1 (2m, Galw, Hvy, Aug 1)
Mister Benedictine 133 4 (2m 4f, Slig, Yld, Aug 8)
Mister Dillon 143 3 (3m, Chel, Gd, Apr 17)
Mister Hotelier (IRE) 133 1 (2m 4f, Wexf, Yld, Mar 17)
Monetary Fund (USA) 132 2 (3m, Chep, GS, Apr 26)
Monkey Kingdom 134 1 (2m 4f, Bang, GS, Mar 22)
Montbazon (FR) 148 3 (2m 1f, Chel, Gd, Mar 14)
Moon Dice (IRE) 140 4 (2m, Tipp, Gd, Oct 6)
Moonshine Lad (IRE) 140 2 (2m 4f, Leop, Hvy, Jan 26)
Moorlands Mist 136 1 (3m, Chep, GS, Dec 7)
More Of That (IRE) 172 1 (3m, Chel, Gd, Mar 13)
Morning Royalty (IRE) 136 4 (2m, Hayd, Hvy, Jan 18)
Moscow Mannon (IRE) 142 2 (2m, Punc, Hvy, Apr 26)
Mosspark (IRE) 141 1 (2m 4f 110y, Hunt, Sft, Feb 20)
Moyle Park (IRE) 137 3 (2m, Leop, Sft, Dec 27)
Mr Fiftyone (IRE) 133 3 (2m, Punc, Hvy, Jan 11)
Mr Mole (IRE) 148 2 (2m, Hayd, Gd, May 11)
Mrs Peachey (IRE) 132 4 (2m 4f, Sand, GS, Dec 7)
My Tent Or Yours (IRE) 173 2 (2m 110y, Chel, GS, Mar 11)
My Wigwam Or Yours (IRE) 139 1 (2m 5f, Newb, Gd, Mar 21)
Native Gallery (IRE) 147 3 (2m 4f, Punc, Hvy, Apr 27)
Never Enough Time (IRE) 150 1 (2m, Leop, Hvy, Feb 9)
Noble Prince (GER) 137 7 (2m 5f, Chel, Gd, Mar 12)
Now This Is It (IRE) 140 3 (2m 1f, Kill, Gd, Aug 31)
Ogee 137 1 (2m 7f, Worc, Gd, Aug 28)
Oilily (IRE) 134 1 (2m 4f, Cork, GF, Jul 12)
On His Own (IRE) 147 6 (2m 4f, Naas, Sft, Oct 28)
On The Bridge (IRE) 144 6 (3m, Chel, Gd, Mar 13)
One Fine Day (IRE) 134 3 (2m, List, Sft, Sep 17)
One Lucky Lady 137 2 (2m 4f, Worc, Gd, Jul 3)
Open Day (IRE) 135 2 (2m 4f, Chep, Gd, Oct 12)
Oscar Hoof (IRE) 135 1 (2m, Kemp, GS, Mar 15)
Oscar Rock (IRE) 141 3 (2m 5f, Newb, Hvy, Dec 28)
Oscars Den (IRE) 133 2 (2m 4f 110y, Chel, Gd, Apr 16)
Oscars Well (IRE) 143 9 (3m, Punc, Hvy, Feb 2)
Our Conor (IRE) 161 3 (2m, Leop, Sft, Dec 29)
Our Man Zebo (IRE) 133 2 (3m, Fair, Yld, Apr 20)
Party Rock (IRE) 145 2 (2m 4f, Live, Sft, Dec 7)
Pas Trop Tard (FR) 132 3 (2m, Muss, Sft, Feb 2)
Pass The Time 132 7 (2m 4f, Chel, GS, Mar 11)
Passage Vendome (FR) 135 2 (2m 2f 50y, Down, Sft, Mar 23)
Pateese (FR) 144 2 (3m 110y, Newb, GS, Nov 29)
Peckhamecho (IRE) 133 6 (2m 4f, Font, Gd, Oct 5)
Pension Plan 140 1 (3m, Ffos, Hvy, Nov 10)
Perfect Gentleman (IRE) 140 1 (2m 4f, Clon, Hvy, Feb 20)
Pine Creek 139 6 (2m 110y, Chel, Gd, Nov 17)
Pineau De Re (FR) 146 3 (3m, Chel, Gd, Mar 13)
Pink Coat 137 1 (2m, Fair, Yld, Nov 30)
Plinth (IRE) 133 3 (2m, Leop, Hvy, Feb 9)
Polly Peachum (IRE) 145 1 (2m 5f 110y, Chel, Gd, Apr 17)
Port Melon (IRE) 134 3 (2m 5f, Chel, Gd, Nov 16)
Portway Flyer (IRE) 132 3 (2m 5f, Kemp, GS, Mar 15)
Prideofthecastle (IRE) 132 1 (2m 4f 110y, Hunt, Sft, Feb 6)
Prima Porta 137 2 (2m 110y, Weth, GS, Nov 2)
Primroseandblue (IRE) 133 3 (2m 4f, Fair, Yld, Nov 30)
Prince Rudi (IRE) 139 3 (2m 6f, Fair, Yld, Apr 21)
Prince Siegfried (FR) 140 (2m, Asco, Sft, Dec 20)
Princely Player (IRE) 138 3 (2m 5f, Chel, GS, Oct 19)
Princeton Plains (IRE) 134 (2m, Fair, Yld, Dec 14)
Ptit Zig (FR) 160 6 (2m 110y, Chel, GS, Mar 11)
Puffin Billy (IRE) 139 5 (2m 110y, Newb, GS, Nov 28)
Pure Faith (IRE) 135 1 (3m 110y, Sout, Gd, Aug 18)
Purple Bay (IRE) 139 2 (2m 1f, Taun, Gd, Apr 10)
Pyrus Gold Wind (IRE) 132 1 (2m 4f, Galw, Sft, Jul 31)
Quartz De Thaix (FR) 145 2 (3m, Chel, Sft, Jan 1)
Que Pasa (IRE) 140 1 (2m 2f, Galw, GF, Sep 10)
Quevega (FR) 145 1 (2m 4f, Chel, GS, Mar 11)
Quickpick Vic (IRE) 145 1 (2m, Leop, Hvy, Jan 26)
Racing Pulse (IRE) 142 1 (2m 6f, Newc, Gd, Dec 12)
Raggletagglegypsy (IRE) 138 3 (2m, Gowr, GF, Jun 23)
Rainbow Peak (IRE) 140 2 (2m 110y, Live, GS, Apr 5)
Rajnagan (IRE) 133 2 (2m 1f, Taun, GF, May 2)
Ranjaan (FR) 133 1 (2m, Kemp, Gd, Nov 25)
Rathlin 146 2 (2m 4f, Punc, Hvy, Apr 27)
Rathvinden (IRE) 149 3 (2m 5f, Chel, Gd, Mar 12)
Rattan (USA) 141 3 (2m 4f, Galw, GF, Sep 11)
Rawnaq (IRE) 143 3 (2m 110y, Chel, Gd, Nov 17)
Real Steel (IRE) 147 2 (2m, Fair, Sft, Apr 6)
Rebel Fitz (FR) 160 1 (2m 4f, Cork, Hvy, Mar 27)
Red Not Blue (IRE) 133 3 (2m 7f, Worc, Gd, Aug 28)
Red Sherlock 148 1 (2m 4f 110y, Chel, Hvy, Jan 25)
Regal Encore (IRE) 132 4 (2m 110y, Sand, Sft, Mar 8)
Renneti (FR) 142 (2m 3f, Lime, Hvy, Dec 27)
Return Spring (IRE) 142 1 (3m, Chel, Sft, Jan 1)
Reve De Sivola (FR) 161 1 (3m 1f, Asco, Sft, Dec 21)
River Maigue (IRE) 140 3 (2m 110y, Sand, GS, Dec 7)
Riverside Theatre 137 9 (3m 110y, Live, Gd, Apr 3)
Robbie 133 2 (2m, Newc, Sft, Mar 28)
Rock On Ruby (IRE) 165 2 (2m 4f, Live, Gd, Apr 3)
Rocky Wednesday (IRE) 140 1 (2m, Leop, Sft, Dec 27)
Rockyaboya (IRE) 137 2 (2m 4f, Slig, Yld, Aug 8)
Rolling Star (FR) 153 1 (2m, Hayd, Sft, Nov 23)
Roman Flight (IRE) 135 2 (2m, Muss, Sft, Feb 12)
Ronaldo Des Mottes (FR) 134 5 (2m, Asco, Sft, Dec 21)
Rory O'moore (IRE) 137 3 (2m 3f, Naas, Sft, Mar 9)
Royal Boy (FR) 150 1 (2m, Kemp, Sft, Jan 11)
Royal Irish Hussar (IRE) 138 1 (2m 110y, Chel, Gd, Nov 16)
Ruacana 139 4 (2m 110y, Sand, GS, Dec 7)
Rubi Ball (FR) 141 2 (2m 6f 110y, Thur, Gd, Nov 28)
Rule The World 163 1 (2m 3f, Naas, Hvy, Jan 18)
Ruler Of All (IRE) 133 3 (2m 1f, Live, GS, Jun 14)
Rum And Butter (IRE) 145 2 (2m 5f, Chel, Gd, Oct 18)
Runswick Royal (IRE) 144 1 (2m 2f, Kels, GS, Feb 13)
Rutherglen 132 5 (2m 1f, Chel, Gd, Mar 14)
Sadler's Risk (IRE) 148 7 (3m, Punc, Hvy, Feb 2)
Saffron Wells (IRE) 133 2 (2m 4f, Sand, Sft, Mar 8)
Sail By The Sea (IRE) 138 1 (2m 1f, Newt, Sft, Apr 1)
Sailors Warn (IRE) 136 1 (2m 2f, Leop, Sft, Mar 2)
Saint Roque (FR) 146 1 (2m 5f, Chel, Gd, Oct 18)
Salubrious (IRE) 156 2 (3m 1f, Asco, Sft, Dec 21)
Sametegal (FR) 149 2 (2m 110y, Chel, Gd, Nov 17)
Sammy Black (GER) 133 2 (2m 6f, Fair, Yld, Apr 21)
Saphir Du Rheu (FR) 162 1 (2m 4f, Ffos, Hvy, Feb 1)
Sausalito Sunrise (IRE) 143 1 (3m, Bang, GS, Apr 12)

Sea Lord (IRE) 149 1 (2m 110y, Pert, Gd, Aug 17)
Security Breach (IRE) 135 3 (2m 5f 190y, Galw, Sft, Aug 3)
Seefood (IRE) 149 2 (3m, Leop, Sft, Dec 28)
Seeyouatmidnight 154 1 (3m, Hayd, Hvy, Feb 15)
Sergeant Mattie (IRE) 134 2 (2m 5f, Plum, Gd, Mar 31)
Seskinane (IRE) 141 1 (2m 4f, Slig, Hvy, May 22)
Seventh Sign 138 1 (3m 110y, Donc, GS, Feb 19)
Sgt Reckless 150 4 (2m 110y, Chel, GS, Mar 11)
Shadow Catcher 138 3 (2m, Cork, Gd, May 24)
Shadow Eile (IRE) 136 2 (2m 2f, Punc, Hvy, Apr 27)
Shamar (FR) 138 3 (2m, Tipp, Gd, Oct 6)
Shamiran (IRE) 136 2 (2m 5f 190y, Galw, Sft, Aug 3)
Shanahan's Turn (IRE) 136 8 (2m 5f, Chel, Gd, Mar 12)
Shanpallas (IRE) 135 1 (2m 4f, Dowr, Gd, May 31)
Shantou Magic (IRE) 137 1 (2m 3f, Mark, Sft, Nov 10)
She Ranks Me (IRE) 133 2 (2m 1f, Taun, Gd, Nov 28)
Sheriff Hutton (IRE) 133 1 (3m 3f, Newt, GF, Aug 3)
Shinrock Paddy (IRE) 136 4 (2m 7f, Nava, Yld, Nov 24)
Shoegazer (IRE) 137 6 (3m 3f, Newt, GF, Aug 3)
Shotavodka (IRE) 144 2 (2m 3f, Newb, Sft, Nov 30)
Si C'etait Vrai (FR) 139 (2m 4f, Punc, Hvy, Apr 27)
Sign Of A Victory (IRE) 137 1 (2m 110y, Newb, GS, Mar 22)
Silk Hall (UAE) 140 1 (2m, Tipp, GF, Jul 21)
Silsol (GER) 140 1 (2m 4f, Ayr, GS, Apr 12)
Silver Eagle (IRE) 136 2 (2m 5f, Chel, GS, Oct 19)
Silver Friend 133 3 (2m, Cork, Hvy, Jan 4)
Sirene D'ainay (FR) 142 (2m 4f, Chel, GS, Mar 11)
Sizing Codelco (IRE) 134 3 (2m, Naas, Sft, Mar 9)
Sizing Machine (IRE) 133 6 (2m 1f, Kill, GF, Jul 18)
Sizing Rio (IRE) 141 3 (2m 4f, Punc, Hvy, Apr 26)
Skibabe (IRE) 133 3 (3m, Clon, Sft, Nov 14)
Smashing (FR) 145 4 (2m 5f, Chel, Gd, Mar 12)
So Fine (IRE) 136 3 (3m, Chel, Gd, Dec 13)
So Young (FR) 158 4 (2m, Punc, Hvy, Apr 26)
Solaras Exhibition (IRE) 135 1 (2m 110y, Stra, GF, Jul 14)
Some Officer (IRE) 133 2 (2m 5f, Lime, Hvy, Mar 16)
Somethingwonderful (IRE) 135 2 (2m, Nava, Sft, Mar 16)
Southfield Theatre (IRE) 152 2 (3m, Chel, Gd, Mar 13)
Special Catch (IRE) 137 3 (2m 2f, Kels, GS, Feb 13)
Speckled Wood (IRE) 134 2 (2m 4f, Fair, Yld, Nov 30)
Spirit Of Shankly 138 2 (2m 4f 110y, Hunt, Sft, Feb 20)
Splash Of Ginge 146 2 (2m 4f, Live, GS, Apr 5)
Stand To Reason (IRE) 133 1 (2m 110y, Newb, Hvy, Dec 28)
Steps To Freedom (IRE) 149 2 (2m, Tipp, GF, Jul 21)
Stocktons Wing (IRE) 133 5 (2m, Fair, Yld, Apr 20)
Stopped Out 144 3 (2m 5f, Newb, Hvy, Dec 28)
Strongpoint (IRE) 140 1 (2m 110y, Pert, GS, Apr 23)
Stuccodor (IRE) 133 2 (2m, Leop, Hvy, Jan 26)
Sullane Chief (IRE) 143 2 (2m 4f, Fair, Hvy, Feb 22)
Supreme Carolina (IRE) 133 2 (3m, Clon, Sft, Nov 14)
Supreme Doc (IRE) 135 2 (2m 2f, Cork, Gd, Aug 25)
Sure Reef (IRE) 139 1 (2m 4f, Leop, Hvy, Jan 26)
Sweet My Lord (FR) 142 3 (2m 6f, Thur, Gd, Oct 24)
Swincombe Flame 135 3 (2m 2f, Punc, Hvy, Apr 27)
Swing Bowler 146 4 (2m, Ayr, GS, Apr 12)
Taglietelle 136 1 (2m 2f 50y, Down, Sft, Mar 23)
Tagrita (IRE) 135 1 (2m 4f, Winc, Hvy, Feb 15)
Tanerko Emery (FR) 148 5 (2m 110y, Chel, Gd, Nov 17)
Tarla (FR) 140 2 (2m 4f, Cork, Hvy, Mar 27)
Ted Veale (IRE) 144 8 (2m, Galw, Hvy, Aug 1)
The Bishop Looney (IRE) 136 3 (3m, Cork, Hvy, Mar 27)
The Crafty Butcher (IRE) 140 1 (3m, Gowr, Yld, Oct 5)
The Game Changer (IRE) 139 2 (2m, Naas, Sft, Mar 9)
The Job Is Right 139 2 (3m, Lime, Hvy, Dec 28)
The Knoxs (IRE) 135 6 (3m 110y, Live, GS, Apr 5)
The Liquidator 145 (2m 110y, Chel, GS, Mar 11)
The New One (IRE) 173 3 (2m 110y, Chel, GS, Mar 11)
The Paparrazi Kid (IRE) 138 1 (2m 4f, Punc, Hvy, Apr 27)
The Skyfarmer 138 1 (2m 1f, Chel, Gd, Dec 13)
The Tullow Tank (IRE) 148 2 (2m 2f, Leop, Hvy, Feb 9)
The Westener Boy (IRE) 133 2 (2m 7f, Nava, Sft, Mar 16)
Theatre Bird (IRE) 137 1 (2m 4f, Leop, Sft, Dec 29)
Thomas Crapper 141 2 (2m 4f 110y, Chel, Gd, Mar 14)
Thomas Edison (IRE) 140 3 (2m, Dowr, Sft, Nov 2)
Thousand Stars (FR) 162 2 (2m, Punc, Hvy, Apr 26)
Three Kingdoms (IRE) 144 (2m 110y, Chel, GS, Mar 11)
Thunder And Roses (IRE) 138 1 (2m 7f, Nava, Sft, Mar 16)
Tidal Bay (IRE) 156 1 (3m 1f, Weth, GS, Nov 2)
Tiger Roll (IRE) 144 1 (2m 1f, Chel, Gd, Mar 14)
Time To Work (IRE) 136 1 (2m, Dowr, Sft, Nov 2)
Timesremembered (IRE) 146 2 (2m 5f, Newb, Hvy, Dec 28)
Tiqris 136 (2m 4f, Winc, GS, Mar 23)
Too Scoops (IRE) 136 6 (2m, Galw, Hvy, Aug 1)
Top Madam (IRE) 147 1 (2m 4f, Slig, Yld, Aug 8)
Top Totti 134 6 (2m 4f, Chel, GS, Mar 11)
Top Wood (FR) 138 4 (3m, Chep, GS, Apr 25)
Tornado Bob (IRE) 140 1 (2m 7f, Worc, Gd, Jun 11)
Totalize 137 2 (2m 1f, Chel, Hvy, Jan 25)
Toubeera 136 1 (3m, Hayd, Hvy, Feb 15)
Trackmate 138 1 (3m, Chel, Gd, Oct 18)
Trucking Along (IRE) 134 2 (2m, Ayr, Hvy, Feb 20)
Trustan Times (IRE) 150 4 (3m, Chel, Gd, Mar 13)
Turban (FR) 141 2 (2m, Cork, Hvy, Jan 4)
Twelve Roses 142 5 (2m 5f, Chel, Gd, Mar 12)
Two Rockers (IRE) 134 9 (3m, Hayd, Sft, Nov 23)
Tzora 134 1 (2m 1f, Newt, Gd, Jun 25)
Ubak (FR) 153 2 (2m 4f, Punc, Hvy, Apr 26)
Ubaltique (FR) 137 1 (2m 3f, Catt, Sft, Jan 22)
Ulzana's Raid (IRE) 133 1 (3m 110y, Ayr, GS, Apr 11)
Un Ace (FR) 145 8 (2m 110y, Chel, GS, Mar 11)
Un Atout (FR) 153 1 (2m 4f, Punc, Hvy, Apr 26)
Un Beau Matin (IRE) 142 1 (2m 2f 50y, Down, Sft, Mar 23)
Un Beau Roman (FR) 142 2 (2m, Punc, Gd, Oct 16)
Un De Sceaux (FR) 164 1 (2m, Gowr, Hvy, Feb 15)
Un Temps Pour Tout (IRE) 149 1 (2m 3f 110y, Asco, Hvy, Feb 15)
Uncle Jimmy (IRE) 142 1 (3m 1f, Warw, Hvy, Jan 11)
Une Artiste (FR) 135 7 (2m 110y, Weth, GS, Nov 2)
Unic De Bersy (FR) 133 2 (2m 4f, Clon, Sft, Nov 14)
Upazo (FR) 145 1 (2m, Fair, Yld, Dec 14)
Upsie (FR) 147 1 (2m, Cork, Hvy, Nov 17)
Upsilon Bleu (FR) 144 2 (2m 2f, Kels, GS, Feb 13)
Upswing (IRE) 133 1 (3m 110y, Newb, Hvy, Feb 8)
Urbain De Sivola (FR) 142 4 (2m 4f 110y, Chel, Gd, Mar 14)
Urban Hymn (FR) 141 1 (3m 110y, Donc, Sft, Jan 25)
Urticaire (FR) 136 2 (2m 4f, Punc, Hvy, Feb 19)
Utopie Des Bordes (FR) 143 5 (2m 6f, Sand, GS, Dec 7)
Valmy Baie (FR) 135 1 (2m 4f, Fair, Hvy, Feb 22)
Valseur Lido (FR) 145 1 (2m, Fair, Sft, Apr 6)
Vaniteux (FR) 150 3 (2m 110y, Chel, GS, Mar 11)
Vasco Du Ronceray (FR) 134 8 (2m 110y, Live, GS, Apr 5)
Vautour (FR) 158 1 (2m 110y, Chel, GS, Mar 11)
Vendor (FR) 139 8 (2m 110y, Newb, Hvy, Feb 8)
Very Wood (FR) 153 1 (3m, Chel, Gd, Mar 14)
Vibrato Valtat (FR) 140 1 (2m 1f, Devo, Hvy, Feb 9)
Vicente (FR) 133 1 (2m 4f, Winc, GS, Mar 23)
Vicenzo Mio (FR) 137 1 (2m, Kemp, Sft, Dec 27)
Vicky De L'oasis (FR) 136 2 (2m, Gowr, Hvy, Mar 22)
Vics Canvas (IRE) 145 1 (2m 7f, Nava, Yld, Nov 24)
Victrix Gale (IRE) 136 3 (3m, List, Sft, Sep 19)
Vieux Lion Rouge (FR) 141 1 (2m 1f, Sedg, Hvy, Feb 20)
Virak (FR) 149 1 (2m 1f, Taun, Hvy, Feb 18)
Volnay De Thaix (FR) 143 5 (2m 4f, Live, GS, Apr 5)
Vulcanite (IRE) 140 1 (2m 110y, Stra, GS, Mar 29)
Waaheb (USA) 146 1 (2m, Cork, Hvy, Jan 4)
Wadswick Court (IRE) 135 2 (2m, Asco, Sft, Feb 15)
Warden Hill (IRE) 134 2 (3m, Bang, GS, Mar 22)
Waterunder (IRE) 135 5 (2m 110y, Sand, GS, Dec 7)
West Wizard (FR) 134 2 (2m, Kemp, Gd, Nov 25)
Western Boy (IRE) 146 7 (2m 110y, Chel, GS, Mar 11)
Whisper (FR) 159 1 (2m 5f, Chel, Gd, Mar 12)
Who Owns Me (IRE) 133 2 (3m 110y, Newb, Hvy, Mar 1)
Wicklow Brave 149 6 (2m 110y, Chel, GS, Mar 11)
Wicklow Gold (FR) 134 1 (2m 5f, Tram, Sft, Dec 12)
Wilde Blue Yonder (IRE) 148 4 (2m 4f, Live, GS, Apr 5)
Willow's Saviour 142 1 (2m, Asco, Sft, Dec 21)
Wounded Warrior (IRE) 134 4 (3m, Fair, Yld, Apr 20)
Wyse Hill Teabags 134 3 (2m 5f 110y, Ayr, GS, Apr 12)
Yorkist (IRE) 136 1 (2m, Newc, Hvy, Feb 22)
Zabana (IRE) 137 1 (2m 4f, Leop, Sft, Jan 25)
Zaidpour (FR) 160 2 (2m 4f, Fair, Yld, Dec 1)
Zamdy Man 150 1 (2m, Hayd, Hvy, Jan 18)
Zarkandar (IRE) 165 4 (3m, Chel, Gd, Mar 13)
Zuider Zee (GER) 140 2 (2m 4f 110y, Hunt, Sft, Nov 12)

TOPSPEED: LAST SEASON'S LEADING CHASERS

KEY: Horse name, best Topspeed figure, finishing position when earning figure, (details of race where figure was earned)

Ackertac (IRE) 138 2 (2m 4f 110y, Sand, Sft, Nov 9)
Al Ferof (FR) 150 5 (2m 5f, Chel, Gd, Mar 13)
Alasi 136 5 (2m 4f 110y, Hunt, GS, Dec 12)
Annacotty (IRE) 149 2 (2m 5f, Chel, Hvy, Jan 25)
Arnaud (IRE) 131 2 (2m 110y, Donc, GS, Jan 25)
Arvika Ligeonniere (FR) 146 3 (2m 1f, Leop, Sft, Dec 27)
Astracad (FR) 133 2 (2m 5f, Chel, Gd, Apr 16)
Baby Run (FR) 136 2 (3m 2f, Live, Sft, Dec 7)
Balder Succes (FR) 153 1 (2m, Live, Gd, Apr 5)
Bally Legend 133 4 (2m 5f, Chel, Gd, Apr 16)
Ballygarvey (FR) 134 4 (2m, Chel, Gd, Nov 15)
Bellenos (FR) 140 2 (2m 1f, Asco, Gd, Mar 30)
Benefficient (IRE) 148 1 (2m 1f, Leop, Sft, Dec 27)
Bennys Mist (IRE) 132 2 (2m 5f 110y, Live, Gd, Apr 4)
Black Thunder (FR) 133 2 (3m 110y, Warw, Hvy, Jan 11)
Bobs Worth (IRE) 138 5 (3m 2f 110y, Chel, Gd, Mar 14)
Bocciani (GER) 139 1 (2m 4f, Mark, Gd, May 10)
Boston Bob (IRE) 148 6 (2m 5f, Chel, Gd, Mar 13)
Brick Red 146 3 (2m 1f, Asco, Gd, Mar 30)
Burton Port (IRE) 131 2 (3m 2f 110y, Newb, Hvy, Mar 1)
Bury Parade (IRE) 137 1 (2m 5f 110y, Asco, Hvy, Jan 18)
Buywise (IRE) 135 1 (2m 5f, Chel, Gd, Apr 16)
Cantlow (IRE) 137 2 (2m 5f, Chel, Gd, Dec 14)
Captain Chris (IRE) 160 1 (2m 5f 110y, Asco, Sft, Feb 15)
Carlingford Lough (IRE) 144 2 (3m, List, Sft, Sep 18)
Cause Of Causes (USA) 132 2 (2m 1f, Fair, Yld, Nov 30)
Champagne Fever (IRE) 149 2 (2m, Chel, GS, Mar 11)
Champion Court (IRE) 155 2 (2m 4f 110y, Hunt, GS, Dec 12)
Chance Du Roy (FR) 137 1 (3m 2f, Live, Sft, Dec 7)
Claret Cloak (IRE) 145 3 (2m, Live, Gd, Apr 3)
Cloudy Too (IRE) 142 2 (2m 5f 110y, Asco, Sft, Feb 15)
Colour Squadron (IRE) 132 3 (2m 5f, Chel, Gd, Dec 14)
Competitive Edge (IRE) 132 2 (2m 1f, Fair, Sft, Jan 19)
Conquisto 143 1 (2m 4f, Live, Gd, Oct 26)
Corrin Wood (IRE) 135 1 (3m 110y, Warw, Hvy, Jan 11)
Cue Card 144 2 (3m, Kemp, Sft, Dec 26)
Dare Me (IRE) 135 1 (2m, Warw, Hvy, Jan 11)
Days Hotel (IRE) 132 2 (2m, Nava, Yld, Nov 10)
De Boitron (FR) 139 1 (2m, Weth, GS, Dec 7)
Defy Logic (IRE) 138 1 (2m 1f, Leop, Sft, Dec 26)
Desert Cry (IRE) 143 2 (2m, Sand, Hvy, Feb 1)
Dodging Bullets 144 4 (2m, Chel, GS, Mar 11)
Doeslessthanme (IRE) 134 5 (2m, Weth, Sft, Jan 11)
Don Cossack (GER) 135 2 (3m 1f, Live, Gd, Apr 4)
Double Ross (IRE) 144 5 (2m 5f 110y, Live, Gd, Apr 4)
Drumshambo (USA) 141 1 (2m 1f, Asco, GS, Nov 2)
Dynaste (FR) 160 1 (2m 5f, Chel, Gd, Mar 13)
Eastlake (IRE) 139 3 (2m 5f 110y, Live, Gd, Apr 4)
Felix Yonger (IRE) 131 2 (2m 3f 120y, Lime, Sft, Dec 26)
Fiendish Flame (IRE) 145 2 (2m 4f, Mark, Gd, May 10)
Flemenstar (IRE) 136 1 (2m, Nava, Yld, Nov 10)
Forpadydeplasterer (IRE) 131 9 (3m, List, Sft, Sep 18)
Fox Appeal (IRE) 136 3 (2m 4f 110y, Kemp, Sft, Feb 22)
French Opera 135 5 (2m 110y, Chel, Gd, Mar 14)
Ghizao (GER) 142 6 (2m 4f 110y, Hunt, GS, Dec 12)
Grandioso (IRE) 136 2 (2m 5f 110y, Asco, Hvy, Jan 18)
Grandouet (FR) 139 6 (2m, Chel, GS, Mar 11)
Grey Gold (IRE) 146 2 (2m 110y, Chep, Hvy, Feb 22)
Hadrian's Approach (IRE) 139 2 (2m 4f 110y, Kemp, GS, Nov 4)
Harry Topper 158 1 (3m, Newb, Hvy, Feb 8)
Hawkes Point 134 2 (3m 5f 110y, Chep, Hvy, Dec 28)
Hidden Cyclone (IRE) 157 2 (2m 5f, Chel, Gd, Mar 13)
Highland Lodge (IRE) 142 2 (3m 3f 110y, Winc, Gd, Oct 27)
Holywell (IRE) 143 1 (3m 1f, Live, Gd, Apr 4)
Hunt Ball (IRE) 151 4 (2m 5f, Chel, Gd, Mar 13)
Indian Castle (IRE) 141 1 (2m 5f, Chel, Hvy, Jan 25)
Jacksonslady (IRE) 132 3 (2m 6f, Galw, Sft, Jul 31)
Just A Par (IRE) 131 1 (3m, Newb, GS, Nov 28)
Kapga De Cerisy (FR) 142 1 (2m 4f 110y, Sand, Sft, Nov 9)
Kid Cassidy (IRE) 152 1 (2m, Chel, Gd, Nov 17)
King Edmund 139 1 (2m 4f 110y, Kemp, Sft, Jan 11)
Lancetto (FR) 138 1 (2m 1f, Asco, Sft, Dec 21)
Lastoftheleaders (IRE) 133 3 (2m 1f, Fair, Sft, Jan 19)
Le Bec (FR) 136 2 (3m 1f 110y, Chel, Gd, Dec 14)
Loose Chips 133 1 (2m 4f 110y, Kemp, Sft, Dec 26)
Lord Windermere (IRE) 144 1 (3m 2f 110y, Chel, Gd, Mar 14)
Lucky Landing (IRE) 135 1 (2m, Weth, Gd, Oct 16)
Lyreen Legend (IRE) 135 6 (3m 2f 110y, Chel, Gd, Mar 14)
Ma Filleule (FR) 152 1 (2m 5f 110y, Live, Gd, Apr 4)
Manyriverstocross (IRE) 144 1 (2m 1f, Asco, Gd, Mar 30)
Medermit (FR) 133 8 (2m 5f, Chel, Gd, Mar 13)
Micheal Flips (IRE) 140 6 (2m 4f, Mark, Gd, May 10)
Mister Marker (IRE) 137 1 (2m 7f 110y, Kels, GS, Feb 13)
Module (FR) 144 3 (2m, Chel, Gd, Mar 12)
Moscow Mannon (IRE) 135 4 (2m, Live, Gd, Apr 5)
Mount Benbulben (IRE) 133 4 (3m, Kemp, Sft, Dec 26)
Mountainous (IRE) 134 1 (3m 5f 110y, Chep, Hvy, Dec 28)
Mr Moonshine (IRE) 131 3 (3m 2f, Live, Sft, Dec 7)
Muirhead (IRE) 131 3 (3m, List, Sft, Sep 18)
Mwaleshi 137 1 (2m, Hayd, Sft, Dec 21)
Nearest The Pin (IRE) 138 2 (2m 4f 110y, Kemp, GS, Mar 15)
Next Sensation (IRE) 135 5 (2m, Live, Gd, Apr 5)
Niceonefrankie 132 1 (2m 3f, Asco, GS, Nov 22)
O'faolains Boy (IRE) 136 1 (3m 110y, Chel, Gd, Mar 12)
Oiseau De Nuit (FR) 142 4 (2m, Chel, Gd, Nov 17)
On His Own (IRE) 143 2 (3m 2f 110y, Chel, Gd, Mar 14)
Oscar Whisky (IRE) 131 1 (2m 4f 110y, Sand, Hvy, Feb 1)
Parsnip Pete 137 1 (2m, Live, Gd, Apr 3)
Pepite Rose (FR) 132 7 (2m 4f, Mark, Gd, May 10)
Perfect Smile (IRE) 131 3 (2m 1f, Fair, Yld, Nov 30)
Poole Master 140 1 (2m 110y, Chep, Hvy, Feb 22)
Quantitativeeasing (IRE) 139 2 (2m 6f, Galw, Sft, Jul 31)
Quentin Collonges (FR) 131 1 (3m 5f 110y, Sand, Gd, Apr 27)
Rajdhani Express 154 3 (2m 5f, Chel, Gd, Mar 13)
Rathlin 139 1 (2m 4f 120y, Kill, Sft, May 12)
Renard (FR) 137 1 (2m 3f 110y, Chep, Hvy, Dec 28)
Riverside Theatre 150 1 (2m 4f 110y, Hunt, GS, Dec 12)
Roalco De Farges (FR) 131 1 (3m 2f 110y, Newb, GS, Mar 22)
Sam Winner (FR) 132 1 (3m 1f 110y, Chel, Gd, Dec 14)
Same Difference (IRE) 139 2 (3m 5f 110y, Sand, Gd, Apr 27)
Savello (IRE) 134 1 (2m 110y, Chel, Gd, Mar 14)
Silviniaco Conti (FR) 147 1 (3m, Kemp, Sft, Dec 26)
Simply Ned (IRE) 148 2 (2m, Live, Gd, Apr 5)
Sire De Grugy (FR) 158 1 (2m 1f, Asco, Hvy, Jan 18)
Sizing Europe (IRE) 140 4 (2m, Chel, Gd, Mar 12)
Smad Place (FR) 135 2 (3m 110y, Chel, Gd, Mar 12)
Some Tikket (IRE) 131 1 (2m 1f, Fair, Sft, Apr 6)
Somersby (IRE) 145 2 (2m, Chel, Gd, Mar 12)
Special Tiara 149 3 (2m, Chel, Gd, Nov 17)
Sraid Padraig (IRE) 131 1 (2m 1f, Fair, Yld, Nov 30)
Stagecoach Pearl 138 2 (2m, Weth, Gd, Oct 16)
Taquin Du Seuil (FR) 131 1 (2m 4f, Chel, Gd, Mar 13)
Tatenen (FR) 132 4 (2m 5f 110y, Live, Gd, Apr 4)
Teaforthree (IRE) 131 9 (3m 5f 110y, Chep, Hvy, Dec 28)
The Disengager (IRE) 133 4 (2m 6f 110y, Mark, Gd, Sep 28)
The Giant Bolster 142 3 (3m 2f 110y, Chel, Gd, Mar 14)
Theatre Guide (IRE) 133 3 (2m 4f 110y, Kemp, GS, Nov 4)
Tidal Bay (IRE) 160 3 (3m 5f 110y, Chep, Hvy, Dec 28)
Torphichen 131 4 (2m 1f, Fair, Sft, Jan 19)
Trifolium (FR) 147 3 (2m, Live, Gd, Apr 5)
Turban (FR) 143 1 (2m 1f, Fair, Sft, Jan 19)
Turn Over Sivola (FR) 135 2 (2m, Live, Gd, Apr 3)
Twinlight (FR) 139 2 (2m 1f, Fair, Sft, Apr 6)
Unioniste (FR) 141 1 (3m 1f, Live, GS, Dec 7)
Urbain De Sivola (FR) 131 3 (2m 4f 110y, Kemp, Sft, Dec 26)
Valdez 142 5 (2m, Chel, GS, Mar 11)
Viva Colonia (IRE) 131 3 (2m 4f, Live, Gd, Oct 26)
Western Warhorse (IRE) 150 1 (2m, Chel, GS, Mar 11)
White Star Line (IRE) 131 1 (3m, List, Sft, Sep 18)
Wishfull Thinking 146 1 (2m 5f, Chel, Hvy, Jan 25)
Wonderful Charm (FR) 132 2 (2m 5f, Chel, Gd, Dec 13)
Woolcombe Folly (IRE) 140 2 (2m 4f, Stra, GS, May 19)
Wyck Hill (IRE) 138 1 (4m 1f, Newc, Hvy, Feb 22)

TOPSPEED: LAST SEASON'S LEADING HURDLERS

KEY: Horse name, best Topspeed figure, finishing position when earning figure, (details of race where figure was earned)

Ahyaknowyerself (IRE) 140 3 (2m, Winc, GS, Nov 9)
Alpha Victor (IRE) 133 1 (3m, Bang, Hvy, Feb 26)
Annie Power (IRE) 139 1 (2m 3f 110y, Asco, GS, Nov 23)
Araldur (FR) 138 4 (3m, Hayd, Gd, May 11)
Arctic Fire (GER) 135 2 (2m 1f, Chel, Gd, Mar 14)
At Fishers Cross (IRE) 131 4 (3m 110y, Newb, Sft, Nov 30)
Ballyalton (IRE) 133 2 (2m 5f, Chel, Gd, Mar 12)
Battle Group 145 1 (3m, Hayd, Gd, May 11)
Beat That (IRE) 138 1 (3m 110y, Live, GS, Apr 4)
Caid Du Berlais (FR) 131 3 (2m 4f 110y, Chel, Gd, Mar 14)
Call Me Bubbles (FR) 132 1 (2m 5f 190y, Galw, Sft, Aug 3)
Captain Cee Bee (IRE) 144 5 (2m 110y, Chel, GS, Mar 11)
Captain Cutter (IRE) 137 1 (2m 5f, Newb, Hvy, Dec 28)
Celestial Halo (IRE) 153 1 (3m 110y, Newb, Sft, Nov 30)
Chris Pea Green 132 3 (2m 4f, Font, Hvy, Feb 23)
Clever Cookie 138 1 (2m 2f, Kels, GS, Mar 1)
Cockney Sparrow 142 1 (2m, Ayr, GS, Apr 12)
Cole Harden (IRE) 135 2 (3m 110y, Live, GS, Apr 4)
Cotton Mill 137 4 (2m, Winc, GS, Nov 9)
Court Minstrel (IRE) 143 2 (2m, Ayr, GS, Apr 12)
Cross Kennon (IRE) 137 3 (3m, Hayd, Gd, May 11)
Dell' Arca (IRE) 139 3 (2m 4f, Live, GS, Apr 5)
Diakali (FR) 144 4 (2m 1f, Chel, Gd, Mar 14)
Don Poli (IRE) 137 1 (2m 4f 110y, Chel, Gd, Mar 14)
Double Ross (IRE) 134 6 (3m, Hayd, Gd, May 11)
Drive Time (USA) 142 4 (2m, Galw, Hvy, Aug 1)
Dunguib (IRE) 139 1 (2m 5f, Nava, Hvy, Feb 16)
Far West (FR) 142 2 (2m, Winc, GS, Nov 9)
Faugheen (IRE) 138 1 (2m 5f, Chel, Gd, Mar 12)
Fingal Bay (IRE) 138 1 (3m, Chel, Gd, Mar 13)
First In The Queue (IRE) 138 1 (2m 110y, Chel, Gd, Oct 18)
Flaxen Flare (IRE) 136 5 (2m 1f, Chel, Gd, Mar 14)
Fox Appeal (IRE) 145 5 (3m, Hayd, Gd, May 11)
Get Me Out Of Here (IRE) 131 8 (2m 110y, Chel, Gd, Nov 17)
Hurricane Fly (IRE) 151 4 (2m 110y, Chel, GS, Mar 11)
Ifandbutwhynot (IRE) 139 2 (2m, Muss, Sft, Jan 1)
Irving 136 9 (2m 110y, Chel, GS, Mar 11)
Jetson (IRE) 141 2 (3m, Hayd, Gd, May 11)
Jezki (IRE) 160 1 (2m 110y, Chel, GS, Mar 11)
Josses Hill (IRE) 143 2 (2m 110y, Chel, GS, Mar 11)
Karinga Dancer 133 5 (2m, Winc, GS, Nov 9)
Kayf Moss 132 1 (2m 4f, Font, Hvy, Feb 23)
Killala Quay 131 4 (2m 5f, Chel, Gd, Mar 12)
Lac Fontana (FR) 141 1 (2m 4f, Live, GS, Apr 5)
Local Hero (GER) 137 3 (2m, Muss, Sft, Jan 1)
Lyvius 133 4 (2m, Muss, Sft, Feb 2)
Magnifique Etoile 133 1 (2m 3f, Stra, Sft, Oct 26)
Make Your Mark (IRE) 136 3 (2m, Galw, Hvy, Aug 1)
Medinas (FR) 135 2 (3m 110y, Newb, Sft, Nov 30)
Meister Eckhart (IRE) 132 2 (2m 4f, Font, Hvy, Feb 23)
Melodic Rendezvous 148 1 (2m, Winc, GS, Nov 9)
Mickie 133 1 (3m 110y, Newb, GS, Nov 29)
Missunited (IRE) 135 1 (2m, Galw, Hvy, Aug 1)
Montbazon (FR) 133 3 (2m 1f, Chel, Gd, Mar 14)
More Of That (IRE) 135 1 (3m, Chel, Gd, Mar 13)
Mr Mole (IRE) 140 2 (2m, Hayd, Gd, May 11)
My Tent Or Yours (IRE) 159 2 (2m 110y, Chel, GS, Mar 11)
Pateese (FR) 137 2 (3m 110y, Newb, GS, Nov 29)
Ptit Zig (FR) 141 6 (2m 110y, Chel, GS, Mar 11)
Rathvinden (IRE) 132 3 (2m 5f, Chel, Gd, Mar 12)
Real Steel (IRE) 131 2 (2m, Fair, Sft, Apr 6)
Reve De Sivola (FR) 139 3 (3m 110y, Newb, Sft, Nov 30)
Rock On Ruby (IRE) 140 3 (2m, Punc, Hvy, Apr 26)
Royal Boy (FR) 136 1 (2m, Kemp, Sft, Jan 11)
Runswick Royal (IRE) 136 4 (2m, Muss, Sft, Jan 1)
Sametegal (FR) 141 5 (2m, Muss, Sft, Feb 2)
Saphir Du Rheu (FR) 135 1 (2m 6f, Sand, GS, Dec 7)
Sea Lord (IRE) 138 1 (2m 110y, Pert, Gd, Aug 17)
Sgt Reckless 141 4 (2m 110y, Chel, GS, Mar 11)
Shamiran (IRE) 131 2 (2m 5f 190y, Galw, Sft, Aug 3)
So Young (FR) 136 4 (2m, Punc, Hvy, Apr 26)
Southfield Theatre (IRE) 136 2 (3m, Chel, Gd, Mar 13)
Splash Of Ginge 140 2 (2m 4f, Live, GS, Apr 5)
Strongpoint (IRE) 134 1 (2m, Muss, Sft, Jan 1)
Swing Bowler 133 4 (2m, Ayr, GS, Apr 12)
The Liquidator 134 (2m 110y, Chel, GS, Mar 11)
The New One (IRE) 156 3 (2m 110y, Chel, GS, Mar 11)
Thousand Stars (FR) 141 2 (2m, Punc, Hvy, Apr 26)
Three Kingdoms (IRE) 133 (2m 110y, Chel, GS, Mar 11)
Timesremembered (IRE) 133 2 (2m 5f, Newb, Hvy, Dec 28)
Trustan Times (IRE) 131 4 (3m, Chel, Gd, Mar 13)
Un Ace (FR) 137 8 (2m 110y, Chel, GS, Mar 11)
Un De Sceaux (FR) 140 1 (2m, Punc, Hvy, Apr 26)
Utopie Des Bordes (FR) 137 5 (2m 6f, Sand, GS, Dec 7)
Valseur Lido (FR) 135 (2m 110y, Chel, GS, Mar 11)
Vaniteux (FR) 142 3 (2m 110y, Chel, GS, Mar 11)
Vautour (FR) 150 1 (2m 110y, Chel, GS, Mar 11)
Volnay De Thaix (FR) 135 5 (2m 4f, Live, GS, Apr 5)
Warden Hill (IRE) 132 2 (3m, Bang, GS, Mar 22)
Western Boy (IRE) 138 7 (2m 110y, Chel, GS, Mar 11)
Whisper (FR) 137 3 (2m 6f, Sand, GS, Dec 7)
Wicklow Brave 139 6 (2m 110y, Chel, GS, Mar 11)
Wilde Blue Yonder (IRE) 140 5 (2m 110y, Chel, GS, Mar 11)
Zaidpour (FR) 140 2 (2m 5f, Nava, Hvy, Feb 16)
Zarkandar (IRE) 145 2 (2m 3f 110y, Asco, GS, Nov 23)

NOTES

V	Sc	Sc	Sc	Sc	Sc	Sc	Sc	Sc	Sc	Sc	Sc	Sc	S	S	S	S	S	S	S	S	S	S	S	S
AP	W	W	W	W	W	W	DP	DP	DP	DP	DP	DP	W	W	W	W	W	W	DP	DP	DP	DP	DP	DP
TNO	F	F	J	J	HF	HF	F	F	J	J	HF	HF	F	F	J	J	HF	HF	F	F	J	J	HF	HF
MOT	Dj	FB	Dj	FB	Dj	FB	Dj	FB	Dj	FB	Dj	FB	Dj	FB	Dj	FB	Dj	FB	Dj	FB	Dj	FB	Dj	FB
8S	2	1	1	0	2	1	3	2	2	1	3	2	3	2	2	∅	3	2	4	3	3	2	4	3

-1 1 1 1 F -1
1 2 1 1 1 2

1 CC SC W F Dj SS V AP TNO MOT 3 1 1 5
D SC DP F Si SS V AP TNO MOT 2 2 1 5
D SC W F CC SS V AP TNO MOT 2 2 1 5
Si SC DP F CC SS V AP TNO MOT 3 1 1 5
1 CC SC W HF Dj SS V 3 1 1 5
D SC DP F Si ST V AP TNO MOT 2 2 1 5
D S W F CC SS V AP TNO MOT 2 2 2 4
1 Si SC DP F FB SS V AP TNO MOT 2 2 1 5
1 Si SC DP J Dj SS V AP TNO MOT 3 1 1 5
1 Si SC DP HF/FB
1 CC S W F FB SS V AP TNO MOT 2 2 2 4
1 CC S W J Dj SS V AP TNO MOT 3 1 2 4
1 CC S W HF/FB
1 Si S DP J FB SS V AP TNO MOT 2 2 2 4